The Financial

Futures Primer

𝕀𝔹

The Financial Futures Primer

Robert W. Kolb

First published 1997

Blackwell Publishers Inc.
350 Main Street
Malden, MA
02148

Blackwell Publishers Ltd.
108 Cowley Road
Oxford OX4 1JF
UK

Library of Congress Cataloging-in-Publication Data

Kolb, Robert W.
  The financial futures primer / Robert W. Kolb.
    p. cm.
  Includes index.
  ISBN 1-57718-070-4
  1. Financial futures. 2. Futures market. I. Title.
HG6024.3.K653   1997
332.63'2—dc21   96-36857
                                                                      CIP

British Library of Congress Cataloging-in-Publication Data

Typeset by AM Marketing.

This book is printed on acid-free paper.

TABLE OF CONTENTS

PREFACE

The Financial Futures Primer provides in one text a comprehensive introduction to the futures markets in general and to financial futures in particular. All of the futures contracts explored in this text are approached from a common pricing framework – the proposition that rational prices preclude arbitrage profits. This guiding principle is introduced in the first chapter and pursued throughout the text.

The text also emphasizes the use of financial futures in risk management. While the book features ample examples of speculative strategies that can be implemented with these instruments, the focus of the application examples is the management of preexisting risk.

From years of teaching futures market courses, I have found that financial futures can be understood best when the discussion begins with a tangible good having no cash flows, such as gold. Therefore, the book begins by considering futures markets in their totality. The analysis of pricing focuses on gold, because gold behaves and is priced like a financial future, but gold has no complicating cash flows. The attention then turns directly to an extended discussion of financial futures. Accordingly, the book is organized as follows.

ORGANIZATION OF THE TEXT

Chapter 1, *Futures Markets: Introduction,* provides an introduction to the institutional framework of the market, including margin, the clearinghouse, and daily settlement. Chapter 2, *Futures Prices,* explores the cost-of-carry model in depth, relating it to the no-arbitrage principle introduced in Chapter 1. Chapter 3, *Using Futures Markets,* discusses the role of speculators in providing market liquidity and in aiding price discovery. Chapter 3 also explores techniques of hedging with futures. Together, Chapters 1–3 provide a comprehensive overview of the market and set the stage for the explicit discussion of financial futures.

Chapters 4–8 consider interest rate futures, stock index futures, and foreign exchange futures. Chapter 4, *Interest Rate Futures: Introduction,* and Chapter 5, *Interest Rate Futures: Refinements,* provide detailed coverage of interest rate futures. Chapter 4 introduces the contracts and covers the basic pricing principles, while Chapter 5 explores key issues (such as the features of the T-bond contract and the implicit options in the contract) in more detail. Chapter 5 can be omitted without loss of continuity. Chapter 6, *Stock Index Futures: Introduction,* and Chapter 7, *Stock Index Futures: Refinements,* follow a similar strategy in treating stock index futures. Chapter 8, *Foreign Exchange Futures,* discusses the contracts, pricing principles, and applications of foreign exchange futures. It also includes basic material on interest rate parity and purchasing power parity conditions.

ACKNOWLEDGMENTS

While this text is a first edition, much of the material contained here is tried and proven. In writing this book, I have drawn heavily on all five editions of *Understanding Futures Markets,* three editions of *Options,* and two editions of *Futures, Options, and Swaps.* Thus, most of the material here has been class-tested in many university courses.

Through all of these editions, I have received the assistance of numerous people, ranging from hundreds of professors to many hundred students. This book has grown out of their contributions and insights, and I am deeply grateful for their efforts. For this edition, I am particularly indebted to George Wang of the Commodity Futures Trading Commission, Peter Alonzi of the Chicago Board of Trade, Tom Gosnell of Oklahoma State University, and Raffaella Cremonesi and Suk Hun Lee of Loyola University of Chicago.

I would also like to thank Andrea Coens for her wonderful copyediting. Producing *The Financial Futures Primer* required the dedicated efforts of a professional production staff. I would like to express my gratitude to Rolf Janke, Editorial Director, Mary Beckwith, Assistant Editor, Jan Phillips, Production Manager, Megan Zuckerman, Graphic Designer, and Diane McCree, Production Editor, for their assistance in putting this project together. Of course, I alone am responsible for any remaining deficiencies.

Robert W. Kolb

■ Chapter 1

Futures Markets: ■ Introduction

OVERVIEW

This chapter lays the foundations essential to understanding how futures markets function. First, we explore the origins of futures markets. We focus on futures markets in the United States, where they are currently the most complete and provide the widest range of trading opportunities. Futures markets, as they now exist in the United States, are a fairly recent development, but understanding their origins helps us understand both the role these markets play today and likely future changes in that role. Forward contracting, however, has existed for many centuries. The ways in which futures markets differ from forward markets, the chapter's second topic, is important for understanding the techniques that can be applied in futures trading today.

The current organization of active futures markets is more important for the potential user than any historical account. Accordingly, the discussion soon focuses on organized futures exchanges as they exist today, with special emphasis on exchanges in the United States. Before entering the arena of the futures market, a prospective trader must understand the organizational form of the futures exchanges, the types of contracts that are traded, and the ways in which futures exchanges compete with each other for business.

The purposes that futures markets serve and the participants in the markets are then briefly characterized in this chapter. These themes are developed further in Chapter 3. Because regulation is important in determining whether futures markets can serve their social function and the interests of the trading parties, the chapter next discusses the regulatory framework, and then closes with a description of futures market taxation.

The Concept of Arbitrage

Throughout this text, we will be concerned with the principles that determine the prices of the financial derivatives we consider. The text consistently employs a no-arbitrage principle to illuminate the pricing principles for each instrument. An **arbitrage opportunity** is a chance to make a riskless profit with no investment. In essence, finding an arbitrage opportunity is like finding free money. The **no-arbitrage principle** states that any rational price for a financial instrument must exclude arbitrage opportunities. This is a minimal requirement for a feasible or rational price for any financial instrument. As we will see in detail in the chapters that follow, this no-arbitrage principle is extremely powerful for understanding what prices can reasonably prevail for all of the instruments addressed in this text.

There are many alternative definitions of "arbitrage." We begin our analysis with a strict definition of what we call **academic arbitrage**. In academic arbitrage it is possible to trade to generate a riskless profit without investment. An **arbitrageur** is a person who engages in arbitrage. For example, shares of IBM trade on both the New York Stock Exchange and the Pacific Stock Exchange. Suppose shares of IBM trade for $110 on the New York market and for $105 on the Pacific Exchange. A trader could make the following two transactions simultaneously:

Buy 1 share of IBM on the Pacific Exchange for $105.
Sell 1 share of IBM on the New York Exchange for $110.

These two transactions generate a riskless profit of $5. Because both trades are assumed to occur simultaneously, there is no investment. Therefore, such an opportunity qualifies as an academic arbitrage opportunity – it affords riskless profits without investment.

In a well-functioning market, such opportunities cannot exist. If they did exist, they would make all of us fabulously wealthy. The existence of such academic arbitrage opportunities is equivalent to money being left lying on the street without being claimed. If you have ever been to Wall Street, you know that there is no money lying on that street. To understand the pricing of derivative instruments, we assume that there are no arbitrage opportunities. This is our no-arbitrage principle. We apply this principle to determine what we can about prices of financial derivatives on the assumption that there are no arbitrage opportunities.

In our example of the IBM share, we assume that there are no transaction costs. We always begin our exploration of pricing relationships under this assumption of perfect markets, so we assume there are no taxes, no transaction costs, and no frictions of any kind. After developing an understanding of pricing relationships in this simple environment, we go on to consider the more realistic world of transaction costs and other market imperfections.

ORIGINS OF FORWARD CONTRACTING

A **forward contract**, as it occurs in both forward and futures markets, always involves a contract initiated at one certain time; performance in accordance with the terms of the contract occurs at a subsequent time. Further, the type of forward contracting to be considered here always involves an exchange of one asset for another. The price at which the exchange occurs is set at the time of the initial contracting. Actual payment and delivery of the good occur later. So defined, almost everyone has engaged in some kind of forward contract.

The following example illustrates a very simple, yet frequently occurring, type of forward contract. Having heard that a highly prized St. Bernard has just given birth to a litter of pups, a dog fancier rushes to the kennel to see the pups. After inspecting the pedigree of the parents, the dog fancier offers to buy a pup from the breeder. The exchange, however, cannot be completed at this time, since the pup is too young to be weaned. The fancier and breeder thus agree that the dog will be delivered in six weeks and that the fancier will pay the $400 in six weeks upon delivery of the puppy. This contract is not a conditional contract; both parties are obligated to complete it as agreed upon.[1] The puppy example represents a very basic type of forward contract. The example could have been made more complicated by the breeder's requiring a deposit, but that would not change the essential character of the transaction. In this example, there is a buyer and a seller. The buyer is said to have a **long position**, while the seller has a **short position**. The act of buying is also called **going long**, and the act of selling is called **going short**. In order for the contract to trade, there must be a long position and a short position. When one trader buys and another sells a futures contract, the transaction generates one contract of trading **volume**.

Figure 1.1 shows the growth of trading volume on U.S. futures exchanges. From the very nature of the trading, there will always be an equal number of long and short positions outstanding. When a contract is first listed for trading, there has been no volume. Assume that the first trade is for one contract, leaving one trader long one contract and one trader short one contract. At this point, there is one open contract, or one contract is obligated for delivery. The **open interest** is the number of open contracts or the number of contracts obligated for delivery. (As we will see later in this chapter, most contracts do not actually lead to delivery.)

From the simplicity of the contract and its obvious usefulness in resolving uncertainty about the future, it is not surprising that such contracts have had a very long history. The origin of forward contracting is not clear. Some authors trace the practice to Roman and

■ **Figure 1.1**

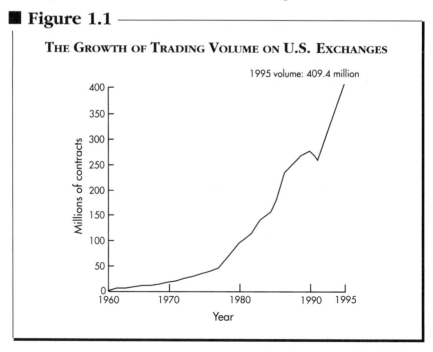

THE GROWTH OF TRADING VOLUME ON U.S. EXCHANGES

1995 volume: 409.4 million

even classical Greek times. Strong evidence suggests that Roman emperors entered forward contracts to provide the masses with their supply of Egyptian grain. Others have traced the origin of forward contracting to India.[2]

While there may not be much agreement about the geographical origins of forward contracting, it is clear that trading originated with contracts similar in form to that of the puppy example. In fact, such contracts continue to be important today, not only among dog lovers, but in markets for credit and foreign exchange as well. Billions of dollars of foreign currencies change hands daily in a very sophisticated market that trades contracts for German marks and English pounds. These contracts are very similar in structure to the puppy contract. While these kinds of forward markets are very large and important, and while they resemble futures markets, this book primarily tries to develop an understanding of futures contracts and the organized exchanges where they trade. Comparing the structure of forward and futures contracts helps illuminate the essential similarities and differences between these two kinds of markets.

FORWARD VERSUS FUTURES MARKETS

While the historical origins of forward contracts are obscure, organized futures markets began in Chicago with the opening of the Chicago Board of Trade in 1848.[3] Despite the loss of records in the great Chicago fire of 1871, it appears that futures contracts, as opposed to forward contracts, were being traded on the Board of Trade by the 1860s. Since then, the basic structure of futures contracts has been adopted by a number of other exchanges, both in the United States and abroad. It is important to understand how futures contracts differ from other forms of forward contracts, such as the puppy example. Forward contracts and futures contracts can be distinguished by several important features of futures markets: the existence of an organized futures exchange, the trading of standardized contracts, the role of a clearinghouse, the system of margins and daily settlement, the ability to close contracts easily, and the regulatory structure of the markets.

THE ORGANIZED EXCHANGE

Futures contracts always trade on an organized exchange. The organization of the Chicago Board of Trade, the oldest and largest futures exchange in the world, is typical. We will use its organizational features to illustrate the institutional characteristics of the other exchanges. The exchange is a voluntary, nonprofit association of its members.[4] **Exchange memberships**, also called **seats**, may be held only by individuals, and these memberships are traded in an active market like other assets. Table 1.1 shows recent membership prices for major futures and security exchanges in the United States. As the prices indicate, these seats are valuable capital assets. Also, the value of these seats fluctuates dramatically, depending mainly on recent and anticipated trading volume.[5]

Exchange members have a right to trade on the exchange and to have a voice in the exchange's operation. Members also serve on committees to regulate the exchange's operations, rules, audit functions, public relations, and the legal and ethical conduct of members. Often administrative officers of the exchange manage the ordinary operation of the exchange and report to the membership.

According to federal law and the rules of the exchange, trading may take place only during official trading hours in a designated trading area called a **pit**. This is a physical location on the floor of the exchange. Each commodity trades in a designated pit. In contrast to the specialist system used on stock exchanges, futures contracts trade by a system of **open outcry**. In this system, a trader must make any offer to buy or sell to all other traders present in the pit. Traders also use an unofficial (but highly developed) system of hand signals to express their wishes to buy or sell. Officially, however, all offers to buy or sell must be made through open outcry.

■ Table 1.1

MEMBERSHIP PRICES OF MAJOR U.S. FUTURES EXCHANGES

Exchange	Membership Price
Chicago Mercantile Exchange	$585,000
Chicago Board of Trade	625,000
New York Mercantile Exchange	500,000
Coffee, Sugar and Cocoa Exchange	140,000
New York Cotton Exchange	86,000

From "Membership Prices of Major U.S. Futures Exchanges," *Futures and Options World*, March 1996. Reprinted by permission of *Futures and Options World*.

Traders in the pit fall into two groups that we can distinguish by their functions. First, a trader can trade for his or her own account and bear the losses or enjoy the profits stemming from this trading. Often, these traders are members of the exchange. Second, a trader could be a broker acting on behalf of his or her own firm or on behalf of a client outside the exchange. For example, the brokers trading on the exchange often represent large brokerage houses such as Merrill Lynch or Prudential Bache. Having distinguished between traders who execute trades for their own accounts and those who execute trades for others, we must realize that certain individuals exercise both functions simultaneously.[6]

Members of the exchange who trade in the pits are typically speculators. A **speculator** is a trader who enters the futures market in pursuit of profit, accepting risk in the endeavor. Some of the traders in the pit that trade for their own accounts may not be full exchange members themselves. It is possible to lease a seat on the exchange from a full member. Also, some exchanges have created special licenses allowing nonmembers to trade in certain contracts in which the exchanges are anxious to build volume. For the most part, a trader in the pit trading for his or her own account is a speculator.

In addition to speculators, many traders are **hedgers**, traders who trade futures to reduce some preexisting risk exposure. Hedgers are often producers or major users of a given commodity. For example, hedgers in wheat might include wheat farmers and large baking firms. Notice that these hedgers do not necessarily need to own the wheat when they hedge. A farmer might hedge by selling his anticipated harvest through the futures market. This could occur even before the farmer plants. Similarly, the baker that will eventually bake the farmer's wheat harvest into bread may hedge an expected need for wheat months before the wheat is actually required. Therefore, hedging is the purchase or sale of futures as a temporary substitute for a transaction in the cash market.[7] For the most part, hedgers are not themselves located on the floor of the exchange. Instead, they trade through a brokerage firm. The brokerage firm communicates the order to the pit and has it executed by a broker in the pit.

Thus, there are two different kinds of brokers. An account executive for a brokerage firm is often called a broker. The account executive could be located in any town or city, and the account executive deals with his or her customers, conveying their orders to the exchange. A second type of broker is a floor broker, a broker on the floor of the exchange who executes orders for other customers. For a typical transaction entered by a trader off-the-floor of the exchange, the order will be given to the customer's broker (account executive), who will transmit the order to the brokerage firm's representatives at the exchange. There, a floor broker, often employed by the brokerage firm, will execute the order on the floor of the exchange.

This organized structure for trading futures contracts differs from the organization of forward markets. Forward markets are loosely organized and have no physical location devoted to the trading.[8] From the puppy example, this difference is clear. Perhaps the best-developed forward market is the market for foreign exchange. It is a worldwide network of participants, largely banks and brokers, who communicate with each other electronically. In the forward market for foreign exchange, there is no organized exchange and no central trading point.[9]

STANDARDIZED CONTRACT TERMS

A second major difference between forward and futures contracts is that futures contracts always have standardized contract terms. The puppy example is typical of a forward contract in its lack of standard-ization. The puppy is not a standardized item; the parties agreed on a particular delivery date, but they could have chosen any other date that was mutually agreeable; and there was no mechanism external to the traders to guarantee that the contract would be fulfilled. By contrast, futures contracts are highly uniform and well-specified com-mitments for a carefully described good to be delivered at a certain time and in a certain manner. Generally, the futures contract specifies the quantity and quality of the good that can be delivered to fulfill the futures contract. The contract also specifies the delivery date and method for closing the contract, and the permissible minimum and maximum price fluctuations permitted in trading.

As an example, consider the Chicago Board of Trade wheat contract. One wheat contract consists of 5,000 bushels of wheat that must be of one of the following types: No. 2 Soft Red, No. 2 Hard Red Winter, No. 2 Dark Northern Spring, or No. 1 Northern Spring. The wheat contract trades for expiration in the following months of each year: July, September, December, March, and May. The Board of Trade also stipulates the delivery terms for completing the contract. To deliver wheat in completion of the contract, the wheat must be in a warehouse approved by the Chicago Board of Trade. These warehouses must be in the Chicago Switching District or the Toledo, Ohio, Switching District.[10] The buyer transmits payment to the seller, and the seller delivers a warehouse receipt to the buyer. The holder of a warehouse receipt has title to the wheat in the warehouse. Delivery can occur on any business day in the delivery month.

The contract also stipulates the minimum price fluctuation, or **tick** size. For wheat, one tick is $^1/_4$ cent per bushel. With 5,000 bushels per contract, this gives a tick size of $12.50 per contract. The contract also specifies a **daily price limit**, which restricts the price movement in a single day. For wheat, the trading price on a given day cannot differ from the preceding day's closing price by more than 20 cents per bushel, or $1,000 per contract. When the contract is trading in its delivery month, this price limit is not in effect. Also, when a commodity enters a particularly volatile period, price limits are generally expanded over successive days. For example, when Iraq invaded Kuwait in 1990, oil prices skyrocketed for several days. On the first day, the futures price was allowed to rise only by the limit. Because the price rose the limit on one day, the price limit was expanded for the next day. For most commodities, price limits expand over several days until there is no limit on how much the price can change in a day. Also, some commodities do not have price limits. Finally, the exchange also controls the trading times for each futures contract. Wheat trades from 9:30 A.M. to 1:15 P.M. Chicago time on each trading day, except for the last day of trading when trading in the expiring contract ceases at noon. The last trading day for the wheat contract is seven business days before the last business day of the delivery month.

Although these rules may appear highly restrictive, they actually stimulate trading. Because the good being traded is so highly standardized, all the participants in the market know exactly what is being offered for sale, and they know the terms of the transactions. This uniformity helps promote liquidity. All futures contracts have such a highly developed framework, which specifies all phases of the transaction. As we saw for wheat, these rules regulate all phases of the market, from the amounts the prices can move to the appropriate ways of making delivery. Each exchange publishes contract terms, and the prospective trader should consult a given contract for these exact details before initiating any trading.

THE CLEARINGHOUSE

To ensure that futures contracts trade in a smoothly functioning market, each futures exchange has an associated clearinghouse. The clearinghouse may be constituted as a separate corporation or it may be part of the futures exchange, but each exchange is closely associated with a particular clearinghouse. The clearinghouse guarantees that all of the traders in the futures market will honor their obligations.[11] The clearinghouse serves this role by adopting the position of buyer to every seller and seller to every buyer. This means that every trader in the futures markets has obligations only to the clearinghouse and has expectations that the clearinghouse will maintain its side of the bargain as well. Thus, the clearinghouse substitutes its own credibility for the promise of each trader in the market.

The clearinghouse takes no active position in the market, but instead interposes itself between all parties to every transaction. In the futures market, the number of contracts bought must always equal the number of contracts sold. So, for every party expecting to receive delivery of a commodity, the opposite trading partner must be prepared to make delivery. If we sum all outstanding long and short futures market positions, the total always equals zero.[12]

Table 1.2 shows the typical trading situation. In the table, we assume that all transactions occur on a single day, say, May 1.

■ Table 1.2

FUTURES MARKET OBLIGATIONS

The oat contract is traded by the Chicago Board of Trade. Each contract is for 5,000 bushels, and prices are quoted in cents per bushel.

(a)	**Party 1**	**Party 2**
	Buys 1 SEP contract for oats at 171 cents per bushel	Sells 1 SEP contract for oats at 171 cents per bushel
(b)	**Party 1**	**Clearinghouse**
	Buys 1 SEP contract for oats at 171 cents per bushel	Agrees to deliver to Party 1 a SEP contract for oats at a price of 171 cents per bushel
(c)	**Party 2**	**Clearinghouse**
	Sells 1 SEP contract for oats at 171 cents per bushel	Agrees to receive from Party 2 a SEP contract for oats and to pay 171 cents per bushel

Party 1 trades on the futures exchange to buy one oats contract of 5,000 bushels for delivery in September. In order for Party 1 to buy the contract, some other participant must sell. In panel (a) of the table it is apparent that Party 1 and Party 2 have exactly complementary positions in the futures market. One party has bought exactly what the other has sold. Notice that the time of delivery, the amount of oats to be delivered, and the price all match. Without a perfect match in all these respects, there could not have been a transaction. In all probability, the two trading parties will not even know each other. It is perfectly possible that each will have traded through a broker from different parts of the country. In such a situation, problems of trust may arise. How can either party be sure that the other will fulfill the agreement?

The clearinghouse exists to solve that problem. As panels (b) and (c) indicate, the clearinghouse guarantees fulfillment of the contract to each of the trading parties. After the initial sale is made, the clearinghouse steps in and acts as the seller to the buyer and acts as the buyer to the seller. In panel (b), the clearinghouse guarantees the buyer of the futures contract, Party 1, that it will deliver at the initially agreed upon time and price. To the seller, Party 2, the clearinghouse guarantees that it will accept delivery at the agreed upon time and price, as panel (c) shows. Figure 1.2 illustrates the same idea graphically. Without a clearinghouse, both parties must deal with each other, and they have direct obligations to one another. With a clearinghouse, each party has obligations to the clearinghouse and the clearinghouse will ensure that they perform.

Because of the clearinghouse, the two trading parties do not need to trust each other or even know each other's identity. Instead, the two traders only have to be concerned about the reliability of the clearinghouse. However, the clearinghouse is a large, well-capitalized financial institution. Its failure to perform on its guarantee to the two trading parties would bring the futures market to ruin. In the history of U.S. futures trading, the clearinghouse has always performed as promised, so the risk of a future default by the clearinghouse is very small.[13]

A more careful examination of panels (b) and (c) from Table 1.2 gives further confidence that the clearinghouse will perform as promised. In total, the clearinghouse has no independent position in oats. It is obligated to receive oats and pay 171 cents per bushel, but it is also obligated to deliver oats and receive 171 cents per bushel. These

■ Figure 1.2

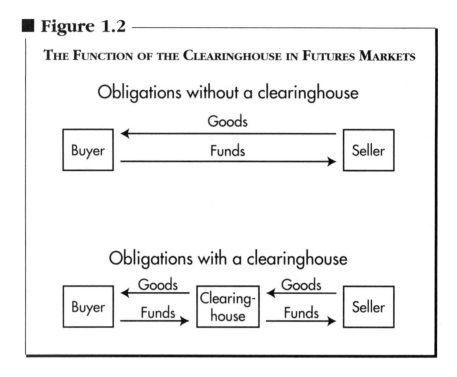

THE FUNCTION OF THE CLEARINGHOUSE IN FUTURES MARKETS

Obligations without a clearinghouse

two obligations net out to zero. Since it maintains no futures market position of its own, the riskiness of the clearinghouse is less than it may appear.[14]

MARGIN AND DAILY SETTLEMENT

In addition to the clearinghouse, there are other safeguards for the futures market. Chief among these are the requirements for margin and daily settlement. Before trading a futures contract, the prospective trader must deposit funds with a broker. These funds serve as a good-faith deposit by the trader and are referred to as **margin**. The main purpose of margin is to provide a financial safeguard to ensure that traders will perform on their contract obligations. The margin requirement restricts the activity of traders, so the exchanges and brokers are anxious that the margin requirements not be unreasonably high. The amount of this margin varies from contract to contract and may vary by broker as well. The margin may be posted in cash, by a bank letter of credit, or in short-term U.S. Treasury instruments. The trader who posts this margin retains title to it.

Types of Margin. In this section, we consider the different types of margins and show how margin requirements would affect a trader holding a single futures position. In the next section, we consider margin rules for more complicated positions.

There are three types of margin. The initial deposit just described is the **initial margin** – the amount a trader must deposit before trading any futures. The initial margin approximately equals the maximum daily price fluctuation permitted for the contract being traded. Upon proper completion of all obligations associated with a trader's futures position, the initial margin is returned to the trader. If one has deposited a security as the margin, then the trader earns the interest that accrues while the security has served as the margin.

For most futures contracts, the initial margin may be 5 percent or less of the underlying commodity's value.[15] It may seem strange that the initial margin is so small relative to the value of the commodity underlying the futures contract. The smallness of this amount is reasonable, however, because there is another safeguard built into the system in the form of **daily settlement** or **marking-to-market**. In the futures market, traders are required to realize any losses in cash on the day they occur. In the parlance of the futures market, the contract is marked-to-the-market.

To understand the process of daily settlement, consult Table 1.2 again and consider Party 1, who bought one contract for 171 cents per bushel. Assume that the contract closes on May 2 at 168 cents per bushel. This means that Party 1 has sustained a loss of 3 cents per bushel. Since there are 5,000 bushels in the contract, this represents a loss of $150, which is deducted from the margin deposited with the broker. When the value of the funds on deposit with the broker reaches a certain level, called the **maintenance margin**, the trader is required to replenish the margin, bringing it back to its initial level. This demand for more margin is known as a **margin call**. The additional amount the trader must deposit is called the **variation margin**. The maintenance margin is generally about 75 percent of the amount of the initial margin. For example, assume that the initial margin was $1,400, that Party 1 had deposited only this minimum initial margin, and that the maintenance margin is $1,100. Party 1 has already sustained a loss of $150, so the equity in the margin account is $1,250. The next day, assume that the price of oats drops 4 cents per bushel, generating an additional loss for Party 1 of $200. This brings the value of the margin account to $1,050, which is below the level of the required maintenance margin. This means that the broker will require Party 1 to replenish the margin account to $1,400, the level of the initial margin. To restore the margin account, the trader must pay $350 variation margin. Variation margin must always be paid in cash.

Figure 1.3 uses the initial margin level of $1,400 and the maintenance margin level of $1,100 to illustrate this process. At the outset, the value of the margin deposited with the broker is $1,400. First the trader has mixed results with some small gains and small losses, with losses predominating. Before long, losses drop the value of the account below $1,100. As the figure shows, the trader must then restore the value, or equity, in the account to $1,400. After this first margin call, the trader has mixed results for a while, followed by large losses. These losses generate a second margin call. Figure 1.3 shows only the required cash flows. The trader could have withdrawn cash whenever the value of the equity exceeded $1,400. However, a trader cannot withdraw funds that would leave the account's equity value below the level of the initial margin.

■ **Figure 1.3**

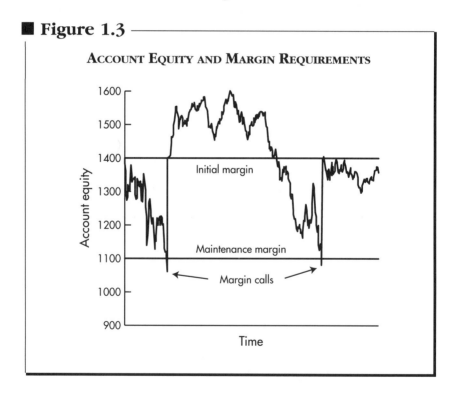

ACCOUNT EQUITY AND MARGIN REQUIREMENTS

Because futures prices change almost every day, each account will have frequent gains and losses. The losses can require a variation margin payment, and the gains may entitle the trader to withdraw cash. For convenience, traders do not want to face a daily margin call in many cases. There are two basic ways to avoid a margin call. First, a trader can deposit securities with a value well in excess of the initial margin. Second, a trader can deposit funds in excess of the initial margin into an interest-bearing account. In either case, such a deposit provides a liquidity pool that will protect the trader from untimely demands for variation margin payments. Similarly, the trader can instruct the broker to sweep profits from his account into an interest-bearing investment. Those funds can be held ready to meet margin calls as required.

This practice of posting maintenance or variation margin and daily settlement helps make the futures market safer. Assume that Party 1 in Table 1.2 posted only the initial margin, the bare minimum to have the trade executed. Also assume that the trader suffered a loss requiring more margin and that the trader was unable or refused to post the required additional margin. The broker in such a situation is empowered to close the futures position by deducting the loss from the trader's initial margin and returning the balance, less commission costs, to the trader. The broker would also close the trader's entire brokerage account as well. Failure to post the required maintenance margin is a violation of a trader's agreement with the broker. Now it becomes apparent why the initial margin is so small. The initial margin needs to cover only one day's price fluctuation, because any losses will be covered by the posting of additional variation margin. Failure to pay variation margin will lead to the futures position being closed out.

Margin Cash Flows. This section traces the flow of margin funds from the trader to the clearinghouse. The margin system functions through a hierarchy of market participants that links the clearinghouse with the individual trader. The members of an exchange may be classified as clearing members or nonclearing members. A **clearing member** is a member of the exchange that is also a member of the clearinghouse. The clearinghouse deals only with clearing members. As a consequence, any nonclearing member must clear his or her trades through a clearing member.

The clearinghouse demands margin deposits from clearing members to cover all futures positions that are carried by that clearing member. For example, a clearing member might be a large broker who executes orders for individual traders and who provides clearing services for some nonclearing members of the exchange. Therefore, the clearing member will impose margin requirements on all of the accounts that it represents to the clearinghouse.

Figure 1.4 shows the margin flows for an individual trader who might trade through a clearing member or a nonclearing member. In the figure, Trader A trades through a broker who is a clearing member. In this case, Trader A deposits margin funds with the clearing member, who makes margin deposits with the clearinghouse. As a second alternative in Figure 1.4, Trader B trades through a broker who is a nonclearing member of the exchange. This broker must arrange to clear all trades with a clearing member. In this situation, Trader B deposits margin funds with his or her broker. This broker deposits margin funds with a clearing member, and the clearing member deposits margin funds with the clearinghouse.

It is not very important whether Traders A and B trade directly through a clearing member or a nonclearing member. Most large brokerage firms are clearing members, so most individual traders who trade through their local broker will be trading through a clearing member. However, many members of each exchange trade for their own accounts as speculators. Few of them are clearing members, so they need to clear their trades through a clearing member.

■ **Figure 1.4**

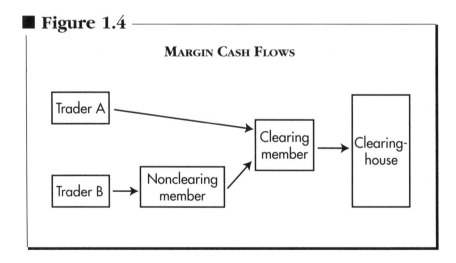

MARGIN CASH FLOWS

MARGINS FOR COMBINATIONS OF FUTURES POSITIONS

As we will explore in Chapter 3, speculators often hold combinations of related futures positions. Such a combined futures position is called a **spread**. For example, a speculator might hold a long position in a wheat futures contract for July delivery and a short position in a wheat futures contract for September delivery. (The speculator would be attempting to profit on a change in the relationship between the prices on the two futures contracts.) Not surprisingly, the prices of the July and September wheat futures contracts are closely related. In this example, both futures positions are in the same commodity. A spread position with both futures positions in the same commodity is called an **intramarket spread**, a **calendar spread** or a **time spread**.[16] The futures contracts in a spread usually have related price movements, which reduces the risk of a spread relative to a single contract. Because the risk of the spread is less than the risk of holding a single outright contract, the exchange imposes lower margin requirements on such spreads. As an example, the wheat contract might have an initial margin requirement of $2,500 for a single futures contract. If a trader holds an intramarket spread in wheat, the margin could be much lower, say $1,500. This lower spread margin covers both contracts in the spread of our example. Thus, the spread margin per contract is less than half the outright margin. All time spreads receive this favorable margin treatment.

In addition to intramarket spreads, there are also spreads between different, but related, commodities. For example, a trader might hold a long futures position in July wheat and a short position in July oats. A spread in two distinct, but related, commodities is called an **intermarket spread**. Not every pair of commodities is sufficiently related to receive treatment as an intermarket spread. For example, there is a close relationship between wheat and oats, but such a close relationship does not exist between wheat and coffee. The exchanges determine which commodity pairs constitute an intermarket spread for purposes of margins. Table 1.3 shows some pairs of commodities that qualify for spread margins. As the table shows, qualification for intermarket spread margining treatment depends on a close economic relationship between the two commodities. Notice that each of these spread margin pairs is for commodities traded on the same exchange. This system results from the fact that each exchange sets its own

■ **Table 1.3**

EXAMPLES OF INTERMARKET SPREADS QUALIFYING FOR SPREAD
MARGIN TREATMENT

Exchange	Commodity Pair
Chicago Board of Trade	Treasury bonds vs. Treasury notes
	Any pair of wheat, corn, or oats
	Any pair of soybeans, soyoil, or soymeal
	Gold vs. silver
Chicago Mercantile Exchange	Eurodollars vs. Treasury bills
	Any pair of foreign currencies (British pound, German mark, Swiss franc, French franc, Japanese yen, Canadian dollar, Australian dollar)
	Any pair of cattle, feeder cattle, or hogs
	Pork bellies vs. hogs

margins. With each exchange establishing its margins independently, there is little opportunity for considering spread relationships between related commodities traded on two different exchanges.

INTERMARKET CROSS-MARGINING

Intermarket cross-margining is a system that establishes a trader's margin requirement by considering the trader's entire portfolio, even if portions of that portfolio are held in different exchanges. In essence, the idea extends the principle of spread margins across exchange boundaries. As an example, Treasury bill and Treasury bond futures prices are clearly related. However, Treasury bill futures trade at the Chicago Mercantile Exchange and Treasury bond futures trade at the Chicago Board of Trade. A margining system that recognizes a spread between bills and bonds would be a system of intermarket cross-margining.

Today there is a limited intermarket cross-margining system. Intermarket cross-margining for futures becomes possible if a trader holds positions on two different exchanges through the same brokerage firm. For example, assume a trader holds a long SEP Treasury bill futures contract and a short SEP Treasury bond contract with her broker, Merrill Lynch. This position would qualify for spread margins, because both sides of the spread are held with the same broker. The broker fulfills the function of identifying the two individual futures positions as two halves of a single spread. However, if the trader held the bill position with Merrill Lynch and the bond position with Salomon Brothers, for example, the position would not qualify for reduced margins.

Some market observers have called for an extension of intermarket cross-margining. Under these proposals, margin rules would consider a trader's full position, not only across different futures exchanges, but across fundamentally different types of instruments. Much of the impetus for such a broad cross-margining system has emerged from studies of the market crash of October 1987. After the crash, the Brady Commission studied the performance of the financial system during that stressful time. As one of their conclusions, the Commission endorsed intermarket cross-margining. Because the Brady Commission focused on equities, we will use stock trading as an example. The principles apply to other kinds of instruments as well. Individual stocks trade on stock exchanges and through the National Association of Securities Dealers Automated Quotation (NASDAQ) system. Options on individual stocks and stock indexes trade on various option exchanges. Stock index futures trade on various futures exchanges, as do options on those stock index futures. Considered in total, equity trading spans a large number of exchanges. There are 13 clearing-houses in the United States, all of which impose margin requirements. With some exceptions, one clearinghouse does not recognize the positions that traders hold at other clearinghouses. As a consequence, each position is margined separately.

Full intermarket cross-margining would consider all types of a trader's total equity position in determining the necessary margin position. Because margin requirements are supposed to reflect the trader's risk exposure, such a system of cross-margining would be highly desirable, since it would monitor the trader's total risk. In many instances, a trader's entire portfolio risk can be less than the sum of the risks represented by the individual pieces. For example, a trader holding a large portfolio of individual stocks, and who sells a stock index futures contract, is essentially a spread trader. Like spread traders in other goods, this trader's total risk exposure might well be less than the risk exposure represented by either the stock portfolio alone or the futures position alone. Under intermarket cross-margining, the margin requirements would recognize the real extent of the trader's risk.

There are at least five benefits of such a cross-margining system. First, the total amount of initial margin required from traders will be less for a given degree of risk protection. This would free capital for other applications, such as meeting variation margin calls. Second, cross-margining would probably require a central clearinghouse to serve the various markets. Such a central clearinghouse would reduce transfers of money between accounts and increase the operational efficiency of the market. Third, lower margin requirements would help attract more traders. Having more traders in the system would contribute to making the markets more liquid. Fourth, such a system would help U.S. exchanges compete with the burgeoning foreign financial markets. Finally, in periods of dramatic price changes, cross-margining would reduce the chances of a forced sell-off by some traders. For example, assume there is a large price rise in the stock market, and consider a trader who owns stocks and is short a stock index futures contract. Rising stock prices generate a loss for a short stock index futures trader. If the margin system requires margin based only on considering the futures position in isolation, the trader would be required to pay variation margin. However, if the trader owns stock and sells a stock index futures contract against it, the rise in stock prices might generate a gain on the stock itself that would fully offset the losses on stock index futures. The economics of such a situation do not require any increase in the trader's margin payments. Only a system of cross-margining could reflect the true economics of this trader's position.

Cross-margining also may involve certain risks. First, reducing margin might free capital for additional trading, not merely as a reserve against future margin calls. Cross-margining might merely mean that the system as a whole holds less margin money, thereby causing an increase in the overall risk of system-wide default. Second, the offsetting positions might diverge from their normal relationships. In this case, there could be losses on both sides of the position instead of a loss on one side coupled with an offsetting gain on the other.

One impediment to full intermarket cross-margining is the 13 clearinghouses themselves. Cross-margining means that clearinghouses may be consolidated or eliminated. Therefore, some clearinghouses are reluctant to open a Pandora's box of cross-margining that may lead to their own demise.

THE SPAN MARGIN SYSTEM

While full cross-margining remains in the future, a partial cross-margining system known as SPAN is already in widespread use. SPAN stands for *Standard Portfolio Analysis of Risk,* and it is in use at most U.S. futures exchanges today. It offers cross-margining between futures and options on futures by considering the entire portfolio in setting margin requirements. The price of an option on a futures contract depends on a number of factors, including the price of the futures, the volatility of price movements on the futures, and the amount of time remaining until the option expires.[17]

The SPAN system considers 16 possible "what if" scenarios to determine the appropriate margin. The 16 scenarios reflect changes in the futures price and changes in the volatility of futures price. Table 1.4 shows the 16 different scenarios. The futures range equals the maintenance margin on a single futures contract and an extreme move is twice the futures range. The SPAN system computes how the value of the portfolio would change under each of the 16 scenarios. The margin requirement equals the largest loss under any of the 16 scenarios. If a trader holds a combination of futures and option on

■ **Table 1.4** ───────────────────────────────

SIXTEEN SPAN SCENARIOS

1. Futures unchanged; Volatility up	9. Futures down 2/3 range; Volatility up
2. Futures unchanged; Volatility down	10. Futures down 2/3 range; Volatility down
3. Futures up 1/3 range; Volatility up	11. Futures up 3/3 range; Volatility up
4. Futures up 1/3 range; Volatility down	12. Futures up 3/3 range; Volatility down
5. Futures down 1/3 range; Volatility up	13. Futures down 3/3 range; Volatility up
6. Futures down 1/3 range; Volatility down	14. Futures down 3/3 range; Volatility down
7. Futures up 2/3 range; Volatility up	15. Futures up extreme move
8. Futures up 2/3 range; Volatility down	16. Futures down extreme move

futures positions, the SPAN system will accurately reflect the risk of the entire position and compute the margin amount commensurate with that level of risk.

VALUE-AT-RISK (VAR)

Value-at-Risk (VAR) is an attempt to measure the entire price risk of a firm's portfolio. Originally developed with a particular eye to measuring the risk of derivatives, the principle applies to all types of financial instruments. The goal is to determine how much the value of the portfolio is likely to change over a certain period. For example, VAR should allow a manager to compute the maximum loss that might be experienced in one day at a 95 percent confidence level. Applying the VAR technique requires determining the price sensitivity of each instrument in the portfolio to the relevant market factors. This can be done in three ways: using historical price performance of the security; simulating the price changes from perturbations in market factors such as interest rates, foreign exchange rate, and market indexes; or by an analytical method that decomposes instruments into more fundamental cash equivalents.

JP Morgan has developed a system of market risk factors called RiskMetrics. JP Morgan provides a vector of these risk factors, updated each day, on the World Wide Web, and these can be downloaded by anyone free of charge. A number of vendors provide software for using the RiskMetric factors. The Bank for International Settlements (BIS) has proposed its own system, and some firms use their own proprietary system of VAR. It would be desirable for there to be a single industry standard for computing VAR, as this would allow meaningful interfirm risk comparisons. Unfortunately, various computational methods give significantly different risk measurements, and standardization of these techniques lies in the future.[18]

CLOSING A FUTURES POSITION

Initially, we discussed the completion of a futures contract through delivery. However, in the discussion of variation margin we noted that the broker might close the position after trading on May 2. The careful reader might remember that the initial trade shown in Table 1.2 called for a September delivery. In view of that fact, it may not seem that the futures position could be closed in May. There are, however, three ways to close a futures position: delivery, offset, and an exchange-for-physicals.

Delivery. Most futures contracts are written to call for completion of the futures contract through the physical delivery of a particular good. As we have seen in our discussion of the wheat contract, delivery takes place at certain locations and at certain times under rules specified by a futures exchange. In recent years, exchanges have introduced futures contracts that allow completion through **cash settlement**. In cash settlement, traders make payments at the expiration of the contract to settle any gains or losses, instead of making physical delivery. Both physical delivery and cash settlement close the contract in the expiration period. However, few futures contracts are actually closed through either physical delivery or cash settlement. For example, in the fiscal year ending September 30, 1995, only about three-fourths of one percent of all contracts traded were settled by either physical delivery or cash settlement. Table 1.5 shows the commodity groups and the percentage of contracts completed by delivery or cash settlement within each group. Only currencies have more than 2 percent of contracts completed by delivery or cash settlement. In the energy, livestock, and wood groups, delivery is extremely

■ Table 1.5

COMPLETION OF FUTURES CONTRACTS VIA DELIVERY OR CASH
SETTLEMENT OCTOBER 1, 1994–SEPTEMBER 30, 1995

Commodity Group	Volume	Delivered or Settled in Cash	
		Contracts	Percentage
Grains	21,093,886	70,548	0.33
Oilseeds	20,687,820	158,003	0.76
Livestock	6,238,509	12,900	0.21
Other Agricultural	12,742,515	60,302	0.47
Energy/Wood	47,941,379	74,978	0.16
Metals	17,393,317	157,323	0.90
Financial Instruments	259,029,356	1,940,293	0.75
Currencies	24,293,644	521,611	2.15
All Commodities	409,420,426	2,995,958	0.73

Source: Commodity Futures Trading Commission, Annual Report, 1995.

rare. Therefore, the vast majority of all contracts initiated must be completed by some means other than delivery or cash settlement.

Offset. By far, most futures contracts are completed through **offset** or via a **reversing trade**. To complete a futures contract obligation through offset, the trader transacts in the futures market to bring his or her net position in a particular futures contract back to zero. Consider again the situation depicted in Table 1.2. The first party has an obligation to the clearinghouse to accept 5,000 bushels of oats in September and to pay 171 cents per bushel for them at that time. Perhaps the trader does not wish to actually receive the oats and wants to exit the futures market earlier, say, May 10. The trader can fulfill the commitment by entering the futures market again and making the reversing trade depicted in Table 1.6.

The first line of Table 1.6 merely repeats the initial trade that was made on May 1. On May 10, Party 1 takes exactly the opposite position by selling 1 SEP contract for oats at the current futures price of 180 cents per bushel. This time the trader transacts with a new entrant to the market, Party 3. After this reversing trade, Party 1's net position is zero. The clearinghouse recognizes this, and Party 1 is absolved from any further obligation. In this example, the price of September oats rose 9 cents per bushel during this period, happily yielding Party 1 a profit of $450. Party 2, the original seller, is not affected by Party 1's reversing trade. Party 2 still has the same commitment, because the clearinghouse continues to stand ready to complete this transaction described in Table 1.2. Now the clearinghouse also assumes a complementary obligation to the new market entrant, Party 3. Note that

■ Table 1.6

THE REVERSING TRADE

	Party 1's Initial Position	Party 2
May 1	Bought 1 SEP contract for oats at 171 cents per bushel	Sold 1 SEP contract for oats at 171 cents per bushel
	Party 1's Reversing Trade	Party 3
May 10	Sells 1 SEP contract for oats at 180 cents per bushel	Buys 1 SEP oats contract at 180 cents per bushel

the position of the clearinghouse has not really changed due to the transactions on May 10. Also, Party 2 and Party 3 have complementary obligations after the new trades, just as Party 1 and Party 2 had complementary obligations after the initial transactions on May 1.

In entering the reversing trade, it is crucial that Party 1 sell exactly the same contract that was bought originally. Note in Table 1.6 that the reversing trade matches the original transaction in the good traded, the number of contracts, and the maturity. If it does not, then the trader undertakes a new obligation instead of canceling the old. If Party 1 had sold one DEC contract on May 10 instead of selling the SEP contract, for example, he or she would be obligated to receive oats in September and to deliver oats in December. Such a transaction would result in holding two positions instead of a reversing trade.

Exchange-for-Physicals (EFP). A trader can complete a futures contract by engaging in an exchange-for-physicals (EFP). In an EFP, two traders agree to a simultaneous exchange of a cash commodity and futures contracts based on that cash commodity. For example, assume that Trader A is long one wheat contract and genuinely wishes to acquire wheat. Also, assume that Trader B is short one wheat contract and owns wheat. The two traders agree on a price for the physical wheat and agree to cancel their complementary futures positions against each other. An EFP differs in certain respects from an offsetting trade. First, the traders actually exchange the physical good. Second, the futures contract was not closed by a transaction on the floor of the exchange. Third, the two traders privately negotiated the price and other terms of the transaction. Because an EFP transaction takes place away from the trading floor of the exchange, it is sometimes known as an **ex-pit** transaction. Federal law and exchange rules generally require all futures trading to take place in the pit. However, the EFP is the one recognized exception to this general rule. EFPs are also known as **against actuals** or **versus cash** transactions.

EXCHANGES AND TYPES OF FUTURES

Since the founding of the Chicago Board of Trade in 1848, futures markets have flourished. The past decade has been a period of extraordinary growth for futures markets, due largely to the development of entirely new types of contracts in foreign exchange, interest rates, and stock indexes. Within the last few years, several new types of contracts have been developed, including futures on stock indexes and options on futures contracts. The future promises to be a period of continued explosive growth for the industry.

WORLDWIDE EXCHANGES

Table 1.7 lists the major U.S. futures exchanges, the date they began trading, and the principal types of contracts they trade. Recent years have seen considerable consolidation in the industry. One of the largest mergers was the union of the Commodity Exchange of New York (COMEX) and the New York Mercantile Exchange (NYME) into the New York Mercantile Exchange with NYMEX and COMEX divisions. Table 1.8 covers some major foreign exchanges. The oldest of these is more than 140 years old. Differences in size among these exchanges are striking, ranging from the New York Cotton Exchange, which by state law can trade only cotton futures, to the very large

■ Table 1.7

U.S. FUTURES EXCHANGES

Exchange and Year Founded	Principal Types of Contracts			
	Physical	Currencies	Interest Rates	Index
Chicago Board of Trade (CBOT) 1848	◆		◆	◆
Chicago Mercantile Exchange (CME) 1919	◆	◆	◆	◆
Coffee, Sugar and Cocoa Exchange (New York) 1882	◆			
Kansas City Board of Trade (KCBT) 1856	◆			◆
Mid-America Commodity Exchange (Chicago) 1880	◆	◆	◆	
Minneapolis Grain Exchange 1881	◆			
New York Cotton Exchange, Inc. 1870	◆	◆		◆
New York Mercantile Exchange 1872	◆			◆

From *Futures 1996 Source Book.* Reprinted by permission of Futures Magazine, 219 Parkadie, Cedar Falls, Iowa 50613.

■ Table 1.8

NON-U.S. FUTURES EXCHANGES

Exchange	Principal Types of Contracts			
	Physical	Currencies	Interest Rates	Stock Index
Bolsa de Mercadorios de Sao Paulo	♦	♦	♦	♦
London International Financial Futures Exchange (LIFFE)	♦	♦	♦	♦
International Petroleum Exchange (London)	♦			
London Futures & Options Exchange (FOX)	♦			
Tokyo International Financial Futures Exchange (TIFFE)		♦	♦	
Osaka Securities Exchange				♦
Tokyo Commodity Exchange	♦			
Tokyo Stock Exchange			♦	♦
Singapore International Monetary Exchange (SIMEX)	♦	♦	♦	♦
Deutsche Boerse			♦	♦
Marche a Terme International de France (MATIF)	♦	♦	♦	♦
Hong Kong Futures Exchange	♦	♦	♦	♦
New Zealand Futures Exchange		♦	♦	♦
Sydney Futures Exchange	♦	♦	♦	♦
Toronto Futures Exchange				♦
Montreal Exchange			♦	♦
Winnepeg Commodity Exchange	♦			
Kuala Lumpur Commodity Exchange	♦			

Sources: *The Wall Street Journal, Futures Magazine, Intermarket Magazine,* various issues.

exchanges, such as the Chicago Board of Trade (CBOT) and the Chicago Mercantile Exchange (CME), which have more than 1,000 members each and trade a wide variety of futures. The futures markets of Chicago alone directly employ more than 40,000 people.

TYPES OF FUTURES CONTRACTS

The types of futures contracts that are traded fall into four fundamentally different categories. The underlying good traded may be a physical commodity, a foreign currency, an interest-earning asset, or an index, usually a stock index. Contracts for more than 50 different goods are currently available. While Chapters 4 through 8 focus specifically on the various types of financial futures, it is useful to have some appreciation for the range of goods that are traded on the futures market.

Agricultural and Metallurgical Contracts. In the agricultural area, contracts are traded in grains (corn, oats, and wheat), oil and meal (soybeans, soymeal, and soyoil, and sunflower seeds and oil), livestock (live hogs, cattle, and pork bellies), forest products (lumber and plywood), textiles (cotton), and foodstuffs (cocoa, coffee, orange juice, rice, and sugar). For many of these commodities, several different contracts are available for different grades or types of the commodity. For most of the goods, there are also a number of months for delivery. The months chosen for delivery of the seasonal crops generally fit their harvest patterns. The number of contract months available for each commodity also depends on the level of trading activity. For some relatively inactive futures contracts, there may be trading in only one or two delivery months in the year. By contrast, an active commodity, such as soybean meal, may have trading in eight delivery months.

The metallurgical category includes the genuine metals, as well as petroleum contracts. These two kinds of goods are really more similar than they appear to be, because both petroleum and metals are highly storable. Among the metals, contracts are traded on gold, silver, platinum, palladium, and copper. Of the petroleum products, heating oil, crude oil, gasoline, and propane are traded on futures markets.

Interest-Earning Assets. Futures trading on interest-bearing assets started only in 1975, but the growth of this market has been tremendous. Contracts are traded now on Treasury bills, notes, and bonds, on Eurodollar deposits, and on municipal bonds. The existing contracts span almost the entire yield curve, so it is possible to trade instruments with virtually every maturity. The CME trades two contracts with three-month maturities, T-bills and Eurodollar time deposits. This allows trading based on anticipated interest rate differentials for the same maturity. In addition, contracts on foreign debt instruments are traded on foreign futures exchanges. For example, major contracts on government bonds are traded on exchanges in London, Paris, Frankfurt, and Tokyo.

Foreign Currencies. Active futures trading of foreign currencies dates back to the inception of freely floating exchange rates in the early 1970s. Contracts trade on the British pound, the Canadian dollar, the Japanese yen, the Swiss franc, and the German mark. Contracts are also listed on French francs, Dutch guilders, and Mexican pesos, but these have met with only limited success and are no longer traded. The foreign exchange futures market represents the one case of a futures market existing in the face of a truly active forward market. The forward market for foreign exchange is many times larger than the futures market. Many people believe that the presence of the forward market deterred the introduction and slowed the growth of futures trading in foreign exchange. Contracts on different currencies are also traded on a number of foreign futures exchanges, as Table 1.8 shows.

Indexes. The last major group of futures contracts is for indexes. Most, but not all, of these contracts are for stock indexes. Beginning only in 1982, these contracts have been quite successful, with trading on market indexes in full swing. Exchanges trade contracts on four different U.S. stock indexes: the Standard and Poor's 500, a Major Market Index, the New York Stock Exchange Index, and the Value Line Index. Foreign exchanges trade futures on foreign stock indexes, such as the trading of the Japanese Nikkei index on the Tokyo Futures Exchange and on the Singapore International Monetary Exchange (SIMEX) as well.

In September 1990, the Chicago Board of Trade and the Chicago Mercantile Exchange began trading futures contracts based on Japanese financial markets. The Chicago Mercantile Exchange trades a contract based on the Nikkei 225 stock index and the Chicago Board of Trade launched a contract based on the TOPIX index of major firms traded on the Tokyo Stock Exchange. Neither contract has met expectations, due in part to the poor performance of the Japanese stock market in recent years. One of the most striking things about these stock index contracts is that they do not admit the possibility of actual delivery. A trader's obligation must be fulfilled by a reversing trade or a cash settlement at the end of trading. Other types of indexes also are traded in futures markets, including a foreign exchange index and an index of municipal bonds.

RELATIVE IMPORTANCE OF COMMODITY TYPES

Figure 1.5 presents another division of futures contracts into eight categories and shows the relative importance of trading in these different categories in the United States in 1995. As Figure 1.5 shows, over

■ Figure 1.5

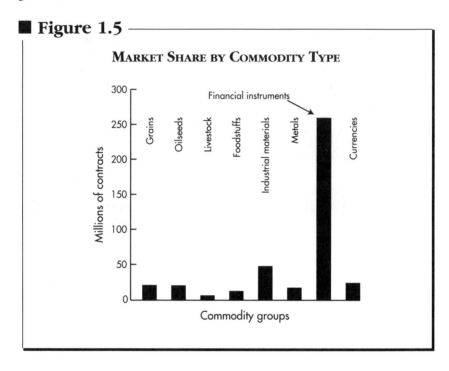

Market Share by Commodity Type

half of the trading volume stems from financial instruments. These include futures contracts based on underlying instruments such as Treasury securities and stock indexes. As we have noted, trading in these contracts began in 1975, so growth in this area has been dramatic. Figure 1.6 shows how the portions of futures trading volume have shifted among these commodity groups over recent years.

Electronic Futures Trading

From the beginning of organized futures exchanges in the mid-1800s to a few years ago, the system of open outcry has been the only method of futures trading. While open outcry continues to dominate futures trading, we are now seeing the emergence of automated trading systems that may eventually change the entire face of the futures markets.

The advent of electronic trading systems also promises to be an important element in global competition among futures exchanges. In futures trading, the U.S. markets are the oldest and best established. In some ways, the members of the U.S. exchanges are the most conservative and wedded to tradition, particularly the tradition of

■ Figure 1.6

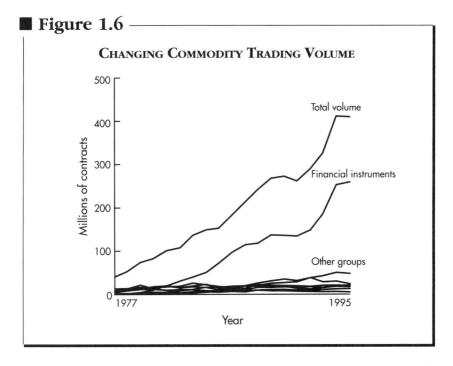

CHANGING COMMODITY TRADING VOLUME

trading in pits through open outcry. Exchange policies are controlled by exchange members. In the Chicago markets, a high proportion of members are individuals who trade for their own accounts. Their livelihood depends upon the trading acumen that they have developed through their years in the trading pits. Electronic trading systems threaten to make those open outcry skills obsolete. Not surprisingly, these members have resisted any threats to the system of open outcry.

New and smaller exchanges have little tradition to confront. Compared to pit trading with open outcry, electronic trading is definitely cheaper to launch. Many traders also believe that electronic systems are operationally superior to pit trading. Further, there are many different electronic trading systems, all of which have their own features. No matter what one believes about the virtues of open outcry versus electronic trading, it is clear that electronic trading is here to stay. Because electronic trading is largely technologically driven, we can expect accelerating change in this area. Some smaller foreign exchanges have a much larger commitment to electronic trading than do the major exchanges. The four largest systems are: GLOBEX, sponsored by the CME and the French exchange MATIF; Project A, sponsored by the CBOT; Access, sponsored by NYMEX; and APT, sponsored by the LIFFE of London. Table 1.9 shows recent volume for these major systems. The remainder of this section provides a brief description of GLOBEX and Project A.

GLOBEX

Because of initial resistance by U.S. traders, exchanges in the United States have been relatively slow to develop electronic trading systems. However, because the U.S. exchanges dominate world futures markets, any system that prevails in the United States will have an extremely good chance of being the dominant electronic trading system in the world. After many delays, GLOBEX began trading in June 1992. GLOBEX was initially developed by the Chicago Mercantile Exchange. The Paris exchange, MATIF, also trades through GLOBEX, and GLOBEX continues to court other exchanges. Transacting on GLOBEX involves seven steps, which are shown in Figure 1.7.

Initially, GLOBEX was created to augment open outcry. Currently, trading on GLOBEX is restricted to hours when the Chicago Mercantile Exchange is not open. However, when one considers the success of electronic trading systems at other exchanges, it seems clear that electronic trading has a future that goes far beyond a mere supplement to pit trading. That future remains obscure, however. In its first year of trading, GLOBEX traded just slightly more than one million contracts. (This is less than one-half of one percent of industry volume.) Ironically, MATIF accounts for more volume on GLOBEX than the CME. At one point, the CBOT was a partner in GLOBEX, but it has

■ Table 1.9

ELECTRONIC FUTURES TRADING

System	Exchange	Country	Recent Monthly Volume
GLOBEX	CME	USA	725,000
APT	LIFFE	United Kingdom	370,000
Access	NYMEX	USA	140,000
Project A	CBOT	USA	117,000

From "Any Time, Any Place," *Risk* 9:3, March 1996, pp. 27–31. Reprinted by permission.

■ Figure 1.7

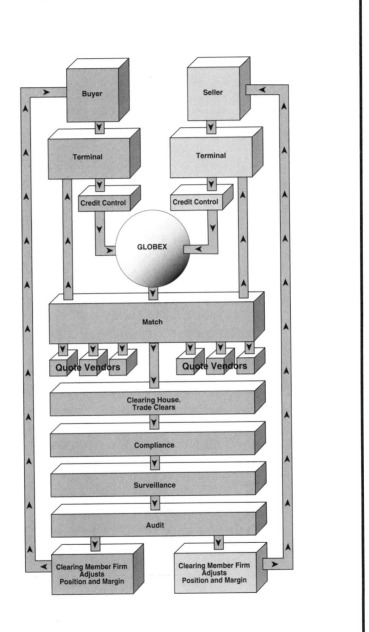

Reprinted by permission of Chicago Mercantile Exchange.

now abandoned that venture and instead launched its own electronic trading system called Project A.

Project A

Project A is an electronic order-entry and matching system operated by the CBOT for off-hours trading of CBOT contracts. The system operates from 2:30 to 4:30 p.m. and from 10:30 p.m. to 6:00 a.m. Chicago time. During the regular trading day, all trading takes place in pits using open outcry. Initially the system allowed for trading of financial futures and options, but this has now been expanded to include agricultural contracts. Trades entered in open-outcry sessions can be offset on Project A, and vice versa.

With its expanded hours, traders can trade CBOT products during the entire time the cash Treasury market is open. Also, overseas traders can trade CBOT contracts during their daylight hours, and the ability to trade CBOT contracts during the Chicago night allows real-time spread trading of CBOT contracts against foreign markets.

Purposes of Futures Markets

Any industry as old and as large as the futures market must serve some social purpose. If it did not, it would most likely have passed from existence some time ago. Traditionally, futures markets have been recognized as meeting the needs of three groups of futures market users: those who wish to discover information about future prices of commodities, those who wish to speculate, and those who wish to hedge. While Chapter 3 discusses the uses that these three groups make of futures markets in detail, it is important to have some understanding of the social function of futures markets before proceeding. Traditionally, speculation is not regarded as socially useful by itself, although it may have socially useful by-products. Thus, there are two main social functions of futures markets – price discovery and hedging.

Price Discovery

Price discovery is the revealing of information about future cash market prices through the futures market. As discussed earlier, in buying or selling a futures contract, a trader agrees to receive or deliver a given commodity at a certain time in the future for a price that is determined now. In such a circumstance, it is not surprising that there is a relationship between the futures price and the price that people expect to prevail for the commodity at the delivery date specified in the futures contract. While the exact nature of that relationship will be considered in detail in Chapter 2, the relationship is predictable to a high degree. By using the information contained in futures prices today, market observers can form estimates of what the price of a given commodity will be at a certain time in the future. The forecasts of future prices that can be drawn from the futures market compare in accuracy quite favorably with other types of forecasts. Futures markets serve a social purpose by helping people make better estimates of future prices, so that they can make their consumption and investment decisions more wisely.

As an example of price discovery and its benefits, consider a mine operator who is trying to decide whether to reopen a marginally profitable silver mine. The silver ore in the mine is not of the best quality, so the yield from the mine will be relatively low. The financial wisdom of operating the mine will depend on the price the miner can obtain for the silver once it is mined and refined. However, the miner must make the decision about the mine today, and the silver will not be ready for market for 15 months. The crucial element in the miner's decision is the future price of silver.

While the price of silver 15 months from now cannot be known with certainty, it is possible to use the futures market to estimate that future price. The price quoted in the futures market today for a silver futures that expires in 15 months can be a very useful estimate of the future price. As we will see in Chapter 2, for some commodities an estimate of the future price of a good drawn from the futures market is one of the best estimates possible. In our example, let us assume that the futures price for silver is high enough to justify operating the mine again. The miner figures that the new mine will be profitable if he can obtain the futures price for the silver when it becomes available in 15 months. In this situation, the miner has used the futures market as a vehicle of price discovery. Farmers, lumber producers, cattle ranchers, and other economic agents can use futures markets the same way. They all use futures market estimates of future cash prices to guide their production or consumption decisions.

HEDGING

Many futures market participants trade futures as a substitute for a cash market transaction. For example, we considered a farmer who sold wheat futures in anticipation of a harvest, and we noted that the farmer used futures as an alternative to the sale of wheat through the cash market. We now consider this classic kind of hedge in more detail. At planting time, the farmer bears a risk associated with the uncertain harvest price his wheat will command. The farmer might use the futures market to hedge by selling a futures contract. If the farmer expects to harvest 100,000 bushels of wheat in nine months, the farmer could establish a price for that harvest by selling 20 wheat futures contracts. (Each wheat contract is for 5,000 bushels.) By selling these futures contracts, the farmer seeks to establish a price today for the wheat that will be harvested in the future. With certain qualifications, this futures transaction protects the farmer from wheat price fluctuations that might occur between the present and the future harvest. The futures transaction served as a substitute for a cash market sale of wheat. A cash market sale was impossible, because the wheat did not actually exist. In this example, the farmer sells wheat in the futures market as a temporary substitute for a future anticipated cash market transaction. Therefore, **anticipatory hedging** is a futures market transaction used as a substitute for an anticipated future cash market transaction.

Hedging transactions can take other forms. For example, consider an oil wholesaler who holds a substantial inventory of gasoline. The wholesaler needs the inventory as a stock from which to service retail customers. If the wholesaler simply holds the stock of gasoline, she must bear the price risk of fluctuating gasoline prices. As an alternative, she can sell crude oil futures as a substitute for selling the gasoline itself. By holding gasoline in her business inventory and selling crude oil futures to offset the risk associated with the gasoline, the wholesaler can reduce her business risk. The wholesaler could have used the cash market directly to reduce risk by simply selling her entire inventory in the cash market. Unfortunately, this method of reducing business risk eliminates the business, because the wholesaler would no longer have the gasoline inventory that is essential to her entire business. Selling futures substitutes for the risk-reducing transaction of selling her entire inventory.

For both of our examples, the hedger uses the futures market as a substitute for a cash market transaction. Both hedgers had a pre-existing risk associated with the commodity being sold. The farmer anticipated harvesting and selling wheat, and he used the futures market as a substitute for a cash market sale of wheat. Even though the farmer did not have wheat on hand when he sold futures, he did have a preexisting risk in wheat. The risk arose from the anticipated holding of the cash wheat at harvest. For the oil wholesaler, the risk was immediate. As prices of oil fluctuate, the value of her gasoline inventory fluctuates as well. Thus, the wholesaler had a preexisting risk associated with the price of oil, and she used the futures market transaction to reduce that risk.

Because hedgers are traders that use futures transactions as substitutes for cash transactions, hedgers are almost always business concerns that deal with a specific commodity. Almost without exception, individual traders are speculators because they enter the futures market in pursuit of profit and increase their risk in the process. By contrast, hedgers have a preexisting risk exposure of some form that leads them to use futures transactions as a substitute for a cash market transaction. Hedging is the prime social rationale for futures trading, and therefore we will give hedging a great deal of attention throughout the book. Chapter 3 explains the use that the hedger makes of the futures markets, while the techniques and applications of hedging are elaborated for specific financial futures markets in Chapters 4 through 8.

Traders in the futures markets are either speculators or hedgers, or the agents of one of these two groups. Yet the benefits provided by the futures market extend to many other sectors of society. The individual interested in forecasts of future prices need not enter the market to benefit. For example, our silver miner did not need to trade any futures to capture the benefits of price discovery. The forecasts are available for the price of the daily newspaper. The chance for hedgers to avoid unacceptable risks by entering the futures market also has wide implications for social welfare. Some individuals would not engage in certain clearly beneficial forms of economic activity if they were forced to bear all of the risk of the activity themselves. Being able to transfer risk to other parties via the futures market enhances economic activity in general. Of course, a general stimulation of economic activity benefits society as a whole.

BROKERS, ADVISORS, AND COMMODITY FUND MANAGERS

We have already seen that speculators and hedgers are traders who trade for their own accounts. Also, we have mentioned that the market utilizes brokers, those individuals who execute trades for a customer, whether a speculator or a hedger. In this section, we consider brokers in more detail, because there are a number of different types of brokers. In addition, this section considers advisors and managers of futures funds, as listed in Table 1.10.

In discussing brokers earlier in this chapter, we focused on an individual who executes orders on the floor of the exchange. We mentioned that such a broker is often the employee of a brokerage firm, such as Merrill Lynch. In the futures market, there are special names for the individuals and firms that execute orders on behalf of others.[19]

FLOOR BROKER (FB)

When an individual off the floor of the exchange places an order, he or she usually does so through an account executive with a brokerage firm. The order is transmitted to the floor of the exchange where it is executed by a **floor broker** – an individual who executes an order for the purchase or sale of a futures contract for another person. There are about 7,500 floor brokers in the United States.

Many floor brokers are members of **broker associations** or **broker groups**. A broker group is an association of floor brokers who band together to fill orders for their customers. The group might be as small as two brokers who cover for each other during vacations or as large as groups of brokers that operate in several markets and share profits and expenses. These broker groups have become an important force among the trading community. For example, there are more than 200 broker groups at the Chicago Mercantile Exchange and more than 100 at the New York Mercantile Exchange.

Broker groups provide some services to the futures community. First, they provide a training ground for new brokers. Second, they

■ **Table 1.10** ───────────────────────────

BROKERS, ADVISORS, AND FUND MANAGERS

1. Floor Broker (FB)	4. Associated Person (AP)
2. Futures Commission Merchant (FCM)	5. Commodity Trading Advisor (CTA)
3. Introducing Broker (IB)	6. Commodity Pool Operator (CPO)

provide a flexible pool of manpower to respond to radical fluctuations in trading volume. Third, they provide an easy way for large brokerage houses to be able to execute in several pits simultaneously. Fourth, the capital of the association stands behind each member of the group. Thus, there is less chance of any single broker defaulting.

These broker groups have become the object of criticism for several reasons. First, the existence of an association might encourage members to trade with each other preferentially, instead of offering a trade to the entire market as the rules require. Second, broker groups were accused of dishonesty in fulfilling customer orders in some important recent legal actions. For example, one member of a broker group might trade for his own account, while another member of the same group might act as a floor broker in executing an order for someone outside the broker group. The temptation exists to give a preferential price to the other member of the broker group at the expense of the outside party. In 1993, the CFTC increased its monitoring of these broker groups and required identification of such cooperative relationships.

FUTURES COMMISSION MERCHANT (FCM)

A **futures commission merchant** is a firm or individual that accepts orders to trade futures on behalf of another party and who accepts money to support such an order. Thus, a brokerage firm that accepts orders to trade futures is a futures commission merchant or FCM. In many cases, the FCM will be a large firm with offices in many cities that accepts orders from individuals and other firms. The FCM transmits these orders to the floor of the exchange where they are executed by a floor broker. The floor broker may be an employee of the FCM, although this is not always the case. Since the mid-1980s, the number of FCMs has declined due to consolidation in the industry and very stiff competition. In 1984, there were approximately 400 FCMs, but that number declined to about 275 by 1996.

INTRODUCING BROKER (IB)

An **introducing broker** is an individual or firm that accepts orders to trade futures, but who does not accept the funds to support such orders. Thus, the FCM accepts money to support the orders (such as margin deposits), but the introducing broker does not. Essentially, the IB finds a customer and solicits that customer's business. However, the IB does not process the trade or hold monies for margin. Instead, the IB works with another broker, called a **carrying broker**, who processes the trade, holds the margin deposit, and provides accounting and documentation of the trades to the customer. The introducing broker and carrying broker share the commissions earned for executing trades. In 1989, the number of IBs peaked at about 1,800. By late 1996, the number of IBs had fallen to about 1,300.

Associated Person (AP)

An **associated person** is an individual who solicits orders, customers, or customer funds, or an individual who supervises anyone who makes such solicitations. Thus, a floor broker or an introducing broker is also an associated person, as is the manager of a branch office of an FCM. This broad category includes most of the professional individuals who make their livings in the futures industry. There were more than 55,000 APs in 1990, but that number fell to about 48,000 by 1996.

Commodity Trading Advisor (CTA)

A **commodity trading advisor** is a person who directly or indirectly advises others regarding their futures trading. This category also applies to individuals who advise the public through written publications or other mass media. Thus, the writer of a futures newsletter that recommends certain positions in the futures market would be a CTA. In 1993, there were more than 2,700 CTAs.

Commodity Pool Operator (CPO)

A **commodity pool operator** is an individual or firm that operates or solicits funds for a commodity pool. A **commodity pool** consists of a collection of funds used to engage in futures trading activities. Typically, a number of individuals contribute funds to form the commodity pool. The pool operator uses those funds to engage in speculative futures trading. The individuals who contributed monies to the pool own a share of the entire pool. Thus, a commodity pool is similar to a mutual fund in which individuals contribute funds for investment in stocks and bonds. There are approximately 1,325 commodity pool operators in the United States.

REGULATION OF FUTURES MARKETS

There are four identifiable tiers of regulation in the futures market: the broker; the exchange and clearinghouse; an industry self-regulatory body, the National Futures Association (NFA); and a federal government agency, the Commodities Futures Trading Commission (CFTC). To a large extent, these tiers overlap, but each regulatory body has its specific duties.

THE BROKER

As we have seen in our discussion of the margin system, the broker essentially represents his or her customers to the exchange and clearinghouse. In the margin system, the clearinghouse holds the clearing member responsible for all of the accounts that clearing member carries. Because of the representations to the industry that the broker makes on behalf of its client, the broker has a duty to keep informed about the activities of its customer and to ensure that those activities are proper. Among futures market participants, the often repeated rule for brokers is "know your customer." The broker is the industry representative in the best position to know a given customer, because the customer gains access to trading directly through the broker.

As we will see in more detail, some kinds of futures trading are not permitted to any traders. Other traders have restrictions on the kind of trading that they should engage in. As an example, let us consider a **position limit**. For a commodity with a position limit, no single trader is allowed to hold more than a certain number of contracts. This rule limits the influence of a single trader on the market and aims to prevent the trader from controlling the futures price.[20] On occasion, some traders have tried to circumvent this rule by trading through different accounts. Often, the broker can detect such a maneuver and has a duty to report such activity. As this example shows, the broker is often in the best position to detect some abuses, because he or she is closest to the customer. The trading of some customers is restricted due to the nature of the customer's business. For example, some financial institutions are allowed to trade only certain types of futures for hedging purposes. The broker for such an institution should not allow prohibited trading.

In general terms, the broker is responsible for knowing the customer's position and intentions, for ensuring that the customer does not disrupt the market or place the system in jeopardy, and for keeping the customer's trading activity in line with industry regulations and legal restrictions.

The futures exchanges and clearinghouses have specific regulatory duties. Many of these duties require the exchange and clearinghouse to control the conduct of exchange and clearing members. To do so, the exchanges formulate and enforce rules for their members and rules for trading on the exchange. Generally, the rules of each exchange are designed to create a smoothly functioning market in which traders can feel confident that their orders will be executed properly and at a fair price. Thus, all exchanges prohibit fraud, dishonorable conduct, and defaulting on contract obligations.

More specifically, exchange rules prohibit **fictitious trading** – trading that merely gives the appearance of transacting without actually changing ownership. Exchange rules prohibit circulating rumors to affect price, disclosing a customer's order, trading with oneself, taking the opposite side of a customer's order, making false statements to the exchange, and failing to comply with a legitimate order by the exchange.

The rules also prohibit **prearranged trading**. A prearranged trade occurs when two futures market participants consult in advance and agree to make a certain trade at a given price. Instead, the rules require that all orders be offered to the entire market through open outcry. The rules prohibit prearranged trading because a prearranged trade is noncompetitive and can be abusive. For example, assume that a floor broker receives an order to buy wheat and that the fair market price for the wheat contract is $4.20 per bushel. In a prearranged trade, the floor broker might agree with a friendly floor trader to buy the contract from him or her at $4.21. With the true market value at $4.20, this practice cheats the customer by $.01 per bushel or $50 per contract. Had the order been offered to the market as the rules require, the order would have been filled at the prevailing price of $4.20. Thus, the prohibition of prearranged trading aims at ensuring that each order is executed at a fair market price.

The rules also prohibit a broker from trading for his or her own account at the customer's requested price before filling a customer's order. The broker who trades for himself or herself before filling a customer's order engages in the prohibited practice called **front**

running. To see why this practice is prohibited, assume that market prices are rising rapidly due to some new information. Assume also that the broker holds a customer order to buy. If the broker executes his or her own order first, the broker's own order will be executed at a more favorable price, because of the quickly rising prices. Thus, front running gives the broker an unfair advantage. As a second example, assume that a broker receives a very large customer order to sell. The broker knows that placing this order will depress the futures price temporarily. The front running broker would enter his or her own order to sell first. The broker's order would be executed at the high price, and the broker would then execute the customer's order. Upon execution of the customer's order, the price falls as the broker anticipated. Now the broker can buy and close his or her position. This gives the broker a profit from front running. In front running, the broker uses his or her special knowledge of order flow or market movement to obtain an unethical and prohibited personal advantage.

Futures exchanges also set daily price limits, position limits, and margin requirements, although the CFTC has a role in each of these types of rules. In addition, each exchange has rules that govern membership on the exchange. For example, exchange rules establish membership requirements and specify how customer complaints are to be resolved. For each of these categories, the rules of the exchange are subject to review by the CFTC. However, the CFTC generally provides broad guidelines within which the exchanges and clearinghouses form their own specific rules.

NATIONAL FUTURES ASSOCIATION (NFA)

In 1974, Congress passed a new law for the regulation of futures markets. Part of that law authorized the futures industry to create one or more self-regulatory bodies. The purpose of these bodies according to the act is "... to prevent fraudulent and manipulative acts and practices, to promote just and equitable principles of trade, in general, to protect the public interest, and to remove impediments to and perfect the mechanism of free and open futures trading." While the law has contemplated more than a single self-regulatory body, the National Futures Association is the only such body in existence. For many classes of market participants, membership in the NFA is mandatory.

The following parties are required to be members of the NFA: Futures Commission Merchants, Commodity Pool Operators, Introducing Brokers, Commodity Trading Advisors, and Associated Persons. Exchanges, banks, and commodity business firms may join the NFA, but membership is not compulsory. Floor traders and floor brokers are not required to be members, because they are subject to exchange regulation. One must be a member of the NFA to do commodity-related business with the public.

The NFA has the responsibility for screening and testing applicants for registration, and it can review personal background information before allowing individuals to register in the various categories of futures professionals. The NFA also requires FCMs and Introducing Brokers to maintain adequate capital and to keep accurate trading records. Finally, the NFA can audit member firms' records and capital adequacy. For serious violations, the NFA can suspend or expel violators from the futures industry. Finally, the NFA operates an arbitration process for resolving trading disputes.

As the NFA states, it seeks to prevent infractions before they occur. By doing so, the NFA helps the futures industry to remain viable by keeping the public trust. However, in assessing the NFA, it is wise to remember that it is an industry self-regulatory body, designed to protect the integrity of the industry and to promote the interests of the industry.

COMMODITY FUTURES TRADING COMMISSION (CFTC)

The Commodity Futures Trading Commission Act of 1974 established the commission. Before this act, commodity futures markets were regulated solely under the Commodity Exchange Act administered through the Department of Agriculture. The new act supplemented, rather than replaced, the Commodity Exchange Act. The CFTC Act brought currency and metal futures under federal regulation.

The CFTC has specific powers under the CFTC Act. One important area of CFTC jurisdiction concerns the approval of new contracts. Before trading, an exchange must submit the newly designed contract to the CFTC for approval. The CFTC is responsible for determining whether trading in such a contract is contrary to the public interest. To receive approval, the contract must show promise of serving an economic purpose, such as making for fairer pricing of the commodity in some way or in making hedging possible. Providing an arena for speculation is not enough justification to show that a futures contract would serve an economic function.

The CFTC also regulates futures market trading rules, including the daily permitted maximum price fluctuation, certain features of the delivery process, and minimum price fluctuation limits. Generally, the CFTC is not involved in determining membership in the exchanges, but it can review complaints of membership exclusion or other unfair treatment by the exchanges. Perhaps the most striking power of the CFTC is the emergency power to intervene in the conduct of the market itself when the commission believes manipulation is present. Also, the CFTC has the power to require competency tests of brokers and commodity representatives. Figure 1.8 shows the overlapping structure of the regulatory bodies.

AIMS OF REGULATION

Futures market regulations today control both entry into and the operation of futures markets. Before a new contract can be traded,

■ Figure 1.8

OVERLAPPING FUTURES MARKET REGULATION

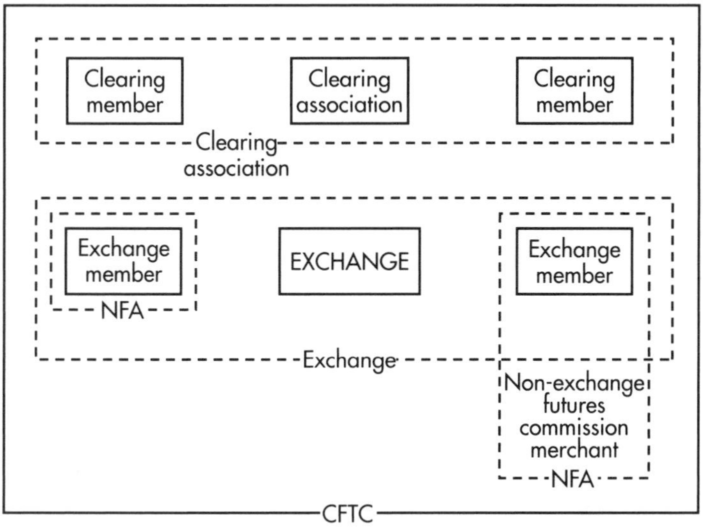

From G. D. Koppenhaver, "Futures Market Regulation," *Economic Perspectives* 11:1, January/February 1987. Reprinted by permission of Federal Reserve Bank of Chicago.

the CFTC must approve the contract for trading. Another dimension of current regulatory practice focuses not on entry but on the operation or performance of futures markets. On the operational side, futures market regulation aims to provide a marketplace in which the social functions of futures markets can be fulfilled. Practices that interfere with the process of price discovery or the efficient transfer of unwanted risk make futures markets perform poorly. For example, practices that make futures prices behave as poor indicators of future spot prices reduce the usefulness of the futures market for price discovery. Also, practices that distort prices can increase the cost of transferring risk. To see more clearly the point of regulation, we consider one of the most feared aspects of future trading abuse, price manipulation.

"It is a felony for a person to manipulate or attempt to manipulate the price of any commodity in commerce or for future delivery."[21] To prove manipulation, the manipulator must be shown to have the ability to set an artificial futures price, must have intended to set an artificial price, and must have succeeded in setting such a price. In essence, an artificial price is a price that does not reflect free demand and supply conditions. By trading in certain ways, it may be possible for a trader or group of traders to move the price in the market from its economically sound or justified price. The basic way of accomplishing this feat is through a market corner or a market squeeze. In a corner or squeeze, a trader or group of traders gains effective control over the pricing mechanism in the futures market.

Given these problems created by price manipulation, it may seem clear that there is a need for government regulation of futures markets. Some observers argue that such governmental regulation is not needed. According to these authors, the exchanges have a strong incentive for self-regulation. Only by attracting the public for trading can the exchange make money as a whole. Therefore, according to this argument, the exchange left to its own devices will be self-regulating, obviating the need for governmental regulation.[22]

In addition to the issue of price manipulation, other areas of concern to regulators include: insider trading, front running, capital formation concerns, and the effect of futures trading on the riskiness of the cash market for commodities. Insider trading is trading on information not available to the public at large. For example, a government clerk working on a forecast of the size of the corn crop has access to information that could be valuable in futures trading. Using such information to guide trading would be a case of insider trading. Recently, insider trading scandals in the stock market have attracted a great deal of public attention. Insider trading in futures markets is not subject to the same limitations as those found in the stock market. Nonetheless, most exchanges have some restrictions on insider trading. Some observers argue that prohibitions against insider futures trading would actually be harmful. Under this view, insider trading contributes to liquidity and to market efficiency.[23]

NEW REGULATORY INITIATIVES

In early 1996, the Securities Exchange Commission (SEC) and the Financial Accounting Standards Board (FASB) were both proposing new rules for disclosure of risk positions in firms' derivatives positions. These proposals were being disseminated in the wake of several major scandals involving significant losses resulting from derivatives trading. The SEC proposal would require firms to disclose quantitative information about market risks in tabular form, would require firms to present sensitivity analyses of their risk positions, would require firms to present qualitative risk information, and would permit firms to disclose value-at-risk information.

The FASB proposal would require all derivatives to be recognized in the firm's financial statements at fair value. For reporting purposes, derivatives would be divided into those that stand alone and those that hedge some other instrument. The hedging derivatives would be divided into those that hedge asset, liabilities, or forecasted transactions. This FASB proposal has come under strong attack by the derivatives industry as failing to allow deferral of gains and losses on hedging transactions. Almost certainly, the SEC and FASB proposals will be revised and the implementation of the resulting rules will be deferred for a few years.[24]

TAXATION OF FUTURES TRADING

In 1981, Congress passed a law regarding the taxation of gains and losses in futures trading that had dramatic effects on the ways in which futures contracts could be used. The new law stipulated that all paper gains and losses on futures positions must be treated as though they were realized at the end of the tax year. For tax purposes, this new law meant that the futures positions must be marked-to-market at the end of the year. Forty percent of any gains or losses are to be treated as short-term gains; 60 percent are to be treated as long-term capital gains or losses. Prior to the passage of the Tax Reform Act of 1986, long-term capital gains were taxed at a lower rate than ordinary income or short-term capital gains. The 1986 law stipulates that all income is taxed at one rate. This change removes the protection of the long-term rates, but the new law also reduced overall tax rates. As a net result, the 1986 law seems to have had little effect on profits from futures trading.

Conclusion

As we have seen in this chapter, forward trading has grown out of a need that has been felt for centuries. With the passage of time and the development of a more complex society, futures markets have emerged as a special kind of forward contracting. With their special characteristics of organized exchanges, clearinghouses, financial safeguards, and standardized contracts, futures markets represent a kind of highly specialized forward trading begun in the middle of the nineteenth century and brought into fruition over the last quarter century.

Futures markets depend on well-developed financial markets and on the existence of widely available homogeneous commodities. The availability of standard commodities depends, in turn, on a sophisticated economic infrastructure, with the key element being an integrated transportation system. Futures markets, almost by their very nature, serve a geographically dispersed group of participants. This means that futures markets also depend on the existence of an elaborate communications system.

With these facts in mind, it is clear that futures markets could not really have developed before they did, when telegraphic communication and a suitable financial environment were coming into existence. Their growth, which has recently accelerated, makes futures markets an important economic phenomenon, and one well worth studying.

Notes

1. The mutual obligation of both buyer and seller of a futures contract is an important feature of the futures market that helps to distinguish futures contracts from options. If you buy a call option,

then you buy the right to obtain a good at a certain price, but the buyer of a call has no obligation. Instead, as the term implies, he has an option to buy something but no obligation to do anything. The buyer of a futures contract, by contrast, undertakes an obligation to make a payment at a subsequent time and to take delivery of the good that is contracted. The initiation of any futures contract implies a set of future obligations.

2. For a discussion of the historical origins of futures contracting, see A. Loosigian, *Interest Rate Futures,* Princeton, NJ: Dow Jones Books, 1980. L. Venkataramanan also discusses the origins of forward contracting in his book, *The Theory of Futures Trading,* New York: Asia Publishing House, 1965.

3. For an account of the early days of the Chicago Board of Trade, see *The Commodity Trading Manual,* Chicago: Chicago Board of Trade, 1989.

4. Scott Chambers and Colin Carter, "U.S. Futures Exchanges as Nonprofit Entities," *Journal of Futures Markets,* 10:1, February 1990, pp. 79–88, analyze the difference that their nonprofit status has on the operation of futures exchanges. They argue that this freedom from profit-maximizing goals stimulates cross-subsidization of the exchanges' products. In a practical sense, this analysis implies that exchanges use profits from successful contracts to subsidize less profitable contracts.

5. See R. Chiang, G. D. Gay, and R. W. Kolb, "Commodity Exchange Seat Prices," *Review of Futures Markets,* 6:1, 1987, pp. 1–12.

6. The practice of trading for one's own account and simultaneously acting as a broker for other parties is known as **dual trading**. In recent months, this practice has come under close scrutiny and some restrictions have been placed on it.

7. This is the classic definition of hedging given by H. Working, "Hedging Reconsidered," *Journal of Farm Economics,* 35, 1953, pp. 544–61.

8. There are some exceptions to this general rule. For example, the London Metals Exchange trades metals forwards, but has a physical trading floor.

9. Chapter 8 discusses the foreign exchange forward market in some detail as a preliminary to the discussion of the foreign exchange futures market.

10. The exchange also controls price differentials for delivery in one location rather than another or the delivery of one grade of the commodity instead of another. For example, if wheat delivery is to be made in Toledo, the delivery price must be two cents per bushel under the contract price.

11. In his article "Market Incompleteness and Divergences Between Forward and Futures Interest Rates," *Journal of Finance*, 35:2, May 1980, pp. 221-34, Edward J. Kane argues that the costliness of the performance guarantees provided by the clearinghouse is sufficient to cause a divergence between the prices of forward and futures contracts.

12. Notice that this is different from the stock market. Stocks represent title to the real assets of the firms, and these are owned by someone at every point in time. The long and short positions in the stock market, when "netted out," always equal the number of shares actually in existence, not zero, as in the futures market.

13. For more on the clearinghouse and its functions, see F. R. Edwards, "The Clearing Association in Futures Markets: Guarantor and Regulator," *Journal of Futures Markets*, 3:4, Winter 1983, pp. 369-92.

14. We might say that the clearinghouse is "perfectly hedged." No matter whether futures prices rise or fall, the wealth of the clearinghouse will not be affected. This is the case since the clearinghouse holds both long and short positions that perfectly balance each other. Chapter 3 focuses on the concept of hedging, and the book pursues this topic through all subsequent chapters.

15. One startling example is for the T-bill futures contract. An initial margin deposit of $1,000-2,500 serves as the security for a contract on $1,000,000 face value of Treasury bills.

16. The terminology for spreads is quite diverse. The definitions used here are not universal.

17. For a comprehensive discussion of options, see R. Kolb, *Options, 3e*, Cambridge, MA: Blackwell Publishers, 1997.

18. For an introduction to VAR and its extensions, see the following three articles: Charles Smithson and Lyle Minton, "Value at Risk," *Risk*, 9:1, January 1996, pp. 25-27; Charles Smithson and Lyle Minton, "Value at Risk (2)," *Risk*, 9:2, February 1996, pp. 38-39; Chris Turner, "VAR as an Industrial Tool," *Risk*, 9:3, March 1996, pp. 38-40. The following three articles document the differing

VAR results from alternative calculation methods: Arturo Estrella, Darryll Hendricks, John Kambhu, Soo Shin, and Stefan Walter, "The Price Risk of Options Positions: Measurement and Capital Requirements," Federal Reserve Bank of New York, *Quarterly Review*, 19:2, Summer/Fall 1994, pp. 27–43; Tanyo Styblo Beder, "VAR: Seductive but Dangerous," *Financial Analysts Journal*, September/October 1995, pp. 12–24; James V. Jordan and Robert J. Mackay, "Assessing Value at Risk for Equity Portfolios: Implementing Alternative Techniques," in Rod Beckstrom, Alyce Campbell, and Frank Fabozzi (ed.) *Handbook of Firm-Wide Risk Management*, Homewood, IL: Irwin, 1996.

19. The definitions used in this section are drawn from various publications of the National Futures Association. Statistics regarding the number of firms and individuals of each classification appear in the 1989 *Annual Report* of the Commodity Futures Trading Commission.

20. Position limits do not apply in the same way to hedgers.

21. G. D. Koppenhaver, "Futures Market Regulation," *Economic Perspectives*, 11:1, January/February 1987.

22. See F. Easterbrook, "Monopoly, Manipulation, and the Regulation of Futures Markets," *Journal of Business*, 59:2, Part 2, April 1986, pp. S103–S127, who argues against such regulation. By contrast, A. Kyle, in "A Theory of Futures Market Manipulations," in R. Anderson, *The Industrial Organization of Futures Markets*, Lexington, MA: D. C. Heath, 1984, argues that squeezes increase the cost of hedging and should therefore be regulated to make them more difficult.

23. See S. Grossman, "An Analysis of the Role of Insider Trading on Futures Markets," *Journal of Business*, April 1986, 59:2, Part 2, pp. S129–S146.

24. See Donald L. Horwitz, "SEC Proposes Rules for Derivatives Disclosure," *Futures Industry*, March/April 1996, pp. 33–35; Phoebe Mix, "FASB Struggles with Derivatives Accounting," *Futures Industry*, March/April 1996, pp. 31–32; and Pat Arbor, "Does FASB Control the Future of Futures?" *Risk*, 9:1, January 1996, p. 19.

■ Chapter 2

Futures Prices

OVERVIEW

Having explored the basic institutional features of the futures market in Chapter 1, we now consider futures prices. In an important sense, the study of the prices in a market provides the essential key to understanding all features of the market. Prices and the factors that determine those prices will ultimately influence every use of the market.

This chapter examines the fundamental factors that affect futures prices. There is little doubt that the determinants of foreign exchange futures prices and orange juice futures prices, for example, are very different. We must also recognize, however, that a common thread of understanding links futures contracts of all types. This chapter follows that common thread, while subsequent chapters explore the individual factors that affect prices for financial futures. Perhaps the most basic and most common factor affecting futures prices is the way in which their prices are quoted. Our discussion of futures prices begins with reading the price quotations that are available every day in *The Wall Street Journal*.

Futures market prices bear economically important relationships to other observable prices as well. An important goal of this chapter is to understand those relationships. The futures price for delivery of coffee in three months, for example, must be related to the spot price, or the current cash price, of coffee at a particular physical location. The **spot price** is the price of a good for immediate delivery. In a restaurant, for example, you buy a cup of coffee at the spot price. The spot price is also called the **cash price** or the **current price**.

This important difference between the cash price and the futures price is called the **basis**. Likewise, the futures price for delivery of coffee in three months must be related in some fashion to the futures price for delivery of coffee in six months. The difference in price for two futures contract expirations on the same commodity is an intracommodity spread. As we will see, the time spread can also be an economically important variable.

Because futures contracts call for the delivery of some good at a particular time in the future, we can be sure that the expectations of market participants help determine futures prices. If people believe that gold will sell for $50 per ounce in three months, then the price of the futures contract for delivery of gold in three months cannot be $100. The connection between futures prices and expected future spot prices is so strong that some market observers believe that they must be, or at least should be, equal.

Similarly, the price for storing the good underlying the futures contract helps determine the relationships among futures prices and the relationship between the futures price and the spot price. By storing goods, it is possible, in effect, to convert corn received in March into corn that can be delivered in June. The difference in price between the March corn futures and the June corn futures must, therefore, be related to the cost of storing corn.

All of these futures pricing issues are interconnected. The basis, the spreads, the expected future spot price, and the cost of storage all form a system of related concepts. This chapter describes the linkages among these concepts that are common to all futures contracts. The discussion begins with the futures prices themselves.

READING FUTURES PRICES

One of the most complete and widely available sources for futures prices is *The Wall Street Journal* (WSJ), which publishes futures prices daily. These prices are reported in a standardized format, as Figure 2.1 shows. The date shown near the top of Figure 2.1 is the day for which the prices were recorded. The publication date of the WSJ is

Figure 2.1

FUTURES PRICE QUOTATIONS

FUTURES PRICES

Tuesday, April 23, 1996

Open Interest Reflects Previous Trading Day

GRAINS AND OILSEEDS

CORN (CBT) 5,000 bu.; cents per bu.

	Open	High	Low	Settle	Change	Lifetime High	Lifetime Low	Open Interest
May	473	479	469½	478½	+ 8½	479	259½	74,519
July	453	461	450	460½	+ 10¼	461	254	163,163
Sept	371½	375	369½	373¾	+ 3¾	391	260	55,979
Dec	335½	338	330	334	....	354	239	125,662
Mr97	341	342¼	336	339¾	− ½	357	279¼	12,932
May	343	343	339	341½	− ½	356	306	1,229
July	343	343	339½	340¾	− ¾	355	284	3,478
Dec	293	294	289	292½	+ ½	302	249¾	3,632

Est vol 100,000; vol Mn 94,934; open int 440,594, −8,850.

OATS (CBT) 5,000 bu.; cents per bu.

	Open	High	Low	Settle	Change	Lifetime High	Lifetime Low	Open Interest
May	252	258¾	249¼	258¾	+ 10	258¾	153½	1,858
July	248½	257½	248½	257½	+ 10	257½	165	4,884
Sept	226½	231	223	231	+ 8½	231½	163	3,663
Dec	227½	232½	223½	232¼	+ 8	232½	160	3,121
Mr97	227½	233½	227½	233½	+ 7	233½	197	214

Est vol 2,400; vol Mn 2,907; open int 13,740, +118.

SOYBEANS (CBT) 5,000 bu.; cents per bu.

	Open	High	Low	Settle	Change	Lifetime High	Lifetime Low	Open Interest
May	818	820	802	812¼	− 1¼	824	602	29,005
July	821½	829½	811½	822	+ ½	832½	599½	80,862
Aug	825	825½	811	820½	+ ½	829½	626	9,778
Sept	805	807	795	804	+ ¾	810	623	5,672
Nov	790	800	784	794	+ 2½	806	585	69,364
Ja97	800	800½	789	799¾	+ 4½	813	650	5,511
Mar	804	804	796	803	+ 2¾	816	679	1,702
May	800	805	798	805	+ 1	818	735	1,443
July	808	808	796	803¼	+ 1¼	820	633	1,966
Nov	719	720	713	717½	+ 4	734	601	1,592

Est vol 65,000; vol Mn 73,929; open int 206,895, +1,664.

SOYBEAN MEAL (CBT) 100 tons; $ per ton.

	Open	High	Low	Settle	Change	Lifetime High	Lifetime Low	Open Interest
May	257.10	259.80	254.00	256.90	....	259.80	181.50	18,766
July	262.00	263.40	258.00	260.90	− .10	263.90	183.00	50,879
Aug	262.50	263.00	258.20	261.00	− .70	263.00	189.50	9,944
Sept	258.20	258.50	255.00	258.00	+ .30	259.00	188.00	6,117
Oct	254.00	254.00	251.00	253.00	+ .30	255.00	190.00	3,542
Dec	253.50	254.00	250.50	253.40	+ .70	254.50	178.00	15,009
Ja97	253.50	254.00	250.50	252.70	+ 1.20	255.50	215.00	795
Mar	254.00	254.00	250.70	252.30	− .40	255.50	227.00	669
May	251.50	251.50	250.00	250.00	− 1.50	256.00	237.50	399

Est vol 25,000; vol Mn 23,759; open int 106,166, +1,698.

SOYBEAN OIL (CBT) 60,000 lbs.; cents per lb.

	Open	High	Low	Settle	Change	Lifetime High	Lifetime Low	Open Interest
May	26.85	26.85	26.38	26.62	− .10	27.85	23.50	17,065
July	27.18	27.24	26.75	27.06	− .03	27.90	23.88	46,493
Aug	27.35	27.37	27.00	27.21	− .06	27.90	24.28	8,449
Sept	27.55	27.55	27.15	27.40	− .04	27.85	24.49	4,256
Oct	27.50	27.53	27.20	27.49	− .03	28.02	24.65	2,908
Dec	27.90	27.92	27.48	27.79	− .02	28.25	24.45	15,188
Ja97	27.75	27.80	27.60	27.80	− .05	28.25	25.12	678
Mar	28.12	28.12	27.80	28.05	− .02	28.40	25.45	454
May		....	....	28.20	+ .03	28.45	25.65	201

Est vol 15,000; vol Mn 15,577; open int 95,713, −786.

WHEAT (CBT) 5,000 bu.; cents per bu.

	Open	High	Low	Settle	Change	Lifetime High	Lifetime Low	Open Interest
May	635	654	635	653½	+ 25½	654	379	9,109
July	609½	619½	602	615½	+ 21	619½	325	60,180
Sept	604	621	601	611	+ 18½	621	374	13,715
Dec	601	619	601	617½	+ 22½	619	362	15,119
Mr97	592	609	592	599	+ 17	609	456½	1,088
July	456	457	450	453	− 2½	465	365	1,081

Est vol 30,000; vol Mn 12,312; open int 100,388, −1,545.

WHEAT (KC) 5,000 bu.; cents per bu.

	Open	High	Low	Settle	Change	Lifetime High	Lifetime Low	Open Interest
May	684½	684½	676	684½	+ 25	684½	368	7,017
July	658¼	658¼	659	658¼	+ 25	658¼	330	21,987
Sept	640	645	631	644½	+ 24¼	645	387	6,776
Dec	630	637	620	630	+ 17	637	437	4,446
Mr97	610	620	610	615½	+ 16½	620	468½	788

Est vol 10,472; vol Mn 5,109; open int 41,022, −428.

WHEAT (MPLS) 5,000 bu.; cents per bu.

	Open	High	Low	Settle	Change	Lifetime High	Lifetime Low	Open Interest
May	82.65	82.90	82.65	82.80	− .10	82.90	73.50	1,223
July	82.65	82.80	82.50	82.80	− .10	82.80	73.75	572
Oct		....	....	79.55	+ .45	79.50	75.50	286
Dec	77.75	78.50	78.50	78.50	+ .15	78.50	75.00	1,510

Est vol 25,000; vol 12,658; open int 59,855, +788.

ORANGE JUICE (CTN) 15,000 lbs.; cents per lb.

	Open	High	Low	Settle	Change	Lifetime High	Lifetime Low	Open Interest
May	132.80	133.90	132.50	133.85	+ .65	138.00	106.50	7,797
July	131.35	132.50	130.60	132.45	+ 1.00	135.00	110.00	7,517
Sept	129.75	130.00	129.25	130.25	+ .35	137.00	113.00	2,952
Nov	126.00	126.00	125.50	125.80	− .10	135.50	117.00	946
Ja97	122.50	122.75	122.30	122.95	+ .15	135.50	117.50	3,065
Mar	124.50	124.50	123.50	124.95	− .05	138.00	120.00	188
May		....	....	126.95	− .05	131.00	119.60	136

Est vol 6,800; vol 5,187; open int 22,603, +311.

METALS AND PETROLEUM

COPPER-HIGH (Cmx.Div.NYM) 25,000 lbs.; cents per lb.

	Open	High	Low	Settle	Change	Lifetime High	Lifetime Low	Open Interest
Apr	123.70	123.70	123.10	123.25	− .45	127.80	110.50	1,540
May	122.05	123.20	121.60	121.70	− 1.05	126.00	107.00	16,250
June	121.70	121.70	120.90	120.60	− .65	122.00	109.00	1,274
July	120.10	120.60	119.30	119.50	− .65	122.90	105.50	16,174
Aug	118.80	118.80	118.80	118.30	− .70	119.50	108.00	565
Sept	118.30	118.30	117.00	117.20	− .75	121.00	105.25	3,885
Oct	116.40	116.40	116.40	116.10	− .65	119.00	108.00	492
Nov	115.00	115.00	115.00	115.50	− .65	116.30	107.00	362
Dec	114.70	114.70	113.80	114.00	− .65	118.80	106.00	5,772
Ja97		....	....	113.10	− .60	118.50	106.00	310
Feb		....	....	112.20	− .55	112.90	106.00	177
Mar	111.80	111.80	111.00	111.20	− .45	115.30	104.75	990
Apr		....	....	110.35	− .40	113.70	104.00	148
May		....	....	109.45	− .35	112.50	103.80	531
June		....	....	108.45	− .30	113.65	103.60	173
July		....	....	107.45	− .25	113.70	103.00	263
Sept		....	....	105.55	− .15	113.70	103.00	232

Est vol 13,000; vol Mn 8,593; open int 49,410, +282.

GOLD (Cmx.Div.NYM) 100 troy oz.; $ per troy oz.

	Open	High	Low	Settle	Change	Lifetime High	Lifetime Low	Open Interest
Apr	392.00	392.00	391.50	391.30	− .20	430.20	385.00	47
June	393.60	394.50	393.30	393.40	− .20	447.00	370.90	102,127
Aug	395.80	396.60	395.70	395.70	− .20	423.00	393.90	20,837
Oct	398.30	398.30	398.30	398.10	− .20	432.20	395.50	5,556
Dec	400.60	401.40	400.50	400.50	− .20	447.50	379.60	24,474
Fb97		....	....	402.90	− .20	428.00	403.50	5,125
Apr	406.00	406.00	406.00	405.40	− .20	428.00	403.50	4,899
June	408.60	408.60	408.60	407.90	− .30	456.00	407.00	6,721
Aug		....	....	410.40	− .30	414.50	414.50	1,005
Oct		....	....	412.90	− .30	426.50	413.30	211
Dec		....	....	415.40	− .30	477.00	402.00	7,401
Ju98		....	....	423.20	− .30	489.50	421.50	5,521
Dec		....	....	431.20	− .30	505.00	424.30	4,867
Ju99		....	....	439.30	− .30	520.00	442.00	3,701
Dec		....	....	455.10	− .30	506.00	439.00	3,520
Ju00		....	....	455.40	− .30	473.50	445.50	3,788
Dec		....	....	463.10	− .30	474.50	451.00	2,585

Est vol 16,000; vol Mn 20,789; open int 202,661, +2,993.

PLATINUM (NYM) 50 troy oz.; $ per troy oz.

	Open	High	Low	Settle	Change	Lifetime High	Lifetime Low	Open Interest
Apr	415.50	415.50	414.50	412.70	− 2.30	467.50	399.00	15
July	408.00	409.50	407.00	407.70	− 0.30	451.90	402.00	19,962
Oct	412.00	412.00	411.00	410.90	− 0.30	441.00	403.50	3,354
Ja97		....	....	413.70	− 0.30	442.00	408.00	1,077

Est vol 1,602; vol Mon 2,716; open int 25,362, −444.

SILVER (Cmx.Div.NYM) 5,000 troy oz.; cnts per troy oz.

	Open	High	Low	Settle	Change	Lifetime High	Lifetime Low	Open Interest
Apr		....	....	531.2	− 0.9	551.0	551.0	1
May	533.0	535.5	531.0	531.5	− 1.0	646.0	475.0	36,482
July	537.5	540.5	536.0	536.7	− 0.8	642.0	480.0	37,584
Sept	542.0	546.0	540.5	541.5	− 0.7	602.0	488.0	11,876
Dec	550.0	552.5	550.0	548.8	− 0.6	670.0	454.0	8,535
Mr97	557.0	561.0	556.0	556.4	− 0.5	611.0	544.0	3,320
May		....	....	561.3	− 0.5	606.0	557.0	779
Jly	569.5	569.5	569.5	566.3	− 0.5	655.0	550.0	1,248
Dec		....	....	579.5	− 0.5	695.0	502.0	1,331
Jl98		....	....	597.7	− 0.5	700.0	700.0	175
Dec	610.0	610.0	610.0	611.7	− 0.5	734.0	584.0	245
Jl99		....	....	633.7	− 0.5	660.0	637.0	297

From *The Wall Street Journal,* April 24, 1996. © 1996 Dow Jones & Company, Inc. Reprinted by permission of The Wall Street Journal. All Rights Reserved Worldwide.

the next business day. As the heading states, the open interest (to be discussed later) pertains to the preceding trading day. Figure 2.1 shows quotations for agricultural and metallurgical futures. In later chapters, we present quotations for financial futures. For each contract, the listing shows the commodity, the exchange where it is traded, the amount of the good in one contract, and the units in which prices are quoted. For example, the very first contract is for the corn contract traded by the CBOT. One contract is for 5,000 bushels, and the prices are quoted in cents per bushel.

At this point a word of warning is appropriate. The information about the contracts shown with the prices is useful, but incomplete. For corn, the type of corn that is traded is not mentioned, nor is the delivery procedure. Further, the WSJ does not give information about daily price limits, and it does not report the tick size. With so much information omitted, a trader should not trade based just on what the WSJ shows. To have a good insight into the price behavior and the price fluctuations of a contract requires additional information, such as that found in the *Commodity Trading Manual* published by the Chicago Board of Trade.

For each of the delivery months, the price listings have a row of data, with the first line going to the contract that matures next, also called the **nearby contract**. Each succeeding line pertains to another maturity month. Contracts that mature later are called **distant** or **deferred contracts**. The first three columns of prices give the opening, high, and low prices for each contract for the day of trading being reported.

The next price column, "Settle," records the **settlement price**, which is the price at which contracts are settled at the close of trading for the day. The settlement price is not always the last trade price of the day, as it would be with stocks. In Chapter 1, we examined the feature of daily settlement. All margin flows are based on the settlement price. If the settlement price brings a trader's equity below the level required for maintenance margin, then the trader will receive a margin call and will have to pay variation margin.

Typically, the settlement price will equal the last trading price for the day, but they are not always the same. Most exchanges have a settlement committee for each commodity, usually comprised of members of the exchange who trade that commodity. This committee meets immediately at the close of trading to establish the settlement price. The committee is responsible for establishing a settlement price that fairly indicates the value of the futures contract at the close of trading. When trading is active and prices are stable at the end of the day, the settlement committee has an easy job. The prices recorded from trades will be continuous, fluctuating little from trade to trade. In such cases the committee may simply allow the final trading price to be the settlement price. Therefore, in many cases the price for the last trade and the settlement price are the same price, but they are conceptually distinct.

Difficulties arise for the settlement committee, however, when a contract has little trading activity. Imagine that the last trade for a particular maturity of a given commodity occurred three hours before the close of trading and that significant information pertaining to that commodity was discovered after that last trade. In this example, the last actual trade price for the contract does not represent what the true economic price would be at the close of trading. In such a case, the settlement committee performs an important function by establishing a settlement price that differs from the price on the last recorded trade.

To establish a settlement price, the members use information on other maturity months for the same commodity. The difference between prices of contracts for different delivery months is very stable, at least relative to the futures prices themselves. So the settlement committee will use that price difference, or spread, to establish the settlement price on the contract that was not recently traded. Even more drastic situations might arise from time to time, but the settlement committee must establish a settlement price even when there is very little information to go on. Having this function performed by a committee helps rule out the possibility that an inaccurate settlement price might be chosen to generate a windfall gain for the person choosing the settlement price.

The next column, after the settlement price, is denoted as "Change." The value in this column is the change in the settlement price from the preceding day to the current day, the day for which prices are reported. The next two columns show the lifetime high and low prices for each contract. Figure 2.1 indicates how radically prices may differ for some contracts over their lives. For the contracts about to mature, the difference between the lifetime highs and lows can be enormous. For the contracts that have just been listed, there has been little time for the lifetime high and low prices to diverge radically.

The final column in Figure 2.1 is headed by the title of "Open Interest," which shows the total number of contracts outstanding for each maturity month. **Open interest** is the number of futures contracts for which delivery is currently obligated. To understand the meaning of this more clearly, assume that the December 1997 widget contract has just been listed for trading, but that the contract has not traded yet. At this point, the open interest in the contract is zero. Trading begins and the first contract is bought. This purchase necessarily means that some other trader sold. This transaction creates one contract of open interest, because there is one contract now in existence for which delivery is obligated.

Subsequent trading can increase or decrease the open interest, as Table 2.1 shows for trading in the incredibly popular widget contract. At $t = 0$, trading opens on the widget contract. The open interest is zero as is volume to date. At $t = 1$, Trader A buys and Trader B sells one widget contract. This transaction creates one contract of volume. After the transaction, the open interest is one contract, because one

■ **Table 2.1**

HOW TRADING AFFECTS OPEN INTEREST

Time	Action	Open Interest
$t = 0$	Trading opens for the popular widget contract.	0
$t = 1$	Trader A buys and Trader B sells 1 widget contract.	1
$t = 2$	Trader C buys and Trader D sells 3 widget contracts.	4
$t = 3$	Trader A sells and Trader D buys 1 widget contract. (Trader A has offset 1 contract and is out of the market. Trader D has offset 1 contract and is now short 2 contracts.)	3
$t = 4$	Trader C sells and Trader E buys 1 widget contract.	3

	Trader	Long Position	Short Position
Ending Positions	B		1
	C	2	
	D		2
	E	1	
	All Traders	3	3

contract is obligated for delivery, as Table 2.1 shows. At $t = 2$, Trader C buys and Trader D sells three widget contracts. The volume resulting from these trades is three contracts and the open interest is now four contracts. At $t = 3$, Trader A sells and Trader D buys one widget contract, creating one more contract of volume. Notice here that Trader A offsets his one contract through a reversing trade. After this offsetting transaction, Trader A is out of the market. Trader D has reversed one of her three contracts. This reduces the open interest by one contract. At $t = 4$, Trader C sells and Trader E buys one widget contract, for one contract of volume. With this transaction, Trader C reverses one contract, but Trader E enters the market. Because Trader E, in effect, takes the place of Trader C for this one contract, the open interest remains at three. The bottom panel of the table summarizes each trader's position and shows how the open interest remains at three contracts.

When a contract is distant from maturity, it tends to have relatively little open interest. As the contract approaches maturity, the open interest increases. Most often the contract closest to delivery, the nearby contract, has the highest level of open interest. As the nearby contract comes very close to maturity, however, the open interest falls. This is due to the fact that traders close their positions to avoid actual delivery. As we saw in Chapter 1, actual delivery is fairly unusual. When the futures contract matures, all traders with remaining open interest must make or take delivery, and the open interest goes to zero. Recall, also, that the open interest figures reported in the WSJ pertain to the day preceding the day for which prices are reported. Figure 2.2 shows the pattern of open interest for the December 1989 S&P 500 futures contract over its life, and Figure 2.3 shows the pattern of trading volume for the same contract. (This contract was the nearby contract at the time of the mini-crash of October 13, 1989.) The open interest and volume of trading follow a predictable pattern, such as the one shown in these two figures. Notice that the peak open interest occurs when the contract has about two to three months remaining until expiration.

In Figure 2.1, beneath the lines for each of the contract maturities, the WSJ reports more trading information. The figure shows the estimated volume for all maturities for a given commodity, followed by the actual volume for the preceding day. Next, the open interest for all contract maturities is shown. Finally, the last number reports the change in the open interest since the preceding day. We may also

■ **Figure 2.2**

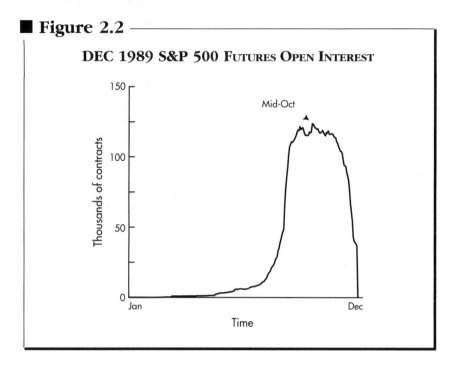

DEC 1989 S&P 500 Futures Open Interest

■ **Figure 2.3**

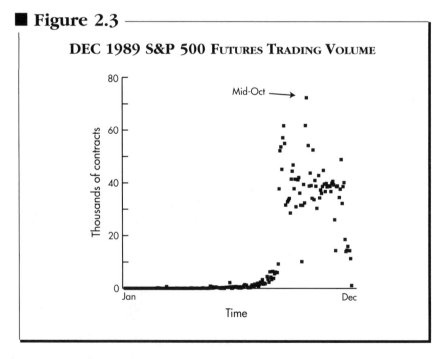

DEC 1989 S&P 500 Futures Trading Volume

note that it is possible for the volume of trading to exceed the number of contracts of open interest. This occurs when trading activity is particularly heavy for a given commodity on a certain day.

THE BASIS AND SPREADS

In this section, we analyze relationships between two prices. The basis is the relationship between the cash price of a good and the futures price for the same good. We also consider spreads. A **spread** is the difference between two futures prices. If the two prices are for futures contracts on the same underlying good, but with different expiration dates, the spread is an **intracommodity spread**. If the two futures prices that form a spread are futures prices for two underlying goods, such as a wheat futures and a corn futures, then the spread is an **intercommodity spread**.

THE BASIS

The basis receives a great deal of attention in futures trading. The **basis** is the current cash price of a particular commodity at a specified location minus the price of a particular futures contract for the same commodity:

$$\text{Basis} = \text{Current Cash Price} - \text{Futures Price}$$

Several features of this definition require explanation. First, the definition of the basis depends upon a cash price of a commodity at a specific location. The cash price of corn, for example, might differ between Kansas City and Chicago, so the basis for those two locations will also differ. Normally, one good cannot sell for different prices in two markets. If such a good had two prices, a trader could buy the commodity in the cheaper market and sell it in the market with the higher price, thereby reaping an arbitrage profit. Prices for corn in Chicago and Kansas City can differ, of course, because of the expense of transporting corn from one location to another. If corn is grown near Chicago, then we might reasonably expect the price of corn in Chicago to be lower than the price of corn in Kansas City. So the basis calculated in considering futures prices may differ, depending upon the geographic location of the spot price that is used to compute the basis.

Usually people speaking of the basis are referring to the difference between the cash price and the nearby futures contract. There is, however, a basis for each outstanding futures contract, and this basis will often differ in systematic ways, depending upon the maturities of the individual futures contracts. Table 2.2 shows spot and futures gold prices for July 11, and illustrates this phenomenon. The cash, or spot, price is the London A.M. fix, or morning quotation, so the basis pertains to London. The futures prices are from the COMEX. The right column shows the basis for each futures contract. The basis is negative for all delivery months in this example. The chart of the basis shows that it is possible to contract for the future sale or purchase of gold at a price that exceeds the current cash price. The difference between the current cash price of $353.70 per ounce and the price of the more distant futures contracts is striking, as much as $37.80 per ounce for the most distant DEC contract.

Futures markets can exhibit a pattern of either normal or inverted prices. In a **normal market**, prices for more distant futures are higher than for nearby futures. For example, the gold prices in Table 2.2 represent a normal market. In an **inverted market**, distant futures prices are lower than the prices for contracts nearer to expiration. The interpretation of the basis can be very important, particularly for agricultural commodities. For many commodities, the fact that the harvest comes at a certain time each year introduces seasonal components into the series of cash prices. Many traders believe that understanding these seasonal factors can be very beneficial for speculation

■ **Table 2.2**

GOLD PRICES AND THE BASIS (JULY 11)

Contract	Prices	The Basis
CASH	353.70	
JUL (this year)	354.10	−.40
AUG	355.60	−1.90
OCT	359.80	−6.10
DEC	364.20	−10.50
FEB (next year)	368.70	−15.00
APR	373.00	−19.30
JUN	377.50	−23.80
AUG	381.90	−28.20
OCT	386.70	−33.00
DEC	391.50	−37.80

and hedging. Also, as will become clear, the basis, such as that shown in Table 2.2, can be used as a valuable information source to predict future spot prices of the commodities that underlie the futures contracts.

A further point about the basis emerges from Table 2.2. Notice that the basis for the nearby contract is only −$.40, about one-thousandth of the cash price. There is good reason that it should be so small. The JUL contract is extremely close to delivery on the date in question, July 11. At delivery, the futures price and the cash price must be equal, except for minor discrepancies due to transportation and other transaction costs. If someone were to trade the JUL contract on the day in question, the trade would be for the delivery of gold within three weeks. The price of gold for delivery within three weeks must closely approximate the current spot price of gold.

When the futures contract is at expiration, the futures price and the spot price of gold must be the same. The basis must be zero, again subject to the discrepancy due to transaction costs. This behavior of the basis over time is known as **convergence**, as Figures 2.4 and 2.5 illustrate. In Figure 2.4, the cash price lies above the futures price. As time progresses, and the futures contract approaches maturity, the basis narrows. At the maturity of the futures contract, the basis is

■ Figure 2.4

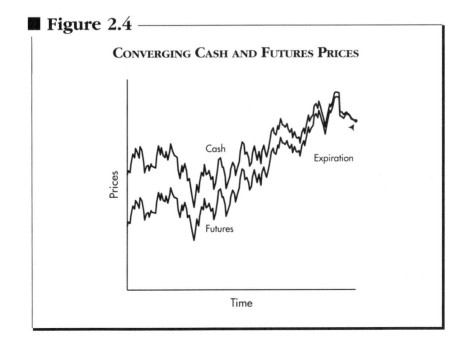

CONVERGING CASH AND FUTURES PRICES

■ **Figure 2.5**

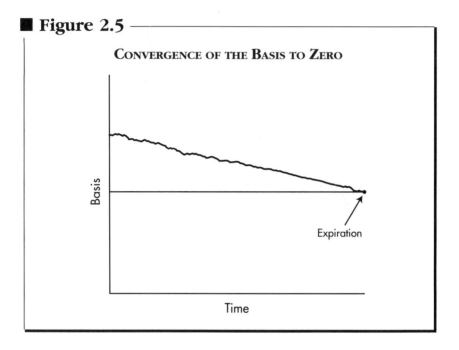

CONVERGENCE OF THE BASIS TO ZERO

zero, consistent with the no-arbitrage requirement that the futures price and cash price be equal at the maturity of the futures contract. Figure 2.5 shows the basis itself, corresponding to the prices in Figure 2.4. The basis is positive, but declines to zero as the futures contract approaches maturity.

Figure 2.6 illustrates one other feature of the basis that is very important for futures trading. The upper portion of the figure shows prices for the MAR S&P 500 futures contract. The graph covers the range from 300 to 400, a 100-point range within which the contract traded between July and its expiration in March of the next year. The bottom portion of Figure 2.6 illustrates how the basis for this contract behaved over the same time interval. This bottom panel also covers a 100-point scale to make the two graphs comparable.

As the graph dramatically reveals, the fluctuation in the basis was much less than the range of fluctuation in the futures price itself. This is almost always the case. The basis is almost always much more stable than the futures price or the cash price, when those prices are considered in isolation. The futures price may oscillate and the cash price may swing widely, but the basis (cash − futures price) tends to be relatively steady. The relatively low variability of the basis is very

■ Figure 2.6

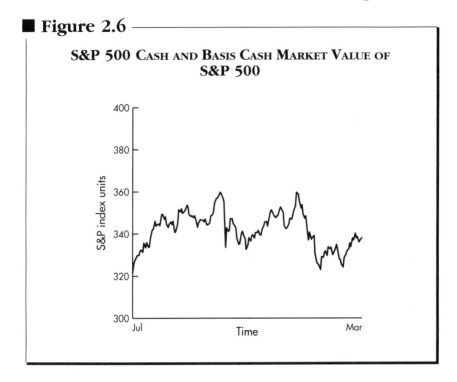

S&P 500 Cash and Basis Cash Market Value of S&P 500

important for hedging and for certain types of speculation, as will be discussed in Chapter 3.

SPREADS

Just as there is an important relationship between each futures contract and the cash price of the commodity, the relationship among futures prices on the same good (an intracommodity spread) is also important, because it indicates the relative price differentials for a commodity to be delivered at two points in time. As we will see, there are strong economic relationships that govern the permissible time spreads that may exist between any two futures contracts.

Spread relationships are important for speculators. Much speculation involves some kind of spread position – the holding of two or more related futures contracts. If a trader hopes to use futures markets to earn speculative profits, an understanding of spread relationships is essential. Since most speculation uses spreads, the search for a profit turns on an ability to identify spread relationships that are

economically unjustified. While the understanding of the spread relationships in a particular commodity requires considerable knowledge
about the commodity itself, certain general principles apply to all
spreads.

Figure 2.7 shows the spread between the S&P 500 futures contract
for JUN of 1989 and the MAR contract for the next year, computed
here as the June price minus the March price. The time period here
is the same used in Figure 2.6. Thus, we can see the stability of the
spread in Figure 2.7 compared to the price itself in Figure 2.6.

MODELS OF FUTURES PRICES

In this section, we consider two models of futures prices. The first
of these is the **cost-of-carry model**. According to this model, futures
prices depend on the cash price of a commodity and the cost of
storing the underlying good from the present to the delivery date of
the futures contract. The second model is the **expectations model**.
According to this view, the futures price today equals the cash price
that traders expect to prevail for the underlying good on the delivery
date of the futures contract. For example, the futures price in January

■ **Figure 2.7**

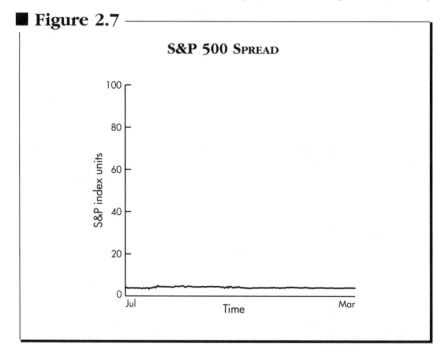

S&P 500 SPREAD

for the JUL contract is the market's January estimate of what the price of corn will be in July when the futures contract expires.

To explore these models, we employ the concept of arbitrage. We begin by assuming that prices in the market do not allow any arbitrage profits. Under this assumption, we ask what futures pricing relationships are permissible. For the sake of simplicity, we begin by assuming that futures markets are perfect. A **perfect market** is a market with no transaction costs and no restrictions on free contracting between two parties. Thus, the analysis begins under the assumptions of an idealized world – a world that allows no arbitrage and that includes no market frictions. Gradually, we develop a more realistic analysis by relaxing these assumptions. This approach allows us to start the analysis within a fairly simple environment and to add complications after we explore the most essential features of the pricing relationships.

THE COST-OF-CARRY MODEL IN PERFECT MARKETS

In this section, we use the concept of arbitrage introduced in Chapter 1 to explore the cost-of-carry model or carrying charge theory of futures prices. The **cost-of-carry** or **carrying charge** is the total cost to carry a good forward in time. For example, wheat on hand in June can be carried forward to, or stored until, December.

Carrying charges fall into four basic categories: storage costs, insurance costs, transportation costs, and financing costs. Storage costs include the cost of warehousing the commodity in the appropriate facility. While storage seems to apply most clearly to physical goods, such as wheat or lumber, it is also possible to store financial instruments. In many cases, the owner of a financial instrument will leave the instrument in a bank vault. For many goods in storage, insurance is also necessary. For example, stored lumber should be protected against fire, and stored wheat should be insured against water damage.

The carrying charges also include, in some cases, transportation costs. Wheat in a railroad siding in Kansas must be carried to delivery in two senses. It must be stored until the appropriate delivery time for a given futures contract, but it must also be physically carried to the appropriate place for delivery. As will become obvious, transportation costs between different locations determine price differentials between those locations. Without question, transportation charges play different roles for different commodities. Transporting wheat from Kansas to Chicago could be an important expense. By contrast, delivery of Treasury bills against a futures contract is accomplished by a wire transfer costing only a few dollars. In almost all cases, the most significant carrying charge in the futures market is the financing cost. For most situations, financing the good under storage over-whelms the other costs.

The carrying charge reflects only the charges involved in carrying a commodity from one time or one place to another. The carrying charges do not include the value of the commodity itself. So, if gold costs $400 per ounce and the financing rate is 1 percent per month, the financing charge for carrying the gold forward is $4 per month ($1\% \times \$400$).

Most participants in the futures markets face a financing charge on a short-term basis that is equal to the repo rate. The **repo rate** is the interest rate on repurchase agreements. In a **repurchase agreement** a person sells securities at one point in time, with the understanding that they will be repurchased at a certain price at a later time. Most repurchase agreements are for one day only and are known, accord-ingly, as overnight repos. The repo rate is relatively low, exceeding the rate on Treasury bills by only a small amount.[1] The financing cost for such goods is so low because anyone wishing to finance a commodity may offer the commodity itself as collateral for the loan. Further, most of the participants in the market tend to be financial institutions of one type or another who have low financing costs anyway, at least for very short-term obligations.

Cash and Futures Pricing Relationships. The carrying charges just described are important because they play a crucial role in determining pricing relationships between spot and futures prices as well as the relationships among prices of futures contracts of different maturities. For present purposes, we will assume that the only carrying charge is the financing cost at an interest rate of 10 percent per year. As an example, consider the prices and the accompanying transactions shown in Table 2.3.

The transactions in Table 2.3 represent a successful cash-and-carry arbitrage. This is a **cash-and-carry arbitrage** because the trader buys the cash good and carries it to the expiration of the futures contract. The trader traded at $t = 0$ to guarantee a riskless profit without invest-ment. There was no investment, because there was no cash flow at $t = 0$. The trader merely borrowed funds to purchase the gold and to carry it forward. The profit in these transactions was certain once

■ Table 2.3

CASH-AND-CARRY GOLD ARBITRAGE TRANSACTIONS

Prices for the Analysis

Spot price of gold	$400
Future price of gold (for delivery in 1 year)	$450
Interest rate	10%

Transaction	Cash Flow
$t = 0$ Borrow $400 for one year at 10%.	+$400
Buy one ounce of gold in the spot market for $400.	−400
Sell a futures contract for $450 for delivery of 1 ounce in 1 year.	0
Total Cash Flow	$0
$t = 1$ Remove the gold from storage.	$0
Deliver the ounce of gold against the futures contract.	+450
Repay loan, including interest.	−440
Total Cash Flow	+$10

the trader made the transactions at $t = 0$. As these transactions show, to prevent arbitrage the futures price of the gold should have been $440 or less. With a futures price of $440, for example, the transactions in Table 2.3 would yield a zero profit. From this example, we can infer the following general rule:

Cost-of-Carry Rule 1:

The futures price must be less than or equal to the spot price of the commodity plus the carrying charges necessary to carry the spot commodity forward to delivery.

We can express Rule 1 mathematically as follows:

$$F_{0,t} \leq S_0(1 + C) \tag{2.1}$$

where:

$F_{0,t}$ = the futures price at $t = 0$ for delivery at time $= t$
S_0 = the spot price at $t = 0$
C = the cost-of-carry, expressed as a fraction of the spot price, necessary to carry the good forward from the present to the delivery date on the futures

As we have seen, if prices do not conform to cost-of-carry rule 1, a trader can borrow funds, buy the spot commodity with the borrowed funds, sell the futures contract, and carry the commodity forward to deliver against the futures contract. These transactions would generate a certain profit without investment, or an arbitrage profit. There would be a certain profit, because it is guaranteed by the sale of the futures contract. Also, there would be no investment, since the funds needed to carry out the strategy were borrowed and the cost of using those funds was included in the calculation of the carrying charge. Such opportunities cannot exist in a rational market. The cash-and-carry arbitrage opportunity arises because the spot price is too low relative to the futures price.

We have seen that an arbitrage opportunity arises if the spot price is too low relative to the futures price. As we now see, the spot price might also be too high relative to the futures price. If the spot price is too high, we have a reverse cash-and-carry arbitrage opportunity. As the name implies, the steps necessary to exploit the arbitrage opportunity are just the opposite of those in the cash-and-carry arbitrage strategy. As an example of the reverse cash-and-carry strategy, consider the prices for gold and the accompanying transactions in Table 2.4.

In these transactions, the arbitrageur sells the gold short. As in the stock market, a short seller borrows the good from another trader and must later repay it. Once the good is borrowed, the short seller sells it and takes the money from the sale. (The transaction is called short selling because one sells a good that he or she does not actually own.) In this example, the short seller has the use of all of the proceeds from the short sale, which are invested at the interest rate of 10 percent. The trader also buys a futures contract to ensure that he or she can acquire the gold needed to repay the lender at the expiration of the futures in one year.

Notice that these transactions guarantee an arbitrage profit. Once the transactions at $t = 0$ are completed, the $12 profit at $t = 1$ year is certain. Also, the trader had no net cash flow at $t = 0$, so the strategy required no investment. To make this arbitrage opportunity impossible, the spot and futures prices must obey cost-of-carry rule 2.

Cost-of-Carry Rule 2:
The futures price must be equal to or greater than the spot price plus the cost of carrying the good to the futures delivery date.

■ Table 2.4

REVERSE CASH-AND-CARRY GOLD ARBITRAGE TRANSACTIONS

Prices for the Analysis

Spot price of gold	$420
Future price of gold (for delivery in 1 year)	$450
Interest rate	10%

Transaction	Cash Flow
$t = 0$ Sell one ounce of gold short.	+$420
Lend the $420 for 1 year at 10%.	−420
Buy 1 ounce of gold futures for delivery in 1 year.	0
Total Cash Flow	$0
$t = 1$ Collect proceeds from the loan ($420 × 1.1).	+$462
Accept delivery on the futures contract.	−450
Use gold from futures delivery to repay short sale.	0
Total Cash Flow	+$12

Expressing this rule mathematically with the notation we introduced earlier:

$$F_{0,t} \geq S_0(1 + C) \qquad (2.2)$$

If prices do not obey this rule, there will be an arbitrage opportunity. Table 2.5 summarizes the transactions necessary to conduct the cash-and-carry and the reverse cash-and-carry strategies.

To prevent arbitrage, we have seen that the two following rules must hold:

To prevent cash-and-carry arbitrage	$F_{0,t} \leq S_0(1 + C)$	(2.1)
To prevent reverse cash-and-carry arbitrage	$F_{0,t} \geq S_0(1 + C)$	(2.2)

Together, Equations 2.1 and 2.2 imply cost-of-carry rule 3:

Cost-of-Carry Rule 3:

The futures price must equal the spot price plus the cost of carrying the spot commodity forward to the delivery date of the futures contract.

■ **Table 2.5** ────────────────────────────

TRANSACTIONS FOR ARBITRAGE STRATEGIES

Market	Cash-and-Carry	Reverse Cash-and-Carry
Debt	Borrow funds.	Lend short sale proceeds.
Physical	Buy asset and store; deliver against futures.	Sell asset short; secure proceeds from short sale.
Futures	Sell futures.	Buy futures; accept delivery; return physical asset to honor short sale commitment.

Expressing rule 3 mathematically, we have:

$$F_{0,t} = S_0(1 + C) \qquad (2.3)$$

Notice that the relationship of Equation 2.3 was derived under the following assumptions: Markets are perfect; that is, they have no transaction costs and no restrictions on the use of proceeds from short sales. It must be acknowledged that this argument explicitly excludes transaction costs. Transaction costs exist on both sides of the market, for purchase or sale of the futures. In many markets, however, transaction costs for short selling are considerably more expensive, which limits the applicability of the reverse cash-and-carry strategy.

Spreads and the Cost-of-Carry. These same cost-of-carry relationships also determine the price relationships that can exist between futures contracts on the same good that differ in maturity. As an example, consider the prices and accompanying arbitrage transactions shown in Table 2.6.

As this example shows, the spread between two futures contracts cannot exceed the cost of carrying the good from one delivery date forward to the next, as cost-of-carry rule 4 states.

Cost-of-Carry Rule 4:
The distant futures price must be less than or equal to the nearby futures price plus the cost of carrying the commodity from the nearby delivery date to the distant delivery date.

■ Table 2.6

GOLD FORWARD CASH-AND-CARRY ARBITRAGE

Prices for the Analysis

Futures price for gold expiring in 1 year	$400
Futures price for gold expiring in 2 years	$450
Interest rate (to cover from year 1 to year 2)	10%

Transaction		Cash Flow
$t = 0$	Buy the futures expiring in 1 year.	+$0
	Sell the futures expiring in 2 years.	0
	Contract to borrow $400 at 10% for year 1 to year 2.	0
	Total Cash Flow	$0
$t = 1$	Borrow $400 for one year at 10% as contracted at $t = 0$.	+$400
	Take delivery on the futures contract.	−400
	Begin to store gold for 1 year.	0
	Total Cash Flow	$0
$t = 2$	Deliver gold to honor futures contract.	+$450
	Repay loan ($400 × 1.1).	−440
	Total Cash Flow	+$10

Expressing rule 4 mathematically, we have:

$$F_{0,d} \leq F_{0,n}(1 + C), \qquad d > n \qquad (2.4)$$

where:

$F_{0,d}$ = the futures price at $t = 0$ for the distant delivery contract maturing at $t = d$

$F_{0,n}$ = the futures price at $t = 0$ for the nearby delivery contract maturing at $t = n$

C = the percentage cost of carrying the good from $t = n$ to $t = d$

As we have seen, if this relationship did not hold, a trader could buy the nearby futures contract and sell the distant contract. The trader would then accept delivery on the nearby contract and carry the good until the delivery of the distant contract, thereby making a profit.

To complete our argument, we analyze what happens if the nearby futures price is too high relative to the distant futures price. To conduct the arbitrage in this case, consider the gold prices and arbitrage transactions shown in Table 2.7. Thus, forward reverse cash-and-carry arbitrage is possible if the nearby futures price is too high relative to the distant futures price. To exclude this arbitrage opportunity, prices must conform to cost-of-carry rule 5.

Cost-of-Carry Rule 5:

The nearby futures price plus the cost of carrying the commodity from the nearby delivery date to the distant delivery date cannot exceed the distant futures price.

Expressing cost-of-carry rule 5 mathematically, we have:

$$F_{0,d} \geq F_{0,n}(1 + C), \quad d > n \quad (2.5)$$

■ Table 2.7

Gold Forward Reverse Cash-and-Carry Arbitrage

Prices for the Analysis

Futures price for gold expiring in 1 year	$440
Futures price for gold expiring in 2 years	$450
Interest rate (to cover from year 1 to year 2)	10%

Transaction	Cash Flow
$t = 0$ Sell the futures expiring in 1 year.	+$0
Buy the futures expiring in 2 years.	0
Contract to lend $440 at 10% from year 1 to year 2.	0
Total Cash Flow	$0
$t = 1$ Borrow one ounce of gold for 1 year.	$0
Deliver gold against the expiring futures.	+440
Invest proceeds from delivery for 1 year.	−440
Total Cash Flow	$0
$t = 2$ Accept delivery on expiring futures.	−$450
Repay one ounce of borrowed gold.	0
Collect on loan of $440 made at $t = 1$.	+484
Total Cash Flow	+$34

From our two arbitrage arguments in Tables 2.6 and 2.7, we have derived the rules expressed in Equations 2.4 and 2.5. To exclude forward:

Cash-and-carry arbitrage $\quad F_{0,d} \leq F_{0,n}(1 + C), \quad d > n \qquad (2.4)$
Reverse cash-and-carry arbitrage $\quad F_{0,d} \geq F_{0,n}(1 + C), \quad d > n \qquad (2.5)$

Following the same pattern of argument we used for spot prices and futures prices, we see that Equations 2.4 and 2.5 imply cost-of-carry rule 6.

Cost-of-Carry Rule 6:

The distant futures price must equal the nearby futures price plus the cost of carrying the commodity from the nearby to the distant delivery date.

We can express cost-of-carry rule 6 mathematically as follows:

$$F_{0,d} = F_{0,n}(1 + C), \qquad d > n \qquad (2.6)$$

If these relationships were ever violated, profit-hungry traders would immediately recognize the chance and trade until prices adjusted to eliminate all of the arbitrage opportunities.

Summary. All of the cost-of-carry relationships explored to this point assumed that markets are perfect. In particular, we assumed that they allowed unrestricted short selling. We made heavy use of these assumptions. For example, we assumed that the borrowing and lending rates were equal, that we could sell gold short and use 100 percent of the proceeds from the short sale, and that it was possible to contract to borrow and lend at forward rates. All of these assumptions require qualifications, which the next section will develop.

The basic rules developed in this section provide a very useful framework for analyzing relationships between cash and futures prices, on the one hand, and spreads between futures prices, on the other. Cost-of-carry rule 3 and Equation 2.3 express the basic cash-futures relationship:

$$F_{0,t} = S_0(1 + C) \qquad (2.3)$$

Cost-of-carry rule 6 and Equation 2.6 express the relationship for two futures prices:

$$F_{0,d} = F_{0,n}(1 + C), \qquad d > n \qquad (2.6)$$

Notice that these two equations have the same form. We therefore use Equation 2.3 to make a final point to summarize the cost-of-carry model in perfect markets. Equation 2.7 says that the cost-of-carry in the perfect market we have been considering equals the ratio of the futures price to the spot price minus 1. In Equation 2.7, the "C" is the **implied repo rate** – the interest rate implied by the difference between the cash and futures prices. Solving Equation 2.3 for the cost-of-carry C, we have:

$$C = F_{0,t}/S_0 - 1 \qquad (2.7)$$

In a well-functioning market, the implied repo rate must equal the actual repo rate. As we have seen in this section, deviations from this relationship lead to arbitrage opportunities in a perfect market. We now consider the qualifications to the basic conclusion that are required by market imperfections.

The Cost-of-Carry Model in Imperfect Markets

In real markets, four market imperfections operate to complicate and disturb the relationships of Equations 2.3 and 2.6. First, traders face transaction costs. Second, restrictions on short-selling frustrate reverse cash-and-carry strategies. Third, borrowing and lending rates are not generally equal as the assumption of perfect markets would imply. Finally, some goods cannot be stored, so they cannot be carried forward to delivery. This section considers each of these in turn.

The main effect of these market imperfections is to require adjustments in the identities expressed by Equations 2.3 and 2.6. Market imperfections do not invalidate the basic framework we have been building. Instead of being able to state an equality as we did in the perfect markets framework leading to Equations 2.3 and 2.6, we will find that market imperfections introduce a certain indeterminacy to the relationship.

Direct Transaction Costs. In actual markets, traders face a variety of direct transaction costs. First, the trader must pay a fee to have an order executed. For a trader off the floor of the exchange, these fees include brokerage commissions and various exchange fees. Even members of the exchange must pay a fee to the exchange for each trade. Second, in every market, there is a bid-asked spread. A market maker on the floor of the exchange must try to sell at a higher price (the **asked price**) than the price at which he or she is willing to buy (the **bid price**). The difference between the asked price and the bid price is the **bid-asked spread**. In our discussion, we will assume that these transaction costs are some fixed percentage of the transaction amount, *T*. For simplicity, we assume that the transaction costs apply to the spot market, but not to the futures market.

To illustrate the impact of transaction costs, we use the same prices with which we began our analysis in perfect markets. Now, however, we consider transaction costs of 3 percent. With transaction costs, our previous arbitrage strategy of buying the good and carrying it to delivery will not work. Table 2.8 shows the results of this attempted arbitrage. With transaction costs, the attempted arbitrage results in a certain loss, not an arbitrage profit.

■ Table 2.8

ATTEMPTED CASH-AND-CARRY GOLD ARBITRAGE TRANSACTIONS

Prices for the Analysis

Spot price of gold	$400
Future price of gold (for delivery in 1 year)	$450
Interest rate	10%
Transaction cost (*T*)	3%

Transaction		Cash Flow
t = 0	Borrow $412 for 1 year at 10%.	$412
	Buy 1 ounce of gold in the spot market for $400 and pay 3% transaction costs, to total $412.	−412
	Sell a futures contract for $450 for delivery of 1 ounce in 1 year.	0
	Total Cash Flow	$0
t = 1	Remove the gold from storage.	$0
	Deliver the ounce of gold to close futures contract.	+450.00
	Repay loan, including interest.	−453.20
	Total Cash Flow	−$3.20

We would have to pay $400 as before to acquire the good, plus transaction costs of 3 percent for a total outlay of $400(1 + T) = $412. We would then have to finance this total until delivery for a cost of $412(1.1) = $453.20. In return, we would only receive $450 upon the delivery of the futures contract. Given these prices, it clearly does not pay to attempt this "cash-and-carry" arbitrage. As Table 2.8 shows, these attempted arbitrage transactions generate a certain loss of $3.20. With transaction costs of 3 percent and the same spot price of $400, the futures price would have to exceed $453.20 to make the arbitrage attractive. To see why this is so, consider the cash outflows and inflows. We pay the spot price plus the transaction costs, $S_0(1 + T)$, to acquire the good. Carrying the good to delivery costs $S_0(1 + T)(1 + C)$. These costs include acquiring the good and carrying it to the delivery date of the futures. In our example, the total cost is:

$$S_0(1 + T)(1 + C) = \$400(1.03)(1.1) = \$453.20$$

Thus, to break even, the futures transaction must yield $453.20. We can write this more formally as:

$$F_{0,t} \leq S_0(1 + T)(1 + C) \tag{2.8}$$

If prices follow Equation 2.8, the cash-and-carry arbitrage opportunity will not be available. Notice that Equation 2.8 has the same form as Equation 2.1, but Equation 2.8 includes transaction costs.

In our discussion of the cost-of-carry model in perfect markets, we saw that futures prices could not be too high relative to spot prices. Otherwise, arbitrage opportunities would be available, as we saw in Table 2.4. We now explore the transactions as shown in Table 2.4, except we include the transaction costs of 3 percent. Table 2.9 shows these transactions.

Including transaction costs in the analysis gives a loss on the same transactions that were profitable with no transaction costs. In the original transactions of Table 2.4 with the same prices, the profit was $12. For perfect markets, Equation 2.2 gave the no-arbitrage conditions for the reverse cash-and-carry arbitrage strategy.

$$F_{0,t} \geq S_0(1 + C) \tag{2.2}$$

■ Table 2.9

ATTEMPTED REVERSE CASH-AND-CARRY GOLD ARBITRAGE

Prices for the Analysis

Spot price of gold	$420
Future price of gold (for delivery in 1 year)	$450
Interest rate	10%
Transaction costs (*T*)	3%

Transaction	Cash Flow
t = 0 Sell 1 ounce of gold short, paying 3% transaction costs. Receive $420(.97) = $407.40.	+$407.40
Lend the $407.40 for 1 year at 10%.	−407.40
Buy 1 ounce of gold futures for delivery in 1 year.	0
Total Cash Flow	$0
t = 1 Collect loan proceeds ($407.40 × 1.1).	+$448.14
Accept gold delivery on the futures contract.	−450.00
Use gold from futures delivery to repay short sale.	0
Total Cash Flow	−$1.86

Including transaction costs, we have:

$$F_{0,t} \geq S_0(1 - T)(1 + C) \qquad (2.9)$$

Combining Equations 2.8 and 2.9 gives:

$$S_0(1 - T)(1 + C) \leq F_{0,t} \leq S_0(1 + T)(1 + C) \qquad (2.10)$$

Equation 2.10 defines the **no-arbitrage bounds** – bounds within which the futures price must remain to prevent arbitrage. In general, transaction costs force a loosening of the price relationship in Equation 2.3. In perfect markets, Equation 2.3 gave an exact equation for the futures price as a function of the spot price and the cost-of-carry. If the futures price deviated from that no-arbitrage price, traders could transact to reap a riskless profit without investment. For a market with transaction costs, Equation 2.10 gives bounds for the futures price. If the futures price goes beyond these boundaries, arbitrage is possible. The futures price can wander within the bounds without offering arbitrage opportunities, however. As an example, consider the bounds implied by the transactions in Table 2.8. If there are no transaction costs, the futures price must be exactly $440 to exclude arbitrage. With the 3 percent transaction costs on spot market transactions, the futures price is free to wander within the range $426.80 to $453.20 without creating any arbitrage opportunity, as Table 2.10 shows.

Figure 2.8 illustrates the concept of arbitrage boundaries. The vertical axis graphs futures prices and the horizontal axis shows the time dimension. The solid horizontal line shows the no-arbitrage condition for a perfect market. In a perfect market, the futures price must exactly equal the spot price times 1 plus the cost of carry, $F_{0,t} = S_0(1 + C)$. With transaction costs, however, we have a lower and an upper bound. If the futures price goes above the upper no-arbitrage bound, there will be a cash-and-carry arbitrage opportunity. This occurs when $F_{0,t} > S_0(1 + T)(1 + C)$. Likewise, if the futures price falls too low, it will be less than the lower no-arbitrage bound. Futures prices that are too low relative to the spot price give rise to a reverse cash-and-carry arbitrage. This opportunity arises when $F_{0,t} < S_0(1 - T)(1 + C)$. Figure 2.8 shows these no-arbitrage boundaries as dotted lines.

∎ Table 2.10

ILLUSTRATION OF NO-ARBITRAGE BOUNDS

Prices for the Analysis

Spot price of gold	$400
Interest rate	10%
Transaction costs (T)	3%

No-Arbitrage Futures Price in Perfect Markets

$$F_{0,t} = S_0(1 + C) = \$400(1.1) = \$440$$

Upper No-Arbitrage Bound with Transaction Costs

$$F_{0,t} \le S_0(1 + T)(1 + C) = \$400(1.03)(1.1) = \$453.20$$

Lower No-Arbitrage Bound with Transaction Costs

$$F_{0,t} \ge S_0(1 - T)(1 + C) = \$400(.97)(1.1) = \$426.80$$

■ Figure 2.8

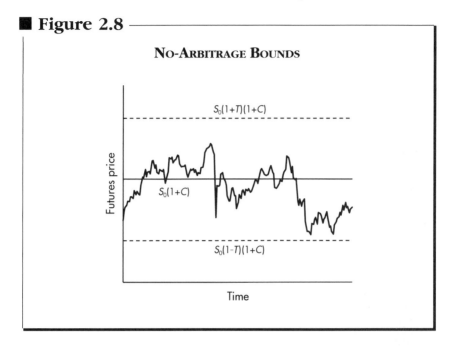

NO-ARBITRAGE BOUNDS

$S_0(1+T)(1+C)$

Futures price

$S_0(1+C)$

$S_0(1-T)(1+C)$

Time

If the futures price stays between the bounds, no arbitrage is possible. If the futures price crosses the boundaries, arbitrageurs will flock to the market to exploit the opportunity. For example, if the futures price is too high, traders will buy the spot commodity and sell the futures. This action will raise the price of the spot good relative to the futures price, thereby driving the futures price back within the no-arbitrage boundaries. If the futures price stays within the boundaries, no arbitrage is possible, and the arbitrageurs will not be able to affect the futures price.

From Figure 2.8, we can note three important points. First, the greater the transaction costs, T, the farther apart will be the bounds. With higher transaction costs, the arbitrage relationships we have been exploring are less binding on possible prices. Second, we have been assuming that all traders in the market face the same percentage transaction costs, T. Clearly, different traders face different transaction costs. For example, a retail trader, who is not an exchange member, can face transaction costs that are much higher than those for a floor trader. It is easily possible for the retail trader to pay as much as 100 times the exchange and brokerage fees paid by a floor trader. Therefore, Figure 2.8 really pertains to a particular trader, not to every trader in the market. Consider a trader facing higher transaction costs of $2T$ instead of T. For this trader, the no-arbitrage bounds would be twice as wide as those in Figure 2.8. Third, we have seen that market forces exist to keep the futures price within the no-arbitrage bounds, and that each trader faces his or her own particular bounds, depending on that trader's transaction costs.

Differences in transaction costs give rise to the concept of **quasi-arbitrage**. Some traders, such as small retail customers, face full transaction costs. Other traders, such as large financial institutions, have much lower transaction costs. For example, exchange members pay much lower transaction costs than do outside traders. Therefore, the quasi-arbitrageur is a potential cash-and-carry or reverse cash-and-carry trader with relatively lower transaction costs. The futures price should stay within the bounds of the lowest transaction cost trader. Once the futures price drifts beyond the bounds of the lowest transaction cost trader, he or she will exploit the arbitrage opportunity. As we have seen, arbitrage activity will drive the futures price back within the no-arbitrage bounds for that trader.

Thus, in the actual market, we expect to see futures prices within the no-arbitrage bounds of the lowest transaction cost trader. This means that traders with higher transaction costs will not be able to exploit any arbitrage opportunities. If prices start to drift away from the perfect markets equality of Equation 2.3, they will be exploited first by the traders with low transaction costs. This exploitation will take place through quasi-arbitrage, because the low transaction cost trader does not face the full transaction costs of an outside trader.

Unequal Borrowing and Lending Rates. In perfect markets, all traders can borrow and lend at the risk-free rate. This is not true in real markets. Generally, traders face a borrowing rate that exceeds the lending rate. In our examples of cash-and-carry and reverse cash-and-carry arbitrage, we have assumed that the two rates were the same. For the cash-and-carry arbitrage, the trader borrows funds, while the trader lends funds in the reverse cash-and-carry arbitrage. Throughout our examples, we assumed that traders could both borrow and lend at a 10 percent rate. If the borrowing and lending rates are not equal, Equation 2.10 requires adjustment to reflect that fact. In Equation 2.10, the upper bound on the futures price comes from the cash-and-carry arbitrage possibility, as shown in Figure 2.8. In the cash-and-carry arbitrage, the trader borrows funds so the borrowing rate is the appropriate rate in the expression for the upper bound.

Analogously, the reverse cash-and-carry trade uses a strategy of lending to fix the lower bound. Thus, the lending rate is appropriate for the expression giving the lower bound. Equation 2.11 reproduces Equation 2.10, but reflects the different borrowing and lending rates:

$$S_0(1 - T)(1 + C_L) \leq F_{0,t} \leq S_0(1 + T)(1 + C_B) \qquad (2.11)$$

where:

C_L = the lending rate
C_B = the borrowing rate

These differential borrowing and lending rates serve to widen the no-arbitrage boundaries that we have been exploring, because generally $C_L < C_B$. We can illustrate the effect of the differential rates by extending the example of Table 2.10 to include unequal borrowing and lending rates. Table 2.11 illustrates the effect of these unequal rates on the no-arbitrage bounds. As the table shows, including differential borrowing and lending rates widens the no-arbitrage boundaries.

Restrictions on Short Selling. In our analysis, we have so far assumed that traders can sell assets short and use the proceeds from

■ Table 2.11

ILLUSTRATION OF NO-ARBITRAGE BOUNDS WITH DIFFERENTIAL BORROWING AND LENDING RATES

Prices for the Analysis

Spot price of gold	$400
Interest rate (borrowing)	12%
Interest rate (lending)	8%
Transaction costs (T)	3%

Upper No-Arbitrage Bound with Transaction Costs and a Borrowing Rate

$$F_{0,t} \leq S_0(1 + T)(1 + C_B) = \$400(1.03)(1.12) = \$461.44$$

Lower No-Arbitrage Bound with Transaction Costs and a Lending Rate

$$F_{0,t} \geq S_0(1 - T)(1 + C_L) = \$400(.97)(1.08) = \$419.04$$

the short sale. In all of our examples, we have also assumed that the short seller has the unrestricted use of all funds arising from the short sale. Consider for a moment, however, the position of the broker who facilitates a short sale. In the stock market, for example, the prospective short seller asks his or her broker to borrow a share from another customer and to sell it on behalf of the short seller. If the short seller received all of the funds from the short sale, the broker would be in a precarious position. The broker has borrowed the share from another customer and must return the share upon demand. If the broker allows the short seller to have all of the proceeds of the short sale, the broker runs a significant risk. The short seller might, for instance, take all of the funds and abscond. Alternatively, the price might move against the short seller and the short seller might not be able to pay to reacquire the stock.

Because of these inherent risks, there are restrictions on short selling in virtually all markets. These restrictions are important, because we found that short selling was a necessary technique for the reverse cash-and-carry arbitrage strategy. If a trader sells the spot good short, Equation 2.2 must hold to prevent arbitrage. Further, from 2.1 and 2.2, we were able to derive the no-arbitrage condition of 2.3 for a perfect market.

In actual markets, there are serious impediments to short selling. First, for some goods, there is virtually no opportunity for short selling. This is particularly true for many physical goods. Second, even when short selling is permitted, restrictions limit the use of funds from the short sale. Often these restrictions mean that the short seller does not have the use of all of the proceeds from the short sale. A typical percentage for the broker to retain is 50 percent, meaning that the short seller would have the use of only 50 percent of the funds.

In the arbitrage relationship of Equation 2.2, we concluded that:

$$F_{0,t} \geq S_0(1 + C)$$

This result assumes unrestricted short selling, so that the short seller had full use of the short sale proceeds, S_0. As we saw, the reverse cash-and-carry transaction employs the short sale, and this arbitrage strategy determines the lower bound for the futures price. To reflect the fact that the short seller does not have use of the proceeds, but only some fraction f, we can recast Equation 2.2 to say:

$$F_{0,t} \geq f S_0(1 + C)$$

where:

f = the fraction of usable funds derived from the short sale

This fraction must lie between zero and one. In a perfect market, $f = 1.0$, and it effectively drops out of the equation. With restricted short selling, we can now rewrite our no-arbitrage conditions. First, for a market that is perfect except for restricting short sales, we have a modification of Equation 2.3:

$$S_0(1 + fC) \leq F_{0,t} \leq S_0(1 + C) \tag{2.12}$$

We can also integrate restricted short selling into our imperfect markets framework of Equation 2.11. Taking into account transaction costs, differential borrowing and lending rates, and restricted short selling, the no-arbitrage bounds are:

$$S_0(1 - T)(1 + fC_L) \leq F_{0,t} \leq S_0(1 + T)(1 + C_B) \tag{2.13}$$

The restrictions on short selling widen the no-arbitrage bounds. Notice now, however, that restricted short selling affects only the reverse cash-and-carry strategy, so restricted short selling affects only the lower bound. The effects are substantial, however. Table 2.12 shows the lower no-arbitrage bounds for restrictions on the use of short sale proceeds. When traders face large restrictions on short selling, there is little chance for reverse cash-and-carry arbitrage. If traders can use only half of the short sale proceeds, the lower no-arbitrage bound is so low that it can have little effect on the futures price. We will see, however, that different traders face different restrictions on using proceeds from a short sale. The differential use of these short sale proceeds is related to the concept of quasi-arbitrage. Traders with better access to short sale proceeds have less than full transaction costs to pay when they engage in cash-and-carry or reverse cash-and-carry trading strategies.

Equation 2.13 expresses the final results of our cost-of-carry model analysis, and it includes transaction costs, differential borrowing and

■ **Table 2.12**

ILLUSTRATION OF NO-ARBITRAGE BOUNDS WITH VARIOUS SHORT SELLING RESTRICTIONS

Prices for the Analysis

Spot price of gold	$400
Interest rate (borrowing)	12%
Interest rate (lending)	8%
Transaction costs (T)	3%

Upper No-Arbitrage Bound with Transaction Costs and a Borrowing Rate

$$F_{0,t} \leq S_0(1 + T)(1 + C_B) = \$400(1.03)(1.12) = \$461.44$$

Lower No-Arbitrage Bound with Transaction Costs and a Lending Rate, f = 1.0

$$F_{0,t} \geq S_0(1 - T)(1 + fC_L) = \$400(.97)[1 + (1.0)(.08)] = \$419.04$$

Lower No-Arbitrage Bound with Transaction Costs and a Lending Rate, f = 0.75

$$F_{0,t} \geq S_0(1 - T)(1 + fC_L) = \$400(.97)[1 + (.75)(.08)] = \$411.28$$

Lower No-Arbitrage Bound with Transaction Costs and a Lending Rate, f = 0.5

$$F_{0,t} \geq S_0(1 - T)(1 + fC_L) = \$400(.97)[1 + (0.5)(.08)] = \$403.52$$

lending rates, and restrictions on short selling. In complexity, it is a far cry from our simple perfect markets/no-arbitrage relationship of Equation 2.3. The two are closely related, however. In terms of Equation 2.13, the perfect markets assumptions can be expressed as:

$T = 0$ so there are no transaction costs
$C_B = C_L = C$ so borrowing and lending rates are equal
$f = 1.0$ so traders have full use of short sale proceeds

If these three conditions hold, we are back to our perfect market assumptions, and Equation 2.13 becomes:

$$(1.0)S_0(1 - 0)(1 + C) \leq F_{0,t} \leq S_0(1 + 0)(1 + C)$$

which reduces to:

$$S_0(1 + C) \le F_{0,t} \le S_0(1 + C)$$
$$F_{0,t} = S_0(1 + C)$$

This final expression is simply Equation 2.3, the perfect markets version of our cost-of-carry model.

Limitations to Storage. Of all commodities, gold is perhaps the most storable. It is chemically stable, it has a high value relative to weight and volume, and so on. Some other commodities cannot be stored very well at all, however. The storability of a commodity is important to futures pricing because the arbitrage strategies that we have been considering depend on being able to store the underlying good. For example, the cash-and-carry arbitrage strategy assumes that a trader can buy a commodity today and store it until a later delivery date on a futures contract. If a commodity cannot be stored, some of the arbitrage strategies that we have been considering will not be available. Therefore, the no-arbitrage bounds we have developed will have to be altered to reflect the actual limitations to storage.

In the cash-and-carry arbitrage strategy, the ability to store the commodity limits the futures price relative to the cash price. As we saw in Equation 2.1, the futures price cannot exceed the cash price by more than the cost-of-carry. To see the importance of this point, imagine a tasty tropical fruit that can be harvested on only one day per year, and assume that the fruit spoils in one day if it is not eaten. These physical characteristics of the fruit make it impossible to store. This limitation to storage means that a cash-and-carry strategy cannot link futures and cash prices. Because the fruit is not storable, we could say that the storage cost is infinite. Thus, Equation 2.1 would merely say that the futures price must be less than infinity. This we already know without a business degree.

While the tropical fruit example is quite fanciful, there are also commodities with very practical limits to storage. The Chicago Mercantile Exchange traded a futures contract on fresh eggs for many years. While eggs can be stored for a while, there are definite limits that cannot be exceeded. Grains and oilseeds play an important role in agricultural futures. While wheat, oats, corn, soybeans, soymeal, and soyoil all store well, they cannot be stored indefinitely. Therefore, when storage is limited, the cash-and-carry strategy is also limited.

The importance of these limitations to storage varies across commodities. As we noted, they are not important for gold, but they can be important for perishable assets.

How Traders Deal with Market Imperfections. We have seen that transaction costs, differential borrowing rates, and restrictions on short selling all act to widen the no-arbitrage bounds that link cash and futures prices. It is also important to realize that these factors have vastly different effects on different traders. Also, they differ widely across markets. This section considers these market imperfections in a practical light.

There are two critical points about transaction costs. First, every trader faces transaction costs on every trade. Second, these costs differ widely across traders. Let us consider two extreme cases. In both instances, we are interested in the marginal transaction cost, because the marginal transaction cost determines whether the trade takes place. Imagine a professor in Miami who occasionally dabbles in the futures market. Such a trader will trade through a brokerage firm. The broker will charge a commission, the floor broker who executes the order will face a bid-asked spread, and the trader will have to pay exchange fees as well. Together these costs could be as low as $15–20, or they could be much higher. In addition, the professor incurs substantial search costs to determine how to trade. These are difficult to quantify. In contrast with our dabbling professor, consider a major gold trading firm, such as Handy and Harmon or Engelhard. Such firms refine silver and gold and trade it worldwide. As part of their commercial enterprise, they operate a futures trading desk to hedge their own risk exposure in the gold market. In addition, the traders on the desk actively trade in the market, searching for the arbitrage opportunities that we have been considering. A large trading firm faces a very low marginal transaction cost.

These differences in transaction costs stem from several sources. First, the firm is already in the market for other business purposes. Unlike the professor who studies the market merely looking for a good trading opportunity, these commercial concerns are already in the market in support of their physical metals business. This presence makes their information-gathering cost much lower than that faced by the professor who trades only occasionally. Second, the commercial concern will typically own an exchange membership and have its own people on the floor. If so, the firm faces no brokerage commission, which is a large cost of each trade for the professor.

A third and major factor is the difference in the chance to sell short. Short selling of metals is effectively closed to the professor, but it is virtually wide open for the metals trading firm. For the professor, selling short, if it is possible at all, will involve substantial limitations on the use of the short sale proceeds. The metals trading firm, by contrast, will hold an inventory of gold. Thus, the trading firm can simulate short selling by merely selling some of its inventory. From a trading perspective, the sale of the gold that the firm already owns is identical to selling gold short. As long as the firm has access to a supply of gold it can sell, it can replicate the trading effect of selling short. For firms with substantial gold stocks, there is virtually no limitation to replicating a short sale. In sum, for many markets, large commercial concerns in the business face very low transaction costs. For them, the market imperfections we have examined are of little practical importance. Thus, in some markets, prices closely approximate the perfect markets pricing relationship of Equation 2.3.

THE CONCEPT OF A FULL CARRY MARKET

In the price quotations of Figure 2.1, we can readily observe different patterns of prices for different commodities. In general, for some commodities, the futures price rises with the maturity of the futures contract. For some commodities, the prices are inversely related to the futures maturity. For yet other commodities, the prices rise and fall, showing no obvious relationship to maturity.

We can group commodities into different types by the degree to which their prices approximate full carry. In a **full carry market**, futures prices conform to Equations 2.3 and 2.6. If prices match the relationships specified in the equation, the market is said to be at full carry. If the futures price is higher than Equations 2.3 and 2.6 indicate, then the market is **above full carry**. If the futures price is less than the full carry price, the market is **below full carry**.

As an example, consider the following data for August 16:

Gold September	410.20
Gold December	417.90
Banker's Acceptance Rate – 90 days	7.80%

Is gold at full carry? In addition to financing, warehousing and insuring gold also have costs. These amounts are negligible for gold in percentage terms, so we ignore them for the present. We begin by annualizing the percentage difference between the two gold prices:[2]

$$\left(\frac{F_{0,d}}{F_{0,n}}\right)^4 = 1.0772$$

Thus, the implied annual percentage difference between the two gold prices is 7.72 percent. This corresponds almost exactly to our interest rate estimate. In fact, this is not surprising because gold is almost always at full carry. From this example, we can see that in a full carry market, prices should be normal. That is, the more distant futures price should exceed the nearby price. Other markets are not at full carry. Some markets are normal at times and near full carry, while they diverge radically from full carry at other times.

We have already seen that a well-developed market for short sales is important in keeping the no-arbitrage bounds tight, so that prices will more closely conform to the full carry relationship. There are five main factors that affect market prices and move them toward or away from full carry: short selling conditions, supply, seasonality of production, seasonality of consumption, and ease of storage.

Ease of Short Selling. We have already seen in our discussion of the cost-of-carry model that short selling restrictions widen the no-arbitrage bounds on futures prices. In the extreme case, where short selling is not permitted, there can be no reverse cash-and-carry arbitrage, so the futures price has no lower no-arbitrage bound. In markets for physical goods, short selling is highly restricted, even though some commercial interests can replicate short selling by reducing their inventories. By contrast, it is very easy to sell financial assets short. For this reason, and for others, financial assets tend to be full carry assets.

Large Supply. If the supply of an asset is large relative to its consumption, the market for the good will more closely approximate a full carry market. On the side of cash-and-carry arbitrage, a large supply makes it easier for traders to acquire the physical good to store for future delivery. Relative to consumption for jewelry or industrial uses, for example, the supply of gold is very large. This factor helps keep gold near full carry. By contrast, the world supply of copper is low relative to consumption. Typical supplies of copper on hand roughly equal three months of production. Markets for copper and other industrial metals are not full carry markets.

Nonseasonal Production. Temporary imbalances in supply and demand tend to cause distortions in normal price relationships. If production is highly seasonal, the stock of a good will be subject to large shifts. Many agricultural commodities have highly seasonal production due to their harvest cycles. In these markets, prices tend to be high for periods immediately prior to the harvest and low for the post-harvest months.

Nonseasonal Consumption. Foodstuffs, such as soybeans, may have seasonal production, but consumption is fairly steady. People like to eat all year. For other goods, production is fairly continuous, but consumption is highly seasonal. For example, contract prices for heating oil often show a seasonal pattern of high prices in winter, while gasoline prices are often relatively high for summer months.

High Storability. The tropical fruit that must be harvested and eaten in a single day is the perfect example of a nonstorable commodity. If the good is nonstorable, cash-and-carry arbitrage strategies cannot link the cash price with the futures price. Thus, the cost-of-carry model is unlikely to apply to a good with poor storage characteristics. To a great extent, most physical commodities traded on futures exchanges have good storage characteristics. Some commodities that were less storable – such as fresh eggs and potatoes – have passed from futures trading. To the extent that a commodity has poor storage characteristics, however, the cost-of-carry model is unlikely to apply.

Convenience Yield

We have seen in the preceding section that various factors cause the array of futures prices to vary from full carry for many commodities. In general, the cost-of-carry model fails to apply when an asset has a **convenience yield** – a return on holding the physical asset. When holding an asset has a convenience yield, the futures price will be below full carry. In an extreme case, the market can be so far below full carry that the cash price can exceed the futures price. When the cash price exceeds the futures price, or when the nearby futures price exceeds the distant futures price, the market is in **backwardation**. An asset has a convenience yield when traders are willing to pay a premium to hold the physical asset at a certain time. For example, natural gas prices tend to be high in the winter – just when people need heat. Likewise, soybean prices are high right before harvest – just when supplies are low and people still want to eat.

To explore the concept of the convenience yield more fully, assume that this is October and the cash price of soybeans is $6.00 per bushel. Harvest is one month away and a trader owns 5,000 bushels of soybeans. The futures price of soybeans for November is $5.50. In this example, the market is in backwardation, because the cash price exceeds the futures price. Under these circumstances, the trader will hold the soybeans from October to November only if he or she has some clear need for owning the beans during this period.

If the trader does not need the physical beans for the next month, he or she can sell the beans and buy a NOV futures contract. This strategy will yield a profit of $.50 per bushel, and it will save a month of carrying costs. Clearly, only a person with a need for physical beans will hold them given the price structure. For example, consider a food processor who still wants beans in October. The food processor might derive a convenience yield from owning beans, but only persons with a business need for the beans, such as a food processor, could derive a convenience yield.

If the bean market is below full carry, it might seem that there is an opportunity for a reverse cash-and-carry arbitrage. This strategy requires selling beans short, but it is clear that short selling will not be possible. Short selling involves borrowing beans from someone else. Because the market is below full carry, no one will lend beans costlessly. Anyone who owns the beans holds them because of the convenience yield they derive. If they owned the beans and received no convenience yield, they would sell them outright in the market and buy the cheaper SEP futures to replace their beans in two months. Lending the beans to someone else so that other party can make money is the last application the holder of the physical beans would consider. Thus, if an asset has a convenience yield, the market can be below full carry, or even in backwardation. Such a situation will not provide a field day for reverse cash-and-carry arbitrage strategies, however, because short selling opportunities will not be available.

SUMMARY

In our exploration of the cost-of-carry model, we have seen that cash-and-carry and reverse cash-and-carry strategies place no-arbitrage bounds on futures prices. Transaction costs, differential borrowing and lending rates, restrictions on short selling, and limitations to storage all act to widen those bounds. Therefore, while the cost-of-carry model reveals much about the determinants of futures prices, it does not provide a complete determination of futures prices.

As we have seen, some commodities have characteristics that promote full carry. These include easy short selling, a large supply of the good, nonseasonal production and consumption, and high storability. Related to these, and also contributing to the applicability of the cost-of-carry model, is the lack of a convenience yield. Because market imperfections and the characteristics of the commodities themselves sometimes combine to force the no-arbitrage bounds apart, other factors help determine where within the no-arbitrage bounds the futures price will lie. Within the no-arbitrage bounds, the market's expectation plays a large role in futures price determination.

FUTURES PRICES AND EXPECTATIONS

Earlier we considered a tropical fruit that can be harvested on only one day per year, July 4. The fruit is so delicate that it must also be consumed on that day or it will spoil. How would a futures contract on such a fruit be priced? As we explore in this section, the cost-of-carry model breaks down for the pricing of such a futures contract.

Cash-and-carry arbitrage strategies do not apply to this fruit, because it cannot be carried. The fruit spoils in one day. Therefore, the cash price and the futures price are not linked by the opportunity to carry the fruit forward. Another way of making the same point is to say that the cost-of-carry is infinite. Thus, any positive cash price is consistent with any positive futures price, no matter how high.

Reverse cash-and-carry strategies also do not apply. For example, assume that the cash price of the fruit is $2 on July 4, and the futures price for delivery in one year is $1. From our discussion of convenience yield, we know that this backwardation is due to the benefit that holding the cash fruit conveys. Therefore, no one would lend the fruit for short selling. Anyone who does not need the fruit for immediate consumption would merely sell it in the cash market and buy the cheaper futures. In sum, short selling would not be possible, so reverse cash-and-carry strategies will not serve to link the cash and futures prices. Because both the cash-and-carry and reverse cash-and-carry strategies fail for this fruit, they impose no-arbitrage bounds on the futures price.

The Role of Speculation

What does determine the futures price? Assume that market participants expect the price of the fruit in the next harvest to be $10 each. This price is the **expected future spot price**. In this event, the futures price must equal, or at least closely approximate, the expected future spot price. If this were not the case, profitable speculative strategies would arise.

As an example, if the futures price were $15, exceeding the expected future spot price of $10, speculators would sell the futures contract and then plan to buy the fruit for $10 on the harvest date. They would then be able to deliver the fruit and collect $15, for a $5 profit, if all went according to plan. By contrast, if the futures price were below the expected future spot price, say at $7, speculators would buy the futures contract, take delivery on the harvest date paying $7, and plan to sell the fruit at the market price of $10.

In short, the presence of speculators in the marketplace ensures that the futures price approximately equals the expected future spot price. Too great a divergence between the futures price and the expected future spot price creates attractive speculative opportunities. In response, profit-seeking speculators will trade as long as the futures price is sufficiently far away from the expected future spot price. We can express this basic idea by introducing the following notation.

$$F_{0,t} \approx E_0(S_t) \tag{2.14}$$

where:

$E_0(S_t)$ = the expectation at $t = 0$ of the spot price
to prevail at time t

Equation 2.14 states that the futures price approximately equals the spot price currently expected to prevail at the delivery date. If this relationship did not hold, there would be attractive speculative opportunities.

Limits to Speculation

With Equation 2.14, we have said that the futures price and the expected future spot price should be approximately equal. Why does this relationship hold only approximately? There are two basic answers to this question, one of which is fairly obvious and the second of which is fairly profound. First, the relationship holds only approximately because of transaction costs. Second, if some participants in the market are more risk averse than others, the futures price can diverge sharply from the expected future spot price.

Transaction Costs. Assume that the fruit has a futures price of $9 and an expected future spot price of $10, and assume that the cost of transacting to take advantage of this discrepancy is $2. With these prices, a trader cannot buy the futures for $9 and plan to make a $1 profit by selling the fruit at its expected future spot price. This opportunity is not profitable with the transaction costs, because the total cost of acquiring the fruit would be the $9 delivery on the futures plus the $2 transaction cost. Transaction costs can keep the futures price from exactly equaling the expected future spot price. This parallels our discussion of transaction costs and their effect on the cost-of-carry model.

Risk Aversion. Traders in futures markets can be classified, at least roughly, into hedgers and speculators. Hedgers have a preexisting risk associated with a commodity and sometimes enter the market to reduce that risk, while speculators trade in the hope of profit. Entering the futures market as a speculator is a risky venture. If people are risk averse, however, they incur risk willingly only if the expected profit from bearing the risk will compensate them for the risk exposure. Without doubt, most participants in financial markets are risk averse, so they seek compensation to warrant their taking a risky position. In the futures markets, speculative profits can come only from a favorable movement in the price of a futures contract.

Assume that the expected future spot price of the fictional fruit is $10.00 and that the corresponding futures price is $10.05. Assume also that there is tremendous uncertainty about what the actual price of the fruit will be. The market expects a cash price of $10 upon harvest, but the fruit is very susceptible to weather conditions, and it is also subject to the dread fictional fruit weevil. For a speculator, there appears to be a $.05 profit available from the strategy of selling the futures, buying fruit for $10.00 at harvest, and delivering against the futures contract. This strategy subjects the speculator to considerable risk if the weather is bad or if the weevil strikes, however. Speculators may decide that the expected profit of $.05 is not worth the risk exposure. If the speculators do not pursue the $.05 expected profit, there will be no market forces to drive the futures price into exact equality with the expected future spot price. Thus, the futures price can differ from the expected future spot price if traders are risk averse.

Summary. The strong principles of the cost-of-carry model place no-arbitrage bounds on futures prices in many instances. In some cases those bounds are very wide, or even nonexistent, due to transaction costs, restrictions on short selling, or the characteristics of the physical commodity. Within the bounds placed by cash-and-carry and reverse cash-and-carry strategies, expectations play a major role in establishing futures prices. We have seen that speculative strategies are available when the futures price does not equal the expected future spot price. Still, these speculative strategies do not ensure exact equality between the futures price and the expected future spot price. The futures price can diverge from the expected future spot price due to transaction costs or due to risk aversion on the part of traders. Of the two, risk aversion is much more important and deserves extended consideration.

FUTURES PRICES AND RISK AVERSION

In this section, we explore in detail two theories of how risk aversion can affect futures prices. We have already seen that risk aversion among speculators can allow the futures price to diverge from the expected future spot price. According to the theory of normal backwardation, this divergence occurs in a systematic way. As a second theory, the Capital Asset Pricing Model (CAPM) relates market prices to a measure of systematic risk. Some scholars have applied the CAPM to futures markets to understand the differences that might exist between futures prices and expected future spot prices.

THE THEORY OF NORMAL BACKWARDATION

Assume for the moment that speculators are rational; that is, they make assessments of expected future prices based on available information. In assessing this information, rational speculators occasionally make mistakes, but on the whole, they process the information efficiently. As a result, their expectations, on average, are realized. This does not imply that they are mistake free. Instead, they make errors of assessment that are not biased. The expectational errors are randomly distributed around the true price that the commodity will have in the future. Assume also that speculators have "homogeneous expectations," that is, they expect the same future spot price.

Such a group of speculators might confront the prices prevailing in a futures market and find that those prices match the expected future spot prices. If the futures price reaches the expected price of the commodity when the futures contract matures, then there is no reason to speculate in futures. If the futures price matches a speculator's expectation of subsequent cash prices for the commodity, then the speculator must expect neither a profit nor a loss by entering the futures market. Yet, by entering the market under such conditions, the speculator would certainly incur additional risk. After all, the trader's expectations might be incorrect. Faced with such a situation, no risk averse speculator would trade, because the speculator would face additional risk without compensation.

Hedgers, taken as a group, need to be either long or short in the futures market to reduce the risk they face in their businesses. For example, a wheat farmer has a long position in cash wheat because he or she grows wheat. The farmer can reduce risk by selling wheat futures. If hedgers are net short, for example, speculators must be net long. For the sake of simplicity, consider a single speculator who is considering whether to take a long position. As just noted, the rational speculator takes a long futures position only if the expected future spot price exceeds the current futures price. Otherwise, the speculator must expect not to make any profit.

The hedger, we assume, needs to be short to avoid unwanted risk. According to this line of reasoning, he must be willing to sell the futures contract at a price below the expected future spot price of the commodity. Otherwise, the hedger cannot induce the speculator to accept the long side of the contract. From this point of view, he, in effect, buys insurance from the speculator. The hedger transfers his unwanted risk to the speculator and pays an expected profit to the speculator for bearing the risk. The payment to the speculator is the difference between the futures price and the expected future spot price. Even so, the speculator does not receive any sure payment. The speculator must still wait for the expected future spot price to materialize to capture the profit expected for bearing the risk.

Thus far, the discussion has focused on a single hedger and a single speculator. It is necessary, however, to try to do justice to the fact that the marketplace is peopled by many individuals with different needs, different levels of risk aversion, and different expectations (heterogeneous expectations) about future spot prices.

Figure 2.9 depicts the situation that might prevail in the futures market for a commodity. It shows the relevant positions of hedgers and speculators as two groups. As the futures price varies, the number of contracts desired by the two groups will vary as well. We assume that hedgers are net short. At no futures price will hedgers, taken as a group, desire a long position in the futures.[3] This is reasonable given the definition of a hedger as one who enters the futures market to reduce a preexisting risk. Line *WX* shows the hedgers' desired position in the futures market for various futures prices. At higher prices, hedgers want to sell more futures contracts, as the downward slope for line *WX* indicates. Lines *WX* and *YZ* are drawn as straight lines, but that is only for convenience. Also, note that the hedgers hedge different amounts depending on the futures price. With low prices, they sell fewer contracts, thereby hedging less of their preexisting risk than they would if futures prices were high.

■ **Figure 2.9** ───────────────────────

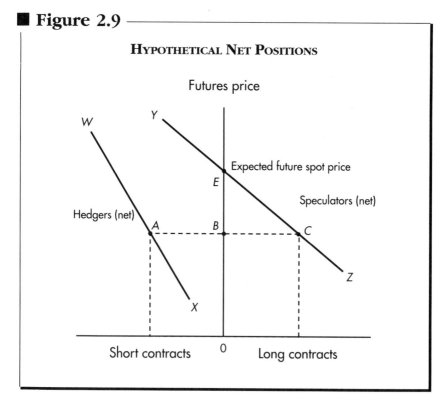

HYPOTHETICAL NET POSITIONS

In Figure 2.9, speculators are willing to hold either long or short net positions as the situation demands. Assuming that the speculators, as a group, correctly assess the appropriate expected future spot price, they will be neither long nor short when the futures price equals the expected future spot price. At that point, speculators hold a zero net position in the futures market. (In such a situation, some speculators would be long, others short, reflecting their divergent opinions. But, in the aggregate, they would hold a net zero position.) Line *YZ* shows the speculators' desired positions as a function of the futures price. If the futures price exceeds the expected future spot price, the speculators will desire to be net short as well as the hedgers. If the futures price lies below the expected future spot price, speculators will want to be net long, holding some position between *E* and *Z* on line *YZ*.

Not all positions shown on the graph are feasible. If the futures price lies above point *E*, then both the hedgers and speculators desire to be short. Yet, the number of outstanding short contracts must equal the number of long contracts. As the figure is drawn, there is only one price at which the market can clear: point *B*. With a price of *B*, the net short position desired by the hedgers exactly offsets the net long position desired by the speculators. This is reflected graphically by the fact that the distance *AB* equals the distance *BC*. Through the typical process by which markets reach equilibrium, the futures market may reach an equilibrium price at *B*, with the futures price lying below the expected future spot price.

Notice that the slope of *WX* (the hedgers' line) is steeper than that of *YZ* (the speculators' line). The more gentle slope of *YZ* expresses the greater risk tolerance of the speculators. For any drop in the futures price below the expected future spot price, *E*, the increase in the speculators' demand for long contracts exceeds the drop in the hedgers' desire to hold the short contracts. Indeed, this must be the case. Economically, the speculators must be more risk tolerant than the hedgers. After all, the speculators in this model accept the risk that the hedgers are unwilling to bear, so the speculators must be more risk tolerant.

This account explains how the futures price can diverge from the expected future spot price, even with no transaction costs. Likewise, if hedgers want to be net long, speculators must be net short. If the speculators are net short, then they can hope to earn a return for their risk-bearing services only if the futures price lies above the expected future spot price. Again, the futures price need not equal the expected future spot price. Instead, the relationship between the futures price and the expected future spot price depends in part on whether the hedgers need to be net short or net long.

Clearly, in this model, the futures price will be below the expected future spot price if the hedgers are net short, as in Figure 2.9. The amount of the discrepancy depends upon the risk aversion of the two groups. For example, assume that the speculators are more risk averse than Figure 2.9 depicts. Higher risk aversion is represented in the graph by the steepness of the hedgers' or speculators' line. If the speculators were more risk averse, their line would be steeper. As a result, at price B the speculators would be willing to hold fewer long contracts and the market would not clear at that price. Instead, the market clearing price would be below B, the exact price depending upon the steepness of the speculators' line. In that case, the market clearing price would be below B and fewer hedgers would be able to hedge.

This approach to determining futures prices originated with John Maynard Keynes and John Hicks. The view that hedgers are net short, as shown in Figure 2.9, is associated with Keynes and Hicks. Over the life of the futures contract, the futures price must move toward the cash price. (This is already clear, since the basis must equal zero at the maturity of the futures contract, as was discussed earlier.) If expectations about the future spot price are correct, and hedgers are net short, then the futures price must lie below the expected future spot price. In such a case, futures prices can be expected to rise over the life of a contract.

The view that futures prices tend to rise over the contract life due to the hedgers' general desire to be net short is known as **normal backwardation**. (Normal backwardation should not be confused with a market that is in backwardation. A market is in backwardation at a given moment if the cash price exceeds the futures price or if a nearby futures price exceeds a distant futures price.) Conversely, if hedgers are net long, then the futures price would lie above the expected future spot price, and the price of the futures contract would fall over its life. This pattern of falling prices is known as a **contango**. Figure 2.10 depicts these price patterns.[4]

Figure 2.10 illustrates the price patterns for futures that we might expect under different scenarios. In considering the figure, assume that market participants correctly assess the future spot price, so that

■ **Figure 2.10** ─────────────────────────────

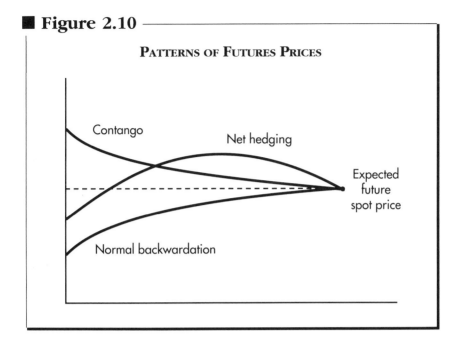

PATTERNS OF FUTURES PRICES

the expected future spot price in the figure turns out to be the actual spot price at the maturity of the futures contract. If the futures price equals the expected future spot price, then the futures price will lie on the dotted line, which equals the expected future spot price. With initially correct expectations, and no information causing a revision of expectations, the futures price should remain constant over its entire trading life.

Alternative conceptions certainly exist, such as the theory of normal backwardation and the contango. If speculators are net long, as Keynes and Hicks believed, then futures prices must rise over the life of the contract if the speculators are to receive their compensation for bearing risk. Prices then follow the path that is labeled "Normal backwardation" in Figure 2.10. With the futures price rising over its life, the speculator earns a return for bearing risk. Notice that the line for normal backwardation terminates at the expected future spot price. This is necessary since the futures price and the spot price must be equal at the maturity of the futures contract, and the figure is drawn assuming that the expected future spot price turns out to be the subsequently observed spot price.

If speculators are net short and are to receive compensation for bearing risk, futures prices must follow a contango, as Figure 2.10

also illustrates. The fall in futures prices, as the contract approaches maturity, gives the short speculators the compensation that induced them to enter the market.

One final possibility, also shown in Figure 2.10, is known as the **net hedging hypothesis**. According to this view, the net position of the hedgers might change over the life of the futures contract. When the contract begins trading, the hedgers are net short and the speculators are net long. In such a situation, the futures price lies below the expected future spot price. Over time, the hedgers gradually change their net position. Eventually, the hedgers are net long, requiring the speculators to be net short. For the speculators to receive their compensation in this case, the futures price must lie above the expected future spot price, as it did in the contango.

Perhaps this account of hedgers changing from being net short to net long over the life of the contract appears dubious, but it is certainly conceivable. Consider grain farmers who wish to hedge the crop that they will produce. To hedge the price risk associated with harvest, they need to be short. Cereal producers have a need for the grain, and they hedge their price risk by being long. To show how the price could follow the pattern suggested by the net hedging hypothesis, imagine that the farmers hedge first. This makes the hedgers net short. Later, the cereal producers begin to hedge their future need for the grain, and the net hedging position of the farmers and cereal producers taken together begins to move toward zero. When it reaches zero, the farmers and cereal producers in the aggregate are neither short nor long. Time passes, and still more cereal producers hedge by going long. Eventually, the long hedgers come to predominate and all hedgers taken together are net long. Under such a condition, the futures price must lie above the expected future spot price if the speculators are to receive compensation for bearing risk.

Even though the theory of normal backwardation originated in about 1920, there is still no broad consensus on whether the theory is true. While the issue has been well studied, different studies focus on different commodities and different time periods, and this has, perhaps, led to widely differing results. In general, it might be too optimistic to assume that all commodities would share the same characteristics. Perhaps the most accurate generalization of these studies is to conclude that there is no overwhelming evidence in support of normal backwardation.[5]

FUTURES PRICES AND THE CAPITAL ASSET PRICING MODEL

The capital asset pricing model (CAPM) has been widely applied to all kinds of financial instruments, including futures contracts. Equation 2.15 expresses the basic relationship of the CAPM:

$$E(R_j) = r + \beta_j [E(R_m) - r] \tag{2.15}$$

where:

$$r = \text{the risk-free rate}$$
$$E(R_j) = \text{expected return on asset } j$$
$$E(R_m) = \text{expected return on the market portfolio}$$
$$\beta_j = \text{the ``beta'' of asset } j$$

The CAPM measures the systematic risk of an asset by β, and β is usually estimated from a regression equation of the following form:

$$r_{j,t} = \alpha_j + \beta_j r_{m,t} + \epsilon_{j,t} \tag{2.16}$$

where:

$$r_{j,t} = \text{the return on asset } j \text{ in the } t^{\text{th}} \text{ period}$$
$$r_{m,t} = \text{the return on the market portfolio } j \text{ in the } t^{\text{th}} \text{ period}$$
$$\alpha_j = \text{the constant term in the regression}$$
$$\epsilon_{j,t} = \text{the residual error for day } t$$

According to the CAPM, only unavoidable risk should be compensated in the marketplace, and traders can avoid much risk through diversification. Even after diversification, risk remains for some assets because the returns of the asset are correlated with the market as a whole. This remaining risk is systematic. In essence, β_j measures the systematic risk of asset j relative to the market portfolio. According to Equation 2.15, an asset with $\beta = 1$ has the same degree of systematic risk as does the market portfolio, and the asset should earn the same return as the market. The risk-free asset has $\beta = 0$, and it should earn the risk-free rate of interest.

As we have seen, futures market trading does not require any investment. However, trading futures does require margin payments, but these are not investments. With no funds invested, there is no capital to earn the risk-free interest rate. Therefore, a futures position should have zero return if $\beta = 0$. If the beta of a futures position exceeds zero, a long position in the futures contract should earn a positive return. For example, for futures position j, assume the following values hold:

$$E(R_m) = .09$$
$$r = .06$$
$$\beta_j = .7$$

According to Equation 2.15, a long position in futures contract j should earn:

$$E(R_j) = \beta_j[E(R_m) - r] = .7(.09 - .06) = .021$$

Thus, positive betas for futures contracts lead to the expectation of rising futures prices. Zero betas would be consistent with futures prices that neither rise nor fall. A negative beta would imply that futures prices should fall.

As with the theory of normal backwardation, approximately equal numbers of studies support and oppose the CAPM as it applies to futures markets. This untidy irresolution may be due to the fact that futures returns are very close to zero. Thus, some studies find average returns significantly different from zero, while others do not. Most studies do seem to find that futures contracts have betas near zero, at least when these betas are measured using conventional techniques. Final resolution of these issues will require more comprehensive data sets and analyses than have been employed to date.

CONCLUSION

While futures markets have a reputation for high risk and wild price swings, this chapter has stressed the underlying rationality of futures prices. We cannot deny that prices vary suddenly and sharply in the futures market, but it is quite possible that these price movements accurately reflect the arrival of new information at the market. Further, it is also apparent that futures prices observe the economic laws detailed earlier. Both the cost-of-carry model and the expected future price framework provide rational procedures for thinking about the behavior of futures prices. It must also be admitted that futures prices, on the whole, conform to these theories.

If the conclusions reached about futures pricing here are correct, then a picture of the usefulness of the market begins to emerge. If prices react rationally to new information, and if spread relationships are strongly interconnected, and if futures prices are good estimates of expected future spot prices, then it is possible to understand the uses that can be made of the market by different elements of society. These different groups in society were identified as those who wish to discover price information by observing futures markets, such as speculators and hedgers. If futures prices closely approximate expected future spot prices, then the price discovery function is well served. Speculators, on the other hand, will have a difficult life, because profitable opportunities will not be abundant. Hedgers, for their part, have an apparent opportunity to reduce their risk exposure with relatively little cost.

The next chapter explores how these different groups use the futures market. The difficulties facing speculators are examined more closely, along with the benefits that the futures markets provide to hedgers and to society as a whole.

NOTES

1. For a very informative and readable account of repurchase agreements, see M. Bowsher, "Repurchase Agreements," *Instruments of the Money Market,* Richmond: Federal Reserve Bank of Richmond, 1981.

2. The ratio of the distant to the nearby futures price defines the interest rate between the two dates $t = n$ and $t = d$. In this example, $d - n$ is 90 days, so we raise the expression to the 4th power to account for the quarterly compounding.

3. By assuming that hedgers will be net short no matter what the futures price, we are merely assuming that their preexisting risk requires a short position. Some potential hedgers would, of course, abandon their risk-reducing short position if the futures price were low enough. However, in so doing, the potential hedger would have abandoned the intention of hedging and would be speculating. This is clear if we recall that the risk-reducing futures trade is to go short.

4. A normal market gives rise to "normal backwardation" and an inverted market is consistent with prices following a "contango." (In the French futures market, you may sometimes encounter the "Last Contango in Paris." Sorry.)

5. For a more extended summary of these studies, see R. Kolb, *Understanding Futures Markets*, 5e, Cambridge, MA: Blackwell Publishers, 1997, Chapter 3.

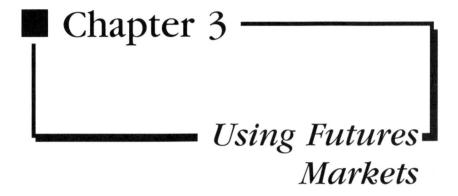

Chapter 3

Using Futures Markets

OVERVIEW

In the two preceding chapters, we discussed the institutional setting of futures markets and the determination of futures prices. This chapter explores three different ways that futures markets serve different elements of society. As we have already noted, futures markets provide a means of price discovery. Second, futures markets provide an arena for speculation. Third, futures markets provide a means for transferring risk, or hedging. This chapter explores each of these contributions of futures markets.

First we will analyze the function of **price discovery** – the revelation of information about the prices of commodities in the future. Because prices in the futures markets provide information that is not readily available elsewhere, the markets serve societal needs. We note that price discovery is open to everyone, the first group of beneficiaries from these markets.

Speculators comprise the second major group to benefit from futures markets. A **speculator** is a trader who enters the futures market in pursuit of profit, thereby accepting an increase in risk. It may seem strange to list an opportunity for speculation as a service to society, but consider the following examples. Casinos provide speculative opportunities for citizens, and that might be reckoned as a public service. Professional and college sports teams also provide a way for people to speculate by betting, illegally in some states and legally in others.

Clearly, sports teams do not exist so that people can bet on them, but the chance to bet is a side effect, and perhaps a side benefit, of the existence of sports. The situation is similar in the futures markets. Futures markets do not exist in order to provide the chance to speculate, but they do provide speculative opportunities. Less obvious is the way in which speculators themselves contribute to the smooth functioning of the futures market. As we show, the speculator pursues profits. As a side effect, the speculator provides liquidity to the market that helps the market function more effectively.

Hedgers are a third major group of futures market users. A **hedger** is a trader with a preexisting risk who enters the futures market in order to reduce that risk. For example, a wheat farmer has price risk associated with the future price of wheat at harvest. By trading in the futures market, the farmer may be able to reduce that preexisting risk. This opportunity to transfer risk is perhaps the greatest contribution of futures markets to society. In many cases, businesses face risks that result from the ordinary conduct of business. Often these risks are undesired, and the futures market provides a way in which risk may be transferred to other individuals willing to bear it. If people know that unwanted risks may be avoided by transacting in the futures market at a reasonable cost, then they will not be afraid to make decisions that will expose them initially to certain risks. They know that they can hedge that risk.

From the point of view of society, hedging has important advantages. Enterprises that are profitable, but that involve more risk than their principals wish to bear, can still be pursued. The unwanted risk can then be transferred in the futures market, and society benefits economically. This is the strongest argument for the existence of futures markets. By providing an efficient means of transferring risk to those individuals in society willing to bear it cheaply, futures markets contribute to the economy.

PRICE DISCOVERY

In Chapter 2 we explored the connection between futures prices and expected future spot prices, focusing on the relationship between futures prices and expected future spot prices. This relationship is crucial for the futures market's ability to fulfill the social function of price discovery. In this section, we consider this issue in more detail.

Students of futures markets admit a close connection between futures prices and expected future spot prices. The question is how the futures market can be used to reveal information about subsequent commodity prices. The usefulness of price forecasts based on futures prices depends on three factors:

1. The need for information about future spot prices.
2. The accuracy of the futures market forecasts of those prices.
3. The performance of futures market forecasts relative to alternative forecasting techniques.

INFORMATION

Many individuals and groups in society need information about the future price of various commodities. For example, with information about the price of gold one year from now, it would be relatively simple to make a fortune. Certainly, speculation would be much more rewarding if one had a private and infallible source of information about future spot prices. Aside from such dreams of wealth, information about future spot prices is also needed for more mundane purposes, such as the planning of future investment and consumption by individuals, corporations, and governmental bodies.

Consider an underpaid college professor who wants to buy a house. Interest rates are high, so taking a long-term mortgage in such times would commit him to a lifetime of large payments. On the other hand, if he does not buy a house, then he cannot take advantage of the tax deduction that the interest portion of the house payments would provide. If interest rates were to drop soon, then it would be reasonable to wait to buy the house. By consulting the financial pages of the newspaper, the professor could find out what the market believed about the future level of interest rates. Futures contracts on long-term Treasury bonds are traded on the Chicago Board of Trade. If the interest rate for a bond to be delivered in six months is three percentage points lower than current interest rates, then there is good reason to expect interest rates will fall over the next six months. In such a situation, the college professor might do well to wait a few months to buy his house.

Another example concerns a furniture manufacturer who makes wooden furniture. Assume that she is printing her catalog now for the next year and must include the prices of the different items of furniture. Setting prices in advance is always a very tricky affair. In addition to other problems, the price she charges will depend upon the expected future price of lumber. The cost of lumber varies greatly, depending largely on the health of the construction industry, so it is difficult for her to know how to include that cost factor in her calculations. One way in which she might deal with this is to use the prices from the lumber futures market to estimate the costs of the wood that she will have to purchase later on. In doing so, she uses the futures markets for their **price discovery** benefit.

In both of these examples, individuals use futures prices to estimate the spot price at some future date. The advisability of such a technique depends on the accuracy of the forecasts drawn from the futures market. Futures prices may, of course, differ from subsequently observed spot prices. If there is a large discrepancy, the futures forecasts may not be very useful. Errors could result from two sources: inaccurate but unbiased forecasts and bias in the forecast itself.

ACCURACY

A forecasting estimator is unbiased if the average value of the forecast equals the value of the variable to be forecasted.[1] Thus, futures prices might provide unbiased forecasts with very large errors. The situation is reminiscent of the joke about the two economists who predicted the unemployment rate for the next year. The first economist predicted that 12 percent of the work force would be unemployed, while the second put the figure at full employment, or zero percent unemployed. The actual rate turned out to be 6 percent, from which the economists cheerfully concluded that, on average, they were exactly right. In forecasting the unemployment rate, one could say that the economists had provided an unbiased forecast but one that had large errors.

As is typical for many commodities, the forecasts from the futures market have large errors. Futures prices fluctuate radically, which means that most of the time they provide an inaccurate forecast of the underlying commodity's spot price at the time of delivery. Without question, the large size of the forecast errors from the futures markets limits the forecasts' reliability.

One might reasonably wonder why there should be such large errors. According to the theory of finance, prices in well-developed markets reflect all available information. As new information becomes available, futures prices adjust themselves very swiftly. Consequently, futures prices tend to exhibit radical fluctuations, which means that the prices will be inaccurate as estimates of subsequent spot prices.

In addition to the large errors that one can observe in futures market forecasts, futures prices may be biased. One possible reason for this was considered in Chapter 2. Futures prices may embody a risk premium that keeps the futures price from equaling the expected future spot price. In general, the possibility of bias is not too great a concern, at least for practical matters. Further, while there is still no real agreement about their existence, there is agreement that, if biases do exist, they are small. In general, the errors in futures forecasts are so large that they tend to drown out any biases that may also be present.

PERFORMANCE

Since forecasts based on futures prices seem to be so poor, why would anyone care about them? Before discarding the forecasts, consider the alternatives. What other forecast might be more accurate? A considerable amount of study on this topic has failed to lead to any final answer. Nonetheless, evidence suggests that forecasts based on futures prices are not excelled by other forecasting techniques. Futures forecasts have been compared to other techniques and have not been found to be inferior. The current situation in forecasts of the foreign exchange rate is typical. For example, compared to professional foreign exchange forecasting firms, some of which charge large fees, the futures price of foreign currency predicts very well. Many professional firms have recently turned in forecasting records with results worse than those of chance.[2]

In spite of the large errors in forecasts based on futures market prices, the futures market seems better than the alternatives. To summarize, the accuracy of futures forecasts is not that good, but it is certainly better than the alternatives, and futures market forecasts are free. Someone needing a forecast of future spot prices should not rely too heavily on any forecast. When relying on some forecasting technique, however, it should be the forecast freely available in the futures market.

SPECULATION

Defining speculation or identifying the speculator in the futures market is always difficult. For our purposes, the following definition of a speculator will prove useful. A **speculator** is a trader who enters the futures market in search of profit and, by so doing, willingly accepts increased risk.[3]

Most individuals have no heavy risk exposure in most commodities. Consider an individual who is neither a farmer nor a food processor, but who has an interest in the wheat market. If she trades a wheat futures contract, then she most likely is speculating in the sense defined previously. She enters the futures market, willingly increases her risk, and hopes for profit.

One might object that this individual does not have a preexisting risk exposure in wheat. In fact, everyone who eats bread does. One's plans for consuming bread may change if wheat prices rise too high. This objection makes a good point. In order to know whether a particular action in the futures market is a speculative trade requires knowledge about the trader's current assets and future consumption plans. For an individual, however, entry into the futures market is most likely to be for speculation. For the woman who traded a wheat futures contract, the size of the wheat contract (5,000 bushels) is so large relative to her needs for wheat that the transaction increases her overall risk. Assuming that she, like most people, is risk averse, she will not expose herself to the additional risk of entering the futures market unless she hopes to profit by doing so. This is what classifies her as a speculator.

Earlier, we also noted that speculators use futures transactions as a substitute for a cash market transaction. For an individual, trading a 5,000 bushel futures contract is unlikely to be a substitute for a cash market transaction, and this criterion also identifies the individual trading wheat as a speculator. Different types of speculators may be categorized by the length of time they plan to hold a position. Traditionally, there are three kinds of speculators: scalpers, day traders, and position traders.

SCALPERS

Of all speculators, scalpers have the shortest horizon over which they plan to hold a futures position. Scalpers aim to foresee the movement of the market over a very short interval, ranging from the next few seconds to the next few minutes. Many scalpers describe themselves as psychologists trying to sense the feel of the trading among the other market participants. In order to do this, they must be in the trading pit; otherwise, they could not hope to see buying or selling pressure building up among the other traders.[4]

Since their planned holding period is so short, scalpers do not expect to make a large profit on each trade. Instead, they hope to make a profit of one or two ticks – the minimum allowable price movement. Many trades by scalpers end in losses or in no profit. If the prices do not move in the scalper's direction within a few minutes of assuming a position, the scalper will likely close the position and begin looking for a new opportunity.

This type of trading strategy means that the scalper will generate an enormous number of transactions. Were he or she to make these transactions through a broker as an off-the-floor participant, the scalper would lose any anticipated profit through high transaction costs. Since scalpers are members of the exchange, or lease a seat from a member, their transaction costs are very low. Scalpers probably pay less than $1 per round-turn in most futures markets, compared to about $25–80 for an off-the-floor trader who trades through a regular broker. Without these very low transaction costs, the scalper's efforts would be hopeless. To sense the direction of the market and to conserve on transaction costs, a scalper needs to be on the floor of the exchange.

In his book, *The New Gatsbys,* Bob Tamarkin explores the personalities of futures traders based on his own experience. Writing about scalpers, he says:

> Many traded by feel rather than by fundamentals, forgetting about things like leading economic indicators, government policies, and even supplies of commodities. They simply tried to catch the market on the way up and ditch it on the way down. In the trading pits they could do it faster and better than any outside speculators because they were squarely in the heart of the action.

Discussing scalpers in general and describing an individual scalper named Paul, Tamarkin tells us:

> Each trader had a theory about what was happening in the next five minutes. If everyone thought the market was going to open higher, but it opened lower, the psychology in the pit changed immediately. It was a herd mentality fed on raw emotion. It was the easy way. Get the trading feel of the crowd in the pit; then jump on board for the move. By the time the public got in, the market ticked that quarter or

half cent, and Paul had his profit. The ultimate price of a commodity may have been determined by supply and demand, Paul thought, but in the interim, emotional factors reigned supreme.[5]

Although it may not be apparent at first glance, scalpers provide a valuable service to the market by their frenzied trading activity. By trading so often, scalpers help supply the market with liquidity. Their trading activity increases the ease with which other market participants may find trading partners. Without high liquidity, some outside traders would avoid the market, which would decrease its usefulness. A high degree of liquidity is necessary for the success of a futures market, and scalpers play an important role in providing this liquidity. We might say that scalpers provide the opportunity for other traders to trade immediately.

To illustrate the role played by scalpers in providing liquidity, consider the following example. An off-the-floor trader might see the most recently quoted price on a ticker machine and desire to trade at that price. If the market is not liquid, then it may be difficult to trade at or near that price for at least two reasons. First, if the market is not liquid, the observed transaction might have occurred some time ago and there may not be anyone willing to trade at that last reported price. Second, without the willing pool of potential traders represented by the scalpers in the pit, the bid-asked spread could be quite wide, making it difficult to trade near the last reported price. The scalpers in the pit are there to seek profit, but they compete with each other to trade. As a result, the presence of the scalpers helps keep the bid-asked price narrow, keep the market more active and price quotations more current, and attract outside traders to the market because they know their orders can be executed near the equilibrium price for the commodity.

In an interesting article, Professor William Silber explores the behavior of scalpers. He arranged to observe all of the transactions of a scalper he identifies only as Mr. X. Mr. X was a trader on the New York Futures Exchange, trading New York Stock Exchange Composite Index futures. For 31 trading days in late 1982 and early 1983, Silber tracked all of Mr. X's trading. Table 3.1 presents some of Silber's results. During this period, Mr. X traded 2,106 times, or about 70 times per day. These transactions involved the purchase and sale (round-turn) of 2,178 contracts.

■ **Table 3.1** ───────────────────────────────

MR. X'S TRADES OVER 31 TRADING DAYS

Total Transactions	2,106
Number of Contracts Traded (Round-turns – buy and sell one contract)	2,178
Number of Trades (Zero net position to a zero net position)	729
Profitable	353 (48%)
Unprofitable	157 (22%)
Scratch	219 (30%)

From William L. Silber, "Marketmaker Behavior in an Auction Market:
An Analysis of Scalpers in Futures Market," *Journal of Finance*
39:4, September 1984, pp. 937–53. Reprinted by permission of the
American Finance Association.

Table 3.1 also shows the number of trades, which Silber defines as going from a zero net position and returning to a zero net position. Fewer than half (48 percent) of these trades were profitable, while 22 percent generated losses. Thirty percent were scratch trades – those with neither a profit nor a loss. The trades generated an average profit of $10.56, or a total trading profit of $7,698.24 over the period. On average a trade took 116 seconds, so the average length of time that Mr. X had a risk exposure was two minutes. The longest trade, hence the longest period of risk exposure, took 547 seconds, or a little over nine minutes. Clearly, Mr. X is reluctant to maintain positions for very long.

Table 3.2 presents one-half hour of Mr. X's trading. During this period, Mr. X made 19 transactions. Notice how Mr. X opens a position, either long or short, and then moves quickly back to a zero position in the market. During this half-hour, Mr. X goes through five trading cycles, beginning and ending the half-hour with a net zero position.

As Silber concludes, the major function that Mr. X provides to the market is liquidity. As a scalper, Mr. X takes the other side of trades coming in from traders off the floor of the exchange. Also, Silber found that Mr. X's trades tended to be more profitable when they were held for a shorter time. For instance, Mr. X's trades taking longer

■ Table 3.2

ONE-HALF HOUR OF MR. X'S TRADING

Transaction	Time	Contracts Traded (Buy +/Sell −)	Net Position
1	10:05:29	2	2
2	10:06:47	−2	0
3	10:08:10	5	5
4	10:09:15	−1	4
5	10:09:49	−2	2
6	10:10:25	−1	1
7	10:11:20	−1	0
8	10:12:56	6	6
9	10:13:29	−3	3
10	10:15:38	−1	2
11	10:16:58	−1	1
12	10:17:23	−1	0
13	10:22:25	−5	−5
14	10:23:11	3	−2
15	10:23:23	2	0
16	10:25:26	5	5
17	10:26:12	−1	4
18	10:26:18	−1	3
19	10:28:12	−3	0

From William L. Silber, "Marketmaker Behavior in an Auction Market: An Analysis of Scalpers in Futures Market," *Journal of Finance* 39:4, September 1984, pp. 937-53. Reprinted by permission of the American Finance Association.

than three minutes were losing trades on average. As Silber concludes: "Scalper earnings compensate for the skill in evaluating market conditions in the very short run and for providing liquidity to the market over the time horizon."[6] This accords with the excerpts from Tamarkin.

DAY TRADERS

Compared to scalpers, day traders take a very farsighted approach to the market. Day traders attempt to profit from the price movements that may take place over the course of one trading day. The day trader closes his or her position before the end of trading each day so that he or she has no position in the futures market overnight. Day traders may trade on or off the floor.

A day trader might follow a strategy such as concentrating activity around announcements from the U.S. government. The Department of Agriculture releases production figures for hogs at intervals that are well known in advance. The day trader may think that the hog figures to be released on a certain day will indicate an unexpectedly high level of production. If so, such an announcement will cause the futures prices for hogs to fall, due to the unexpectedly large future supply of pork. To take advantage of this insight, the day trader would sell the hog contract prior to the announcement and then wait for prices to fall after the announcement. Such a strategy could be implemented without holding a futures market position overnight. Therefore, it is a suitable strategy for a day trader to pursue. (To avoid drastic effects on markets, government announcements are often made late in the day, after the affected market closes.)

The scalper's strategy of holding a position for a very short interval is clearly motivated, but it is not so apparent why day traders limit themselves to price movements that will occur only during the interval of one day's trading. The basic reason is risk. Day traders believe that it is too risky to hold a speculative position overnight; too many disastrous price movements could occur.

To see the danger of maintaining a position overnight, consider a position in orange juice concentrate traded by the Citrus Associates of the New York Cotton Exchange. In late November, a trader holds a short position in orange juice futures. The weather in Florida is crucial for orange juice prices, and the trader checks the weather forecast for Florida that day before trading closes. There seems to be no possibility of damaging weather in the next few days, so he maintains his position overnight. Unexpectedly, a strong cold front pushes into Florida and destroys a large portion of the orange crop, which, in November, is still on the trees and not yet mature. Naturally, futures prices soar on the opening of trading the next day, and the trader who held his position overnight suffers a large loss. In fear of such sudden developments, day traders close their positions each day before trading stops.

The overwhelming majority of speculators are either scalpers or day traders, which indicates just how risky it can be to take a position home overnight. As the close of trading approaches each day, the pace of trading increases. Typically, 25 percent of the day's trading volume occurs in the last half hour of trading. The last five minutes are particularly frenetic as traders attempt to close all of their open positions.

A **position trader** is a speculator who maintains a futures position overnight. On occasion they may hold them for weeks or even months. There are two types of position traders, those holding an **outright position** and those holding a **spread position**. Of the two strategies, the outright position is far riskier.

Outright Positions. An outright position trader might adopt the following strategy if she believed that long-term interest rates were going to rise more than the market expected over the next two months. As interest rates rise, the futures prices, representing the price of bonds, must fall. However, the trader does not really know when during the next two months the rise in rates will occur. To take advantage of her belief about the course of interest rates, she could sell the futures contract on U.S. Treasury bonds traded at the Chicago Board of Trade and hold that position over the next two months. If she is correct, there will be a sharp rise in rates not correctly anticipated by the market, and futures prices will fall. She can then offset and reap her profit.

The danger in this trader's outright position is clear. If she has made a mistake, and interest rates fall unexpectedly, then she will suffer a large loss. The outright position offers a chance for very large gains if she is correct, but it carries with it the risk of very large losses as well. For most speculators, the risks associated with outright positions are too large. The expected trading life of a new trader is about six months, but it is much shorter for outright position traders.

Spread Positions. More risk-averse position traders may trade spreads. Intracommodity spreads involve differences between two or more contract maturities for the same underlying deliverable good. In contrast, intercommodity spreads are price differences between two or more contracts written on different, but related, underlying goods. For example, the difference between the July wheat and corn contracts would be an intercommodity spread. The spread trader trades two or more contracts with related price movements, the goal being to profit from changes in the relative prices.

Consider the case of a spread speculator who believes that the difference between the futures price of wheat and corn is too high.

Such a trader believes that the intercommodity spread between wheat and corn is inconsistent with the justifiable price differential between the two goods. Wheat normally sells at a higher price per bushel than corn, but for this trader the differential in prices is too large. On February 1, the following closing prices could be observed for the JUL wheat and corn contracts, quoted in cents per bushel.

JUL Wheat	329.50
JUL Corn	229.00

The trader believes that this difference of more than one dollar is too large and is willing to speculate that the price of corn will rise relative to the price of wheat. Accordingly, the trader transacts as shown in the top panel of Table 3.3.

Figure 3.1 shows the prices for the JUL corn and wheat contracts for the relevant period. Prices are expressed in cents per bushel. As the figure shows, prices of both corn and wheat did not change dramatically, but both prices fell after February 1, with wheat prices falling more than corn. Because the trader was short wheat and long corn, the price movements gave a profit on the wheat side of the trade and a loss on the corn side. However, the drop in wheat prices was greater than the drop in corn prices, giving an overall profit on

■ Table 3.3

AN INTERCOMMODITY SPREAD

The wheat and corn contracts are both for 5,000 bushels.

Date	Futures Market
February 1	Sell 1 JUL wheat contract at 329.50 cents per bushel. Buy 1 JUL corn contract at 229.00 cents per bushel.
June 1	Buy 1 JUL wheat contract at 282.75 cents per bushel. Sell 1 JUL corn contract at 219.50 cents per bushel. Corn Loss: −$.095 per bushel × 5,000 bushels = −$475.00 Wheat Profit: $.4675 per bushel × 5,000 bushels = $2,337.50 Total Profit: $1,862.50

■ Figure 3.1

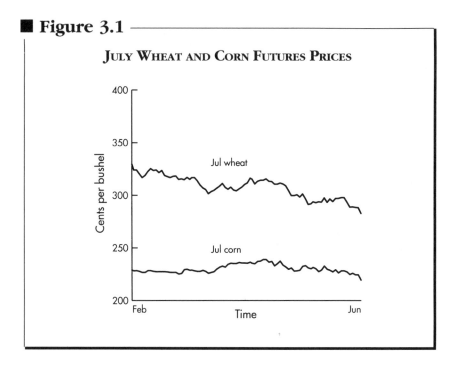

July Wheat and Corn Futures Prices

the spread position. Figure 3.2 tracks the profits that the trader enjoyed from February 1 to June 1.

In this example, the trader correctly bet that the price of corn would rise relative to the price of wheat. As it happened, both prices fell, but the price of wheat fell more, giving an overall profit on the transaction. However, this result is not necessary for the trader to have a profit. For example, if wheat and corn both rose, but corn rose more, the trade would still be profitable. In a spread trade, only the relative prices matter, not the absolute prices.

Other types of spread strategies are also possible. In an intra-commodity spread, a trader takes a position in two or more maturity months for the same good. The belief behind this strategy is that the relative prices between delivery dates for the same commodity will change, generating a profit for the trader. Whereas an outright position only requires a belief about the price movement of one commodity, a spread position focuses on the relative price movements between two or more commodities, or contract maturities.

The classification of speculators into scalpers, day traders, and position traders is useful, but it should not obscure the fact that

■ Figure 3.2

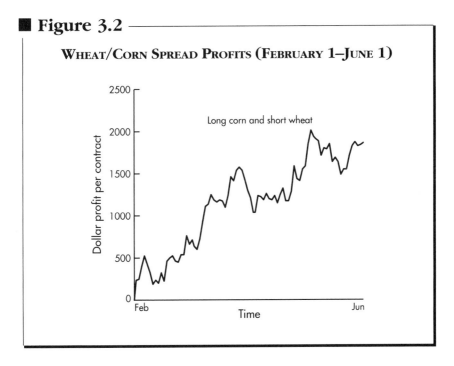

WHEAT/CORN SPREAD PROFITS (FEBRUARY 1–JUNE 1)

individuals can have multiple speculative strategies. A particular trader can easily merge his or her activities as a scalper and a position trader. Those individuals actively trading in the pits take advantage of all types of opportunities that might become available.

SPECULATIVE PROFITS

In this section, we review several dimensions of speculative trading. First, we consider the available evidence on speculator success and failure for individuals. We have already seen that scalpers seem to make speculative profits. Here, we examine the results of several studies of overall trader performance. Second, we evaluate the practices and profits for some technical trading systems. Third, we consider the aims and performance of commodity pools. Finally, we analyze speculative profits in an efficient markets setting.

EVIDENCE ON SPECULATIVE PROFITS

For the most part, speculative profits and losses are difficult to observe. Most traders cherish the privacy of their brokerage accounts. This privacy allows them to enjoy their profits and lick their trading wounds in private and also to tell "fish stories" about their trading prowess. Nonetheless, there are several studies that assess the trading results of speculators. A prime source of this information comes from the CFTC report in which traders with large positions are required to report those positions. This information is made public, although it is presented only in aggregate form. Therefore, it is possible to determine what large (above the reporting requirements) and small (below the reporting requirements) traders are doing in the aggregate. Note that this is not the same as being able to examine a sample of actual trading for particular individuals.

The studies on the magnitude of speculative profits do not reach a consensus, and some of the methodologies employed have been criticized. Nonetheless, there appears to be little reason to think that speculators make large profits, particularly after considering transaction costs. Rather, the results of some gains and some losses might be broadly consistent with speculators trading futures contracts that are fairly priced.

TECHNICAL TRADING SYSTEMS

In futures markets, more than any other segment of the financial markets, technical trading systems seem to find favor. This can be verified by browsing through a recent issue of *Futures* and noting the many advertisements for various technical trading systems. **Technical analysis** is a method of analyzing markets that uses only market data (prices, volume, open interest, and similar information) to predict future price movements. For example, technical analysts believe certain price formations suggest that futures prices will rise. Other formations, according to technical analysis, portend a price decline. We do not explore the methods of technical analysis here, but many books cover the subject.[7] Instead, we want to explore the evidence on whether technical analysis can generate speculative profits.

To have any chance of success, technical analysis depends on the existence of patterns in futures prices. In most markets, scholars find that price patterns do exist, but that these patterns are not sufficiently strong to permit technical trading strategies to generate a profit. To make a trading profit, including covering transaction costs, would require very significant patterns. Many studies are based on simulations of trading systems, instead of systems that are in actual use. While many of these studies suggest that technical analysis may have some merit, this is a very controversial area and the final word has not yet been written on this subject. If technical analysis is useful in futures trading, that result would stand in contrast to findings for other financial markets.[8]

A **commodity fund** or a **commodity pool** is a financial institution that accepts funds from a variety of participants and uses those funds to speculate in the futures market. As such, its organization is similar to a mutual fund. We have noted that trading futures does not require investment as such. Thus, the commodity funds use their customers' funds for two purposes: margin deposits and earning interest. The interest-earning portion provides a pool of funds for future margin calls. Gains and losses for the funds come from futures trading and from the interest that is being earned. Most funds rely strongly on technical analysis for their trading strategies.

What performance can we expect from commodity funds? To analyze this question, we make two initial assumptions. First, we assume that patterns in futures prices are not sufficient to allow technical analysis to generate profits. Second, we assume that the futures price equals the expected future spot price. Under these two restrictions, we would expect the futures trading portion of the commodity fund to neither lose nor profit. Under our assumptions, the fund might trade, but the expected payoff on each trade would be zero. For the interest-earning portion of their assets, we would expect the invested assets to earn the money market rate of interest. Under these assumptions, we expect a commodity fund to underperform a buy-and-hold money market investment, due to the transaction costs that the fund incurs in its trading strategy. To succeed, the commodity fund must be able to earn speculative profits, presumably through technical trading systems, since most funds rely largely on those systems.

Typically, commodity funds use only about 30 percent of invested funds as margin deposits. Thus, the bulk of the money received sits in a money market investment. Second, returns are often negative. Third, even when funds earn positive returns, they typically do not outperform their inherent level of systematic risk. That is, they do not beat the market. Fourth, even if funds are not attractive as investments in themselves, they might be useful in reducing risk when added to a portfolio of stocks and bonds. Evidence on this point is mixed. Fifth, past performance is not a good guide to future performance. In sum, the evidence seems fairly consistent with an efficient markets perspective. Funds do not seem to be an exciting investment vehicle, but they may be a useful tool in some circumstances.

HEDGING

In contrast to the speculator, the **hedger** is a trader who enters the futures market in order to reduce a preexisting risk. If a trader trades futures contracts on commodities in which he or she has no initial position, and in which he or she does not contemplate taking a cash position, then the trader cannot be a hedger. The futures transaction cannot serve as a substitute for a cash market transaction. Having a position, in this case, does not mean that the trader must actually own a commodity. An individual or firm who anticipates the need for a certain commodity in the future or a person who plans to acquire a certain commodity later also has a position in that commodity. In many cases, a hedger has a certain **hedging horizon** – the future date when the hedge will terminate. For example, a farmer can anticipate that he or she will want to hedge from planting to the harvest. In other cases, there will be no specific horizon. We begin with two examples in which hedgers have definite hedging horizons.

A Long Hedge

The idea that you may be at risk in a certain commodity without actually owning it may be a confusing idea to some. Yet consider the following example. Silver is an essential input for the production of most types of photographic films and papers, and the price of silver is quite volatile. For a film manufacturer, there is considerable risk that profits could be dramatically affected by fluctuations in the price of silver. If production schedules are to be maintained, it is absolutely essential that silver be acquired on a regular basis in large quantities. Assume that the film manufacturer needs 50,000 troy ounces of silver in two months and confronts the silver prices shown in Table 3.4 on May 10. The current spot price is 1052.5 cents per ounce, and the price of the JUL futures contract lies above that at 1068.0, with the SEP futures contract trading at 1084.0.

◼ Table 3.4

SILVER FUTURES PRICES ON MAY 10

The COMEX trades a silver contract for 5,000 troy ounces.

Contract	Price (cents per troy ounce)
Spot	1052.5
JUL	1068
SEP	1084

Fearing that silver prices may rise unexpectedly, the film manufacturer decides that the price of 1068.0 is acceptable for the silver that he will need in July. He realizes that it is hopeless to buy the silver on the spot market at 1052.5 and to store the silver for two months. The price differential of 15.5 cents per ounce would not cover his storage costs. Also, the manufacturer will receive an acceptable level of profits even if he pays 1068.0 for the silver to be delivered in July. To pay a price higher than 1068.0, however, could jeopardize profitability seriously. With these reasons in mind, he decides to enter the futures market to hedge against the possibility of future unexpected price increases, and accordingly, he enters the trades shown in Table 3.5.

Taking the futures price as the best estimate of the future spot price, the manufacturer expects to pay 1068.0 cents per ounce for silver in the spot market two months from now in July. At the same time, he buys ten 5,000 ounce JUL futures contracts at 1068.0 cents per ounce. Since he buys a futures contract in order to hedge, this transaction is known as a **long hedge**. The trader is also purchasing a futures contract in anticipation of needing the silver at a future date, so these transactions also represent an **anticipatory hedge**. Time passes, and by July the spot price of silver has risen to 1071.0 cents per ounce, three cents higher than expected. Needing the silver, the manufacturer purchases the silver on the spot market, paying a total of $535,500. This is $1,500 more than expected. Since the futures contract is about to mature, the futures price must equal the spot price, so the film manufacturer is able to sell his ten futures contracts at the same price of 1071.0 cents per ounce, making a three cent profit on each ounce, and a total profit of $1,500 on the futures

■ Table 3.5

A LONG HEDGE IN SILVER

Date	Cash Market	Futures Market
May 10	Anticipates the need for 50,000 troy ounces in two months and expects to pay 1068 cents per ounce, or a total of $534,000.	Buys ten 5,000 troy ounce JUL futures contracts at 1068 cents per ounce.
July 10	The spot price of silver is now 1071 cents per ounce. The manufacturer buys 50,000 ounces, paying $535,500.	Since the futures contract is at maturity, the futures and spot prices are equal, and the ten contracts are sold at 1071 cents per ounce.
	Opportunity loss: −$1,500	Futures profit: $1,500

Net Wealth Change = 0

position. The cash and futures results net to zero. In the cash market, the price was $1,500 more than expected, but there was an offsetting futures profit of $1,500, which generated a net wealth change of zero.

THE REVERSING TRADE AND HEDGING

One peculiar feature of these transactions is that the manufacturer did not accept delivery on the futures contract but offset the contract instead. Rather than accepting delivery on a contract, it usually is better to reverse the trade because offsetting saves on transaction costs and administrative difficulties. The short trader has the right to choose the delivery destination and the long trader must fear that the short trader will select an unpalatable destination. Instead of taking delivery, the long trader can acquire the physical commodity from normal suppliers. The hedger in this example could have achieved the same result by accepting delivery. If delivery were accepted on the futures contract, the silver would have been secured at a price of 1068.0, which is what happened when the reversing trade was used.

A Short Hedge

Although the long silver hedge involved the purchase of a futures contract, hedges do not necessarily involve long futures positions. A **short hedge** is a hedge in which the hedger sells a futures contract. As an example, we assume the same silver prices and a date of May 10, as shown in Table 3.4. A Nevada silver mine owner is concerned about the price of silver, since she wants to be able to plan for the profitability of her firm. If silver prices fall, she may be forced to suspend production. Given the current level of production, she expects to have about 50,000 ounces of silver ready for shipment in two months. Considering the silver prices shown in Table 3.4, she decides that she would be satisfied to receive 1068.0 cents per ounce for her silver.

To establish the price of 1068.0 cents per ounce, the miner decides to enter the silver futures market. By hedging, she can avoid the risk that silver prices might fall in the next two months. Table 3.6 shows the miner's transactions. Notice that these are exactly the mirror image of the film manufacturer's transactions. Anticipating the need to sell 50,000 ounces of silver in two months, the mine operator sells ten 5,000 ounce futures contracts for July delivery at 1068.0 cents

■ Table 3.6

A Short Hedge in Silver

Date	Cash Market	Futures Market
May 10	Anticipates the sale of 50,000 troy ounces in two months and expects to receive 1068 cents per ounce, or a total of $534,000.	Sells ten 5,000 troy ounce July futures contracts at 1068 cents per ounce.
July 10	The spot price of silver is now 1071 cents per ounce. The miner sells 50,000 ounces, receiving $535,500.	Buys 10 contracts at 1071.
	Profit $1,500	Futures loss: −$1,500
	Net Wealth Change = 0	

per ounce. On July 10, with silver prices at 1071.0 cents per ounce, the miner sells the silver and receives $535,000. This is $1,500 more than she originally expected. In the futures market, however, the miner suffers an offsetting loss. The futures contracts she sold at 1068.0, she offsets in July at 1071.0 cents per ounce. Once again, the profits and losses in the two markets offset each other, and produce a net wealth change of zero.

Viewing the results from the vantage point of July, it is clear that the miner would have been $1,500 richer if she had not hedged. She would have received $1,500 more than originally expected in the physicals market, and she would have incurred no loss in the futures market. However, it does not follow that she was unwise to hedge. In hedging, the miner and the film manufacturer both decided that the futures price was an acceptable price at which to complete the transaction in July.

DO HEDGERS NEED SPECULATORS?

Hedging is often viewed as the purchasing of insurance. According to this view, hedgers trade in the futures market and speculators bear the risk that the hedgers try to avoid. Naturally, the speculators demand some compensation for this service. In Chapter 2, the theories of normal backwardation and the contango were considered as explanations of the way in which speculators might receive compensation for bearing risk. In considering the two sides of the silver example, however, no speculators were needed to assume position trades. The long and short hedgers balanced each other out perfectly.

While the example is artificial, it illustrates an important point. Hedgers, as a group, need speculators to take positions and bear risk only for the mismatch in contracts demanded by the long and short hedgers. To the extent that their positions match, position trading speculators are not needed for the job of bearing risk. This helps explain why the risk premiums, if there are any, are not large. In this example, the hedgers do not need speculators to act as position traders. However, even if long and short hedgers were always in balance, the market would still need the liquidity provided by scalpers, such as Mr. X, the scalper we studied earlier.

CROSS-HEDGING

In the examples of a long and short hedge in silver, the hedgers' needs were perfectly matched with the institutional features of the silver markets. The goods in question were exactly the same goods traded on the futures market, the cash amounts matched the futures contract amounts, and the hedging horizons of the miner and film manufacturer matched the delivery date for the futures contract. In actual hedging applications, it will be rare for all factors to match so well. In most cases the hedged and hedging positions will differ in (1) time span covered, (2) the amount of the commodity, or (3) the particular characteristics of the goods. In such cases, the hedge will be a **cross-hedge** – a hedge in which the characteristics of the spot and futures positions do not match perfectly.

As an example, consider the problem faced by a film manufacturer who uses silver, a key ingredient in manufacturing photographic film. Film production is a process industry, with more or less continuous production. However, COMEX silver futures trade for delivery in January, March, May, July, September, and December. The film manufacturer will also need silver in February, April, and so on. Thus, the futures expiration dates and the hedging horizon for the film manufacturer do not match perfectly. Second, consider the differences in quantity between the futures contract and the film manufacturer's needs. The COMEX contract is for 5,000 troy ounces of silver. The film manufacturer will likely need many thousands of ounces, so it will be fairly easy for the manufacturer to choose and trade a number of contracts that will bring the quantity of silver futures close to the actual need. However, if a hedger needed to hedge 7,500 ounces, he or she might have a problem choosing between one or two contracts. Finally, consider the differences in the physical characteristics of the silver underlying the futures contract and the silver used in manufacturing film. To produce film, silver needs to be in pellet form, and it does not need to be as pure as silver bullion. Also, the pellets contain other metals besides silver. The COMEX silver contract specifies that deliverable silver must be in 1,000 ounce ingots that are 99.9 percent pure. In other words, the silver in the futures contract is extremely pure and refined, not like the adulterated silver products that are typically used in industry. Thus, the film manufacturer will have to hedge his or her industrial silver with pure silver bullion.

Cross-hedging is often particularly problematic in the interest rate futures market. Financial instruments are extremely varied in their characteristics, such as risk level, maturity, and coupon rate. By contrast, really active futures contracts are only traded on a few different types of interest-bearing securities.

When the characteristics of the position to be hedged do not perfectly match the characteristics of the futures contract used for the hedging, the hedger must be sure to trade the right number and kind of futures contract to control the risk in the hedged position as much as possible. In general, we cannot expect a cross-hedge to be as effective in reducing risk as a direct hedge. We consider cross-hedging in more detail in later chapters.

RISK-MINIMIZATION HEDGING

In our first examples, we considered hedges when the hedger had a definite horizon in view. Often, the hedger will not want to hedge for a specific future date. Instead, the hedger may want to control a continuing risk on an indefinite basis. Consider, for example, a soy dealer who holds an inventory of soybeans. From this inventory, the dealer meets orders from her customers. As her inventory becomes low, she periodically replenishes her own inventory from cash market sources. The inventory that she holds will fluctuate in value with the price of soybeans. However, she can reduce the fluctuations in the value of her inventory by selling futures contracts, as the following case study shows.

Assume that today is June 19, 1989, and that the dealer's inventory is one million bushels. The cash price of beans has been very volatile in recent months and is near a high, as Figure 3.3 shows. Therefore, the dealer decides to hedge by selling soybean futures. After she sells futures, she will be long the physical soybeans in her inventory and short soybean futures. If the hedge works, the risk of the combined cash/futures position should be less than the cash position alone.

With an inventory of one million bushels, and a soybean contract calling for 5,000 bushels, it might seem wise to sell one bushel in the futures market for each bushel in the cash market. This would call for selling 200 soybean contracts. However, a 1:1 hedge may not be optimal. In our example, the dealer wants to minimize her preexisting risk that comes from holding her soybean inventory. We assume that she holds a given bean inventory for business reasons, and we treat that inventory decision as fixed. The dealer's problem is to choose the number of futures contracts that will minimize her risk. Thus, we define the **hedge ratio** (HR) as the number of futures contracts to hold for a given position in the commodity:

■ **Figure 3.3**

SOYBEAN CASH PRICES (MARCH 27, 1989–JUNE 4, 1990)

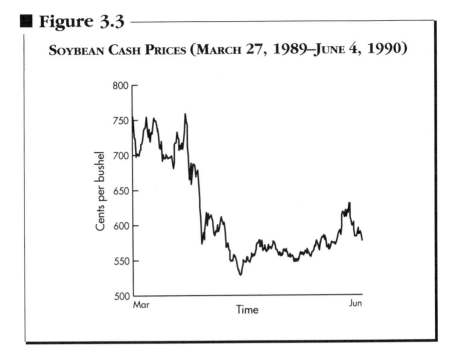

$$\text{HR} = \frac{\text{Futures Position}}{\text{Cash Market Position}} \qquad (3.1)$$

The dealer will trade HR units of the futures to establish the futures market hedge. After establishing the hedge, the trader has a portfolio, *P*, that consists of the spot position plus the futures position. The profits and losses on the portfolio for one day will be:

$$P_{t+1} - P_t = S_{t+1} - S_t + \text{HR}(F_{t+1} - F_t) \qquad (3.2)$$

Note that in our initial discussion we considered that the dealer might hedge each bushel in her cash position with one bushel of futures. In that case, the hedge ratio would be −1.0, the negative sign indicating a short position. Generally, if the trader is long the cash commodity, the futures position will be short. Likewise, if the trader is short the cash good, the futures position will be long.

Now, however, the dealer wants to choose the hedge ratio that will minimize the risk of the portfolio of the spot beans and the futures position. The variance of the combined position depends on the variance of the cash price, the variance of the futures price, and the covariance between the two prices. It is a basic statistical rule that the variance of returns on a portfolio, P, of one unit of the spot asset and HR units of a futures contract is given by Equation 3.3:

$$\sigma_P^2 = \sigma_S^2 + HR^2\sigma_F^2 + 2\,HR\rho_{SF}\sigma_S\sigma_F \qquad (3.3)$$

where:

σ_P^2 = variance of the portfolio, P_t
σ_S^2 = variance of S_t
σ_F^2 = variance of F_t
ρ_{SF} = correlation between S_t and F_t

The dealer minimizes the variance by choosing a hedge ratio defined as follows:[9]

$$HR = \frac{\rho_{SF}\sigma_S\sigma_F}{\sigma_F^2} = \frac{COV_{SF}}{\sigma_F^2} \qquad (3.4)$$

where:

COV_{SF} = the covariance between S_t and F_t

As a practical matter, the easiest way to find the risk-minimizing hedge ratio is to estimate the following regression:

$$S_t = \alpha + \beta F_t + \epsilon_t \qquad (3.5)$$

where:

α = the constant regression parameter
β = the slope regression parameter
ϵ = an error term with zero mean and standard deviation of 1.0

The estimated β from this regression is the risk-minimizing hedge ratio, because the estimated β equals the sample covariance between the independent (F_t) and dependent (S_t) variables divided by the

sample variance of the independent variable. This is exactly the definition we gave of the risk-minimizing hedge ratio in Equation 3.4.

From the regression estimation, we also obtain a measure of hedging
effectiveness. The coefficient of determination, or R^2, is provided by
the regression estimate. Conceptually:

R^2 = portion of total variance in the cash price changes
statistically related to the futures price changes

Thus the R^2 will always be a number between 0 and 1.0. The closer
to 1.0, the better the degree of fit in the regression between the cash
and the futures and the better chance for our hedge to work well.

There are at least three possible measures of S_t and F_t that we might
be tempted to employ in the regression of Equation 3.5 – price levels,
price changes, and percentage price changes. There has been considerable controversy regarding the proper measure. While this controversy is not fully resolved, we recommend using either the change
in price or the percentage change in price, not the price level. If the
general range of prices over the estimation period is fairly stable,
the price change measure will be satisfactory. If the price changes
dramatically, using percentage price changes will give better results.

We now apply this regression approach to the problem of our
soybean dealer as of June 19, 1989, using 60 days of daily data to
estimate the following regression equation:

$$\Delta C_t = \alpha + \beta \Delta F_t + \epsilon_t$$

where:

ΔC_t = change in cash price on day t
ΔF_t = change in futures price on day t

Estimating the regression gives the following parameter estimates:

$$\hat{\alpha} = .6976$$
$$\hat{\beta} = .8713$$
$$R^2 = .56$$

With the estimated $\beta = .8713$, the model suggests selling .8713 bushels
in the futures market for each bushel in inventory. With one million

bushels in inventory and a futures contract of 5,000 bushels, the model suggests selling 174 contracts, because:

$$.8713 \times (1,000,000/5,000) = 174.26 \text{ contracts}$$

From the estimation of the model, we see that the regression accounts for 56 percent of the variance of the cash price change during our sample period. This is an important point, because the regression chose an estimate of β to maximize the R^2. This provides no certainty that we can expect similar results beyond the estimation period. To this point in our example, we have used the data that would actually be available to a trader on June 19, 1989. We assume that our soybean dealer estimated her hedge ratio and placed the hedge at the close of business on June 19. Next, we want to evaluate the performance of the hedge.

Figure 3.4 shows how soybeans performed from June 20, 1989, through June 4, 1990, when we assume that the dealer offset in the futures market, thereby ending the hedge. The graph in Figure 3.4 shows the wealth change from June 20 forward for one contract of

■ Figure 3.4

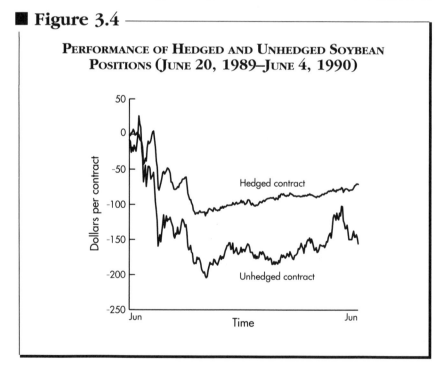

PERFORMANCE OF HEDGED AND UNHEDGED SOYBEAN
POSITIONS (JUNE 20, 1989–JUNE 4, 1990)

cash soybeans and for a contract (5,000 bushels) of cash soybeans hedged with .8713 futures contracts. As the figure shows, in late summer 1989, soybean prices fell dramatically. From the time the hedge was placed until October 1989, soybean prices fell about $2.00 per bushel. During the same interval, the hedge position lost about $1.00 per bushel. From autumn 1989 through May 1990, prices drifted somewhat higher.

Comparing the unhedged and the hedged strategies, we see that both lost money. However, the hedged strategy avoided about 50 percent of the loss associated with the drop in cash prices. Over the life of the hedge, the unhedged bushel of soybeans lost $1.56 and the hedged bushel lost $.71. On the inventory of one million bushels, this represents a benefit of $850,000 from hedging. We can also see from Figure 3.4 that the hedged position had much less variance than the cash position. For an unhedged bushel, the standard deviation of the price change was $.0815 per day. For the hedged position, the standard deviation was $.0431.

Several special points need to be made about this particular hedge. First, we see that the hedge made money because the short position in the futures gave profits as soybean prices fell. We must realize that bean prices could have risen just as easily. In that event, the futures position in the hedge would have lost money. This brings us to the second point. Hedging aims at reducing risk, not generating profits. In this case, the goal was to reduce variance, which the hedge did. Had bean prices risen, the hedge would also have reduced variance, and would have been successful in attaining its goal. Thus, the hedger must expect an equal chance of monetary gains and losses from placing a hedge. However, with a good hedge, the variance can be reduced substantially.

The period we chose for our analysis was a special time in the bean market. There may have been an attempted manipulation of the July 1990 soybean futures contract by the Italian grain firm Ferruzzi. Thus, our estimation period consisted of the run-up in prices that culminated in the market crisis of July 1990. The beginning portion of our hedging period included the price collapse that resulted after Ferruzzi was forced from the market. These events disturbed the normal price relationship between cash and futures prices for soybeans, so this period would be difficult for any hedging model. Nonetheless, the hedge worked fairly well in reducing the volatility of the bean dealer's inventory value. Given the collapsing prices, the hedge also saved her about $850,000.

CONCLUSION

In this chapter we have explored the three major uses that observers and traders make of futures markets. We began by considering the function of price discovery, a service of futures markets that can be enjoyed by traders and nontraders alike. We considered the way in which producers could use information from the futures market to guide their production decisions. If futures prices provide a good guide to future spot prices, then futures markets reveal price information that helps society allocate capital more efficiently.

The futures market attracts speculators – traders who enter the futures market in pursuit of profit, willingly increasing their risks to do so. We classified speculators according to the length of time they planned to hold a futures position as scalpers, day traders, and position traders. We noted that spread trading is an important form of speculative trading and considered different spread trading techniques.

We examined the available evidence on the profitability of speculative trading. We found that studies disagree considerably on the magnitude and even the existence of speculative trading profits. We briefly considered the performance of technical trading systems, where we once again found different conclusions in the academic literature. Commodity funds have become important speculative trading vehicles in recent years. We analyzed the evidence on the performance of commodity funds, and again found no evidence of overwhelming trading acumen.

Hedging is one of the most important social functions of futures markets. A hedger is a trader who enters the futures market in an effort to reduce a preexisting risk. We saw that traders can hedge by being either long or short in the futures market. Except for providing liquidity, we noted that hedgers needed speculative position traders only to absorb an imbalance between long and short hedgers. Much hedging activity involves an imperfect match between the characteristics of the asset being hedged and the asset underlying a futures contract. Hedging in such a situation is called cross-hedging. We gave examples of how traders might use the market to hedge in such a situation. In many instances, hedgers will want to employ risk-minimization techniques for a given position. We showed that it is possible to derive the correct futures position to minimize a given initial risk using a statistical analysis of historical data. Using actual soybean data, we followed a strategy from beginning to end for hedging soybeans over the 1989–1990 period.

NOTES

1. For a more formal treatment of the property of unbiasedness in estimators, see J. Maddala, *Introduction to Econometrics,* New York: Macmillan, 1988.
2. See R. Levich, "Currency Forecasters Lose Their Way," *Euromoney,* August 1983, pp. 140–47. Chapter 8 discusses the forecasting accuracy of professional currency forecasters in more detail.
3. Some authors attempt to distinguish speculators from investors. The usual difference between the two definitions seems to lie in their respective attitudes toward risk and the length of time they expect to hold their positions. Speculators are contrasted only with hedgers, so any investor in the futures market, no matter how conservative, would be regarded as a speculator for the purposes of this book.
4. On the floor of the exchanges, different commodities are traded in different pits. A pit is really an area of the floor, surrounded by steps or risers, which are usually about five steps high. The arrangement allows traders to see and communicate with each other. The term "pit" is really synonymous with trading in futures, as indicated by the title of Frank Norris' novel, *The Pit,* which is the story of futures trading in wheat.
5. B. Tamarkin, *The New Gatsbys: Fortunes and Misfortunes of Commodity Traders,* New York: William Morrow, 1985, pp. 26, 43.
6. W. L. Silber, "Marketmaker Behavior in an Auction Market: An Analysis of Scalpers in Futures Markets," *Journal of Finance,* September 1984, 39:4, pp. 937–53.
7. See, for example, *Commodity Trading Manual,* Chicago: Chicago Board of Trade, 1989, and Martin J. Pring (ed.), *The McGraw-Hill Handbook of Commodities and Futures,* New York: McGraw-Hill, 1985.

8. For a more complete survey of technical trading systems, see R. Kolb, *Understanding Futures Markets,* 5e, Cambridge, MA: Blackwell Publishers, 1997, Chapter 4.

9. To find the risk-minimizing hedge ratio, we take the derivative of the portfolio's risk in Equation 3.3 with respect to HR, set the derivative equal to zero, and solve for HR:

$$\frac{d\,\sigma_P^2}{d\,\text{HR}} = 2\,\text{HR}\,\sigma_F^2 - 2\,\rho_{CF}\sigma_C\sigma_F = 0$$

$$\text{HR} = \rho_{CF}\frac{\sigma_C}{\sigma_F} = \frac{\text{COV}_{CF}}{\sigma_F^2}$$

Chapter 4

Interest Rate Futures: Introduction

OVERVIEW

This chapter explores one of the most successful and exciting innovations in the history of futures markets – the emergence of interest rate futures contracts. Since the first contracts were traded on October 20, 1975, the market has expanded rapidly. In spite of a number of relatively unsuccessful contracts that have been introduced, such as commercial paper and Certificate Delivery GNMA contracts, the market has been a huge success. By fall 1995, open interest exceeded $2.6 trillion (face value) of underlying financial instruments, up from just $800 billion in 1990 and $300 billion in 1987. From inception, the interest rate futures market has come to represent about one-half of the entire futures market, and most industry observers expect the continued growth of the futures market to center around financial instruments.

Almost all of the activity in the U.S. interest rate futures is concentrated in two exchanges, the Chicago Board of Trade (CBOT) and the International Monetary Market (IMM) of the Chicago Mercantile Exchange (CME). The Board of Trade specializes in contracts at the longer end of the maturity spectrum, with active contracts on long-term Treasury bonds and ten-year, five-year, and two-year Treasury notes. In addition, the CBOT trades a municipal bond contract. By contrast, the International Monetary Market has successful contracts with very short maturities, trading contracts for three-month Treasury bills and Eurodollar Deposits. While this chapter discusses features of many different contracts, we focus on the most important contracts: the T-bond contract and three T-note contracts traded on the CBOT, along with the T-bill and Eurodollar contracts traded on the IMM of the CME. For the most part, these are highly active contracts that differ widely in their contract terms and the maturities of the underlying instruments. Figure 4.1 presents price quotations for key contracts.

Interest Rate Futures Contracts

To understand the interest rate futures market, we need to understand the specifications for the different contracts. Among all the different types of futures contracts, interest rate futures exhibit the most variety, with the characteristics of the futures contracts being tailored to the particular attributes of the underlying instruments. We begin by considering the contract specifications for the major short-maturity contracts.

Treasury Bill Futures

The T-bill futures contract, traded by the International Monetary Market of the Chicago Mercantile Exchange, calls for the delivery of T-bills having a face value of $1,000,000 and a time to maturity of 90 days at the expiration of the futures contract. The contracts trade for delivery in March, June, September, and December. The delivery dates are chosen to make newly issued 13-week T-bills immediately deliverable against the futures contract. Also, a previously issued one-year T-bill will have 13 weeks until maturity, and it can also be delivered against the T-bill futures contract. The IMM permits delivery on the three business days following the last day of trading.

Price quotations for T-bill futures use the IMM Index, which is a function of the discount yield (DY):

$$\text{IMM Index} = 100.00 - \text{DY} \qquad (4.1)$$

where:

DY = Discount yield, e.g., 7.1 is 7.1 percent

■ Figure 4.1

PRICE QUOTATIONS FOR MAJOR INTEREST RATE FUTURES CONTRACTS

INTEREST RATE

TREASURY BONDS (CBT)-$100,000; pts. 32nds of 100%

	Open	High	Low	Settle	Change	Lifetime High	Lifetime Low	Open Interest
June	110-14	110-17	109-30	110-08	– 8	121-23	93-06	343,237
Sept	109-27	109-27	109-13	109-23	– 8	120-29	102-06	26,095
Dec	109-05	109-07	108-31	109-06	– 8	120-15	107-00	5,344
Mr97	....	....	....	108-25	– 8	120-00	106-20	936

Est vol 255,000; vol Mn 257,787; op int 275,671, –8,669.

TREASURY BONDS (MCE)-$50,000; pts. 32nds of 100%

	Open	High	Low	Settle	Change	Lifetime High	Lifetime Low	Open Interest
June	110-11	110-12	109-30	110-05	– 11	121-09	98-10	11,115

Est vol 4,400; vol Mn 5,031; open int 11,167, +625.

TREASURY NOTES (CBT)-$100,000; pts. 32nds of 100%

	Open	High	Low	Settle	Change	Lifetime High	Lifetime Low	Open Interest
June	108-06	108-09	107-30	108-05	– 2	114-26	102-10	288,551
Sept	107-25	107-28	107-24	107-28	– 3	114-26	106-09	35,093
Dec	107-07	107-09	107-07	107-09	– 2	113-30	105-29	2,409

Est vol 65,000; vol Mn 61,838; open int 326,073, +3,188.

5 YR TREAS NOTES (CBT)-$100,000; pts. 32nds of 100%

	Open	High	Low	Settle	Change	Lifetime High	Lifetime Low	Open Interest
June	106-15	106-15	106-08	106-13	– 1	111-07	05-025	176,873
Sept	....	....	....	06045	– 1	10-305	05-015	11,448

Est vol 31,500; vol Mn 26,405; open int 188,356, +2,218.

2 YR TREAS NOTES (CBT)-$200,000, pts. 32nds of 100%

	Open	High	Low	Settle	Change	Lifetime High	Lifetime Low	Open Interest
June	03105	03112	103-09	03112	– 0.7	105-19	102-26	17,379

Est vol 11,100; vol Mn 380; open int 17,386, +66.

30-DAY FEDERAL FUNDS (CBT)-$5 million; pts. of 100%

	Open	High	Low	Settle	Change	Lifetime High	Lifetime Low	Open Interest
Apr	94.790	94.790	94.780	94.785	+ .05	94.980	94.980	4,201
May	94.73	94.73	94.72	94.73	....	95.05	94.49	4,250
June	94.71	94.71	94.70	94.71	....	95.20	94.48	4,628
July	94.69	94.69	94.69	94.69	– .01	95.34	94.66	2,894
Aug	94.68	94.68	94.67	94.68	– .01	95.39	94.61	1,352
Sept	94.63	94.64	94.62	94.64	– .01	95.43	94.54	1,158
Oct	94.55	94.56	94.54	94.56	– .01	95.51	94.41	907
Nov	....	....	....	94.48	– .02	95.54	94.35	215
Dec	....	....	....	94.43	– .03	94.56	94.37	41
Ja97	....	....	....	94.37	– .04	95.35	94.34	111

Est vol 888; vol Mn 282; open int 19,842, +80.

MUNI BOND INDEX (CBT)-$1,000; times Bond Buyer MBI

	Open	High	Low	Settle	Change	Lifetime High	Lifetime Low	Open Interest
June	112-08	112-10	111-30	112-07	+ 6	120-29	108-23	11,627

Est vol – – 2,300; vol Mn 3,949; open int 11,635, +137.
The index: Close 113-26; Yield 6.42.

TREASURY BILLS (CME)-$1 mil.; pts. of 110%

	Open	High	Low	Settle	Chg	Discount Settle	Chg	Open Interest
June	95.00	95.01	95.00	95.01	....	4.99	....	9,527
Sept	94.85	94.85	94.83	94.84	....	5.16	....	5,087
Dec	....	....	....	94.66	....	5.34	....	793

Est vol 562; vol Mn 619; open int 15,407, +260.

LIBOR-1 MO. (CME)-$3,000,000; points of 100%

	Open	High	Low	Settle	Chg	Discount Settle	Chg	Open Interest
May	94.59	94.59	94.58	94.59	....	5.41	....	15,513
June	94.59	94.60	94.59	94.60	....	5.40	....	4,662
July	94.58	94.59	94.58	94.59	....	5.41	....	4,238
Aug	94.57	94.57	94.56	94.57	....	5.43	....	1,383
Sept	94.50	94.50	94.49	94.49	– .01	5.51	+ .01	833
Oct	....	....	....	94.44	– .01	5.56	+ .01	200
Nov	....	....	....	94.37	– .03	5.63	+ .03	320
Dec	94.07	94.09	94.06	94.10	– .02	5.90	+ .02	1,145
Ja97	....	....	....	94.28	– .01	....	+ .01	220

Est vol 1,332; vol Mn 1,735; open int 28,561, +187.

EURODOLLAR (CME)-$1 million; pts of 100%

	Open	High	Low	Settle	Chg	Yield Settle	Chg	Open Interest
May	94.54	94.55	94.54	94.55	....	5.45	....	17,564
June	94.56	94.56	94.53	94.55	....	5.45	....	380,507

As an example, a discount yield of 8.32 percent implies an IMM Index value of 91.68. The IMM adopted this method of price quotation to ensure that the bid price would be below the asked price, the relationship prevailing in most markets. Price fluctuations may be no smaller than one tick, or one **basis point**. Given the fact that the instruments are priced by using a discount yield and a contract size of $1,000,000, a one basis point movement in the interest rate generates a price change of $25.00. Equation 4.2 gives the price that must be paid at delivery for the cash market bill:

$$\text{Bill Price} = \$1,000,000 - \frac{DY \ (\$1,000,000)(DTM)}{360} \qquad (4.2)$$

where:

DTM = Days until maturity

With a discount yield of 8.32 percent on the futures contract, the price to be paid for the T-bill at delivery would be $979,200:

$$\text{Bill Price} = \$1,000,000 - \frac{.0832(\$1,000,000)(90)}{360} = \$979,200$$

If the futures yield rose to 8.35 percent, the delivery price would be $979,125, changing $25 for each basis point. Many futures contracts have a daily price limit, a constraint on how much the futures price is allowed to move in a single day of trading. For example, in former times the limit for the T-bill contract was 60 basis points, or $1,500, in either direction from the previous day's settlement price. The contract specifications have been changed and now there is no limit on the daily price fluctuation.

Figure 4.1 presents price quotations for T-bill futures. These quotations are similar in structure to those for other futures contracts. The first four columns of figures give the open, high, low, and settlement quotations in terms of the IMM Index. The "Chg" column shows the change in the IMM Index from the previous day's settlement. Under the heading "Discount" are the settlement discount yield and the change in the settlement discount yield. Notice that the settlement discount yield plus the settlement IMM Index always sum to 100.0. Similarly, the change in the IMM Index and the change in the discount yield are always equal in magnitude but opposite in sign. The last column gives the open interest for each contract maturity. The final line of the quotations reports the volume, open interest across all maturities, and the change in the open interest since the previous day.

Although the contract specifications call for the delivery of a T-bill having 90 days to maturity, delivery of 91- or 92-day bills is also permitted with a price adjustment. The price can be adjusted by substituting the correct number of days until maturity in Equation 4.2. In any event, all of the delivered T-bills must be of the same maturity. Upon delivery, the short trader must deliver the T-bills and the long trader must pay the invoice amount. The invoice amount is:

$$\text{Invoice Amount} = \$1,000,000 - \frac{\text{T-bill Yield } (\$1,000,000)(\text{DTM})}{360}$$

$$(4.3)$$

The actual delivery process extends over two business days. On the first day, the short trader gives notice to the IMM Clearinghouse that he or she will deliver. The Clearinghouse assigns the delivery to an outstanding long trader. The two traders communicate with their own and the other trader's banks to alert the banks to the impending transactions. To consummate the transaction, the short trader delivers the bills and the long trader pays the short trader. This is accomplished through wire transfers between the banks of the two traders. Figure 4.2 diagrams the delivery process followed by the IMM Clearinghouse.

EURODOLLAR FUTURES

Eurodollar deposits are U.S. dollar deposits held in a commercial bank outside the United States. These banks may be either foreign banks or foreign branches of U.S. banks. The deposits are normally nontransferable and cannot be used as collateral for loans. London dominates the Eurodollar deposit market, so rates in this market are often based on **LIBOR**, the **London Interbank Offered Rate**. LIBOR is the rate at which banks are willing to lend funds to other banks in the interbank market. LIBOR is an important rate in international finance; for example, many loans to developing countries have been priced as LIBOR plus some number of percentage points.

■ Figure 4.2

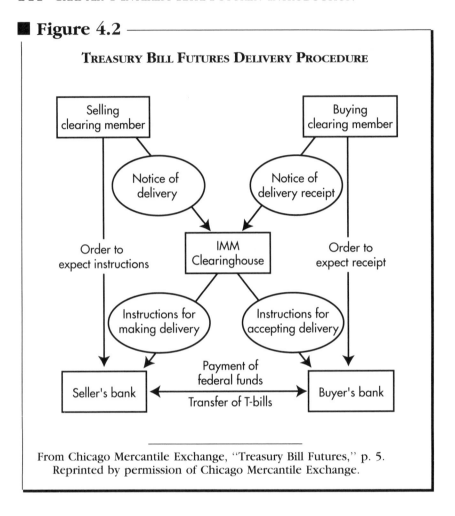

Treasury Bill Futures Delivery Procedure

From Chicago Mercantile Exchange, "Treasury Bill Futures," p. 5. Reprinted by permission of Chicago Mercantile Exchange.

Eurodollar futures, like T-bill futures, trade on the IMM of the CME. Eurodollar futures have come to dominate the market for short-term contracts and greatly exceed the T-bill contract in volume and open interest. Like the T-bill contract, the instrument underlying the Eurodollar contract has a three-month maturity. Unlike the T-bill contract, the underlying good is not a bond but a time deposit held in a commercial bank. Also, unlike the T-bill contract, there is no actual delivery on the Eurodollar contract. Instead, the contract is fulfilled by cash settlement.

The Eurodollar futures contract was the first contract to use cash settlement rather than the delivery of an actual good for contract fulfillment. We have already noted that Eurodollar deposits are non-transferable, a feature that by itself precludes delivery. As a result, the IMM requires fulfillment of a contract by a cash payment based on its measure of Eurodollar rates. To establish the settlement rate at the close of trading, the IMM determines the three-month LIBOR rate. It then uses this rate indication to establish the final settlement price. The rules of the exchange are quite explicit:

> The final settlement price shall be determined by the Clearing House as follows. On the last day of trading the Clearing House shall determine the London Interbank Offered Rate (LIBOR) for three-month Eurodollar Time Deposit funds both at the time of termination of trading and at a randomly-selected time within the last 90 minutes of trading. The final settlement price shall be 100 minus the arithmetic mean, rounded to the nearest 1/100th of a percentage point, of the LIBOR at these two times.
>
> To determine the LIBOR at either time the Clearing House shall select at random 12 reference banks from a list of no less than 20 participating banks that are major banks in the London Eurodollar market. Each reference bank shall quote to the Clearing House its perception of the rate at which three-month Eurodollar Time Deposit funds are currently offered by the market to prime banks. These rates must be confirmed in writing by telex before they are accepted as official; only after confirmation will they be used to determine the final settlement price. The two highest and the two lowest quotes shall be eliminated. The arithmetic mean of the remaining eight quotes shall be the LIBOR at that time. If for any reason there is difficulty in obtaining a quote within a reasonable time interval from one of the banks in the sample, that bank shall be dropped from the sample, and another shall be randomly selected to replace it.[1]

The use of a number of banks with polling at two separate times and confirmation required in writing is designed to thwart any attempted manipulation of the final settlement price. Since its inception in 1981, this procedure has worked very well, with Eurodollar futures having grown very rapidly. Once the final settlement price is determined, traders with open positions settle with cash through the normal marking-to-market procedure. This fulfills their obligation and the contract expires.

Prior to the final trading day, the daily settlement price depends on the quotations in the futures market. In a sense, the futures price appears free to wander from the spot market values except for the final day of trading. This is an illusion, however. Consider, for example, the second to last trading day. Traders know that tomorrow the futures settlement price will be set equal to the average LIBOR actually available from banks. Therefore, the price today cannot be very different from today's cash market LIBOR. If it did differ significantly, traders would enter the market to buy or sell futures and would expect to reap their profit when the futures price is pegged to the cash market LIBOR. This same argument holds for every other day prior to expiration as well, so the Eurodollar futures contract must behave as though there will be an actual delivery at the contract's expiration. We will see evidence of this relationship later.

For the Eurodollar contract, the contract size is for $1,000,000, with the yield being quoted on an add-on basis. The add-on yield is given by:

$$\text{Add-on Yield} = \left(\frac{\text{Discount}}{\text{Price}}\right)\left(\frac{360}{\text{DTM}}\right) \tag{4.4}$$

For example, assume the discount yield is 8.32 percent. We have already seen that this discount yield gives a price of $979,200 for a $1 million face value three-month T-bill. Therefore, the dollar discount is $20,800 and 90 days remain until the bill will mature. With these values we have:

$$\text{Add-on Yield} = \left(\frac{\$20,800}{\$979,200}\right)\left(\frac{360}{90}\right) = .0850$$

Add-on yields exceed corresponding discount yields. In our example, the discount yield is 8.32 percent, and the add-on yield equivalent is 8.5 percent. However, for both measures, a shift of one basis point is worth $25 on a $1,000,000 contract. Note also that these yields and relationships vary with maturity, so the statements made here hold only for three-month maturities.

Figure 4.1 shows price quotations for Eurodollar futures from *The Wall Street Journal*. The quotations have the same structure as the T-bill futures examined in the previous section, but the yields are add-on yields. Like the T-bill contract, the Eurodollar contract uses the IMM Index. Thus, the quoted price is:

$$\text{IMM Index} = 100.00 - \text{LIBOR} \tag{4.5}$$

The relationship between the T-bill and Eurodollar futures yields is very stable. Using data on a pair of September contracts, Figure 4.3 shows the settlement yields for both contracts over the lives of the contracts, with Eurodollar yields exceeding T-bill yields. The relationship between the two is very steady. To emphasize this strong correspondence between these yields, we estimated the following regression for this pair of contracts using daily data:

Change in Eurodollar Yield$_t$ = α + β Change in T-bill Yield$_t$ + e_t

The results were:

Change in Eurodollar Yield$_t$ =
$$-0.00045 + 1.0621 \text{ Change in T-bill Yield}_t$$

with an R^2 of 0.9119 and a *t*-statistic for β of 56.00, based on 305 observations. What the graph strongly indicates, the regression confirms: There is an extremely strong relationship between the level of T-bill and Eurodollar yields. Notice also that the Eurodollar yield lies above the T-bill yield. From the regression we can see that Eurodollar

■ Figure 4.3

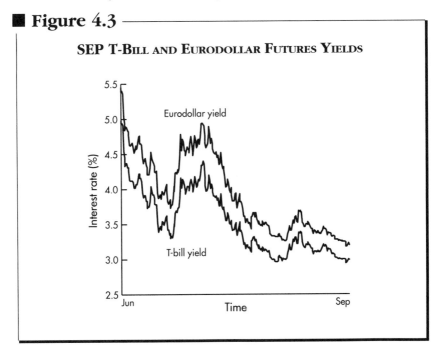

SEP T-Bill and Eurodollar Futures Yields

yields move just slightly more than 1:1 for a change in T-bill yields, because the estimated β = 1.0621. Later in this chapter, we explore some speculative strategies based on the relationship between these two yields.

Treasury Bond Futures

Of all futures contracts, the T-bond contract is one of the most complex and most interesting. The complexity of the contract stems from the delivery rules under which it is traded and from the wide variety of bonds that can be delivered to fulfill the contract. For the T-bill contract, delivery takes place within a very narrow span of time, but the Chicago Board of Trade, which trades the T-bond contract, employs a radically different delivery procedure.

In spite of its peculiarities, the T-bond contract is perhaps the single most successful futures contract ever introduced. Starting in August 1977, its success has been amazing. In 1986, for example, more than 52 million T-bond futures contracts were traded, and in 1995 this figure exceeded 88 million. With a face value per contract of $100,000, this represents an underlying value of more than $8.8 trillion. This single contract accounted for more than 50 percent of the CBOT's total volume of futures and options contracts.

Figure 4.1 presented quotations for T-bond futures from *The Wall Street Journal*. The structure of these quotations parallels the others we have already examined. The first four columns of figures give the open, high, low, and settlement price for the contract, with the quotations in points and 32nds of par. For example, a quoted price of 97–26 means that the contract traded for 97 and 26/32nds of par. The decimal equivalent of this value is 97.8125 percent of par. With a par value of $100,000 per contract, the cash price would be $97,812.50. The next column shows the change since the previous settlement in 32nds. The next column shows the bond yield implied by the futures price, followed by the change in the bond yield since the previous settlement. The final column of figures gives the open interest per contract. The final line in the quotations gives the usual volume and open interest information.

For the T-bond contract, the minimum price fluctuation is 1/32nd of one full percentage point of face value. This means that the minimum price fluctuation per contract is $31.25 [(1/32)(.01)($100,000)]. In normal market conditions, the daily price limit is three full points, or 96 32nds, for a daily price limit of $3,000 per contract, which can be expanded in periods of high volatility.

Delivery against the T-bond contract is a several day process that the short trader can trigger to cause delivery on any business day of the delivery month. Like the T-bill and Eurodollar contracts, the T-bond contract trades for delivery in March, June, September, and December. Delivery can be made on any business day of the delivery month, with the short trader choosing the exact delivery day. To effect delivery, the short trader initiates a delivery sequence that extends over three business days. Figure 4.4 shows the delivery procedure for T-bond futures, a procedure that applies to other Board of Trade contracts, such as the T-note futures contracts.

The **first position day** is the first permissible day for the short trader to declare his or her intention to make delivery, with the delivery taking place two business days later. The first permissible day for such an announcement falls in the month preceding the delivery month, since delivery can occur as soon as the first business day of the delivery month. If the short declares the intention to deliver on any other day besides the first position day, then that day is called **position day**. On position day, the short trader announces the intention to deliver on the second business day thereafter.

The second day in the delivery sequence is the **notice of intention day**. On this day, the Clearing Corporation matches the short trader with the long trader having the longest outstanding position, and identifies the short and long traders to each other. The short trader is then obligated to make delivery to that particular long trader on the next business day. The third and final day of the delivery sequence is **delivery day**, when the actual transaction takes place. On this day the short delivers the financial instrument to the long trader and receives payment. The long trader then has all rights of ownership in the T-bonds that were delivered in fulfillment of the contract.

For the T-bond futures contract, a wide variety of bonds may be delivered against the contract at any one time. The rules of the Board of Trade call for the delivery of $100,000 worth of T-bonds having at least 15 years remaining until maturity or to their first permissible call date.

Table 4.1 presents some key dates in the delivery process for both the T-bond and T-note futures contracts, and Table 4.2 shows the T-bonds eligible for delivery in 1996. The first two columns of Table 4.2 list the coupon rate and maturity date. The rest of the table lists

■ Figure 4.4

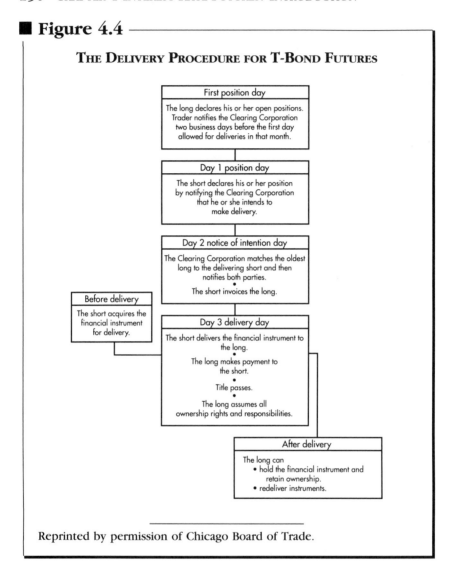

THE DELIVERY PROCEDURE FOR T-BOND FUTURES

Reprinted by permission of Chicago Board of Trade.

conversion factors for each bond and each maturity date. (These conversion factors are explained shortly.)

As Table 4.2 shows, more than 25 different bonds could be delivered against the DEC 96 contract. Coupons on these bonds range from 6 percent to 11.25 percent and the maturities range from 2015 to 2026. With all of these bonds outstanding, quite a few different bonds will be deliverable against the T-bond contract for years to come.

■ Table 4.1

Contract Expiration	First Position	First Notice	First Delivery	Last Trading	Last Delivery
MAR 97	FEB 27	FEB 28	MAR 3	MAR 21	MAR 31
JUN	MAY 29	MAY 30	JUN 2	JUN 20	JUN 30
SEP	AUG 28	AUG 29	SEP 2	SEP 19	SEP 30
DEC	NOV 26	NOV 28	DEC 1	DEC 19	DEC 31

THE DELIVERY SEQUENCE FOR T-BOND AND T-NOTE FUTURES EXPIRING IN 1997

The fact that some bonds are cheap, and some expensive, suggests that there may be an advantage to delivering one bond rather than another. If there is such an advantage, why did the CBOT allow several bonds to be delivered against the contract? These considerations are intimately related and have an important impact on the contract design. The significant differences in maturity and coupon rates among these bonds cause large price differences. Because the short trader chooses whether to make delivery, and which bond to deliver, we might expect that only the cheapest bond would ever be delivered.

To eliminate an incentive to deliver just one particular bond, the CBOT initiated a system of conversion factors which alters the delivery values of different bonds as a function of their coupon rate and term-to-maturity. The conversion factors in Table 4.2 are based on a hypothetical bond with 20 years to maturity and an 8 percent coupon rate. A quick glance at Table 4.2 shows only one such bond existed in the fall of 1996.

For purposes of delivery, the CBOT adjusts the price of every bond using a conversion factor that is specific to a given bond and a particular futures contract expiration. The invoice amount is calculated according to Equation 4.6:

$$\text{Invoice Amount} = \text{DSP}(\$100,000)(\text{CF}) + \text{AI} \qquad (4.6)$$

where:

DSP = decimal settlement price (e.g., 96–16 = .965)
CF = conversion factor
AI = accrued interest

■ Table 4.2

DELIVERABLE T-BONDS AND CONVERSION FACTORS

Coupon	Maturity	JUN 96	SEP 96	DEC 96
6.000	Feb 15, 2026	0.7747	0.7751	0.7757
6.125	Aug 15, 2023	0.8076	0.8079	0.8086
6.875	Aug 15, 2025	0.8738	0.8740	0.8744
7.125	Feb 15, 2023	0.9043	0.9044	0.9049
7.250	May 15, 2016	0.9260	0.9266	0.9268
7.250	Aug 15, 2022	0.9184	0.9185	0.9189
7.500	Nov 15, 2024	0.9441	0.9445	0.9444
7.500	Nov 15, 2016	0.9501	0.9505	0.9506
7.625	Nov 15, 2022	0.9589	0.9592	0.9592
7.625	Feb 15, 2025	0.9581	0.9580	0.9583
7.875	Feb 15, 2021	0.9867	0.9865	0.9868
8.000	Nov 15, 2021	0.9998	1.0000	0.9998
8.125	May 15, 2021	1.0132	1.0133	1.0131
8.125	Aug 15, 2021	1.0134	1.0132	1.0133
8.125	Aug 15, 2019	1.0131	1.0128	1.0130
8.500	Feb 15, 2020	1.0526	1.0522	1.0522
8.750	May 15, 2017	1.0751	1.0750	1.0744
8.750	May 15, 2020	1.0790	1.0789	1.0784
8.750	Aug 15, 2020	1.0795	1.0790	1.0789
8.875	Aug 15, 2017	1.0883	1.0877	1.0875
8.875	Feb 15, 2019	1.0907	1.0901	1.0899
9.000	Nov 15, 2018	1.1030	1.1027	1.1021
9.125	May 15, 2018	1.1149	1.1146	1.1138
9.250	Feb 15, 2016	1.1224	1.1215	1.1210
9.875	Nov 15, 2015	1.1824	1.1816	1.1803
10.625	Aug 15, 2015	1.2542	1.2525	1.2512
11.250	Feb 15, 2015	1.3111	1.3089	1.3073

From Chicago Board of Trade, World Wide Web site. Reprinted by permission of Chicago Board of Trade.

Each term requires comment. The **decimal settlement price** is simply the decimal equivalent of the quoted price, which is expressed in "points and 32nds of par." The $100,000 reflects the contract amount. The conversion factor attempts to adjust for differences in coupons and maturities among the deliverable bonds.

The conversion factor for any bond can be approximated quite accurately by following two rules:

1. Assume that the face value of the bond to be delivered is $1.
2. Discount the assumed cash flows from the bond at 8 percent using the bond pricing equation.

The result approximates the conversion factor for the bond in question. This will only be an approximation, however, because the official conversion factors reflect quarterly intervals between the present and the delivery date. Exact conversion factors are available in the form shown as Table 4.2 from the Chicago Board of Trade.[2] The conversion factors can also be found from these formulas:

For bonds with an even number of full semiannual periods until maturity:

$$CF = \sum_{t=1}^{n} \frac{C_t}{1.04^t} + \frac{1}{1.04^n} \qquad (4.7)$$

For bonds with an uneven number of full semiannual periods until maturity:

$$CF = \frac{\sum_{t=1}^{n} \dfrac{C_t}{1.04^t} + \dfrac{1}{1.04^n} + C_t}{1.04^{.5}} - .5C_t \qquad (4.8)$$

where:

CF = conversion factor
C_t = semiannual coupon payment in dollars assuming a $1 face value bond
n = the number of full semiannual periods remaining from the bond before maturity (or call if the bond is callable)

As examples, we will compute the conversion factors for the SEP 96 and DEC 96 deliveries of the 7¼ bond maturing on May 15, 2016. As we have seen, on September 1, 1996, there were 39 full semiannual periods until maturity on this bond, 38 in the years from November 15, 1996, through November 15, 2016, and one from November 15, 2015, to maturity on May 15, 2016. There were no excess complete quarters, so we can use the simpler formula. Assuming a $1 face value, the semiannual coupon would be $.03625 = .5(.0725).

$$CF = \sum_{t=1}^{39} \frac{.03625}{1.04^t} + \frac{1}{1.04^{39}}$$

$$= .709938 + .216621$$

$$= .9266$$

This matches the conversion factor in the table of .9266.

As a second example, we compute the conversion factor for the same bond for delivery on the DEC 96 contract. On December 1, 1996, we saw that this bond had 38 full semiannual periods and an excess complete quarter before it matures. Therefore, we use the second version of the conversion factor formula. We have:

$$CF = \frac{\sum_{t=1}^{38} \frac{.03625}{1.04^t} + \frac{1}{1.04^{38}} + .03625}{1.04^{.5}} - .5(.03625)$$

$$= \frac{.702085 + .225285 + .036250}{1.04^{.5}} - .018125$$

$$= .9268$$

This value matches the .9268 of Table 4.2.

Looking closely at the conversion factors in Table 4.2, we note that the closer the coupon rate is to 8 percent, the closer the conversion factor will be to 1. For a bond with an 8 percent coupon, the conversion factor would equal 1.0. This makes sense, because the conversion factor would be calculated by discounting an 8 percent coupon instrument at 8 percent. For bonds with coupon rates above 8 percent, the shorter the maturity, the closer the conversion factor will be to 1. Just the opposite holds for bonds with coupon rates below 8 percent. In general, if yields are 8 percent across all maturities, the conversion factors will be proportional to the bonds' market prices. This is exactly the desired situation, since the delivery value of a bond should be proportional to its market value.

With a flat term structure and yields at 8 percent, there is no advantage to delivering any bond rather than another. The correlative of this proposition is somewhat disturbing and very important for T-bond futures. If the term structure is not flat, or if yields are not equal to 8 percent, then there is some bond that is better to deliver than the other permissible bonds. This bond is known as the **cheapest-to-deliver**. Among T-bond futures traders, the concept of the cheapest-to-deliver bond is well known. Most brokerage houses have computer systems that show the cheapest-to-deliver T-bonds on a real time basis. Since this feature is well known, futures prices tend to track the cheapest-to-deliver bond, which may change over time.

The interplay of actual bond market prices and the conversion factor biases noted here determine which bond will be the cheapest-to-deliver at any given moment. Prior to actual delivery, some bond will be the cheapest to acquire and to carry to delivery. We have already noted that the cost-of-carry relationship considers the net financing cost of carrying an asset to delivery. In the T-bond futures market, the net financing cost is the price that must be paid for funds less the coupon rate obtained by holding the bond itself. Therefore, at any particular moment, the cheapest-to-deliver bond will be the bond that is most profitable to deliver. In Chapter 5, we explain how to find the cheapest-to-deliver bond in more detail.

Why did the CBOT adopt this cumbersome system of conversion factors, particularly since it introduces biases into the market? As we have seen, a substantial deliverable supply of the spot commodity is a necessary condition for a successful futures contract. If the supply of the deliverable commodity is insufficient, then opportunities for market corners and squeezes can arise. To ensure a large deliverable supply, the CBOT allowed a wide range of bonds to qualify for delivery. With many bonds eligible for delivery, it is necessary to adjust bond prices to reflect their varying market values.

In futures markets, the short trader usually has choices to make in the delivery process. For example, we have noted that the short trader chooses the exact delivery day in the delivery month and chooses which deliverable bond to deliver. Therefore, the short trader has a number of options embedded in the futures position. These timing and quality options have a value to the seller, so they effectively reduce the prices that we observe in futures markets. Assessing the value of these options for the seller becomes quite complicated. We consider them briefly later in this chapter, and again in Chapter 5.

Treasury Note Futures

T-bonds and T-notes share a very similar structure, but they differ in the term to maturity at which they are initially offered. Both instruments pay semiannual coupons. Just as the spot market instruments are very similar, the T-bond and T-note futures contracts are very similar as well.

There are three T-note futures contracts trading at the Chicago Board of Trade. While similar in structure, these contracts are based on notes of varying maturities. Nominally, the contracts are designated as ten-, five-, and two-year contracts. However, a range of maturities is deliverable against each contract, with maturity being measured on the first day of the delivery month. Deliverable maturities on 21 months to two years for the two-year contract, four years three months to five years three months for the five-year contract, and six years six months up to ten years for the ten-year contract. The contract size for the five- year and ten-year contracts is $100,000 of face value, but it is $200,000 for the two-year contract. By having a larger denomination for the two-year contract, the CBOT brings the volatilities of the contracts into the same range. This difference in the volatility of the underlying bonds leads to differences in price quotations. For the two-year, the tick size is one-quarter of a 32nd, while the five-year contract has a one-half of a 32nd tick size. Each contract allows for a range of deliverable maturities, thereby increasing the deliverable supply for each contract.

The T-note and T-bond contracts use the same system of conversion factors as the T-bond contract, and they have the same delivery system. The ten-year and five-year contracts have substantial trading volume and open interest. The two-year contract started trading on June 22, 1990. Although the trading volume and open interest on this contract increased in the years following its inception, it still remains quite small compared to the five-year and ten-year contracts. Price movements of T-bonds and T-notes are closely related.

Pricing Interest Rate Futures Contracts

Introduction

Interest rate futures trade in markets that are virtually always at full carry. In other words, the cost-of-carry model provides a complete understanding of the price structure of interest rate futures contracts.

To understand why the cost-of-carry model fits interest rate futures, recall our discussion in Chapter 2. There we identified five features of the underlying good that promote full carry: ease of short selling, large supply of the underlying good, nonseasonal production, nonseasonal consumption, and ease of storage.

The goods that underlie the major interest rate futures contracts meet these conditions very well. First, bonds are created and mature in a nonseasonal way, so the restrictions on seasonality are met almost perfectly. Second, storage is virtually effortless. Most Treasury securities exist only in computer records, and are not even committed to paper. Third, the supply is incredibly ample. For the most important contracts, the underlying instruments are highly liquid debt instruments. For the three T-note contracts, the T-bond contract, and the T-bill contract, the underlying instruments are all issues of the U.S. Treasury. These instruments are available in huge supply and trade in a highly liquid market. The Eurodollar bond contract deals with deliverable supply by avoiding delivery completely. It uses cash settlement. Finally, short selling is very well developed in this market. Because these securities are held in such large amounts by futures market participants, these traders can simulate short selling by selling some of their inventory of Treasury securities. Therefore, it appears that interest rate futures prices should behave like the cost-of-carry model in a perfect market. That is, interest rate futures markets should be at full carry.

In Chapter 2 we considered the cost-of-carry model in perfect markets and concluded that the futures price should equal the spot price plus the cost of carrying the spot good forward to delivery on the futures contract:

$$F_{0,t} = S_0(1 + C) \tag{2.3}$$

We also concluded that a similar relationship must hold between a nearby futures price and a distant futures price:

$$F_{0,d} = F_{0,n}(1 + C) \tag{2.6}$$

where:

$F_{0,t}$ = current futures price for a contract that expires at time t
S_0 = current spot price
C = percentage cost-of-carry between two dates
$F_{0,n}$ = nearby futures price
$F_{0,d}$ = distant futures price

Finally, if we assumed that the only carrying cost is the financing cost, we also concluded that dividing the futures price by the spot price yielded an **implied repo rate**:

$$\frac{F_{0,t}}{S_0} = 1 + C \qquad (2.7)$$

where:

C = the implied repo rate

As we will see, the model applies very well to interest rate futures. However, we must take into account some of the peculiarities of debt instruments.

The Cost-of-Carry Model in Perfect Markets

In this section, we apply the cost-of-carry model to interest rate futures under the assumption of perfect markets. In addition, we assume that the only carrying charge is the interest rate to finance the holding of a good, and we assume that we can disregard the special features of a given futures contract. For example, we ignore the options that sellers of futures contracts may hold, such as the option to substitute various grades of the commodity at delivery or the option to choose the exact delivery date within the delivery month, and we ignore the differences between forward and futures prices that may result from the daily resettlement cash flows on the futures contract. In summary, we are assuming:

1. markets are perfect,
2. the financing cost is the only carrying charge,
3. we can ignore the options that the seller may possess, and
4. we can ignore the differences between forward and futures prices.

Later in this chapter, we will relax these assumptions.

Each interest rate futures contract we have considered specifies the maturity of the deliverable bond. For example, the T-bill futures contract requires that a deliverable T-bill must have a maturity of 90–92 days. This requirement applies on the delivery date. As we saw in Chapter 2, the cash-and-carry strategy involves selling a futures contract, buying the spot commodity, and storing it until the futures delivery date. Then the trader delivers the good against the futures contract. For example, if the futures price of gold is too high relative to the cash market price of gold, a trader could engage in a cash-and-carry arbitrage. Part of this strategy would involve buying gold, storing until the futures expiration, and delivering the gold against the futures contract.

To apply this strategy in the interest rate futures market, we must be very careful. For example, if a T-bill futures contract expires in 77 days, we cannot buy a 90-day T-bill and store it for future delivery. If we attempt to do so, we will find ourselves with a 13-day T-bill on the delivery date. This will not be deliverable against the futures contract. Therefore, to apply a cash-and-carry strategy, a trader must buy a bond that will still have or come to have the correct properties on the delivery date. For our T-bill cash-and-carry strategy, the trader must secure a 167-day T-bill to carry for 77 days. Then the bill will have the requisite 90 days remaining until expiration on the delivery date.

We illustrate the cash-and-carry strategy with an example. Consider the data in Table 4.3. The yields used in Table 4.3 are not the discount yields of the IMM Index, but the yields calculated according to the bond pricing formula. The example assumes perfect markets, including the assumption that one can either borrow or lend at any of the riskless rates represented by the T-bill yields. These restrictive assumptions will be relaxed momentarily. The data presented in Table 4.3, and the assumptions just made, mean that an arbitrage opportunity

■ **Table 4.3**

INTEREST RATE FUTURES AND ARBITRAGE

Today's Date: January 5

Futures	Yield According to the Bond Pricing Formula
MAR Contract (Matures in 77 days on March 22)	12.50%
Cash Bills:	
167-day T-bill (Deliverable on MAR futures)	10
77-day T-bill	6

is present. Since the futures contract matures in 77 days, the spot 77-day rate represents the financing cost to acquire the 167-day T-bill, which can be delivered against the MAR futures contract on March 22. This is possible because the T-bill that has 167 days to maturity on January 5 will have exactly 90 days to maturity on March 22.

As the transactions presented in Table 4.4 indicate, an arbitrage opportunity exists because the prices and interest rates on the three instruments are mutually inconsistent. To implement a cash-and-carry strategy, a trader can sell the MAR futures and acquire the 167-day T-bill on January 5. The trader then holds the bill for delivery against the futures contract. The trader must finance the holding of the bill during the 77-day interval from January 5 to delivery on March 22. To exploit the rate discrepancy, the trader borrows at the short-term rate of 6 percent and uses the proceeds to acquire the long-term T-bill. At the maturity of the futures, the long-term T-bill has the exactly correct maturity and can be delivered against the futures contract. This strategy generates a profit of $2,235 per contract. Relative to the short-term rate, the futures yield and the long-term T-bill yield were too high. In this example, the trader acquires short-term funds at a low rate (6 percent) and reinvests those funds at a higher rate (10 percent). It may appear that this difference generates the arbitrage profit, but that is not completely accurate, as the next example shows.[3]

Consider the same values as shown in Table 4.3, but now assume that the rate on the 77-day T-bill is 8 percent. Now the short-term

■ Table 4.4

CASH-AND-CARRY ARBITRAGE TRANSACTIONS

January 5
Borrow $956,750 for 77 days by issuing a 77-day T-bill at 6%.
Buy 167-day T-bill yielding 10% for $956,750.
Sell MAR T-bill futures contract with a yield of 12.50% for $970,984.

March 22
Deliver the originally purchased T-bill against the MAR futures contract and collect $970,984.
Repay debt on 77-day T-bill that matures today for $968,749.

$$\begin{array}{rr} \text{Profit:} & \$970,984 \\ & -\ 968,749 \\ \hline & \$\quad 2,235 \end{array}$$

rate is too high relative to the long-term rate and the futures yield. To take advantage of this situation, we reverse the cash-and-carry procedure of Table 4.4, as Table 4.5 shows. In other words, we now exploit a reverse cash-and-carry strategy. With this new set of rates, the arbitrage is more complicated, since it involves holding the T-bill that is delivered on the futures contract. In this situation, the arbitrageur borrows $955,131 for 167 days at 10 percent and invests these funds at 8 percent for the 77 days until the MAR futures matures. The payoff from the 77-day investment of $955,131 will be $970,984, exactly enough to pay for the delivery of the T-bill on the futures contract. This bill is held for 90 days until June 20 when it matures and pays $1,000,000. On June 20, the arbitrageur's loan on the 167-day T-bill is also due, and equals $998,308. This trader repays this debt from the $1,000,000 received on the maturing bill. The strategy yields a profit of $1,692. Notice in this second example that the trader borrowed at 10 percent and invested the funds at 8 percent temporarily. This shows that it is the entire set of rates that must be consistent and that arbitrage opportunities need not only involve misalignment between two rates.

■ Table 4.5

REVERSE CASH-AND-CARRY ARBITRAGE TRANSACTIONS

January 5
Borrow $955,131 by issuing a 167-day T-bill at 10%.
Buy a 77-day T-bill yielding 8% for $955,131 that will pay $970,984 on March 22.
Buy one MAR futures contract with a yield of 12.50% for $970,984.

March 22
Collect $970,984 from the maturing 77-day T-bill.
Pay $970,984 and take delivery of a 90-day T-bill from the MAR futures contract.

June
Collect $1,000,000 from the maturing 90-day T-bill that was delivered on the futures contract.
Pay $998,308 debt on the maturing 167-day T-bill.

	Profit:	$1,000,000
	−	998,308
	$	1,692

From our analyses in Chapter 2, we know that the reverse cash-and-carry strategy involves selling an asset short and investing the proceeds from the short sale. In our example of Table 4.5, the short sale is the issuance of debt. By issuing debt, the arbitrageur literally sells a bond. In Chapter 2, we also noted that a trader could simulate a short sale by selling from inventory. The same is true for interest rate futures. For example, a bank that holds investments in T-bills can simulate a short sale by selling a T-bill from inventory.

To this point, we have considered a cash-and-carry strategy in Table 4.4 and a reverse cash-and-carry strategy in Table 4.5. These two examples show that there must be a very exact relationship among these rates on the different instruments to exclude arbitrage opportunities. If the yield on the MAR futures is 12.50 percent and the 167-day spot yield is 10 percent, there is only one yield for the 77-day T-bill that will not give rise to an arbitrage opportunity, and that rate is 7.15 percent. To see why that is the case, consider two ways of holding a T-bill investment for the full 167-day period of the examples:

1. hold the 167-day T-bill, or
2. hold a 77-day T-bill followed by a 90-day T-bill that is delivered on the futures contract.

Since these two ways of holding T-bills cover the same time period and have the same risk level, the two positions must have the same yield to avoid arbitrage. For the examples, the necessary yield on the 77-day T-bill can be found by using an equation expressing the yield on a long-term instrument as being equal to the yield on two short-term positions:

$$(1.10)^{167/360} = (1 + x)^{77/360}(1.1250)^{90/360}$$

This equation holds only if the rate, x, on the 77-day T-bill equals 7.1482 percent.

We can also express the same idea in terms of the prices of the bills. To illustrate this point, consider the prices of three securities. The first is a 167-day bill that yields 10.00 percent and pays $1 upon maturity. Second is a T-bill futures with an underlying bill having a $1 face value. With a yield of 12.50 percent, the futures price will be $.970984. Finally, the third instrument matures in 77 days, has a face value of $.970984, and yields 7.1482 percent.

$$P_{167} = \frac{\$1}{(1 + r_{167})^{167/360}} = \frac{\$1}{1.1^{167/360}} = .956750$$

$$P_F = \frac{\$1}{(1 + r_{fut})^{90/360}} = \frac{\$1}{1.1250^{90/360}} = .970984$$

$$P_{77} = \frac{\$.970984}{(1 + r_{77})^{77/360}} = \frac{\$.970984}{1.071482^{77/360}} = .956750$$

The third instrument is peculiar, with its strange face value. However, this is exactly the payoff necessary to pay for delivery on the futures contract in 77 days. Notice also that the 77-day bill and the 167-day bill have the same price. They should, because both prices of $.956750 are the investment now that is necessary to have a $1 payoff in 167 days. The futures yield and the 167-day yield were taken as fixed. The yield on the 77-day bill, 7.1482 percent, is exactly the yield that must prevail if the two strategies are to be equivalent and to prevent arbitrage.

The Financing Cost and the Implied Repo Rate. With these prices, and continuing to assume that the only carrying cost is the financing charge, we can also infer the implied repo rate. We know that the ratio of the futures price divided by the spot price equals 1 plus the implied repo rate. As we have seen, the correct spot instrument for our example is the 167-day bill, because this bill will have the appropriate delivery characteristics when the futures matures. Thus, we have:

$$1 + C = \frac{P_F}{P_{167}} = \frac{.970984}{.956750} = 1.014878$$

The implied repo rate, C, is 1.4878 percent. This covers the cost-of-carry for 77 days from the present to the expiration of the futures. We can annualize this rate as follows:

$$1.014878^{360/77} = 1.071482$$

The annualized repo rate is 7.1482 percent. This exactly matches the interest rate on the 77-day bill that will prevent arbitrage. Therefore, assuming that the interest cost is the only carrying charge, the cost-of-carry equals the implied repo rate.

This equivalence between the cost-of-carry and the implied repo rate also leads to two rules for arbitrage.

1. If the implied repo rate exceeds the financing cost, then exploit a cash-and-carry arbitrage opportunity: borrow funds; buy the cash bond; sell futures; hold the bond and deliver against futures.
2. If the implied repo rate is less than the financing cost, then exploit a reverse cash-and-carry arbitrage opportunity: buy futures; sell the bond short and invest proceeds until futures expires; take delivery on futures; repay short sale obligation.

The Futures Yield and the Forward Rate of Interest. We have seen that the futures price of an interest rate futures contract implies a yield on the instrument that underlies the futures contract. We call this implied yield the futures yield. Now we continue to assume that the financing cost is the only carrying charge, that markets are perfect, that we can ignore the options that the seller of a futures contract may possess, and that the price difference between forward contracts and futures contracts is negligible. Under these conditions, we can show that the futures yield must equal the forward rate of interest.

We continue to use the T-bill futures contract as our example. The T-bill futures, like many other interest rate futures contracts, has an underlying instrument that will be delivered when the contract expires. If we consider a SEP contract, it calls for the delivery of a 90-day T-bill that will mature in December. The futures yield covers the 90-day span of time from delivery in September to maturity in December. Given the necessary set of spot rates, it is possible to compute a forward rate to cover any given period.

To illustrate the equivalence between futures yields and forward rates under our assumptions, we continue to use our example of a T-bill with a 167-day holding period. Let us assume the following spot yields:

For a 167-day bill   10.0000%
For a 77-day bill   7.1482%

These two spot rates imply a forward rate to cover the period from day 77 to day 167:

$$(1 + r_{0,167})^{167/360} = (1 + r_{0,77})^{77/360}(1 + r_{77,167})^{90/360}$$

Substituting values for the spot bills and solving for the forward rate, $r_{77,167}$, gives:

$$(1.10)^{167/360} = (1.071482)^{77/360}(1 + r_{77,167})^{90/360}$$

$$(1 + r_{77,167})^{90/360} = \frac{(1.10)^{167/360}}{(1.071482)^{77/360}} = \frac{1.045205}{1.014877} = 1.029884$$

$$1 + r_{77,167} = 1.1250$$

$$r_{77,167} = .1250$$

Therefore, the forward rate, to cover day 77 to day 167, is 12.50 percent. As we saw earlier, the futures yield is also 12.50 percent for the T-bill futures that expires on day 77. Therefore, the futures yield equals the forward rate for the same period. In deriving this result, we must bear our assumptions in mind: markets are perfect, the financing cost is the only carrying charge, and we ignore the seller's options and the difference between forward and futures prices.

THE COST-OF-CARRY MODEL FOR T-BOND FUTURES

In this section we apply the cost-of-carry model to the T-bond futures contract. In essence, the same concepts apply, with one difference. The holder of a T-bond receives cash flows from the bond, which affects the cost-of-carry that the holder of the bond actually incurs. For example, assume that the coupon rate on a $100,000 face value T-bond is 8 percent and the trader finances the bond at 8 percent. In this case, the net carrying charge is zero – the earnings offset the financing cost.

To illustrate this idea, let us assume that, on January 5, a T-bond that is deliverable on a futures contract has an 8 percent coupon and costs 100.00. The trader faces a financing rate of 7.1482 percent for the 77 days until the futures contract is deliverable. Because the T-bond has an 8 percent coupon rate, the conversion factor is 1.0 and plays no role. With an 8 percent coupon, the accrued interest from the date of purchase to the delivery date on the futures is:

$$(77/182)(.04)(100,000) = \$1,692$$

Therefore, the invoice amount will be $101,692. If this is the invoice amount in 77 days, the T-bond must cost the present value of that amount, discounted for 77 days at the 77-day rate of 7.1482 percent. This implies a cost for the T-bond of $100,200. If the price is less than $100,200, a cash-and-carry arbitrage strategy will be available. Under these circumstances the cash-and-carry strategy would have the cash flows shown in Table 4.6.

The transactions in Table 4.6 show that the futures price must adjust to reflect the accrual of interest. The bond in Table 4.6 had no coupon payment during the 77-day interval, but the same adjustment must be made to account for cash throwoffs that the bondholder receives during the holding period.

The Cost-of-Carry Model in Imperfect Markets

We now relax our assumption of perfect markets and see how the cost-of-carry model applies to interest rate futures. Specifically, we will focus on the possibility that the borrowing and lending rates may differ. We continue to ignore the seller's options and the price differences between forward and futures contracts. Thus, in this section we analyze the cost-of-carry model for the situation in which:

1. the borrowing rate exceeds the lending rate,
2. the financing cost is the only carrying charge,
3. we can ignore the options that the seller may possess, and
4. we can ignore the differences between forward and futures prices.

In Chapter 2 we saw that allowing the borrowing and lending rates to differ leads to an arbitrage band around the futures price. For

■ Table 4.6

Cash-and-Carry Transactions for a T-Bond

January 5
Borrow $100,200 for 77 days at the 77-day rate of 7.1482%.
Buy the 8% T-bond for $100,200.
Sell one T-bond futures contract for $101,692.

March 22
Deliver T-bond; receive invoice amount of $101,692.
Repay loan of $101,692.

Profit: 0

example, let us assume that the borrowing rate is 25 basis points, or one-fourth of a percentage point, higher than the lending rates. Continuing to use our T-bill example, we have:

Instrument	Lending Rate	Borrowing Rate
77-day bill	7.1482	7.3982
167-day bill	10.0000	10.2500

These assumptions approximate real market conditions. For example, a bank might be able to lend funds to the government by buying a T-bill. To borrow, however, the bank might have to transact at a somewhat higher repo rate.

When it was possible to both borrow and lend at the same rate, our earlier examples showed that the futures yield must be 12.50 percent. Now, with these different borrowing and lending rates, we want to determine how the futures yield can vary from 12.50 percent. To do this we apply the cash-and-carry and reverse cash-and-carry strategies. In both cases, we find the futures price that gives exactly a zero gain or loss on the strategy.

In the cash-and-carry strategy, we sell the futures and borrow in order to buy a good that we can deliver on the futures contract. Table 4.7 details the transactions with unequal borrowing and lending rates. The table illustrates the highest futures yield and lowest futures price that gives a zero profit with the unequal borrowing and lending rates. From this example, we see that the futures yield can be as low as

■ **Table 4.7**

CASH-AND-CARRY TRANSACTIONS WITH UNEQUAL BORROWING
AND LENDING RATES

January 5
Borrow $956,750 for 77 days at the 77-day borrowing rate of 7.3982%.
Buy 167-day T-bill yielding 10% for $956,750.
Sell one T-bill futures contract with a yield of 12.2760% for $971,468.

March 22
Deliver the originally purchased T-bill against the MAR futures contract and collect $971,468.
Repay debt on 77-day T-bill that matures today for $971,468.

Profit: 0

12.2760 percent without generating an arbitrage opportunity. This futures yield implies that the futures price can be as high as $971,468 and still not generate an arbitrage opportunity.

We now consider the reverse cash-and-carry strategy. Here, we will borrow long-term to finance a short-term investment and we purchase the futures. When the futures expires, we accept delivery and hold the delivered good until the bond matures. Table 4.8 illustrates the transactions that show how high the futures yield can be and how low the futures price can be without providing an arbitrage opportunity.

From the transactions in Table 4.8, we see that the futures yield can be as high as 12.9751 percent without providing an arbitrage opportunity. Similarly, the corresponding futures price can be as low as $969,961 without creating an arbitrage opportunity.

With equal borrowing and lending rates in our earlier examples, we saw that the futures yield had to be exactly 12.50 percent and the futures price had to be $970,984. The unequal borrowing and lending rates create a no-arbitrage band for the futures. Now the futures yield must fall in the range from 12.2760 to 12.9751 percent, and the futures price must lie in the range $969,961 to $971,468. As

■ Table 4.8

REVERSE CASH-AND-CARRY TRANSACTIONS WITH UNEQUAL BORROWING AND LENDING RATES

January 5
Borrow $955,743 at the 167-day borrowing rate of 10.25%.
Buy a 77-day T-bill yielding 7.1482% for $955,743.
Buy one MAR futures contract with a futures yield of 12.9751% for $969,961.

March 22
Collect $969,961 from the maturing 77-day T-bill.
Pay $969,961 and take delivery of a 90-day T-bill on the futures contract.

June
Collect $1,000,000 from the maturing 90-day T-bill that was delivered on the futures contract.
Pay $1,000,000 debt on the maturing 167-day T-bill.

Profit: 0

long as the futures yield and futures price stay within these respective ranges, arbitrage will not be possible.

A PRACTICAL SURVEY OF INTEREST RATE FUTURES PRICING

If markets are perfect, if the only carrying charge is the financing cost, if we ignore the seller's options, and if we ignore differences between futures and forward prices, we have seen how the cost-of-carry model specifies an exact futures yield and futures price. If we allow market imperfections in the form of unequal borrowing and lending rates, we have seen that the cost-of-carry model leads to a no-arbitrage band of possible futures prices. Now we provide a practical approach to include other market imperfections in our analysis.

In Chapter 2 we considered transaction costs, a typical market imperfection. There we saw that transaction costs lead to a no-arbitrage band of possible futures prices. In essence, transaction costs increase the no-arbitrage band just as unequal borrowing and lending rates do. In Chapter 2, we also considered impediments to short selling as a market imperfection that would frustrate the reverse cash-and-carry arbitrage strategy. From a practical perspective, restrictions on short selling are relatively unimportant in interest rate futures pricing. First, supplies of deliverable Treasury securities are plentiful, and government securities have little (or zero) convenience yield. Second, because Treasury securities are so widely held, many traders can simulate short selling by selling T-bills, T-notes, or T-bonds from inventory. Therefore, restrictions on short selling are unlikely to have any pricing effect.

In our analysis of the cost-of-carry model, we found that the futures yield must equal the forward rate of interest, under our assumptions. By assuming that we could ignore the difference between forward and futures prices, we implicitly assumed that we could ignore the effect of daily resettlement cash flows on pricing. However, in Chapter 2 we saw that daily resettlement cash flows could affect pricing of the futures contract if the price of the cash commodity were correlated with interest rates. In the interest rate futures market, the underlying goods are highly correlated with interest rates. Therefore, we might expect to find differences between futures and forward prices, and between futures and forward yields. In Chapter 2, we saw that a negative correlation between the price of the cash commodity and interest rates would lead to a futures price that is less than the forward price. This is exactly the situation with interest rate futures, because bond prices fall as interest rates rise. Therefore, we would expect the futures price to be less than the forward price. However, most studies indicate that this is not a serious problem in general. From a practical point of view, this difference is unlikely to be critical.

In the construction of interest rate futures contracts, we have seen that the seller of a futures contract possesses timing and quality options that may be valuable. For example, the seller of a T-bond futures possesses a timing option because she can decide which day of the delivery month to deliver. Likewise, the seller possesses a quality option, because she can decide which bond to deliver. The buyer of the futures knows that the seller acquires these options by selling the futures. Therefore, the futures price must adjust to account for those options. This means that the futures price with the seller's options must be less than it would be if it had no options attached.

Studies have shown that the seller's options can have significant value. We consider this issue in more detail in Chapter 4. Here we note that these options have sufficient value to be of practical importance in using interest rate futures.

INTEREST RATE FUTURES PRICING: AN EXAMPLE

We conclude our discussion of interest rate futures pricing in this chapter by applying the cost-of-carry model to actual market data. For this illustration, we consider the difference between a JUN and SEP T-bond futures prices. Under the simplifying assumptions made earlier, we would expect these two prices to be closely related by the financing cost of carrying a bond from June to September. We know that market imperfections, the difference between futures and forward prices, and the seller's options might all disturb this relationship. Nonetheless, we expect the main component of this price difference to be tied to the financing cost from September to December.

To apply this idea to actual data, we use the JUN T-bill futures contract to provide a proxy for the financing rate to hold a T-bond from June to September. To accept delivery on the JUN T-bond futures and carry the delivered bond forward to the September delivery involves paying the invoice price to acquire the bond, financing the bond for three months at the JUN T-bill rate, receiving the accrued interest on the bond (which we estimate as having an 8 percent coupon rate), and selling the SEP futures. In a perfect market, this strategy should yield a zero profit. In other words, we expect the quantity:

$$F_{0,d} + AI - F_{0,n}(1 + C) = 0 \qquad (4.9)$$

where:

$F_{0,d}$ = SEP T-bond futures price
$F_{0,n}$ = JUN T-bond futures price plus accrued interest due
at delivery
C = three month cost-of-carry estimated from JUN T-bill
futures
AI = interest accrued from T-bond in September, estimated at
$2,000 per contract (8 percent per year on $100,000
for one quarter)

Figure 4.5 graphs the value of Equation 4.9 for a one contract position. In an absolutely perfect market, we expect the value to be zero. As Figure 4.5 shows, it is extremely close to zero. The minimum value is –$202, and the maximum value is $48. Thus, the graph of the value

■ **Figure 4.5**

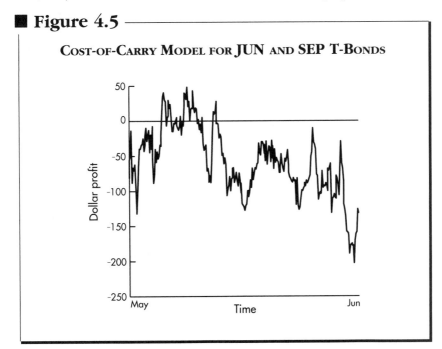

COST-OF-CARRY MODEL FOR **JUN** AND **SEP** T-BONDS

of Equation 4.9 ranges from −2/10 of 1 percent to +1/20 of 1 percent. These values are all the closer considering the crude estimate of the accrued interest and the fact that we did not even attempt to find the cheapest-to-deliver bond. Presumably, a more exacting analysis would lead to yet smaller discrepancies.

Speculating with Interest Rate Futures

In the interest rate futures market, it is possible to speculate by holding an outright position, or by trading a spread. An outright position, such as buying a T-bill futures, is a simple bet on the direction of interest rates. More sophisticated speculative strategies involve trading spreads. As we discussed in Chapter 3, a spread speculation involves a bet on a change in the relationship between two futures prices. In this section we consider some basic speculative strategies and illustrate them with examples.

The concept of a speculative profit is a very slippery notion, as we discussed in Chapter 3. A speculator might earn accounting profits that constitute a justifiable return to the application of his capital and energies. This is different from economic profit or an economic rent, which would be a profit in excess of return for the use of capital and the bearing of risk. Accounting profits are consistent with market efficiency, but economic profits are not. As the speculative strategies of this section are considered, it is important to keep these different conceptions of profit in mind.

Speculating with Outright Positions

For a speculator with an outright position in futures, the speculation is very simple. The long trader is betting that interest rates will fall so that the price of the futures will rise. The short trader is betting that interest rates will rise so that the futures price will fall.

As an example of an outright speculation, we consider a trader who anticipated rising interest rates on September 20, 1990, following the Iraqi invasion of Kuwait. In particular, the trader believes that short-term rates will rise, so she trades the Eurodollar contract as shown in Table 4.9. To profit from rising rates, the trader must be short in interest rate futures. Accordingly, she sells one DEC 90 Eurodollar contract at 90.30. Five days later, interest rates have risen and the futures contract trades at 90.12. Satisfied with the profit, she sells,

■ Table 4.9

SPECULATING WITH EURODOLLAR FUTURES

Date	Futures Market
September 20	Sell 1 DEC 90 Eurodollar futures at 90.30.
September 25	Buy 1 DEC 90 Eurodollar futures at 90.12.

Profit: 90.30 − 90.12 = .18

Total Gain: 18 basis points × $25 = $450

for a gain of 18 basis points. Because each basis point is worth $25, her total profit is $450.

SPECULATING WITH SPREADS

For the most part, speculation with interest rate futures relies on spread trading. An intracommodity spread is typically a speculation on the term structure of interest rates, for example, a spread between the nearby and distant T-bill futures. An intercommodity spread can be a speculation on the changing shape of the yield curve, or it can be a speculation on shifting risk levels between different instruments. For example, T-bills and T-bonds have the same default risk, so a bond/bill spread is a yield curve speculation. Often, an inter-commodity spread is a speculation on changing risk levels between different instruments, for example, a spread between T-bills and Euro-dollars. Of course, a given spread could combine features of both term structure and risk structure speculations. This section illustrates various types of spread speculation.

An Intracommodity T-Bill Spread. Table 4.10 presents a series of spot rates and futures rates for T-bills. As the spot rates show, the yield curve slopes upward, with three-month bills yielding 10 percent and 12-month bills yielding 12 percent. The table shows three futures contracts, with the nearby contract maturing in three months. For the futures contracts, the futures yields are consistent with the term structure given by the spot rates, in the sense that the futures yields equal the forward rates from the term structure. Faced with such circumstances, particularly with a very steep upward sloping yield curve, a speculator might believe that the term structure would flatten within six months. Even if one were not sure whether rates were

■ Table 4.10

SPOT AND FUTURES T-BILL RATES FOR MARCH 20

Time to Maturity or Futures Expiration	Spot Rates	Futures Contract	Futures Yield	IMM Index
3 months	10.00%	JUN	12.00%	88.0
6 months	11.00	SEP	12.5	87.5
9 months	11.50	DEC	13.5	86.5
12 months	12.00			

going to rise or fall, the speculator could still profit from a T-bill futures spread by entering the transactions shown in Table 4.11.

If the yield curve flattens, the yield spread between successively maturing futures contracts must narrow. Currently, the yield spread between the DEC and SEP futures contracts is 100 basis points. By buying the more distant DEC contract and selling the SEP contract, the trader bets that the yield differential will narrow. If the yield curve flattens, no matter whether the general level of rates rises or falls, then this spread strategy gives a profit. As Table 4.11 shows, yields have fallen dramatically by April 30. The yield on the DEC contract has fallen from 13.50 percent to 11.86 percent and the SEP yield has

■ Table 4.11

SPECULATION ON T-BILL FUTURES

Date	Futures Market
March 20	Buy the DEC T-bill futures at 86.50. Sell the SEP T-bill futures at 87.50.
April 30	Sell the DEC T-bill futures at 88.14. Buy the SEP T-bill futures at 89.02.

Profits:

DEC	SEP
88.14	87.50
−86.50	−89.02
1.64	−1.52

Total Gain: 12 basis points × $25 = $300

moved from 12.50 percent to 10.98 percent. For the profits on this speculative strategy, the important point is that the yield spread has changed from 100 basis points to 88 basis points. This generates a profit on the spread of 12 basis points, or $300 because each basis point change represents $25. The same kind of result could have been obtained in a market with rising rates, as long as the yield curve flattens.

This example shows that all interest rate futures intracommodity spreads are speculations on the changing shape of the yield curve. No matter what change in the shape of the yield curve is anticipated, there is a way to profit from that change by trading the correct interest rate futures spread.

A T-Bill/T-Bond Spread. To illustrate the use of spreads more completely, consider a flat yield curve, with the rates shown in Table 4.12. Here all rates, spot and futures, are at 12 percent, representing a perfectly flat yield curve. If a trader believes that the yield curve is going to become upward sloping, two strategies could take advantage of this belief. First, the trader could use an intracommodity spread similar to the spread of Table 4.11. Since the speculator anticipates a positively sloping yield curve, he or she could sell the distant T-bill futures and buy the nearby T-bill futures. This spread would be speculating that the yield curve would become upward sloping for the very low maturity instruments represented by the T-bills.

With an upward sloping yield curve, however, we would expect the greatest difference in yields between short maturity and long maturity instruments, that is, between T-bills and T-bonds. This implies that long-term yields are expected to rise relative to short-term yields. To take advantage of this anticipated change in yields, the trader might use an intercommodity spread, as shown in Table 4.13.

■ Table 4.12

Spot and Futures Yields, June 20

Cash Market	Yield	Futures Market	Yield	Price
3-month T-bill	12.00%	SEP T-bill	12.00%	88
6-month T-bill	12.00	DEC T-bill	12.00	88
10-3/8s 2007-12	12.00	SEP T-bond	12.00	
		DEC T-bond	12.00	

■ **Table 4.13** ─────────────────────────────────────

INTERCOMMODITY SPREAD SPECULATION

Date	Futures Market
June 20	Sell the DEC T-bond futures at 69–29 with a yield of 12%. Buy the DEC T-bill futures at 88.00 with a yield of 12%.
October 24	Buy the DEC T-bond futures at 65–24 with a yield of 12.78%. Sell the DEC T-bill futures at 87.80 with a yield of 12.20%.

Profits:

T-bond	T-bill
69–29	87.80
−65–24	−88.00
4–05	−.20
= $4,156.25	= −$500

Total Profit: $3,656.25

If long-term yields are expected to rise relative to short-term yields, the best spread strategy calls for selling the futures contract on a long-term instrument while buying a futures on a short-term instrument. This is exactly the course pursued by a speculator who transacts as shown in Table 4.13. With yields at 12 percent, the T-bond instrument has a price of 69–29, and the T-bill futures price is 88.00. By October 14, yields have moved as anticipated, with T-bond futures yields at 12.778 percent and the T-bill futures at 12.20 percent. For the T-bond contract, this gives a price change of 4–05. Since each 32nd of a point of par represents $31.25 on a T-bond futures contract, this gives a total profit on the T-bond contract of $4,156.25. On the T-bill side, rates have not risen as rapidly, only 20 basis points. Since each basis point represents $25, there is a loss on the T-bill futures of $500. When the T-bill loss is offset against the T-bond gain, the net profit from the speculation is $3,656.25.

In this example, we assumed that one T-bond and one T-bill contract were traded. Often such a procedure will not be the best, since different futures contracts have different price volatilities. In this case, the T-bond yield moved almost four times as much as the T-bill yield, but the T-bond price moved more than eight times as much in terms of dollars. This difference in the sensitivity of prices can be very important, both for speculating and for hedging. Notice, also, that both contracts were traded for the same futures delivery month. This shows that a speculative strategy focusing on yield curve changes need not employ different futures maturities. It will be necessary, however, to use either different futures expiration months, or different contracts.

A T-Bill/Eurodollar (TED) Spread. Another basic kind of speculation possible in the interest rate futures market is a speculation on the changing risk structure of interest rates. In these days of a continuing international debt crisis, there is danger for banks heavily engaged in international lending, with great fear of widespread default on the part of many third world nations. A speculator might view this situation as offering potential opportunity. If the crisis developed, we might expect to find a widening of the yield spread between T-bill deposits and Eurodollar deposits, for example. This widening yield spread would reflect the changing perception of the risk involved in holding Eurodollar deposits in the face of potentially very large loan losses. In February, assume that yields for the DEC T-bill and Eurodollar futures contracts are 8.82 and 9.71 percent, respectively. If the full riskiness of the banks' position has yet to be understood, we might expect the yield spread to widen. This would be the case whether interest rates were rising or falling. To take advantage of this belief, a trader could sell the DEC Eurodollar contract and buy the DEC T-bill contract, as Table 4.14 shows.

Since the trader expects the yield spread to widen, he or she sells the Eurodollar contract and buys the T-bill contract for Index values of 90.29 and 91.18, respectively. Later, on October 14, the yield spread of the example has, in fact, widened, with T-bill yields having moved up slightly so the spread has widened by 27 basis points, which means a profit of $675 on the speculation.

Perhaps the single most important point about speculation can be emphasized using this example. Virtually everyone is aware of the problems being faced by banks involved in international lending, with articles appearing almost daily in *The Wall Street Journal*. Therefore, the futures prices must already have embedded in them the market's expectation of the future yield spread between T-bills and Eurodollars.

■ Table 4.14

INTERCOMMODITY SPREAD IN SHORT-TERM RATES	

Date	Futures Market
February 17	Sell one DEC Eurodollar futures contract with an IMM Index value of 90.29. Buy one DEC T-bill futures contract yielding 8.82% with an IMM Index value of 91.18.
October 14	Buy one DEC Eurodollar futures contract with an IMM Index value of 89.91. Sell one DEC T-bill futures contract yielding 8.93% with an IMM Index value of 91.07.

Profits:

Eurodollar	T-bill
90.29	91.07
−89.91	−91.18
.38	−.11

Total Profit: 27 basis points × $25 = $675

By engaging in the speculative strategy discussed here, a trader speculates against the rest of the market. It was not enough to expect yield spreads to widen, but the trader must have expected them to widen more than the market expected. And the trader must have been right to make a profit. This spread relationship is so well known that it has a name – the TED spread (Treasury/Eurodollar).[4]

Notes Over Bonds, the NOB Trade. Like the TED spread, other strategies are sufficiently popular to earn nicknames. The NOB is a speculative strategy for trading T-note futures against T-bond futures. The term "NOB" stands for "Notes over Bonds." As we have seen, prices of bonds and notes are strongly correlated. Because the T-bonds underlying the T-bond futures contract have a longer duration than the T-notes underlying the T-note futures contract, a given change in yields will cause a greater price reaction for the T-bond futures contract. The NOB spread is designed to exploit that fact. Thus, the NOB spread is essentially an attempt to take advantage of either changing levels of yields or a changing yield curve by using an intermarket spread.

If yields rise by the same amount on both instruments, one can expect a greater price change on the T-bond. Assume a trader is long the T-bond futures and short the T-note futures. An equal drop in rates will give a profit on the long T-bond futures that exceeds the loss on the T-note futures, giving a profit on the spread.

The NOB can also be used to trade based on expectations of a changing yield curve shape. For example, assume a trader expects the yield curve to become more steeply upward sloping. This implies that yields on the long maturities (T-bonds) would rise relative to yields on shorter maturities (T-notes). To take advantage of this belief, the trader should sell T-bond futures and buy T-note futures. If a trader expects the yield curve to become more downward sloping, the trader would buy T-bond futures and sell T-note futures. Notice that this speculation only concerns the relative yields, not the levels.

HEDGING WITH INTEREST RATE FUTURES

In this section we explore the concept of hedging with interest rate futures. We present a series of examples, progressing from simple cases to more complex situations. In essence, the hedger in interest rate futures attempts to take a futures position that will generate a gain to offset a potential loss in the cash market. This also implies that the hedger takes a futures position that will generate a loss to offset a potential gain in the cash market. Thus, the interest rate futures hedger is attempting to reduce risk, not to make profits.

A LONG HEDGE EXAMPLE

A portfolio manager learns on December 15 that he will have $972,000 to invest in 90-day T-bills six months from now. Current yields on T-bills stand at 12 percent and the yield curve is flat, so forward rates are all 12 percent as well. The manager finds the 12 percent rate attractive and decides to lock it in by going long in a T-bill futures contract maturing on June 15, exactly when the funds become available for investment. As Table 4.15 shows, the manager anticipates the cash position on December 15 and buys one T-bill futures contract to hedge the risk that yields might fall before the funds are available for investment on June 15. With the current yield and, more importantly, the forward rate on T-bills of 12 percent, the portfolio manager expects to be able to buy $1,000,000 face value of T-bills because:

$$\$972,065.42 = \$1,000,000/(1.12)^{.25}$$

■ Table 4.15

A Long Hedge with T-Bill Futures

Date	Cash Market	Futures Market
December 15	A portfolio manager learns he will receive $972,065 in six months to invest in T-bills. Market Yield: 12% Expected face value of bills to purchase: $1,000,000.	The manager buys one T-bill futures contract to mature in six months. Futures price: $972,065
June 15	Manager receives $972,065 to invest. Market yield: 10% $1,000,000 face value of T-bills now costs $976,454. Loss = −$4,389	The manager sells one T-bill futures contract maturing immediately. Futures yield: 10% Futures price: $976,454 Profit = $4,389
	Net wealth change = 0	

The hedge is initiated and time passes. On June 15, the 90-day T-bill yield has fallen to 10 percent, confirming the portfolio manager's fears. Consequently, $1,000,000 face value of 90-day T-bills is worth:

$$\$976,454.09 = \$1,000,000/(1.10)^{.25}$$

Just before the futures contract matures, the manager sells one JUN T-bill futures contract, making a profit of $4,388.67. But in the spot market the cost of $1,000,000 face value of 90-day T-bills has risen from $972,065 to $976,454, generating a cash market loss of $4,389. However, the futures profit exactly offsets the cash market loss for a zero change in wealth. With the receipt of the $972,065 that was to be invested, plus the $4,389 futures profit, the original plan may be executed, and the portfolio manager purchases $1,000,000 face value in 90-day T-bills.[5]

By design, this example is extremely artificial in order to illustrate the long hedge. Notice that the yield curve is flat at the outset, and only its level changes. Figure 4.6 portrays the kind of yield curve shift that was assumed. This idealized yield curve shift is unlikely to occur.

■ Figure 4.6

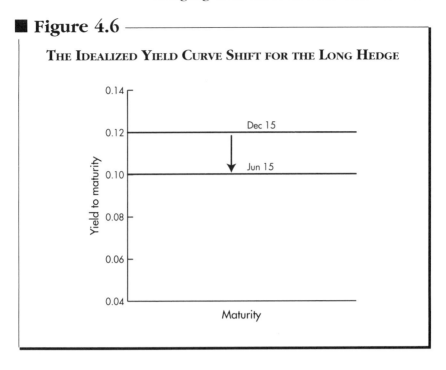

THE IDEALIZED YIELD CURVE SHIFT FOR THE LONG HEDGE

Also, the assumption of a flat yield curve plays a crucial role in accounting for the simplicity of this example. If the yield curve is flat, spot and forward rates are identical. When one "locks-in" some rate via futures trading, a forward rate must be the one locked-in, as the next example shows. Also, we assumed the portfolio manager received exactly the right amount of funds at exactly the right time to purchase $1,000,000 of T-bills. These unrealistic assumptions are gradually relaxed in the following examples.

A Short Hedge. A government securities dealer agrees to sell another firm $1,000,000 face value of 90-day T-bills in four months for $967,000, a price that implies a yield of 14.37 percent. The forward rate (for a 90-day T-bill beginning in four months) from the yield curve also equals 14.37 percent, and the yield on the futures contract is also 14.37 percent. Assume also that the current 90-day T-bill spot rate is 13 percent. The difference, measured in yields at the outset, is −1.37 percent (13 percent − 14.37 percent). Table 4.16 shows the security dealer's position in the cash and futures markets. If rates fall below the expected 14.37 percent, the security dealer will have to deliver T-bills worth more than the $967,000 he will receive. To

■ Table 4.16

A Short Hedge Using T-Bill Futures

Date	Cash Market	Futures Market
Time = 0	The security dealer commits to selling $1,000,000 face value of 90-day T-bills in 4 months for $967,000. Implied yield: 14.37% Spot yield: 13.00%	The security dealer buys one T-bill futures contract that matures in 4 months. Future price: $967,000 Futures yield: 14.37%
Time = 4 mos.	Spot yield is 14.37%. The security dealer delivers $1,000,000 of T-bills and receives $967,000 as expected. Profit = 0	The security dealer sells one T-bill futures contract. With yields at 14.37%, the futures price is $967,000. Loss = 0

Net wealth change = 0

protect against this eventuality, the dealer buys one T-bill futures contract with a futures price of $967,000 and a futures yield of 14.37 percent.

Time passes and the market's expectations are realized. Four months after the hedge is opened, the 90-day T-bill yield is 14.37 percent, as implied by the forward rate. In the cash market, the security dealer delivers T-bills worth the anticipated amount of $967,000 and receives $967,000, generating no profit or loss. In the futures market, the futures yield has been constant at 14.37 percent, generating no profit or loss there either.

This example is instructive because of what it reveals about the basis and its role in hedging with interest rate futures. In futures markets for commodities, a constant basis helps ensure an effective hedge. Not so with interest rate futures. Figure 4.7 depicts the movement of the basis over time for this example of a short hedge. Measuring the basis as (Spot Yield – Futures Yield), the basis certainly changed dramatically – 1.37 percent in four months. But this change in the basis did not interfere with the effectiveness of the hedge, because it was completely anticipated by the hedger. The security dealer looked to the forward rate for the time the hedge was to be lifted to

■ Figure 4.7

CHANGES IN THE BASIS OVER TIME FOR THE SHORT HEDGE

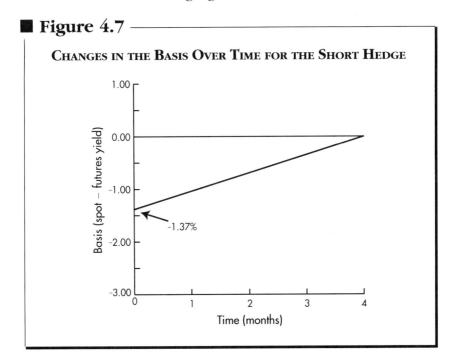

determine what price to demand for the T-bills to be sold. Consequently, the hedger using interest rate futures need not be concerned about all changes in the basis, but only unanticipated changes, i.e., changes not consistent with the expectations embedded in the yield curve at the time the hedge is initiated.

We can make the same point in another way. For the interest rate futures market, we are concerned with the difference between the forward rate and the futures yield. The forward rate is estimated from the term structure at the time the hedge is initiated for the time the hedge is to be terminated. The forward rate of interest is the rate pertaining to the instrument being hedged. For good hedging performance in the interest rate futures market, this difference between the forward rate and the futures yield needs to be constant, as it was in the short hedge example. The next two examples illustrate the importance of changes in this difference between the forward rate and the futures yield.

THE CROSS-HEDGE

The financial vice president of a large manufacturing firm has decided to issue $1 billion worth of 90-day commercial paper in three months.

The outstanding 90-day commercial paper of the firm yields 17 percent, or 2 percent above the current 90-day T-bill rate of 15 percent. Fearing that rates might rise, the vice president decides to hedge against the risk of increasing yields by entering the interest rate futures market.

He decides to hedge the firm's commercial paper in the T-bill futures market, since rates on commercial paper and T-bills tend to be highly correlated. Since one type of instrument is being hedged with another, this hedge becomes a **cross-hedge**. In general, a cross-hedge occurs when the hedged and hedging instruments differ with respect to: (1) risk level, (2) coupon, (3) maturity, or (4) the time span covered by the instrument being hedged and the instrument deliverable against the futures contract. This means that the vast majority of all hedges in the interest rate futures markets are cross-hedges. The hedge being contemplated by the vice president is a cross-hedge, because the commercial paper and the T-bill differ in risk. Assuming that the commercial paper is to be issued in 90 days (and that the T-bill futures contract matures at the same time) ensures that the commercial paper and the T-bill delivered on the futures contract cover the same time span.

Therefore, the vice president decides to sell 1,000 T-bill futures contracts to mature in three months. Table 4.17 shows the transactions. The futures price is $963,575, implying a futures yield of 16 percent. Notice that this differs by 1 percent from the current 90-day T-bill yield of 15 percent. Time passes, and in three months the futures yield has not changed, remaining at 16 percent. However, since the futures contract is about to mature, the spot and futures rates are now equal. Consequently, the trade incurs no gain or loss on the futures contract.

In the cash market the 90-day commercial paper spot rate at the end of the hedging period has become 18 percent, not the 17 percent that was the original 90-day spot rate at the initiation date of the hedge. Since the vice president *thought* he was locking in the 17 percent spot rate, he expected to receive $961,509,400 for the commercial paper issue. But the commercial paper rate at the time of issue was 18 percent, so the firm received only $959,465,798. This appears to be a loss in the cash market of $2,043,602. However, this is only appearance. The vice president may have thought that he was locking in the prevailing spot rate of 17 percent at the time the hedge was initiated, but such a belief was unwarranted. By hedging the

■ Table 4.17

A Cross-Hedge Between T-Bill Futures and Commercial Paper

Date	Cash Market	Futures Market
Time = 0	The Financial V.P. plans to sell 90-day commercial paper in 3 months in the amount of $1 billion, at an expected yield of 17%, which should net the firm $961,509,400.	The V.P. sells 1,000 T-bill futures contracts to mature in 3 months with a futures yield of 16%, a futures price per contract of $963,575, and a total futures price of $963,575,000.
Time = 3 mos.	The spot commercial paper rate is now 18%, the usual 2% above the spot T-bill rate. Consequently, the sale of the $1 billion of commercial paper nets $959,465,798, not the expected $961,509,400. Opportunity loss = ?	The T-bill futures contract is about to mature, so the T-bill futures rate = spot rate = 16%. The futures price is still $963,575 per contract, so there is no gain or loss. Gain/loss = 0

Net wealth change = ?

issuance of the commercial paper, the vice president should have expected to lock in the three-month forward rate for 90-day commercial paper.

Figure 4.8 clarifies these relationships by presenting yield curves for T-bills and commercial paper. The yield curves are consistent with the data of the preceding discussion. At the outset of the hedge, the 90-day spot T-bill rate is .15, and the commercial paper rate equals .17. The 180-day spot rates are .154989 and .174989 for T-bills and commercial paper, respectively. The shape of the yield curves gives sufficient information to calculate the forward, and hence the futures, rates for the time span covering the period from day 90 to day 180.

Using the following notation:

$r_{b,e}$ = the rate on a bond to begin at time b
and to be held until time e,

■ **Figure 4.8**

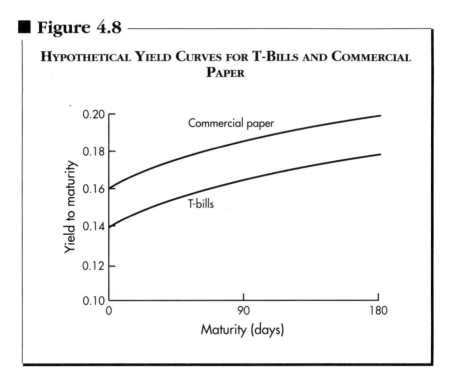

Hypothetical Yield Curves for T-Bills and Commercial Paper

it is necessarily the case that:

$$(1 + r_{0,6})^5 = (1 + r_{0,3})^{.25}(1 + r_{3,6})^{.25}$$

From Figure 4.8 it is clear that, for T-bills, $r_{0,6}$ = .154989 and $r_{0,3}$ = .15. Therefore:

$$(1.154989)^5 = (1.15)^{.25}(1 + r_{3,6})^{.25}$$

and $r_{3,6}$ = .16. That is, the T-bill forward rate for the period to cover from three to six months hence must be 16 percent. By exactly analogous reasoning, the corresponding commercial paper forward rate must be 18 percent:

$$(1.174989)^5 = (1.17)^{.25}(1 + r_{3,6})^{.25}$$

Therefore, $r_{3,6}$ = .18 for commercial paper.

These forward rates, evaluated at time = 0, are the expected future rates to prevail on three-month T-bills and commercial paper beginning in three months. Consequently, the implied yield on the commercial paper of this example is .18, not the .17 that the vice president attempted to lock in.

Now it is possible to understand exactly why the vice president was unable to lock in 17 percent, even though it was the spot rate prevailing at the time the hedge was initiated. The reason is simply this: For the time period over which the commercial paper was to be issued (from three to six months in the future), the market believed the 90-day commercial paper rate would be 18 percent in three months. The futures price and yield reflected this belief. Although the vice president desired a 17 percent rate, the market's expected rate was 18 percent, and by entering the futures contract the vice president locked in the 18 percent rate. Therefore, the opportunity loss of Table 4.17 is only apparent. The vice president's expectation of issuing the commercial paper at 17 percent was completely unwarranted. Instead, the vice president should have expected to issue the commercial paper at the market's expected rate of 18 percent. Then he would have expected to net $959,465,798 for the firm, which is exactly what happened in the example.

A CROSS-HEDGE WITH FAULTY EXPECTATIONS

In the preceding example, the vice president misunderstood the nature of the futures market. If the vice president had understood everything correctly, Table 4.17 would have shown a zero total wealth change. Thus far, all of the examples have been of perfect hedges – those leaving total wealth unchanged. Sometimes, however, even when the hedge is properly initiated with the appropriate expectations, those expectations can turn out to be false. In such cases, the hedge will not be perfect; total wealth will either increase or decrease.

To illustrate this possibility, assume the same basic hedging problem as in the cross-hedge example. In particular, assume that the vice president wishes to hedge the same issuance of commercial paper and that the yield curves are as shown in Figure 4.8. The actions and expectations of the vice president, shown in Table 4.18, are exactly correct. The yield curve implies that, in 90 days, the 90-day T-bill and commercial paper rates will stand at 16 and 18 percent, respectively.

■ **Table 4.18**

A Cross-Hedge With Faulty Expectations

Date	Cash Market	Futures Market
Time = 0	The Financial V.P. decides to sell 90-day commercial paper in 3 months in the amount of $1 billion, at an expected yield of 18%, which should net the firm $959,465,798.	The V.P. sells 1,000 T-bill futures contracts to mature in 3 months, with a futures yield of 16%, a futures price per contract of $963,575, and a total futures price of $963,575,000.
Time = 3 mos.	The spot commercial paper rate was expected to be 18% at this time, but is really 18.5%. Consequently, the sale of the $1 billion of commercial paper nets $958,452,098, not the expected $959,465,798.	The T-bill futures contract is about to mature, so the T-bill futures rate = spot rate = .1625. The futures price is $963,056 per contract, so there is a gain per contract of $519, and a total gain on the 1,000 contracts of $519,000.
	Opportunity loss = −$1,013,700	Gain = +$519,000
	Net wealth change = −$494,700	

However, in this instance, assume that these expectations formed are incorrect. During the 90-day period before the commercial paper was issued, the market came to view the commercial paper as being riskier than was previously thought, and the economy experienced a higher rate of inflation than anticipated. Historically, assume that the yield premium of commercial paper had been 2 percent above the T-bill rate, consistent with Figure 4.8. But now, due to the perception of increased risk for commercial paper, the yield differential widens to 2.25 percent. Then assume that in three months the T-bill rate happens to be 16.25 percent, rising due to greater than anticipated inflation. Under these assumptions, the commercial paper rate is 18.5 percent, not the originally expected 18 percent.

As Table 4.18 reveals, the total gain on the futures position is $519,000. Due to the commercial paper rate being 18.5 percent, and not the originally anticipated 18 percent, there is a loss on the commercial paper of $1,013,700. Since the error in expectation was .5 percent on the commercial paper, but only .25 percent on the T-bills, the gain on the futures does not offset the total loss of the commercial paper. This results in a net wealth change of −$494,700. However, the loss would have been −$1,013,700 without the futures hedge.

In general, real world hedges will not be perfect. Rates on both sides of the hedge tend to move in the same direction, but by uncertain amounts. On occasion rates can even move in opposite directions, generating enormous gains or losses. In the example just discussed, assume that the commercial paper rate turned out to be 18.5 percent, but that the T-bill rate was 15.75 percent – *below* the expected 16 percent. In this case, the loss on the commercial paper would be −$1,013,700, and the loss on the futures would be −$1,568,000 for a total loss of −$2,581,700, because the firm loses on both sides of the hedge. Such an outcome is unlikely, but it is a possible result of which hedgers should be aware.

CONCLUSION

In this chapter, we have considered the contract specifications of the most important interest rate futures contracts. We have explored the proper pricing of futures contracts using the cost-of-carry framework and have seen how interest rate futures are related to the term structure of interest rates.

We have noted some difficulties in applying the simplest form of the cost-of-carry relationship to interest rate futures, particularly to the T-bond futures contract. The breakdown of the arbitrage conditions gives expectations of future interest rates a role in determining interest rate futures prices.

If interest rate futures prices are not determined by strict cost-of-carry relationships, there may be ample reward to various speculative strategies. The chapter concluded by exploring some simple speculative strategies, as well as more complex relationships involving several instruments. In the next chapter, we continue our exploration of interest rate futures by considering the pricing performance and the hedging use of interest rate futures.

Notes

1. Chicago Mercantile Exchange, "Inside Eurodollar Futures," p. 19.

2. The best way to secure a regular source of conversion factors, as well as much other useful information, is to visit the CBOT's site on the World Wide Web.

3. For studies of this approach to pricing T-bill futures, see I. Kawaller and T. Koch, "Cash-and-Carry Trading and the Pricing of Treasury Bill Futures," *Journal of Futures Markets*, 4:2, Fall 1984, pp. 115–23.

4. See the Chicago Mercantile Exchange, "Market Perspectives," February 1987, 5:1, pp. 1–4. See also the Chicago Mercantile Exchange, "The TED Spread," *Financial Strategy Paper*, 1987.

5. For simplicity, we use easier price and yield calculations in many of these hedging examples, abstracting from the full complexity of market yield calculations.

■ Chapter 5

└── *Interest Rate Futures:* ■ *Refinements*

OVERVIEW

Chapter 5 builds on the foundation of Chapter 4. Having already explored the fundamental features of interest rate futures, we now turn to refining our understanding of these important markets. Thus, Chapter 5 considers more closely some of the same issues addressed in Chapter 4. In addition, we examine some new issues, such as the informational efficiency of the interest rate futures market.

The T-bond contract is perhaps the most important futures contract ever devised. It also happens to be one of the most complicated. We begin this chapter with a detailed analysis of the T-bond contract. This analysis lays the foundation for a richer understanding of how to apply interest rate futures to speculate and to manage risk. Next, we consider the informational efficiency of the interest rate futures markets. A market is efficient with respect to some set of information if prices in the market fully reflect the information contained in that set. There have been many studies of informational efficiency for interest rate futures, and we review the results of those studies.

In Chapter 4 we saw that interest rate futures should be full carry markets. However, this conclusion requires some qualifications. Taking the T-bond contract as a model, we analyze the special features of the contract and show how those features can make full carry

191

difficult to measure. For example, seller's options have important implications for the theoretically correct futures price.

Many traders use interest rate futures to manage risk. The techniques for risk management are quite diverse and increasingly sophisticated. Essentially two different sets of techniques apply, depending upon the nature of the risk. Therefore, we consider applications for short-term interest rate futures first and then conclude the chapter by examining the applications of long-term interest rate futures.

THE T-BOND FUTURES CONTRACT IN DETAIL

In Chapter 4 we explored the basic features of the T-bond futures contract. In this section, we first review what we know about the contract from Chapter 4. Then we develop a more complete analysis of the contract. This procedure provides a richer understanding of the contract which helps us understand how to use interest rate futures for speculation and risk management.

REVIEW OF THE T-BOND CONTRACT

In our discussion of the T-bond futures contract in Chapter 4, we noted that the contract calls for the delivery of $100,000 principal amount of U.S. Treasury bonds that have at least 15 years to maturity of their first call date at the time of delivery. We noted that the delivery procedure stretched over three business days, with actual delivery occurring on the third day, which could be any business day of the delivery month.

For any particular futures contract expiration, a variety of bonds will be deliverable. These bonds can be of any coupon rate and any maturity above the minimum. In many cases, the bonds that are deliverable will include some recently issued Treasury bonds that may not even have existed when the contract was first listed for trading.

Without some adjustment, one of these bonds is likely to be much better to deliver than the others. For example, if the contract allowed the delivery of any bond without a price adjustment, every trader would want to deliver the cheapest bond. To make the variety of bonds permitted for delivery comparable, the CBOT uses a system of conversion factors. Essentially, the conversion factor for a given bond is found by assuming that the bond has a face value of $1 and discounting all of the bond's cash flows at 8 percent. Chapter 4 gave the exact formulas for finding the conversion factors. While the conversion factors eliminate much of the inequalities between various bonds, they do not do a complete job. As a consequence, there is still a particular bond that is cheapest-to-deliver among the bonds permitted for delivery.

As another complication, we noted in Chapter 4 that the seller of the T-bond futures possesses several options. For example, the seller chooses which bond to deliver and which day to make delivery. These and other options have significant value, as we explore next.

THE CHEAPEST-TO-DELIVER BOND

In this section we show how to determine which bond will be cheapest-to-deliver, and we show how to find the exact invoice amount, including all the nuances in computing accrued interest. First, we analyze the cheapest-to-deliver bond when some time remains before expiration, but there will be no coupon payment. Second, we consider the case when a coupon payment intervenes between the beginning of the holding period and the futures expiration.

The Case of No Intervening Coupons. Assume today is June 16, 1997, and the JUN 97 T-bond futures settlement price is 93–00. A short trader decides to make today her position day and to deliver against her futures contract. The actual delivery date will be June 18, 1997. She is considering two bonds and wants to know exactly how much she will receive for each and which she should deliver. The two bonds are:

Maturity	Coupon	Price	JUN 97 CF
May 15, 2019	7.25	82–16	.9231
Nov. 15, 2018	9.875	108–16	1.1899

We want to determine the exact invoice amount for each bond and which bond is cheapest-to-deliver.

To answer these questions, we first compute the cash price and invoice amounts for $100,000 face value of these bonds. The total price depends upon the stated price plus the accrued interest (AI). In Chapter 4 we saw that a bond accrues interest for each day based on the coupon rate and the principal amount. In the market, the actual calculation also depends upon the number of days in a half-year, as Table 5.1 shows.

■ Table 5.1

Days in Half-Years

Interest Period	Interest Paid on 1st or 15th		Interest Paid on Last Day	
	Regular Year	Leap Year	Regular Year	Leap Year
January to July	181	182	181	182
February to August	181	182	184	184
March to September	184	184	183	183
April to October	183	183	184	184
May to November	184	184	183	183
June to December	183	183	184	184
July to January	184	184	184	184
August to February	184	184	181	182
September to March	181	182	182	183
October to April	182	183	181	182
November to May	181	182	182	183
December to June	182	183	181	182
1 year (any 2 consecutive half-years)	365	366	365	366

Source: Treasury Circular No. 300, 4th Rev.

Both bonds have the same coupon dates each year, May 15 and November 15, so both are on the May-November cycle. As Table 5.1 shows, for a regular year, there are 184 days in the May-November half-year. From May 15 to June 18 is 34 days. Therefore, the accrued interest for each bond is:

7.25% bond: AI = (34/184)(.5)(.0725)($100,000) = $670
9.875% bond: AI = (34/184)(.5)(.09875)($100,000) = $912

From Chapter 4:

Invoice Amount = DFP($100,000)(CF) + AI

where:

DFP = decimal futures price (e.g., 96-16 = .965)
CF = conversion factor
AI = accrued interest

With a June 16 futures settlement price of 93-00, invoice amounts are:

7.25% bond: .9300($100,000)(.9231) + $670 = $86,518
9.875% bond: .9300($100,000)(1.1899) + $912 = $111,573

Thus, the two bonds have radically different invoice amounts; the 9.875 percent bond has an invoice amount 29 percent greater than the 7.25 percent bond.

To complete delivery, the short trader must deliver one bond and receive the invoice amount. Which should she deliver? The decision depends upon the difference between the invoice amount and the cash market price, which is the profit from delivery. The bond that is most profitable to deliver is the cheapest-to-deliver bond. In other words, the short trader will select the bond to deliver to maximize profit. For a particular bond I, the profit π_i is:

$$\pi_i = \text{Invoice Amount} - (P_i + AI_i)$$
$$= (DFP_i)(\$100,000)(CF_i) + AI_i - (P_i + AI_i)$$

Because the accrued interest is included in the invoice amount and subtracted as a payment being made by surrendering the bond, the profit simplifies to:

$$\pi_i = DFP_i(\$100,000)(CF_i) - P_i \qquad (5.1)$$

To find the cheapest-to-deliver bond, the short trader will compute the profitability for each deliverable bond. The bond with the maximum profit is the cheapest-to-deliver.[1] For the two bonds, the profit from delivery is:

For the 7.25% bond:
$$\pi = .9300(\$100,000)(.9231) - \$82,500 = \$3,348$$
For the 9.875% bond:
$$\pi = .9300(\$100,000)(1.1899) - \$108,500 = \$2,161$$

Thus, delivering the 7.25 percent bond is more profitable, so it is cheaper-to-deliver.

Which bond is cheaper-to-deliver depends on the level of interest rates. Figure 5.1 shows the profits from delivery for three bonds:

25 year; 7% coupon
16 year; 14% coupon
20 year; 8% coupon

The 20-year, 8 percent coupon bond is the nominal bond that underlies the futures contract. It has a conversion factor of 1.0, as do all 8 percent coupon bonds. Therefore, the profit from delivery on an 8 percent coupon bond will always be zero if the futures and bond are priced fairly, as Figure 5.1 shows. The practice of using conversion factors does not introduce any biases for an 8 percent coupon bond.

As Figure 5.1 shows, bias is possible for the other two bonds with coupon rates that differ from 8 percent. If interest rates are below 8 percent, Figure 5.1 shows that there is an advantage to delivering the 16-year bond. By contrast, if yields exceed 8 percent, it is better to

■ Figure 5.1

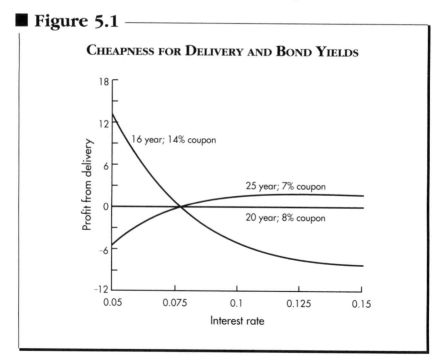

CHEAPNESS FOR DELIVERY AND BOND YIELDS

deliver the 25-year bond. At one point in Figure 5.1, a trader can be indifferent about which bond to deliver. Notice that when yields are exactly 8 percent, the profit from delivery for all three bonds is zero. We can extract a general rule from this analysis. When interest rates are below 8 percent, there is an incentive to deliver short maturity/high coupon bonds. When interest rates exceed 8 percent, there is an incentive to deliver long maturity/low coupon bonds. Expressing the same idea in terms of duration, a trader should deliver low duration bonds when interest rates are below 8 percent and high duration bonds when interest rates are above 8 percent.

The Case of Intervening Coupons. So far, we have dealt with the cheapest-to-deliver bond when there are no coupon payments to consider. We now consider which bond is cheapest-to-deliver when a bond pays a coupon between the beginning of the cash-and-carry holding period and the futures expiration. To find the cheapest-to-deliver bond before expiration, we apply the cash-and-carry strategy. The bond with the greatest profit at delivery from following the cash-and-carry strategy will be the cheapest-to-deliver.

We assume that a trader buys a bond today and carries the bond to delivery. We compare the cash flows associated with that carry relative to the invoice amount based on today's futures price. Of course, we cannot know the future cash flows with certainty. In particular, the futures price might change. However, we make our computation assuming that interest rates and futures prices remain constant. For this analysis, we must consider the estimated invoice amount plus our estimate of the cash flows associated with carrying the bond to delivery.

The estimated invoice amount depends on three factors:

1. today's quoted futures price,
2. the conversion factor for the bond we plan to deliver, and
3. the accrued interest on the bond at the expiration date.

Acquiring and carrying a bond to delivery involves three cash flows as well:

1. pay today the quoted price plus accrued interest,
2. finance the bond from today until expiration, and
3. receive and invest any coupons paid between today and expiration.

We can bring all of these factors together by considering the time line in Figure 5.2.

Today we purchase a bond and finance it until delivery. Between today and delivery, we receive and invest a coupon. At delivery, we surrender the bond and receive the invoice amount. Thus, we have:

$$\text{Estimated Invoice Amount} = \text{DFP}_0 \$100,000(\text{CF}) + \text{AI}_2$$

Estimated Future Value of the Delivered Bond =

$$(P_0 + \text{AI}_0)(1 + C_{0,2}) - \text{COUP}_1(1 + C_{1,2})$$

where:

P_0 = quoted price of the bond today, $t = 0$
AI_0 = accrued interest as of today, $t = 0$
$C_{0,2}$ = interest factor for $t = 0$ to expiration at $t = 2$
COUP_1 = coupon that will be received before delivery at $t = 1$
$C_{1,2}$ = interest factor from $t = 1$ to $t = 2$
DFP_0 = decimal futures price today, $t = 0$
CF = conversion factor for a particular bond and the specified futures expiration
AI_2 = accrued interest at $t = 2$

■ Figure 5.2

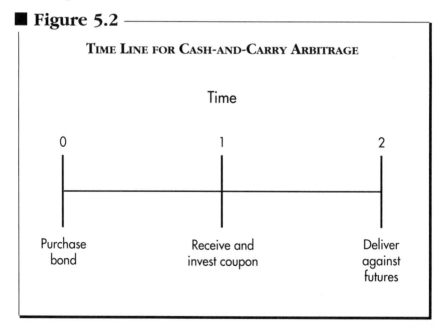

Time Line for Cash-and-Carry Arbitrage

Time

0   1   2

Purchase bond   Receive and invest coupon   Deliver against futures

The short trader will maximize profit by choosing to deliver the cheapest-to-deliver bond. For bond I, the expected profit from delivery is the estimated invoice amount less the estimated value of what will be delivered:

$$\pi = DFP_0(CF) + AI_2 - [(P_0 + AI_0)(1 + C_{0,2}) - COUP_1(1 + C_{1,2})] \tag{5.2}$$

As an illustration, assume that today is April 15, 1997, and we want to find the cheapest-to-deliver bond for the JUN 97 futures expiration. We illustrate the computation with the two bonds we have already considered, with different prices for the different date.

Maturity	Coupon	Price	JUN 97 CF
May 15, 2019	7.25	81-00	.9231
Nov. 15, 2018	9.875	106-16	1.1899

We assume that the bonds will be financed and the coupons invested at the repo rate of 10 percent and that the settlement price of the JUN 97 T-bond futures on April 15 is 91-00. We assume a $100,000 face value and a target delivery date of June 30, 1997. Figure 5.3 shows all of the dates and the number of days between dates.

The semiannual coupons for the two bonds are $3,625 for the 7.25 percent bond and $4,938 for the 9.875 percent bond. Both bonds

■ **Figure 5.3**

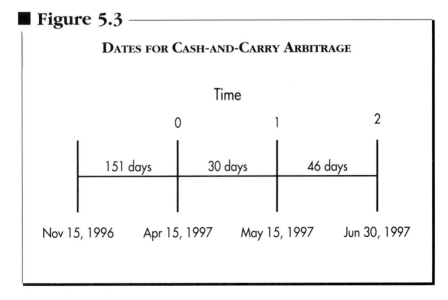

DATES FOR CASH-AND-CARRY ARBITRAGE

Time

0   1   2

151 days   30 days   46 days

Nov 15, 1996   Apr 15, 1997   May 15, 1997   Jun 30, 1997

paid their last coupon on November 15, 1996, 151 days ago. For a regular year, the November-May half-year has 181 days. Therefore, the accrued interest as of April 15 for the bonds is:

For the 7.25% bond: $AI_0 = \$3,625(151/181) = \$3,024$
For the 9.875% bond: $AI_0 = \$4,938(151/181) = \$4,120$

The amount to be financed for each bond is:

For the 7.25% bond: $P_0 + AI_0 = \$81,000 + \$3,024 = \$84,024$
For the 9.875% bond: $P_0 + AI_0 = \$106,500 + \$4,120 = \$110,620$

Next we consider the accrued interest that will accumulate by the delivery date. From May 15, 1997, to June 30, 1997, is 46 days in a half-year of 184 days. Therefore, the bonds will have the following accrued interest on June 30, 1997:

For the 7.25% bond: $AI_2 = \$3,625(46/184) = \$906$
For the 9.875% bond: $AI_2 = \$4,938(46/184) = \$1,235$

With a futures price of 91–00 on April 15, 1997, the $DFP_0 = .91$. The estimated invoice amount for the two bonds is:

For the 7.25% bond: $.91(\$100,000)(.9231) + \$906 = \$84,908$
For the 9.875% bond:
   $.91(\$100,000)(1.1899) + \$1,235 = \$109,516$

Next, we compute the financing rates. On April 15, 76 days remain until the projected delivery date, so $C_{0,2} = .10(76/360) = .0211$. From May 15, 1997, until June 30, 1997, is 46 days, so $C_{1,2} = .10(46/360) = .0128$. Finally, we are in a position to compute the profits from delivery. Table 5.2 summarizes all of these intermediate calculations.

■ **Table 5.2**

DATA FOR CHEAPEST-TO-DELIVER BONDS

Bond	P_0	AI_0	$C_{0,2}$	$C_{1,2}$	DFP_0	CF	AI_2
7.25%	81,000	$3,024	0.02	0.01	0.91	0.9231	906
9.875%	106,500	$4,120	0.02	0.01	0.91	1.1899	1,235

Using the values in Table 5.2, we compute the expected profit from delivering each bond. For the 7.25 percent bond:

$$\pi = (.91)(100,000)(.9231) + 906$$
$$- [(81,000 + 3,024)(1.0211) - (3,625)(1.0128)]$$
$$= 84,908 - 85,797 + 3,671$$
$$= \$2,782$$

For the 9.875 percent bond:

$$\pi = (.91)(100,000)(1.1899) + 1,235$$
$$- [(106,500 + 4,120)(1.0211) - 4,938(1.0128)]$$
$$= 109,516 - 112,954 + 5,001$$
$$= \$1,563$$

For the 7.25 percent bond, the profit from delivery is $2,782, but delivering the 9.875 percent bond generates only $1,563. Therefore, the 7.25 percent bond is cheaper-to-deliver.

The Cheapest-to-Deliver Bond and the Implied Repo Rate. We can also analyze the same situation using the implied repo rate. Here the implied repo rate for the given period equals the net cash flow at delivery divided by the net cash flow when the carry starts:

$$\text{Implied Repo Rate} = \frac{\text{Net Cash Flow over Horizon}}{\text{Net Cash Flow at Inception}}$$

The numerator consists of cash inflows of the invoice amount, plus the future value of the coupons at the time of delivery, less the cost of acquiring the bond initially. The denominator consists of the cost of buying the bond. Therefore, in terms of our notation:

$$\text{Implied Repo Rate} = \frac{DFP_0(100,000)(CF) + AI_2 + COUP_1(1 + C_{1,2}) - (P_0 + AI_0)}{(P_0 + AI_0)}$$

For the 7.25 percent bond we have:

$$\text{Implied Repo Rate} = \frac{.91(100,000)(.9231) + 906 + 3,625(1.0128) - (81,000 + 3,024)}{(81,000 + 3,024)} = .0542$$

For the 9.875 percent bond:

$$\text{Implied Repo Rate} = \frac{.91(100,000)(1.1899) + 1,235 + 4,938(1.0128) - (106,500 + 4,120)}{(106,500 + 4,120)} = .035$$

Annualizing these rates, for the 7.25 percent bond we have $(.0542)(360/76) = 25.67$ percent and for the 9.875 percent bond we have $(.0352)(360/76) = 16.67$ percent. Thus, the low coupon 7.25 percent bond has a higher implied repo rate, suggesting that this bond is better than the 9.875 percent bond to carry to delivery. From this example, we can draw the following rule about the cheapest-to-deliver bond before expiration: The cheapest-to-deliver bond has the highest implied repo rate in a cash-and-carry strategy.

If the implied repo rate equals the borrowing rate, the cash-and-carry arbitrage transaction leaves a zero profit. To illustrate this principle, we focus on the 9.875 percent bond and the cash-and-carry transactions of Table 5.3. As the example of Table 5.3 shows, financing a cash-and-carry arbitrage at the implied repo rate yields a zero profit.

To summarize, we state some general rules about how to conduct arbitrage if the cost of funds varies from the implied repo rate. The

■ Table 5.3

TRANSACTIONS SHOWING IMPLIED REPO RATES

April 15, 1997
Borrow $110,620 for 76 days at implied repo rate of 16.67%.
Buy $100,000 face value of 9.875 T-bonds maturing on Nov. 15, 2018, for a total price of $110,620 including accrued interest.
Sell one JUN 97 T-bond futures contract at the current price of 91–00.

May 15, 1997
Receive coupon payment of $4,938 and invest for 46 days at 10%.

June 30, 1997 (Assuming futures is still at 91–00)
Deliver the bond and receive invoice amount of $109,516.
From the invested coupon receive $4,938 + $4,938(.10)(46/360) = $5,001
Repay debt: $110,620 + $110,620(.1667)(76/360) = $114,513

Net Profit = $109,516 + $5,001 − $114,513 = −$4 ≈ 0 (given rounding error)

transactions we have considered assumed that the futures price did not change and that markets were perfect. In particular, for the reverse cash-and-carry arbitrage, the assumption that the trader had full use of the short sale proceeds was critical. Subject to these restrictions, and the elaboration of the next section, the general rules hold.

1. Cash-and-carry arbitrage nets a zero profit if the actual borrowing cost equals the implied repo rate.
2. If the effective borrowing rate is less than the implied repo rate, one can earn an arbitrage profit by cash-and-carry arbitrage, i.e., buy the cash bond and sell the futures.
3. If the effective borrowing rate exceeds the implied repo rate and if one can sell bonds short, then one can earn an arbitrage profit by reverse cash-and-carry arbitrage, i.e., sell the bond short, buy the futures, and cover the short position at the expiration of the futures.

WHY THEY CALL IT RISK ARBITRAGE

In this section we add more realism to our analysis of arbitrage by considering the peculiarities of the T-bond futures contract in still greater detail. As we will show, market realities add a risk component to both the cash-and-carry and reverse cash-and-carry arbitrage. These complications take our arbitrage framework out of the realm of "academic arbitrage" and show why all arbitrage in the T-bond futures market is really "risk arbitrage." The sources of risk are different for the cash-and-carry and reverse cash-and-carry strategies, and the risks stem from three sources: intervening coupon payments that must face reinvestment, the use of conversion factors, and the options that the seller possesses. In this section, we consider the risks generated by the reinvestment problem and the use of conversion factors. We also treat the seller's options in a general way.

Frustrations to Cash-and-Carry Arbitrage. A closer examination of Table 5.3 shows some potentially risky elements of the cash-and-carry arbitrage. First, the debt was financed at a constant rate throughout the 76–day carry period. Second, the trader actually was able to invest the coupon at the expected reinvestment rate of 10 percent. Third, the futures price did not change over the horizon. We consider each of these problems in turn.

Assume that the trader in Table 5.3 finances the acquisition of the T-bond with overnight repos. The overnight repo rate changes each day, so the financing cost could drift upward. With an increasing financing cost, the transactions of Table 5.3 will not end in a zero profit. Instead, they will give a loss. Therefore, the transactions in Table 5.3 are potentially risky, depending upon the financing rate for the bond. Second, assume that the bond is financed for the entire period at the implied repo rate of 16.67 percent. Also assume that short-term rates drift lower, so that the coupon can only be invested at 8 percent, not the 10 percent shown in Table 5.3. Now the reinvested coupons will only grow to $4,988, not the $5,001 shown in the table. Therefore, the changing rate will generate a loss. These two examples illustrate the risks that remain inherent in a supposedly riskless cash-and-carry strategy. We now turn to a bigger danger, a change in the futures price that can affect the cash flows from the cash-and-carry strategy.

In the transactions of Table 5.3, we assumed that the futures price did not change over the life of the contract. With the financing rates given, the cash-and-carry transactions yielded a zero profit. Now let us assume that the financing of the bond and the investment of the coupon work out exactly as Table 5.3 shows. However, now we consider a drop in the futures price from 91–00 when the contract is initiated to 89–00 at expiration. Such a change in the futures price is entirely feasible, and we need to consider the effect of this changing price on the cash flows from the cash-and-carry strategy.

Table 5.4 presents the same transactions as the zero profit cash-and-carry transactions of Table 5.3. The only difference between the two tables results from a drop in the futures price from 91–00 to 89–00 over the life of the contract. With a futures expiration price of 89–00, the actual invoice amount is:

$$\text{Invoice Amount} = .89(\$100,000)(1.1899) + \$1,235 = \$107,136$$

The drop in the futures price has generated daily resettlement cash inflows of $2,000 over the life of the contract. With the reduced invoice amount, however, the cash-and-carry transactions generate a loss. As the transactions show, the reason for the loss is that futures price fluctuations generate gains or losses on a $1 for $1 basis. For example, a two point drop in the futures price generates a gain of $2,000 in this case. However, when the futures price changes by $1,

▪ Table 5.4

TRANSACTIONS SHOWING IMPLIED REPO RATES

April 15, 1997
Borrow $110,620 for 76 days at implied repo rate of 16.67%.
Buy $100,000 face value of 9.875 T-bonds maturing on Nov. 15, 2018,
for a total price of $110,620 including accrued interest.
Sell one JUN 94 T-bond futures contract at the current price of 91-00.

May 15, 1997
Receive coupon payment of $4,938 and invest for 46 days at 10
percent.

June 30, 1997 (Assuming futures has fallen to 89-00)
Between April and June, the futures price has fallen from 91-00 to
89-00, generating cash inflows of $2,000.
Deliver the bond and receive invoice amount of $107,136.
From the invested coupon receive $4,938 + $4,938(.10)(46/360) =
$5,001
Repay debt: $110,620 + $110,620(.1667)(76/360) = $114,513

Net Profit = $2,000 + $107,136 + $5,001 − $114,513 = −$376

the delivery value of the bond changes by $1 times the conversion factor, which exceeds 1.0 in our example. This makes it possible for the supposedly riskless transaction to generate a loss. The dropping futures price generates $2,000 in daily resettlement profits, but it reduces the invoice amount from $109,516 to $107,136, a drop of $2,380. Thus, the changing price generates a new profit of $2,000 and a new loss of $2,380, for a net loss of $376, which differs by the rounding error of $4 from the value in Table 5.4.

Frustrations to Reverse Cash-and-Carry Arbitrage. In reverse cash-and-carry transactions, a trader sells an underlying good short and buys a futures contract. The trader then invests the proceeds from the short sale, planning to take delivery on the futures and return the borrowed commodity. Table 5.5 shows the reverse cash-and-carry transactions that are the mirror image of Table 5.3. In Table 5.5, the transactions generate a zero profit. The profit must be zero, because the transactions are exact complements to the transactions in Table 5.3.

We now consider the risk elements inherent in the reverse cash-and-carry transactions. First, all of the same risk elements that plagued

■ Table 5.5

TRANSACTIONS SHOWING IMPLIED REPO RATES

April 15, 1997
Sell short $100,000 face value of 9.875 T-bonds maturing on Nov. 15, 2018, for a total price of $110,620 including accrued interest.
Buy one JUN 97 T-bond futures contract at the current price of 91-00.
Lend $110,620 for 76 days at implied repo rate of 16.67 percent.

May 15, 1997
Borrow $4,938 for 46 days at 10% and make coupon payment of $4,938.

June 30, 1997 (Assuming futures is still at 91-00)
Collect investment: $110,620 + $110,620(.1667)(76/360) = $114,513.
Accept delivery of the bond and pay invoice amount of $109,516.
Pay debt from funds borrowed to make coupon payment: $4,938 + $4,938(.10)(46/360) = $5,001

Net Profit = $114,513 − $109,516 − $5,001 = −$4 ≈ 0 (given rounding error)

the cash-and-carry strategy apply to the reverse cash-and-carry strategy as well. The trader of Table 5.5 could have lost if she had been forced to invest the short sale proceeds at less than the implied repo rate. If she had been forced to pay more than 10 percent on the borrowings to pay the coupon, the transactions would have resulted in a loss also. Finally, if futures prices had risen, she would have had daily resettlement inflows that were less than the rise in the invoice amount, and these would have generated losses as well.

In addition to these sources of risk that plague cash-and-carry and reverse cash-and-carry strategies alike, the reverse cash-and-carry strategy faces other special risks stemming from the seller's options. In Table 5.5 we made several implicit assumptions. We assumed that the short futures trader delivered on June 30, 1997, and that the short trader delivered exactly the same bond that the trader of Table 5.5 sold short.

From Chapter 4 we know that the short trader of a T-bond futures has several options associated with the delivery. First, the short trader holds a **quality option** – the option to choose which bond to deliver. In Chapter 4, we noted that there are typically more than 20 deliverable bonds, and the short trader can deliver any of these. Therefore, the reverse cash-and-carry trader cannot be sure that she will receive a particular bond in the delivery. If the delivered bond is not the same bond that she sold short, she must go into the market to buy the bond that will allow her to cover the short sale. Of course, this exposes her to the risk that the price of the 9.875 percent bond could have changed. The seller of a T-bond futures contract also possesses a second important option. The **timing option** is the seller's option to choose the day of delivery. From Chapter 4 we know that delivery can occur on any business day in the delivery month. Therefore, the reverse cash-and-carry trader cannot be sure that delivery will occur on a particular date. This also exposes the trader of Table 5.5 to risk, because she cannot be sure that the delivery will occur on June 30. In addition to the quality and timing options, the short trader also possesses some other highly specialized options that add to the risk of the reverse cash-and-carry transactions. These options make the reverse cash-and-carry transactions extremely risky.[2]

INTEREST RATE FUTURES MARKET EFFICIENCY

A market is informationally efficient if prices in that market fully reflect all information in a given information set. If the market is efficient with respect to some information set, then that information cannot be used to direct a trading strategy to beat the market. A trader beats the market by consistently earning a rate of return that exceeds the risk-adjusted market equilibrium rate of return. There are three commonly distinguished forms of the market efficiency hypothesis: the weak form, the semi-strong form, and the strong form. These versions of market efficiency are distinguished by their information sets. The weak form efficiency hypothesis asserts that information contained in the past history of price and volume data cannot be used to beat the market. The semi-strong form asserts that traders cannot rely on public information to beat the market. The strong form asserts that even private information is insufficient to allow a trader to beat the market.

We have seen that cash-and-carry and reverse cash-and-carry arbitrage strategies rely only on observable prices. Thus, successful arbitrage strategies violate weak form efficiency. For example, large divergences between forward and futures rates of interest would generate important academic arbitrage opportunities. Because the futures market is a zero-sum game, in the absence of transaction costs, one participant's profits imply offsetting losses for others.

For these reasons, users of any market should be concerned about market efficiency. This is true whether one is a speculator or a hedger. Researchers have long recognized the importance of market efficiency as well. This section reviews the development of research on interest rate futures market efficiency and draws conclusions about the efficiency based on the state of research to date. In spite of the attention that has been focused on the efficiency question, only T-bill and T-bond futures contracts have been explored well in published works. Almost all of these analyses focus on divergences between forward rates implied by spot market positions and futures market positions. This focus on rate discrepancies means that the tests have sought evidence of academic arbitrage opportunities in the interest rate futures market. Many early tests were based on a less than full understanding of the conditions under which market efficiency could be judged.

Early tests of futures market efficiency focused exclusively on differences between forward rates and futures rates on T-bills. Differences between these rates were sometimes interpreted without further ado as evidence of market inefficiency. Immediate difficulties with this conclusion arose because different researchers arrived at radically different conclusions, some finding efficiency and others finding gross inefficiencies. From preceding chapters, we know that forward and futures rates can differ for at least two basic reasons: market imperfections or the influence of daily resettlement. Many of the earliest researches into efficiency did not take these two factors into adequate consideration, yet both are important.

Attempts to evaluate academic arbitrage opportunities in the T-bill futures market involve taking complementary positions in the futures market and in the spot market. The difference in the futures and forward yields must be sufficiently large to cover considerable transaction costs if there is to be genuine academic arbitrage. While many studies neglect the full magnitude of these transaction charges, more recent studies find potential for arbitrage even after transaction costs.

Depending on the exact way in which the arbitrage attempt is conducted, a trader must incur a variety of transaction costs. To see the full magnitude of these expenses, consider the misaligned futures and cash T-bill prices in Table 5.6. We explored these prices in Chapter 4. The transaction costs incurred to exploit this misalignment depend

■ **Table 5.6**

INTEREST RATE FUTURES AND ARIBTRAGE

Today's Date: January 5

Futures	Yield According to the Bond Pricing Formula
MAR Futures Contract	
(Matures in 77 days on March 22)	12.50%
Cash Bills	
167-Day T-bill	
(Deliverable on MAR Futures)	10.00
77-Day T-bill	6.00

on the trader's initial position in the spot or futures market. With no position in either market, the trader must pay all transaction costs from the gross trading profits to capture an academic arbitrage profit. If an opportunity is attractive enough to show a profit, even after paying full transaction costs, it can be considered **pure arbitrage**.

If the trader already holds a portfolio of T-bills, for example, then some transaction costs can be avoided. Some of the costs have already been paid, and they should be considered as sunk costs for the analysis of the arbitrage. If a trader with an initial portfolio can successfully engage in arbitrage, then the profitable transaction is regarded as **quasi-arbitrage**. In discussing pure arbitrage and quasi-arbitrage, we refer to academic arbitrage.

To exploit the rate discrepancies in Table 5.6 via pure arbitrage, the trader must be able to pay a variety of transaction costs:

1. Issuing a 77-day T-bill is equivalent to borrowing. The most credit-worthy traders can borrow a T-bill for about 50 basis points above its current yield. For $956,750 for 77 days, the borrowing cost is about $1,023. Consider also that the acquisition of the $956,750 might be through the issuance of a term repo agreement.

2. To buy a 167-day T-bill, a trader must pay the asked price for the bill, even if he or she is a market participant, which could involve an additional cost of about $100. If not a participant in the spot T-bill market, the trader must trade through a broker and pay a commission as well.

3. In selling the MAR futures contract, a trader can receive only the bid price, thereby increasing costs about $25. If he or she is not a trader on the IMM, the trader must pay commission costs as well.
4. Delivering the T-bill also has costs, because the short trader in the futures market bears all costs of delivery. These costs might be about $50.
5. Paying off the due bill also involves transactions costs of the wire transfer and record keeping, which might be $25.

This list of transaction charges is only an indication of the additional expenses that a trader might face in an arbitrage attempt. Many of the charges shown in the list are difficult to gauge, and different market participants face different levels of expense. Nonetheless, the expenses are large and can offset a substantial difference between forward and futures yields. In addition, a trader also faces a cost not shown in the list. To find an arbitrage opportunity, a trader must search for it, and the cost of searching for the opportunity must be included in the calculation of the arbitrage profit.

From the list of transaction costs, we see that some market participants are in a much better position than others. If a participant has a portfolio of spot T-bills, has a very good credit rating, is a trader on the futures exchange, and has a network of computerized information sources already in operation, then the transaction costs incurred in attempting to conduct an arbitrage operation are much smaller. This is the difference between pure arbitrage and quasi-arbitrage. For pure arbitrage, the yield discrepancy must be large enough to cover all transaction costs faced by a market outsider. For quasi-arbitrage, the trader faces less than full transaction costs.

How can we assess the variety of evidence on the efficiency of the interest rate futures market? Several years ago, it appeared the weight of evidence favored efficiency, but today it appears that weight is beginning to shift. In attempting to summarize this evidence in a single sentence, it appears that persistent inefficiencies continue to exist in these markets, but the size of the inefficiencies may not be large enough to reward a change in professions. Studies generally do no reflect the search cost or the use of human capital required to find and exploit the alleged arbitrage opportunity.

We must also remember that most studies have focused on the existence of arbitrage opportunities. Arbitrage, however, is the grossest kind of inefficiency. A market may well have no arbitrage opportunities and still be inefficient. If risky positions can be taken in the futures market, and those risky positions earn returns in excess of a risk-adjusted normal return, then the futures market would still be inefficient. Few tests of such possibilities have been conducted, probably due to the difficulty in defining a risk-adjusted normal return. The ones that have been conducted reach divergent conclusions.

APPLICATIONS: EURODOLLAR AND T-BILL FUTURES

In Chapter 4 we considered speculative strategies and some hedging strategies. In this section we explore alternative risk management strategies using short-term interest rate futures. We proceed by considering a series of examples. Taken together, these examples provide a handbook of techniques for a variety of risk management strategies. All of these strategies turn on protection against shifting interest rates.

CHANGING THE MATURITY OF AN INVESTMENT

Many investors find themselves with an existing portfolio that may have undesirable maturity characteristics. For example, a firm might hold a six-month T-bill and realize that it will have a need for funds in three months. By the same token, another investor might hold the same six-month T-bill and fear that those funds might have to face lower reinvestment rates upon maturity in six months. This investor might prefer a one-year maturity. Both the firm and the investor could sell the six-month bill and invest for the preferred maturity. However, spot market transaction costs are relatively high, and many investors prefer to alter the maturities of investment by trading futures. The two examples that follow show how to use futures to accomplish both a shortening and lengthening of maturities.

Shortening the Maturity of a T-Bill Investment. Consider a firm that has invested in a T-bill. Now, on March 20, the T-bill has a maturity of 180 days, but the firm learns of a need for cash in 90 days. Therefore, it would like to shorten the maturity so it can have access to its funds in 90 days, around mid-September.

For simplicity, we assume that the short-term yield curve is flat with all rates at 10 percent on March 20. For convenience, we assume a 360-day year to match the pricing conventions for T-bills. The face value of the firm's T-bill is $10 million. With 180 days to maturity and a 10 percent discount yield, the price of the bill is given by:

$$P = FV - [DY(FV)(DTM)]/360$$

where:

$$P = \text{bill price}$$
$$FV = \text{face value}$$
$$DY = \text{discount yield}$$
$$DTM = \text{days until maturity}$$

Therefore, the 180-day bill is worth $9,500,000. If the yield curve is flat at 10 percent, the futures yield must also be 10 percent, and the T-bill futures price must be $975,000 per contract. Starting from an initial position of a six-month T-bill, the firm of our example can shorten the maturity by selling T-bill futures for expiration in three months, as Table 5.7 shows. On March 20, there was no cash flow, because the firm merely sold futures. On June 20, the six-month bill is now a three-month bill and can be delivered against the futures. In Table 5.7, the firm delivers the bills and receives the futures invoice amount of $9,750,000. (Although we have assumed the futures price did not change, this does not limit the applicability of our results. No matter how the futures price changed from March to June, the firm would still receive a total of $9,750,000. We assume that this occurs in June instead of over the period.) The firm has effectively shortened the maturity from six months to three months.

Lengthening the Maturity. Consider now, on August 21, an investor who holds a $100 million face value T-bill that matures in 30 days on September 20. She plans to reinvest for another three months after the T-bill matures. However, she fears that interest rates might fall

■ **Table 5.7** ——————————————————————————————

TRANSACTIONS TO SHORTEN MATURITIES

Date	Cash Market	Futures Market
March 20	Holds six-month T-bill with a face value of $10,000,000, worth $9,500,000. Wishes a three-month maturity.	Sell 10 JUN T-bill futures contracts at 90.00, reflecting the 10% discount yield.
June 20		Deliver cash market T-bills against futures; receive $9,750,000.

unexpectedly. If so, she would be forced to reinvest at a lower rate than is now reflected in the yield curve. The SEP T-bill futures yield is 9.8 percent, as is the rate on the current investment. She finds this rate attractive and would like to lengthen the maturity of the T-bill investment. She knows that she can lengthen the maturity by buying a September futures contract and taking delivery. She will then hold the delivered bills until maturity in December.

With a 9.8 percent discount futures yield, the value of the delivery unit is $975,500. With $100 million coming available on September 20, the investor knows she will have enough funds to take delivery of ($100,000,000/$975,500) = 102.51 futures contracts. Therefore, she initiates the strategy presented in Table 5.8.

On August 21, she held a bill worth $99,183,333, assuming a yield of 9.8 percent. With the transactions of Table 5.8, she had no cash flow on August 21. With the maturity of the T-bill in September, the investor received $100,000,000 and used almost all of it to pay for the futures delivery. She also received $499,000, which we assume she invested at 9.8 percent for three months. In December, this investment would be worth $499,000 + $499,000(.098)(90/360) = $511,226. With the T-bills maturing in December, the total proceeds will be $102,511,226, from an investment that was worth $99,183,333 on

■ Table 5.8

TRANSACTIONS TO LENGTHEN MATURITIES

Date	Cash Market	Futures Market
August 21	Holds 30-day T-bill with a face value of $100,000,000. Wishes to extend the maturity for 90 days.	Buy 102 SEP T-bill futures contracts, with a yield of 9.8%.
September 20	30-day T-bill matures and investor receives $100,000,000. Invest $499,000 in money market fund.	Accept delivery on 102 SEP futures, paying $99,501,000.
December 19	T-bills received on SEP futures mature for $102,000,000.	

August 21. This gives her a discount yield of 9.8 percent over the four-month horizon from August to December.

Notice that this transaction locked in the 9.8 percent on the futures contract. In this example, this happens to match the spot rate of interest. However, the important point to recognize is that lengthening the maturity involves locking into the futures yield, no matter what that yield may be. Thus, for the period covered by the T-bill delivered on the futures contract, the investment will earn the futures yield at the time of contracting.

Fixed and Floating Loan Rates

In recent years interest rates have fluctuated dramatically. These fluctuating rates generate interest rate risk that few economic agents are anxious to bear. For example, in housing finance, home buyers seek fixed rate loans, because the fixed rate protects the borrower against rising rates. By the same token, lenders may be unwilling to offer fixed rate loans, because they fear that their cost of funds might rise. With fixed rate lending, and a rising cost of funds, the lender faces a risk of paying more to acquire funds than it is earning on its fixed rate lending. Therefore, many lenders want to make floating rate loans.

In this section, we show how the borrower who receives a floating rate loan can effectively convert this loan into a fixed rate loan, thereby protecting against rises in interest rates. Similarly, for a lender who feels compelled to offer fixed rate loans, we show how the lender can use the futures markets to make the investment perform like a floating rate loan. Either the borrower or lender can bear the interest rate risk. Whichever party bears the interest rate risk can hedge the risk through the futures market. In a floating rate loan, the borrower bears or hedges the risk. In a fixed rate loan, the lender bears or hedges the risk.

In this section we consider a single transaction from two points of view, the lender's and the borrower's. First, we assume that the loan is a floating rate loan and that the borrower hedges the interest rate risk associated with the loan. Second, we consider a fixed rate loan in which the lender hedges the interest rate risk.

Converting a Floating Rate to a Fixed Rate Loan. A construction firm plans a project that will take six months to complete at a total cost of $100 million. The bank offers to provide the funds for six

months at a rate 200 basis points above the 90-day LIBOR rate. However, the bank insists that the loan rate for the second quarter will
be 200 basis points above the 90-day LIBOR rate that prevails at that
date. Also, the construction company must pay interest after the first
quarter. Principal plus interest is due in six months.

Today is September 20 and the current 90-day LIBOR rate is 7.0
percent. The DEC Eurodollar futures yield is 7.3 percent. Based on
these rates and the borrowing plan, the construction company will
pay 9 percent for the first three months and 9.3 percent for the second
three months. These rates give the following cash flows from the
loan:

September 20	Receive principal	+ $100,000,000
December 20	Pay interest	− 2,250,000
March 20	Pay interest and principal	− 102,325,000

The cash flows for September and December are certain. However,
the cash flow in March depends upon the LIBOR rate that prevails
in December. The firm expects a 9.3 percent rate, which equals the
futures yield for the DEC futures plus 200 basis points. However,
between September and December, that rate could rise. For example,
if the spot 90-day LIBOR rate in December is 7.8 percent, the firm
will pay 9.8 percent and the total interest due in March will be
$125,000 higher than expected.

The construction firm decides to lock into the 7.3 futures yield
and its expected 9.3 borrowing rate so that it will know its borrowing
cost. Starting with a floating rate loan and transacting to fix the interest
rate is called creating a **synthetic fixed rate loan**. Table 5.9 shows
how the construction company trades to protect itself from a jump
in rates. At the outset, the firm accepts the floating rate scheme for
its loan and sells 100 DEC Eurodollar futures. If rates rise, the short
futures position will give enough profits to pay the additional interest
expense on the second quarter's loan.

As Table 5.9 shows, LIBOR rises by 50 basis points to 7.8 percent.
This implies a borrowing rate of 9.8 percent for the second quarter,
as the table shows. However, the rise in rates has created a futures
profit of $125,000 = 50 basis points times $25 per basis point times
100 contracts. The table shows that the firm pays $125,000 more
interest in the second quarter than anticipated due to the jump in rates.
However, this is exactly offset by the futures profit.[3] In September, the

■ Table 5.9

SYNTHETIC FIXED RATE BORROWING

Date	Cash Market	Futures Market
September 20	Borrow $100,000,000 at 9.00% for three months and commit to extend the loan for three additional months at a rate 200 basis points above the three-month LIBOR rate prevailing at that time.	Sell 100 DEC Eurodollar futures contracts at 92.70, reflecting the 7.3% yield.
December 20	Pay interest of $2,250,000. LIBOR is now at 7.8%, so borrow $100,000,000 for three months at 9.8%.	Offset 100 DEC Eurodollar futures at 92.20, reflecting the 7.8% yield. Produces profit of $125,000 = 50 basis points × $25 per point × 100 contracts.
March 20	Pay interest of $2,450,000 and repay principal of $100,000,000.	
	Total Interest Expense: $4,700,000	Futures Profit: $125,000
	Net Interest Expense After Hedging: $4,575,000	

firm expected to pay a total of $4,575,000 in interest for the loan. Counting the futures profit, this is exactly the interest that the firm pays because it hedged. By trading in the futures market, the construction firm changed its floating rate loan into a fixed rate loan.

Converting a Fixed Rate to a Floating Rate Loan. We now consider the same transaction from the lender's point of view. If the construction company really wants a fixed rate loan, let them have it, reasons the bank. The bank's cost of funds equals the 90-day LIBOR rate, we assume. The bank expects to pay 7.0 percent for funds this quarter and 7.3 percent next quarter, or an average rate of 7.15 percent over the six months of the loan. Therefore, the bank decides to make a fixed rate six-month loan to the construction company at 9.15 percent. The bank's expected profit is the 200 basis point spread between the lending rate and the bank's LIBOR-based cost of funds. The bank expects to secure the funds by borrowing:

September 20	Borrow principal	+ $100,000,000
	Make loan to construction company	− $100,000,000
December 20	Pay interest	− $1,750,000
March 20	Receive principal and interest from construction company	+ $104,575,000
	Pay principal and interest	− $101,825,000

If all goes as expected, the bank's gross profit will be $1,000,000. Having made a fixed rate loan, however, the bank is at risk of rising interest rates. For example, if LIBOR rises by 50 basis points to 7.8 percent for the second quarter, the bank will have to pay an additional $125,000 in interest. To avoid this risk, the bank transacts as shown in Table 5.10. Notice how they almost exactly match the transactions of the construction company, except that the bank has a lower borrowing rate. If interest rates rise, the bank's cost of funds rises, just

■ **Table 5.10** ───────────────────────

SYNTHETIC FLOATING RATE LENDING

Date	Cash Market	Futures Market
September 20	Borrow $100,000,000 at 7.00% for three months and lend it for six months at 9.15%.	Sell 100 DEC Eurodollar futures contracts at 92.70, reflecting the 7.3% yield.
December 20	Pay interest of $1,750,000. LIBOR is now at 7.8%, so borrow $100,000,000 for three months at 7.8%.	Offset 100 DEC Eurodollar futures at 92.20, reflecting the 7.8% yield. Produces profit of $125,000 = 50 basis points × $25 per point × 100 contracts.
March 20	Pay interest of $1,950,000 and repay principal of $100,000,000.	
	Total Interest Expense: $3,700,000	Futures Profit: $125,000

Net Interest Expense After Hedging: $3,575,000

as was the case for the construction company with a floating rate loan. Both the construction company and the bank were able to hedge by selling Eurodollar futures.

With the rise in rates, the bank paid $125,000 more interest than it expected. However, this increased interest was offset by a futures market gain. Originally, the bank wanted to shift the interest rate risk to the construction company. However, as the transactions of Table 5.10 show, the bank is able to give the construction company the fixed rate loan it desires and still avoid the interest rate risk. In essence, the bank creates a **synthetic floating rate loan**. For its customer it offers a fixed rate loan, but the bank transacts in the futures market to make the transaction equivalent to having given a floating rate loan.

STRIP AND STACK HEDGES

In the example of the synthetic fixed rate loan and synthetic floating rate lending, the interest rate risk focused on a single date. Often, the period of the loan covers a number of different dates at which the rate might be reset. For example, the construction company of our previous example makes a more realistic assessment of how long it will take to complete a project. Instead of six months, the construction firm realizes the project will take a year.

The bank insists on making a floating rate loan for three months at a rate 200 basis points above the LIBOR rate prevailing at the time of the loan. On September 15, the construction company observes the following rates:

Three-month LIBOR	7.00%
DEC Eurodollar	7.30
MAR Eurodollar	7.60
JUN Eurodollar	7.90

For these four quarters, the firm expects to finance the $100,000,000 at 9.00, 9.30, 9.60, and 9.90 percent, respectively. Therefore, the construction company expects to borrow $100,000,000 for a year at an average rate of 9.45 percent. This gives a total expected interest cost of $9,450,000.

A Stack Hedge Example. The construction firm decides to lock in this borrowing rate by hedging with Eurodollar futures. To implement the hedge, the firm sells 300 DEC Eurodollar futures. The firm hopes to protect itself against any changes in interest rates between

September and December. In December, the futures will expire and the firm will offset the DEC futures and replace them with MAR futures. This is a **stack hedge**, because all of the futures contracts are concentrated, or stacked, in a single futures expiration.

We now consider how the construction firm fares with a single change in interest rates over the next year. Shortly after the firm enters the hedge, LIBOR rates jump by 50 basis points. Therefore, the firm's borrowing costs for the next three quarters are:

December-March	9.80%
March-June	10.10
June-September	10.40

For simplicity, we consider only one interest rate change, so the firm secures these rates. Table 5.11 shows the construction firm's transactions and the results of the hedge. The firm hedges its $100,000,000 loan with 300 contracts, or $300,000,000 of underlying Eurodollars. After taking the loan, the first quarter's rate is fixed at 9.00 percent. Therefore, the firm is at risk for $100,000,000 for three quarters. Because the maturity of the Eurodollars that underlie the futures is only one quarter, it requires three times as much futures value as its spot market exposure.

With the shift in rates, the firm must pay $9,825,000 in interest, which is more than the expected $9,450,000 when the firm took the loan. This difference is due to the across-the-board interest rate rise of 50 basis points. The same interest rate rise generates a futures trading profit of $375,000. Thus, the futures profit exactly offsets the increase in interest costs, and the construction firm has successfully hedged its interest rate risk using a stack hedge.

A Danger in Using Stack Hedges. We now consider a potential danger in using a stack hedge of this type. In the example, the stack hedge worked perfectly because all interest rates changed by the same 50 basis points. As a result, the stack hedge gave a perfect hedge and the construction firm had no changes in its anticipated total borrowing cost. The same stack hedge might have performed very poorly if interest rates had changed in a somewhat different fashion.

For example, after the loan agreement is signed, the funds are received, and the same stack hedge is implemented, assume there is a single change in futures yields as follows. The DEC futures yield rises from 7.3 to 7.4 percent, the MAR futures yield rises from 7.6 to

■ Table 5.11

Results of a Stack Hedge

Date	Cash Market	Futures Market
September 20	Borrow $100,000,000 at 9.00% for three months and commit to roll over the loan for three quarters at 200 basis points over the prevailing LIBOR rate.	Sell 300 DEC Eurodollar futures contracts at 92.70, reflecting the 7.3% yield.
December 20	Pay interest of $2,250,000. LIBOR is now at 7.8 percent, so borrow $100,000,000 for three months at 9.8%.	Offset 300 DEC Eurodollar futures at 92.20, reflecting the 7.8% yield. Produces profit of $375,000 = 50 basis points × $25 per point × 300 contracts.
March 20	Pay interest of $2,450,000 and borrow $100,000,000 for three months at 10.10%.	
June 20	Pay interest of $2,525,000 and borrow $100,000,000 for three months at 10.40%.	
September 20	Pay interest of $2,600,000 and principal of $100,000,000.	
	Total Interest Expense: $9,825,000	Futures Profit: $375,000
	Interest Expense Net of Hedging: $9,450,000	

8.3 percent, and the JUN futures yield jumps from 7.9 to 8.6 percent, as Figure 5.4 shows. With this change in rates, the construction firm will have the following borrowing costs and interest expenses:

September–December	9.00%	$2,250,000
December–March	9.40	2,350,000
March–June	10.30	2,575,000
June–September	10.60	2,650,000

■ Figure 5.4

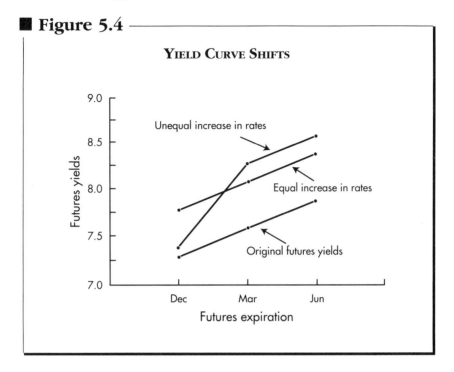

This change in rates gives the same increase in borrowing costs from the initially expected level of $9,450,000 to $9,825,000. However, there is one important difference. The DEC futures yield changed by only 10 basis points. Therefore, the futures profit on 300 DEC Eurodollar contracts is only $75,000 = 10 basis points times $25 per basis point times 300 contracts. Now the net borrowing cost after hedging is $9,750,000. This is $300,000 more than initially expected.

The graph of Figure 5.4 shows the original position for the DEC, MAR, and JUN Eurodollar futures yields. In our first example of a stack hedge, we assumed that all futures yields rose by 50 basis points. The rates after this equal jump are shown in the graph. We then considered an unequal increase in rates and the effectiveness of the stack hedge. Figure 5.4 shows those unequal rates for which the stack hedge was so ineffective. With the unequal increase in rates, the futures yield curve has steepened considerably. The DEC futures yield increased slightly, but the MAR futures yield increased more, as did the JUN futures yield. The poor performance of the stack hedge was due to this unequal change in rates.

A Strip Hedge. The stack hedge of the previous example was really hedging against a change in the DEC futures yield, because all of the contracts were stacked on that single futures expiration. Instead of using a concentration of contracts on a single expiration, a **strip hedge** uses an equal number of contracts for each futures expiration over the hedging horizon.

For our example of a $100,000,000 financing requirement at risk for three quarters, we have seen that a Eurodollar hedge requires 300 contracts. In a strip hedge, the construction firm would sell 100 Eurodollar contracts each of the DEC, MAR, and JUN futures. With the strip hedge in place, each quarter of the coming year is hedged against shifts in interest rates for that quarter. To illustrate the effectiveness of this strip hedge for an unequal increase in rates, Table 5.12 shows the results for the construction firm example.

The strip hedge of Table 5.12 works perfectly. The superior performance of the strip hedge results from aligning the futures market hedges with the actual risk exposure of the construction firm. Because the construction firm faced interest rate adjustments each quarter, it needed to hedge the interest rate risk associated with each quarter. This it could do through a strip hedge, but not through a stack hedge.

Strip versus Stack Hedges. From the example of the strip hedge, it appears that a strip hedge will always be superior to a stack hedge. While there are many circumstances where a strip hedge will be preferred, it is not always better than a stack hedge. Our earlier example of a firm that had a six-month horizon used a stack hedge with great success. Here the stack hedge exactly matched the timing of the firm's interest rate exposure, whereas a strip hedge would not have worked as well. The important point is to use a strip or stack hedge as required to match the timing of the futures hedge to the timing of the cash market risk exposure.

There is also a practical consideration that often leads hedgers to use a stack hedge when theory might favor a strip hedge. To implement a strip hedge requires trading more distant contracts. In our example, the construction firm traded the nearby, second, and third contracts. There is not always sufficient volume and liquidity in distant contracts to make such a strategy viable. Strips work well with Eurodollar futures because Eurodollar futures now have sufficient volume in distant contracts to make them attractive. This has not always been the case, however. When distant contracts lack liquidity, the hedger must trade off the advantages of a strip hedge with the potential lack of liquidity in the distant contracts. For the dominant interest rate futures contracts, strips work well because of the great liquidity in these markets.

■ Table 5.12

RESULTS OF A STRIP HEDGE

Date	Cash Market	Futures Market
September 20	Borrow $100,000,000 at 9.00% for three months and commit to roll over the loan for three quarters at 200 basis points over the prevailing LIBOR rate.	Sell 100 Eurodollar futures for each of: DEC at 92.70, MAR at 92.40, and JUN at 91.90.
December 20	Pay interest of $2,250,000. LIBOR is now at 7.8%, so borrow $100,000,000 for three months at 9.8%.	Offset 100 DEC Eurodollar futures at 92.60. Produces profit of $25,000 = 10 basis points × $25 per point × 100 contracts.
March 20	Pay interest of $2,450,000 and borrow $100,000,000 for three months at 10.10%.	Offset 100 MAR Eurodollar futures at 91.70. Produces profit of $175,000 = 70 basis points × $25 per point × 100 contracts.
June 20	Pay interest of $2,525,000 and borrow $100,000,000 for three months at 10.40%.	Offset 100 JUN Eurodollar futures at 91.40. Produces profit of $175,000 = 70 basis points × $25 per point × 100 contracts.
September 20	Pay interest of $2,600,000 and principal of $100,000,000.	
	Total Interest Expense: $9,825,000	Futures Profit: $375,000
	Interest Expense Net of Hedging: $9,450,000	

HEDGING WITH T-BOND FUTURES

This section begins with an example of a cross-hedge of AAA corporate bonds. The example shows that a simple hedging rule of using $1 of futures per $1 of bonds can lead to horrible hedging results. This example leads to a discussion of alternative hedging techniques focusing on hedging with T-bonds.

In all previous hedging examples, the hedged and hedging instruments were very similar. Often, however, the need arises to hedge an instrument very different from those underlying the futures contract. The effectiveness of a hedge depends on the gain or loss on both the spot and futures sides of the transaction. But the change in the price of any bond depends on the shifts in the level of interest rates, changes in the shape of the yield curve, the maturity of the bond, and its coupon rate.

To illustrate the effect of the maturity and coupon rate on hedging performance, consider the following example. A portfolio manager learns on March 1 that he will receive $5 million on June 1 to invest in AAA corporate bonds paying an annual coupon of 5 percent and having 10 years to maturity. The yield curve is flat and is assumed to remain so over the period from March 1 to June 1. The current yield on AAA bonds is 9.5 percent. Since the yield curve is flat, the forward rates are also all 9.5 percent, so the portfolio manager expects to acquire the bonds at that yield. However, fearing a drop in rates, he decides to hedge in the futures market to lock in the forward rate of 9.5 percent.

The next step is to select the appropriate hedging instrument. The manager considers two possibilities: T-bills or T-bonds. However, the AAA bonds have a 5 percent coupon and a ten-year maturity, which do not match the coupon and maturity characteristics of either the T-bills or T-bonds deliverable on the respective futures contracts. The deliverable T-bills have a zero coupon and a maturity of only 90 days, while the deliverable T-bonds have a maturity of at least 15 years and an assortment of coupons. For this example, assume that the deliverable T-bond is a 20-year, 8 percent coupon bond.

To explore fully the potential difficulties of this situation, we consider hedging the AAA position with T-bill and T-bond futures. We ignore T-notes to dramatize the need to match coupon and maturity characteristics. For the bills and bonds, we assume the yields are 8 and 8.5 percent, respectively. Table 5.13 presents the hedging transactions and results for the T-bill hedge.

Because $5 million is becoming available for investment, assume the manager buys $5 million face value of T-bill futures contracts. Time passes, and by June 1 yields have fallen by 42 basis points on both the AAAs and the T-bills, respectively. The price of the corporate

■ Table 5.13

A CROSS-HEDGE BETWEEN CORPORATE BONDS AND T-BILL FUTURES

Date	Cash Market	Futures Market
March 1	A portfolio manager learns he will receive $5 million to invest in 5%, 10-year AAA bonds in 3 months, with an expected yield of 9.5% and a price of $717.45. The manager expects to buy 6,969 bonds.	The portfolio manager buys $5 million face value of T-bill futures (5 contracts) to mature on June 1 with a futures yield of 8.0% and a futures price, per contract, of $980,944.
June 1	AAA yields have fallen to 9.08%, causing the price of the bonds to be $739.08. This represents a loss, per bond, of $21.63. Since the plan was to buy 6,969 bonds, the total loss is (6,969 × $21.63) = −$150,739.	The T-bill futures yield has fallen to 7.58%, so the futures price = spot price = $981,900 per contract, or a profit of $956 per contract. Since 5 contracts were traded, the total profit is $4,780.
	Loss = −$150,739	Gain = $4,780

Net wealth change = −$145,959

bond is $739.08, or $21.63 higher than the anticipated price of $717.45. Since the manager expected to buy 6,969 bonds, this means that the total additional outlay would be $150,739 (6,969 × $21.63), and this represents the loss in the cash market. In the futures market, rates also fell 42 basis points, generating a futures price increase of $956 per contract. Because five contracts were bought, the futures profit is $4,780. However, the loss in the cash market exceeds the gain in the futures market, for a net loss of $145,959. Note that this loss results even though rates changed by the same amount on both investments.

Consider now the same hedging problem, but assume we implement the hedge using $5 million face value of T-bond futures. Table 5.14 presents the transactions and results. Again yields fall by 42 basis points on both instruments. Consequently, the effect on the cash

■ Table 5.14 ─────────────────────────────

A Cross Hedge Between Corporate Bonds and T-Bond Futures

Date	Cash Market	Futures Market
March 1	A portfolio manager learns he will receive $5 million to invest in 5%, 10-year AAA bonds in 3 months, with an expected yield of 9.5% and a price of $717.45. The manager expects to buy 6,969 bonds.	The portfolio manager buys $5 million face value of T-bond futures (50 contracts) to mature on June 1 with a futures yield of 8.5% and a futures price, per contract, of $96,875.
June 1	AAA yields have fallen to 9.08%, causing the price of the bonds to be $739.08. This represents a loss, per bond, of $21.63. Since the plan was to buy 6,969 bonds, the total loss is (6,969 × $21.63) = −$150,739.	The T-bond futures yield has fallen to 8.08%, so the futures price = spot price = $100,750 per contract, or a profit of $3,875 per contract. Since 50 contracts were traded, the total profit is $193,750.
	Loss = −$150,739	Gain = $193,750

Net wealth change = +$43,011

market is the same, but the total futures gain is $193,750, more than offsetting the loss in the cash market and generating a net wealth change = +$43,011.

If the goal of the hedge is to secure a net wealth change of zero, a gain is appropriately viewed as no better than a loss. It is only by accident of rates moving in the appropriate direction that the gain was not a loss anyway. Recall that all of the simplifying assumptions were in place – a flat yield curve with rates on both instruments moving in the same direction and by the same amount. However, as noted earlier, the coupon and maturity of the hedged and hedging instruments do not match. All three instruments, the bond, the T-bill futures, and the T-bond futures, have different durations, reflecting different sensitivities to interest rates. Consequently, for a given shift in yields (e.g., 42 basis points), the prices of the three instruments will change by different amounts. Therefore, a simple hedge of $1 in the futures market per $1 in the cash market is unlikely to produce satisfactory results.

ALTERNATIVE HEDGING STRATEGIES

We have seen that simple approaches to hedging interest rate risk often give unsatisfactory results, due to mismatches of coupon and maturity characteristics. For the best possible hedges, we need strategies that take these coupon and maturity mismatches into consideration. This section chronicles some of the major strategies for hedging interest rate risk, starting from simple models and going on to more complex models.

Face Value Naive (FVN) Model. According to the FVN model, the hedger should hedge $1 of face value of the cash instrument with $1 face value of the futures contract. For example, a hedger wishing to hedge $100,000 face value of bonds would use one T-bond futures contract. The example we just considered used this strategy. The FVN strategy neglects two critically important factors:

1. By focusing on face values, the FVN model completely neglects potential differences in market values between the cash and futures positions. Therefore, keeping face value amounts equal between the cash and futures market can result in poor hedges because the market values of the two positions differ.
2. The FVN model neglects the coupon and maturity characteristics that affect duration for both the cash market good and the futures contract.

Because of these deficiencies, we will not consider the FVN model further.

Market Value Naive (MVN) Model. The MVN model resembles the FVN model, except it recommends hedging $1 of market value in the cash good with $1 of market value in the futures market. For example, if a $100,000 face value bond has a market value of $90,000 and the $100,000 face value T-bond futures contract is priced at 80-00, the MVN model would recommend hedging the cash bonds with $1.125 = (90/80)$ futures contracts.

Because it considers the difference between market and face value, the MVN model escapes the first criticism lodged against the FVN model. However, the MVN model still makes no adjustment for the price sensitivity of the two goods. Therefore, we dismiss the MVN model without further consideration.

Conversion Factor (CF) Model. The CF model applies only to futures contracts that use conversion factors to determine the invoice amount, such as T-bond and T-note futures. The intuition of this model is to adjust for differing price sensitivities by using the conversion factor as an index of the sensitivity.

In particular, the CF model recommends hedging $1 of face value of a cash market security with $1 of face value of the futures good times the conversion factor. As we have seen for T-bond and T-note futures, there are many deliverable instruments with different conversion factors. To apply the CF model, we must determine which instrument is cheapest-to-deliver and use the conversion factor for that instrument. Assuming we have identified the cheapest-to-deliver security, the hedge ratio (HR) is given by:

$$\text{HR} = -\left(\frac{\text{Cash Market Principal}}{\text{Futures Market Principal}} \right) (\text{Conversion Factor}) \quad (5.3)$$

The negative sign indicates that one must take a futures market position opposite to the cash market position. For example, if the hedger is long in the cash market, the hedger should sell futures.

As an example, assume that a bond manager wishes to hedge a long position of $500,000 face value of bonds with T-bond futures. We assume the cheapest-to-deliver bond has a conversion factor of 1.2. In this situation, the manager should sell $600,000 worth of T-bond futures [$500,000(1.2)] or six contracts. The CF model attempts to secure the same amount of principal value of bonds on both the cash and futures sides of the hedge. This method is useful principally when one contemplates delivering a cash market bond against a futures contract.

Basis Point (BP) Model. The BP model focuses on the price effect of a one basis point change in yields. For example, we have seen that a change of one basis point causes a $25 change in the futures price of a T-bill or Eurodollar contract. Assume that today is April 2 and that a firm plans to issue $50 million of 180-day commercial paper in six weeks. For a one basis point yield change, the price of 180-day commercial paper will change twice as much as the 90-day T-bill futures contract, assuming equal face value amounts. In other words, on $1 million of 180-day commercial paper, a one basis point yield change causes a $50 price change. In an important sense, the commercial paper will be twice as sensitive to a change in yields.

To reflect this greater sensitivity, we can use the BP model to compute the following hedge ratio:

$$HR = -\frac{BPC_C}{BPC_F} \qquad (5.4)$$

where:

BPC_C = dollar price change for a 1 basis point change in the cash instrument

BPC_F = dollar price change for a 1 basis point change in the futures instrument

The ratio BPC_C/BPC_F indicates the relative number of contracts to trade. In our commercial paper example, the cash basis price change (BPC_C) is twice as great as the futures basis price change (BPC_F), so the hedge ratio is −2.0.

To explore the effect of this weighting, consider the following BP model hedge of the commercial paper. Planning to issue commercial paper, the firm will lose if rates rise, because the firm will receive less cash for its commercial paper. As it needs to sell the commercial paper, it is now long commercial paper and must hedge by selling futures. With a −2.0 hedge ratio and a $50 million face value commitment in the cash market, the firm should sell 100 T-bill futures contracts.

Table 5.15 presents the BP model transactions. After rates on both sides of the contract move by 45 basis points, we have the following result. In the cash market, the firm receives $112,500 less than anticipated for its commercial paper. This loss, however, is exactly offset by the price movement on the $100 million of T-bills underlying the futures position. The BP model helped identify the correct number of futures to trade for each unit in the cash market. By contrast, the FVN model would have suggested trading only 50 futures, which would have hedged only half of the loss.

Sometimes the yields may not change by the same amount as they did in Table 5.15. In that case, the hedger may wish to incorporate the relative volatility of the yields into the hedge ratio. For example,

■ Table 5.15

Hedging Results with the BP Model for the Commercial Paper Issuance

April 2

Cash Market	Futures Market
Firm anticipates issuing $50 million in 180-day commercial paper in 45 days at a yield of 11%.	Firm sells 100 T-bill June futures contracts yielding 10% with an index value of 90.00.

May 15

Spot market and futures market rates have both risen 45 basis points. The spot rate is now 11.45% and the futures market yield is 10.45%.

Cash Market Effect	Futures Market Effect
Each basis point move causes a price change of $50 per million-dollar face value. Firm will receive $112,500 less for the commercial paper, due to the change in rates. (45 basis points × $50 × 50 contracts = −$112,500)	Each basis point increase gives a futures market profit of $25 per contract. Futures Profit = 45 basis points × +$25 × 100 contracts = +$112,500

Net wealth change = 0

---

assume that the commercial paper rate is 25 percent more volatile than the T-bill futures rate. In other words, a 100 basis point rise in the T-bill futures rate normally might be accompanied by a 125 basis point rise in the commercial paper rate. To give the same total price change in the futures market as in the cash position, we would need to consider that difference in volatility in determining the hedge ratio. In that case, the hedge ratio becomes:

$$HR = -\left(\frac{BPC_C}{BPC_F}\right) RV \qquad (5.5)$$

where:

RV = volatility of cash market yield relative to futures yield, normally found by regressing the yield of the cash market instrument on the futures market yield

If we incorporate RV, assumed to be 1.25, into our commercial paper hedge, the transactions would appear as shown in the top portion of Table 5.16. Now the hedge ratio is:

$$\text{HR} = -\left(\frac{\$50}{\$25}\right) 1.25 = -2.5$$

Consequently, the hedger sells 125 T-bill futures contracts. Assume again that the T-bill yields rise by 45 basis points. Also, true to its greater relative volatility, the commercial paper yield moves 56 basis points, 1.25 times as much. Because more T-bill futures were sold, the T-bill futures profit still almost exactly offsets the commercial paper loss.

Regression (RGR) Model. One way of calculating a hedge ratio for interest rate futures is the regression technique we considered in Chapter 3. The hedge ratio found by regression minimizes the variance

■ Table 5.16

HEDGING RESULTS WITH THE BP MODEL ADJUSTED FOR RELATIVE YIELD VARIANCES FOR THE COMMERCIAL PAPER ISSUANCE

April 2

Cash Market	Futures Market
Firm anticipates issuing $50 million in 180-day commercial paper in 45 days at a yield of 11%.	Firm sells 125 T-bill June futures contracts yielding 10% with an index value of 90.00.

May 15

Spot market rates have risen 56 basis points to 11.56% and futures rates have risen 45 basis points to 10.45%.

Cash Market Effect	Futures Market Effect
Each basis point move causes a price change of $50 per million-dollar face value. Firm will receive $140,000 less for the commercial paper, due to the change in rates.	Each basis point increase gives a futures market profit of $25 per contract.
56 basis points × $50 × 50 contracts = −$140,000	Futures Profit = 45 basis points × +$25 × 125 contracts = +$140,625

Net wealth change = +$625

of the combined futures-cash position during the estimation period. This estimated ratio is applied to the hedging period.

For the RGR model the hedge ratio is:

$$HR = \frac{COV_{C,F}}{\sigma_F^2} \qquad (5.6)$$

where:

$COV_{C,F}$ = covariance between cash and futures
σ_F^2 = variance of cash and futures

As noted in Chapter 3, this hedge ratio is the regression coefficient found by regressing the change in the cash position on the change in the futures position. These changes can be measured as dollar price changes or as percentage price changes.

$$\Delta C_t = \alpha + \beta \Delta F_t + \epsilon_t$$

The RGR model uses the hedge ratio that gives the lowest sum of squared errors for the data used in the estimation. Using the estimated hedge ratio for an actual hedge assumes that the relationship between the price changes on the futures and cash instruments does not change dramatically between the sample period and the actual hedging period.

This is a practical assumption. If the relationship is basically unchanged, then the estimated hedge ratio will perform well in the actual hedging situation. Fundamental shifts in the relationship between the price of the futures contract and the cash market good can lead to serious hedging errors. This danger is present in all hedging situations, but may be exacerbated in interest rate hedging. Without doubt, the RGR model has proven its usefulness in the market for the traditional futures contracts, and it has been adapted for use in the interest rate futures market by Louis Ederington, Charles Franckle, Joanne Hill, and Thomas Schneeweis.[4]

However, there are some problems in applying the RGR model to interest rate hedging. First, since it involves statistical estimation, the technique requires a data set for both cash and futures prices. This data may sometimes be difficult to acquire, particularly for an attempt to hedge a new security. In such a case, no cash market data would even exist, and a proxy would have to be used. Second, the RGR model does not explicitly consider the differences in the sensitivity of different bond prices to changes in interest rates. As the examples of Tables 5.13 and 5.14 indicate, this can be a very important factor. The regression approach does include the different price sensitivities indirectly, however, since their differential sensitivities will be reflected in the estimation of the hedge ratio. Third, any cash bond will have a predictable price movement over time. The price of any instrument will equal its par value at maturity. The RGR model does not consider this change in the cash bond's price explicitly, but the sample data should reflect this price movement tendency. Fourth, the hedge ratio is chosen to minimize the variability in the combined futures-cash position over the life of the hedge. Since the RGR hedge ratio depends crucially on the planned hedge length, one might reasonably prefer a hedging technique focusing on the wealth position of the hedge when the hedge ends.[5] After all, the wealth change from the hedge depends on the gain or loss when the hedge is terminated, not on the variability of the cash-futures position over the life of the hedge. In spite of these difficulties, the RGR model is a useful way to estimate hedge ratios, both for traditional commodities and, to a lesser extent, for interest rate hedging.

Price Sensitivity (PS) Model. The PS model has been designed explicitly for interest rate hedging.[6] The PS model assumes that the goal of hedging is to eliminate unexpected wealth changes at the hedging horizon, as defined in Equation 5.7:

$$dP_i + dP_F (N) = 0 \qquad\qquad (5.7)$$

where:

dP_i = unexpected change in the price of the cash market instrument

dP_F = unexpected change in the price of the futures instrument

N = number of futures to hedge a single unit of the cash market asset

Equation 5.7 expresses the goal that the unexpected change in the value of the spot instrument, denoted by I, and the futures position, denoted by F, should together equal zero. If this is achieved, the wealth change, or hedging error, is zero. Instead of focusing on the variance over the period of the hedge, the PS model uses a hedge ratio to achieve a zero net wealth change at the end of the hedge.

The problem for the hedger is to choose the correct number of contracts, denoted by N in Equation 5.7, to achieve a zero hedging error. Equation 5.8 gives the correct number of contracts to trade (N), per spot market bond:

$$N = -\left(\frac{R_F P_i D_i}{R_i FP_F D_F}\right) RV \tag{5.8}$$

where:

R_F = 1 + the expected futures yield
R_i = 1 + the expected yield to maturity on asset I
FP_F = the futures contract price
P_i = the price of asset I expected to prevail at the hedging horizon
D_i = the duration of asset I expected to prevail at the hedging horizon
D_F = the duration of the asset underlying futures contract F expected to prevail at the hedging horizon
RV = the volatility of the cash market asset's yield relative to the volatility of the futures instrument's yield

In nontechnical terms, Equation 5.8 says that the number of futures contracts to trade for each cash market instrument to be hedged is the number that should give a perfect hedge, assuming that yields on the cash and futures instrument change by the same amount. To explore the meaning and application of this technique, consider again the AAA bond hedges of Tables 5.13 and 5.14. The large hedging errors resulted from the different price sensitivities of the futures instruments and the AAA bonds.

Table 5.17 presents the data needed to calculate the hedge ratios for hedging the AAA bonds with T-bill or T-bond futures. Here we assume that the cash and futures market assets have the same volatilities, so $RV = 1.0$. For the T-bill hedge:

$$N = -\frac{(1.08)(-\$717.45)(7.709)}{(1.095)(\$980,944)(.25)} = .022244$$

■ Table 5.17 ─────────────────

DATA FOR THE PRICE SENSITIVITY HEDGE

Cash Instrument		T-Bill Futures		T-Bond Futures	
P_i	$717.45	FP_i	$980,944	FP_F	$96,875
D_i	7.709	D_F	.25	D_F	10.143
R_i	1.095	R_F	1.08	R_F	1.085
		N	.02224	N	.005577
		Number of Contracts to Trade	155	Number of Contracts to Trade	39

The hedger should sell .022244 T-bill futures per AAA bond to be hedged. Because the portfolio manager plans to buy 6,969 bonds, he should hedge this commitment by trading 155 (actually, 155.02) T-bill futures. For the T-bond hedge:

$$N = -\frac{(1.085)(-\$717.45)(7.709)}{(1.095)(\$96,875)(10.143)} = .005577$$

With 6,969 bonds to hedge, the portfolio manager should sell 39 (actually, 38.8667) T-bond futures.

With either of these hedges, the same shift in yields on the AAA bonds and the futures instrument should give a perfect hedge. Table 5.18 presents the performance of these two hedges for the same 42 basis point drop in rates used in Tables 5.13 and 5.14.

With the given hedges and the same drop in yields, the first line of Table 5.18 shows that the T-bill hedge gave a futures gain of

■ Table 5.18 ─────────────────

PERFORMANCE ANALYSIS OF PRICE SENSITIVITY FUTURE HEDGE

	Cash Market	T-Bill Hedge	T-Bond Hedge
Gain/Loss	−$150,742	+$148,203	+$150,608
Hedging Error	–	$2,539	$134
Percentage of Cash Market Loss Hedged		98.32%	99.91%

$148,203 to offset the loss on the AAA bonds of $150,742. The futures gain on the T-bond hedge is $150,608. The next line shows the size of the hedging error for the T-bill and T-bond hedges, while the final line gives the percentage of the cash market loss that was hedged. The T-bill hedge was 98.32 percent effective, while the T-bond hedge was 99.91 percent effective. Both hedges were almost perfect. The slight errors were due to rounding error and to the large change in interest rates. In these examples, the PS model worked very effectively. In actual hedging situations, one could not hope for such nearly perfect results, since yields need not change by the same amount on all instruments all of the time.

Conclusion. It is difficult to compare all of the hedging models reviewed in this section, because they differ so much in aim and complexity. The naive hedges, FVN and MVN, are probably appropriate only for hedging short-term instruments with short-term futures contracts. The Conversion Factor model is essentially a naive model applicable to futures contracts with the structure of T-note or T-bond futures contracts.

The most widely used technique is some version of the PS model, although the Regression model is often also employed. In fact, it has been shown that the PS and RGR models are equivalent when the hedging horizon is instantaneous.[7] Because of problems in acquiring data for the RGR model, the PS model appears to be preferred.

In a number of papers, Joanne Hill and Thomas Schneeweis find that the RGR model is an effective hedging tool.[8] However, D. Lasser finds the RGR model to perform no better than various naive models.[9] Raymond Chiang, Gerald Gay, and Robert Kolb find that the PS model is more effective than naive models in hedging the risk of corporate bonds.[10] A. Toevs and D. Jacob offer a useful comparison of a number of hedging strategies, including the naive models and the RGR model, in which they find the PS model to be the most effective.[11] Finally, Ira Kawaller argues that the RGR approach is inferior to the BP or PS approaches to hedging.[12] Table 5.19 summarizes the various approaches to hedging.

CONCLUSION

Interest rate futures constitute one of the most exciting and complex financial markets. Only in recent years have the uses of the market begun to mature, and there remain many potential users who could

■ Table 5.19

SUMMARY OF ALTERNATIVE HEDGING STRATEGIES

Hedging Model	Basic Intuition
Face Value Naive (FVN)	Hedge $1 of cash instrument face value with $1 of futures instrument face value.
Market Value Naive (MVN)	Hedge $1 of cash instrument market value with $1 of futures instrument market value.
Conversion Factor (CF)	Find ratio of cash market principal to futures market principal. Multiply this ratio by the conversion factor for the cheapest-to-deliver instrument.
Basis Point (BP)	For a 1 basis point yield change, find the ratio of the cash market price change to the futures market price change. (Sometimes weighted by the relative volatility of interest rates on the cash market instrument compared to the futures instrument interest rate.)
Regression (RGR)	For a given cash market position, use regression analysis to find the futures position that minimizes the variance of the combined cash/ futures position.
Price Sensitivity (PS)	Using duration analysis, find the futures market position designed to give a zero wealth change at the hedging horizon. (Sometimes weighted by the relative volatility of interest rates on the cash market instrument compared to the futures instrument interest rate.)

benefit from the market. As we have seen, interest rate futures have many applications, including bond portfolio management. Interest rate futures can also be used to control foreign interest rate risk, to manage public utilities and insurance companies, to hedge mortgage financing risk, and to reduce risk in creative financing arrangements. Other uses abound and are just starting to be explored.

NOTES

1. We ignore the differences between the three-day settlement process in futures markets and the one-day settlement procedures common in the cash market.

2. For a more detailed explanation of the seller's options in T-bond futures see Chapter 8 of R. Kolb, *Understanding Futures Markets,* 5e, Cambridge, MA: Blackwell Publishers, 1997.

3. We ignore the daily resettlement feature and the interest that could have been earned on the $125,000 futures profit in the second quarter.

4. See L. Ederington, "The Hedging Performance of the New Futures Market," *Journal of Finance,* 34:1, March 1979, pp. 157-70; C. Franckle, "The Hedging Performance of the New Futures Market: Comment," *Journal of Finance,* 35:5, December 1980, pp. 1272-79; and J. Hill and T. Schneeweis, "Risk Reduction Potential of Financial Futures," in G. Gay and R. Kolb, *Interest Rate Futures: A Comprehensive Introduction,* Richmond, VA: Robert F. Dame, 1982, pp. 307-24.

5. The dependence of the RGR hedge ratio on the planned length of the hedging period was proven by C. Franckle, "The Hedging Performance of the New Futures Market: Comment," *Journal of Finance,* 35:5, December 1980, pp. 1272-79.

6. See R. Kolb and R. Chiang, "Improving Hedging Performance Using Interest Rate Futures," *Financial Management,* 10:4, 1981, pp. 72-79; and "Duration, Immunization, and Hedging with Interest Rate Futures," *Journal of Financial Research,* 10:4, Autumn 1982, pp. 161-70.

7. A. Toevs and D. Jacob, "Futures and Alternative Hedge Ratio Methodologies," *Journal of Portfolio Management,* 12:3, Spring 1986, pp. 60-70.

8. For an example, see J. Hill and T. Schneeweis, "Risk Reduction Potential of Financial Futures," in G. Gay and R. Kolb, *Interest Rate Futures: Concepts and Issues,* Englewood Cliffs, NJ: Prentice Hall, 1982, pp. 307-24.

9. D. Lasser, "A Measure of Ex-Ante Hedging Effectiveness for the Treasury-Bill and Treasury-Bond Futures Markets," working paper.

10. R. Chiang, G. Gay, and R. Kolb, "Interest Rate Hedging: An Empirical Test of Alternative Strategies," *Journal of Financial Research,* 6:3, Fall 1983, pp. 187-97.

11. A. Toevs and D. Jacob, "Futures and Alternative Hedge Ratio Methodologies," *Journal of Portfolio Management,* 12:3, Spring 1986, pp. 60-70.

12. See I. G. Kawaller, "Choosing the Best Interest Rate Hedge Ratio," *Financial Analysts Journal*, 48:5, September/October 1992, pp. 74-77.

■ Chapter 6

■ Stock Index Futures: Introduction

OVERVIEW

Everyone who follows the financial news hears predictions about the future of the stock market. Usually these predictions refer to the future movement of some stock market index. With the advent of stock index futures trading in 1982, these pundits can now trade to take advantage of their insights. (Perhaps they should be required to do so.) In addition to providing a chance to speculate, stock index futures also have a role in hedging various kinds of portfolio risk.

Currently, dramatic changes in stock index futures are under way. Previously successful contracts have greatly diminished importance, while new contracts begin to gain ascendancy. This chapter begins our exploration of stock index futures and the indexes upon which they are based. We focus on four stock market indexes and the futures contracts that are based on them. These indexes are: the Major Market Index (MMI), the Standard and Poor's 500 (S&P 500), the New York Stock Exchange (NYSE) index, and the Nikkei index. Several other contracts trade inactively, so this chapter considers only these four most important indexes.[1]

Successful trading of the index contracts requires a thorough understanding of the construction of the indexes. When the differences and interrelationships among the indexes are understood, it is easier to understand the differences among the futures contracts that are based on those indexes. The differences among the indexes should not be exaggerated, however. The kinds of risk and the expected changes in the levels of the indexes are predicted by the **Capital Asset Pricing Model** (CAPM). The CAPM expresses the relationship between the returns of individual stocks and partially diversified portfolios, on the one hand, and the broad indexes on the other.

As is the case with all futures contracts, the exact construction of the contracts is very important for the trader. No-arbitrage conditions constrain the possible deviations between the price of the futures contract and the level of the underlying index. Cash-and-carry strategies keep the futures price from being too high relative to the price of the stock market index. Similarly, the availability of reverse cash-and-carry strategies keeps the futures price from being too low relative to stock prices. In other words, potential arbitrage strategies constrain the basis for stock index futures as these strategies do for other types of futures contracts.

The Four Indexes

The four indexes, the Major Market Index, the Standard and Poor's 500, the New York Stock Exchange Composite index, and the Nikkei index, are familiar names, but few people are actually acquainted with how these indexes are computed. For an understanding of stock index futures, however, a thorough knowledge of the indexes is indispensable. In general, stock market indexes can be value weighted or price weighted. In a **value weighted index**, each stock in the index affects the index value in proportion to the market value of all shares outstanding, while a **price weighted index** is one that gives a weight to each stock that is proportional to its stock price. In a value weighted index, IBM and Microsoft would have roughly equal weights, because their market values are similar. By contrast, in a price weighted index a small capitalization firm could have a much higher weight than a much larger firm if the small capitalization firm had a high stock price but relatively few outstanding shares. Of the indexes we consider, the MMI and Nikkei indexes are price weighted, while the S&P 500 and NYSE indexes are value weighted.

All four indexes exclude dividends, which means that the indexes do not reflect the full appreciation that the market has enjoyed over any given period. The omission of dividends is very important for understanding the pricing of the futures contracts as well. As we will see in our discussion of pricing, the presence of dividends is a major factor.

THE MAJOR MARKET INDEX

In the early 1980s, the Chicago Board of Trade attempted to launch a futures contract based on the most famous of all stock market indexes – the **Dow Jones Industrial Average** (DJIA). After prolonged legal maneuvering, Dow Jones succeeded in preventing the futures contract from trading. In response, the American Stock Exchange created the Major Market Index (MMI) and licensed the index to the CBOT to provide the underlying index for a futures contract. Starting in the fall of 1993, the American Stock Exchange licensed the MMI to the Chicago Mercantile Exchange, and MMI stock index futures now trade on the CME.

The MMI consists of 20 stocks chosen so that the MMI behaves as much as possible like the DJIA, which consists of 30 stocks. In fact, most MMI stocks are also included in the DJIA. The MMI is computed by adding the share prices of the 20 stocks comprising the index and dividing by the MMI divisor. Similarly, the DJIA is computed by adding the prices of the 30 represented shares and dividing by the Dow Jones divisor. For both indexes, the divisor is used to adjust for stock splits, mergers, stock dividends, and changes in the stocks included in the index. The MMI is constructed so that the MMI value is about one-fifth of the DJIA.

For both the MMI and the DJIA, the index can be computed according to the following formula:

$$\text{Index} = \frac{\sum_{i=1}^{N} P_i}{\text{Divisor}} \qquad (6.1)$$

where:

P_i = price of stock I

Because the indexes depend on the number of dollars from summing all the prices, the MMI and DJIA do not reflect the percentage change in the price of a share. For example, consider a stock that doubles from $1 to $2, and contrast this price change with a stock that moves from $100 to $101. In the first case, a stock has increased 100 percent, while in the latter case, a stock has increased just 1 percent. For the MMI and the DJIA, both stock price changes have the same effect on the index, because the index depends on the sum of the prices, not the percentage price changes of the individual stocks.

Both the MMI and DJIA use a divisor to compute the index value. The divisors used in computing the indexes are designed to keep the index value from changing due to stock splits or stock dividends or due to a substitution of one stock for another in the index. To see how the divisor functions, assume that Dow Jones decides to delete Navistar International from the index and replace it with Dow Chemical. We also assume that Navistar is priced at 6.00, Dow Chemical trades at 47.00, and the current value of the index is 1900.31, with a divisor of .889. Assuming that the sum of the 30 stock prices is $1,689.375, the substitution of Dow for Navistar will generate a new total of prices of $1,730.375, which equals the old sum ($1,689.375) plus the current price of the new stock ($47) minus the current price of the deleted stock ($6). If the divisor is not changed, the new index value will be 1946.43. Thus, the substitution of one stock for another, with no change in the divisor, manufactures a jump in the DJIA of 46 points. Obviously, this cannot be permitted or the index will become meaningless as a barometer of stock prices.

For the index to reflect the level of prices in the market accurately, simply substituting one stock for another should not change the index. The same principle holds for stock dividends and stock splits. Therefore, the divisor must change to accommodate the change in stocks or the stock dividend or the stock split. In our example of substituting Dow Chemical for Navistar, the divisor must change to maintain a constant index value of 1900.31 with the new total of prices of 1730.375. Therefore, the new divisor must satisfy the following equation:

$$1900.31 = \frac{1730.375}{\text{New Divisor}}$$

$$\text{New Divisor} = \frac{1730.375}{1900.31} = .9106$$

Thus, to keep the index value unchanged, the new divisor must be .9106. Generalizing from this example, we see that Equation 6.2 gives the value for the new divisor:

$$\text{New Divisor} = \frac{\text{New Sum of Prices}}{\text{Index Value Before Substitution}} \qquad (6.2)$$

To find the new divisor, compute the new sum of prices that results from substituting one firm for another. Then divide this sum by the original index value.

THE NIKKEI INDEX

The Nikkei index is a price weighted index like the MMI. It is the most widely followed and quoted index for the Japanese stock market and it includes 225 of the largest Japanese firms, including Sony, Fuji Photo Film, Honda, Toyota, Yamaha, NEC, Citizen Watch, and Nippon Telephone and Telegraph. Membership in the 225 stocks occurs only due to special events such as mergers and liquidations. In the 1980s, there were only eight substitutions.

Shares in the Japanese stock market are classified as First Section or Second Section. Stocks in the First Section are the larger and more important firms in the economy, and all Nikkei shares are in the first section. The Nikkei index had a spectacular run-up during the last half of the 1980s, and a serious fall in the early 1990s. In 1980 the Nikkei stood at about 12,000 and increased to over 38,000 by 1990. From 1990 through 1992, it fell dramatically and stood at about 18,000 by the end of 1993, but recovered to the 20,000 range by 1996.

THE S&P 500 INDEX

Of the four indexes, the S&P 500 index is the most widely used in the U.S. finance industry. For example, many managers are judged by comparing the performance of their portfolios to the performance of the S&P 500. The index is based on 500 firms which come from various industries and most of which are listed on the New York Stock Exchange.[2] Together, these 500 firms comprise approximately 80 percent of the total value of the stocks listed on the New York Stock Exchange.

Each of the stocks in the index has a different weight in the calculation of the index, and the weight is proportional to the total market value of the stock (the price per share times the number of shares outstanding). Therefore, the S&P 500 index is a value weighted index. This contrasts with the composition of the MMI, the DJIA, and the Nikkei which assign equal weight to each stock price. The value of the S&P 500 index is reported relative to the average value during the period of 1941–1943, which was assigned an index value of 10. As a simplified example of the way the index is computed, assume that the index consists of only three securities, ABC, DEF, and GHI. Table 6.1 shows how the value of the three firms would be weighted to calculate the index. For each stock, the total market value of the outstanding shares is computed. In the table, the three firms' shares have a total value of $19,000. If the value in the 1941–1943 period had been $2,000, the current level of the index would be calculated as shown in the table, where X is the current index level with a value of 95.00. Mathematically, the calculation of the index is given by:

$$\text{S\&P Index}_t = \left(\frac{\sum_{i=1}^{500} N_{i,t} P_{i,t}}{\text{O.V.}} \right) 10 \qquad (6.3)$$

■ Table 6.1

Calculation of S&P 500

	Outstanding Shares		Price		Value
Company ABC	100	×	$50	=	$ 5,000
Company DEF	300	×	40	=	12,000
Company GHI	200	×	10	=	2,000
		Current Market Valuation		=	$19,000

If the 1941–43 value were $2,000, then $19,000 is to $2,000 as X is to 10.

$$\frac{\text{Current Market Valuation}}{\text{1941–43 Market Valuation}} \quad \frac{\$19,000}{\$2,000} = \frac{X}{10}$$

$$\$190,000 = \$2,000X$$

$$95.00 = X$$

From Chicago Mercantile Exchange, "Inside S&P 500 Stock Index Futures." Reprinted by permission of Chicago Mercantile Exchange. © Standard & Poor's. S&P 500® is a trademark of The McGraw-Hill Companies, Inc. Reprinted by permission.

where:

O.V. = original valuation in 1941-43
$N_{i,t}$ = number of shares outstanding for firm I
$P_{i,t}$ = price of shares in firm I

The weights of each firm change as their prices rise and fall relative to other firms represented in the index. Firms such as Exxon, AT&T, and IBM represent large shares of the index, while other firms have only a minuscule impact. The index is computed on a continuous basis during the trading day and reported to the public. There is considerable variability in the performance of the index over time, even though it is a large portfolio of the very largest and most stable firms. As we will see in the next chapter, recent developments in the stock index futures market have given new importance to the volatility of stock market indexes.

THE NEW YORK STOCK EXCHANGE COMPOSITE INDEX

The New York Stock Exchange Composite index is broader than the S&P 500, since it includes all of the approximately 1,700 stocks listed on the New York Stock Exchange. The largest 50 companies account for about 40 percent of the value of the NYSE capitalization.

The weight of each stock in the index is proportional to its value, just as is the case with the S&P 500 index. Therefore, the NYSE index is a value weighted index. The NYSE and S&P 500 indexes are calculated using a similar method. However, the NYSE Composite index takes its base date as December 31, 1965. At any subsequent point in time, the value of the NYSE index is given by:

$$\text{NYSE Index}_t = \left(\frac{\sum_{t=1}^{1720} N_{i,t} P_{i,t}}{\text{O.V.}} \right) 50.0 \qquad (6.4)$$

where:

O.V. = original value of all shares on the NYSE as of
       December 31, 1965

Equation 6.4 says that the value of the NYSE index equals the current value of all shares listed on the NYSE divided by the December 1965 base value, with the result being multiplied by 50 as a simple scaling device. This gives an initial value of 50.00 for the index. By late 1974, the index stood at 32.89, was as high as 81.02 in 1980, and was about 330 in 1996.

Comparison of the Indexes

Because we will consider four futures contracts, it is important to understand the relationships among the four underlying indexes, since such knowledge is important in choosing the most appropriate contract for speculation or hedging. For hedging, the choice of an index depends on the relationship between the good being hedged and the characteristics of the index. For speculation, the volatility of the index is particularly important.

As we know from portfolio theory, the more fully diversified a portfolio is, the less unsystematic risk it should contain. With less unsystematic risk, the total risk should be lower. Based on the December 1995 futures contracts, the standard deviation of the daily percentage changes in the indexes was as follows:

MMI	.00523
Nikkei	.01621
S&P 500	.00501
NYSE	.00476

As we might expect, the more stocks in the index, the less volatile the percentage price change. Also, because big firms tend to be more stable than small firms, we would expect a value weighted index to be less volatile than an equally weighted index. Notice, however, that the Nikkei is significantly more volatile than the U.S. indexes.

In spite of differences in volatility, the correlations among the U.S. indexes are high, typically exceeding 85 percent. The correlations between the Nikkei index and the U.S. indexes are significantly lower. We might expect these results, because each index is based on a diversified portfolio. As the S&P 500 index represents about 80 percent of the value of NYSE stocks, there is an extremely high correlation between the S&P 500 and NYSE Composite indexes. The correlation between the MMI and the other two U.S. indexes is somewhat lower, reflecting the less diversified character of the MMI. Table 6.2 presents a correlation matrix of the daily percentage changes for the December 1995 futures contracts based on the four indexes. The S&P 500 and

■ **Table 6.2**

CORRELATION OF DAILY PERCENTAGE CHANGES IN INDEX VALUES

	MMI	Nikkei	S&P 500	NYSE
MMI	1.0000	0.1185	0.8930	0.8957
Nikkei		1.0000	0.1291	0.1471
S&P 500			1.0000	0.9844
NYSE				1.0000

© Standard & Poor's. S&P 500® is a trademark of The McGraw-Hill Companies, Inc. Reprinted by permission.

NYSE are the most closely correlated. This is due to the large number of identical stocks and the great diversification represented by these portfolios, in addition to the fact that both of these indexes are value weighted indexes. The great similarity in these indexes suggests that one index might be a good substitute for either of the other two for hedging or risk management purposes. The Nikkei is not well correlated with any U.S. index, suggesting the potential diversification benefits available from investing across the U.S. and Japanese markets.

STOCK INDEX FUTURES CONTRACTS

All four futures contracts share certain basic similarities in terms of the calculation of their value and the method by which they are settled. Table 6.3 summarizes these features. All four contracts are

■ **Table 6.3**

SUMMARY OF STOCK INDEX FUTURES CONTRACTS

Contract	Contract Size	Index Composition	Index Weighting
MMI	$500 × Index	20 blue-chip stocks, mostly in the DJIA	Price
Nikkei	$5 × Index	225 first section shares	Price
S&P 500	$500 × Index	500 mostly NYSE stocks	Market value
NYSE	$500 × Index	All NYSE common stocks	Market value

settled in cash, so there is no delivery in the stock index futures market, and all four contracts trade on the March, June, September, December cycle. Each futures contract has its respective index's current value multiplied by some dollar amount as the underlying contract value. For the S&P 500, the NYSE Composite, and the MMI, the multiplier is $500. For the Nikkei, the multiplier is $5. These values are set by the exchange and determine the contract size.

In early 1996, the indexes and the futures contracts had the following values:

Futures	Index	Futures Contract Value
MMI	580.76	$290,380
Nikkei	20,915.44	104,577
S&P 500	650.03	325,015
NYSE	348.77	174,385

Therefore, values range widely across the four indexes and will fluctuate as market prices vary.

With the futures contracts being stated in terms of so many dollars times the value of the index, the dollar change in the futures contracts can be quite different. The relative dollar change in the different futures will depend on some factors that we have already considered, such as the different volatilities of the indexes and the correlations among the indexes. Table 6.4 presents data based on the indexes to illustrate comparative volatilities. These data are based on daily absolute changes in the December 1995 futures contract. The first line of

■ **Table 6.4**

DAILY ABSOLUTE CHANGES IN THE INDEXES

	December 1995 Futures Contract			
	MMI	Nikkei	S&P 500	NYSE
Mean Change	1.9031	198.03	1.8115	1.0672
Standard Deviation	1.6816	190.07	1.8516	0.9398
Implied Mean Change for Futures	$951.54	$990.16	$1,055.74	$533.61
Implied Mean Standard Deviation for Futures	$840.79	$950.33	$925.80	$469.92

data shows the average absolute daily change in the index values for the four indexes. To compare the dollar volatility of the futures contracts, the last two lines of Table 6.4 present the dollar changes implied for the futures. For example, the average absolute daily change in the MMI index times the futures contract multiplier of $500 is $951.54, and the standard deviation in dollars is $840.79.

STOCK INDEX FUTURES PRICES

Figure 6.1 presents price quotations for stock index futures. The organization of the quotations is similar to those of other commodities. Like most financial futures, stock index futures essentially trade in a full carry market. Therefore, the cost-of-carry model provides a virtually complete understanding of stock index futures pricing. When the conditions of the cost-of-carry model are violated, arbitrage opportunities arise. For a cash-and-carry strategy, a trader would buy the stocks that underlie the futures contract and sell the futures. The trader would then carry these stocks until the futures expiration. The cash-and-carry strategy is attractive when stocks are priced too low relative to the futures. In a reverse cash-and-carry strategy, the trader would sell the stocks short and invest the proceeds, in addition to buying the futures. The reverse cash-and-carry strategy is attractive when stocks are priced too high relative to the futures. Thus, any discrepancy between the justified futures and cash market prices would lead to a profit at the expiration of the futures, simply by exploiting the appropriate strategy. From Chapter 2, the basic cost-of-carry model for a perfect market with unrestricted short selling was given by Equation 2.3:

$$F_{0,t} = S_0(1 + C) \qquad (2.3)$$

where:

$F_{0,t}$ = futures price at $t = 0$ for delivery at time t
S_0 = spot price at $t = 0$
C = the percentage cost of carrying the good from $t = 0$ to time t

THE COST-OF-CARRY MODEL FOR STOCK INDEX FUTURES

Applying Equation 2.3 to stock index futures faces one complication – dividends. Holding the stocks gives the owner dividends; however,

■ Figure 6.1

QUOTATIONS FOR STOCK INDEX FUTURES

INDEX

S&P 500 INDEX (CME) $500 times index

	Open	High	Low	Settle	Chg	High	Low	Open Interest
June	652.00	655.20	650.15	655.00	+2.95	673.20	553.95	177,760
Sept	656.35	660.80	655.60	660.50	+3.00	677.80	559.70	6,070
Dec	662.70	666.00	661.40	666.00	+2.95	681.80	612.70	2,716
Mr97	668.20	671.10	667.30	671.25	+2.40	681.20	656.80	162

Est vol 65,587; vol Mn 66,748; open int 186,708, –103.
Indx prelim High 651.59; Low 647.70; Close 651.59 +3.70.

S&P MIDCAP 400 (CME) $500 times index

	Open	High	Low	Settle	Chg	High	Low	Open Interest
June	234.45	235.55	234.35	235.45	+1.00	237.90	202.45	8,538

Est vol 594; vol Mn 468; open int 8,597, +5.
The index: High 234.35; Low 232.65; Close 234.34 +1.69

NIKKEI 225 STOCK AVERAGE (CME)-$5 times index

	Open	High	Low	Settle	Chg	High	Low	Open Interest
June	22260.	22335.	22220.	22305.	+ 45	22335.	14655.	29,561
Sept	22380.	22440.	22320.	22410.	+ 50	22440.	17440.	138

Est vol 1,144; vol Mn 1,486; open int 29,724, +602.
The index: High 22216.54; Low 22104.80; Close 22119.88 –4.01

GSCI (CME)-$250 times nearby index

	Open	High	Low	Settle	Chg	High	Low	Open Interest
June	212.40	212.90	210.00	211.10	+1.40	212.90	176.40	13,690

Est vol 280; vol Mn 108; open int 13,711, +37.
The index: High 215.79; Low 212.12; Close 215.55 +3.20

CAC-40 STOCK INDEX (MATIF)-FFr 200 per index pt.

	Open	High	Low	Settle	Chg	High	Low	Open Interest
Apr	2117.0	2124.0	2109.0	2112.5	– 8.5	2124.0	1879.0	31,385
May	2107.5	2113.5	2100.0	2102.0	– 8.5	2113.5	1860.0	14,160
June	2089.0	2092.0	2079.5	2081.5	– 8.5	2092.5	1799.0	26,408
Sept	2098.0	2103.0	2098.0	2092.5	– 8.5	2103.0	1777.0	10,214
Mr97	2142.0	2142.0	2132.0	2133.5	– 9.5	2142.0	1921.0	3,035
Sept	2126.0	2126.0	2126.0	2125.5	– 9.5	2126.0	2009.5	3,435
Mr98	....	....	2184.5	– 8.5	2120.0	2115.0	700

Est vol 28,190; vol Mn 28,531; open int 89,337, +6,259.

FT-SE 100 INDEX (LIFFE)-£25 per index point

	Open	High	Low	Settle	Chg	High	Low	Open Interest
June	3851.0	3858.0	3831.0	3843.0	–21.0	3877.0	3490.0	60,076
Sept	3866.0	3866.0	3849.0	3856.0	–19.5	3876.0	3452.5	3,116

Est vol 9,927; vol Mn 8,494; open int 63,273, –1,017.

DAX-30 GERMAN STOCK INDEX (DTB)
DM 100 times index

	Open	High	Low	Settle	Chg	High	Low	Open Interest
June	2545.0	2560.0	2538.5	2552.5	+ .18	2560.0	2152.0	149,946
Sept	2563.0	2576.5	2560.0	2572.0	+ .08	2575.0	2295.5	3,988

Est vol 16,814; vol Mn 14,210; open int 154,067, –1,023.
The index: High 2555.74; Low 2538.92; Close 2549.12 –.01

ALL ORDINARIES SHARE PRICE INDEX (SFE)
A$25 times index

	Open	High	Low	Settle	Chg	High	Low	Open Interest
June	2308.0	2335.0	2303.0	2330.0	+34.0	2396.0	2068.0	78,457
Sept	2336.0	2336.0	2335.0	2358.0	+36.0	2358.0	2235.0	1,073
Dec	....	....	2370.0	+34.0	2340.0	2225.0	117
Mr97	....	....	2394.0	+34.0	2343.0	2310.0	158

Est vol 12,258; vol Mn 6,269; open int 79,805, +8,289.
The index: High na; Low na; Close na

From *The Wall Street Journal,* April 24, 1996, p. C16. © 1996 Dow Jones & Company, Inc. Reprinted by permission of The Wall Street Journal. All Rights Reserved Worldwide. © Standard & Poor's. S&P 500® is a trademark of The McGraw-Hill Companies, Inc. Reprinted by permission.

each of the indexes is simply a price index. The value of the index at any time depends solely on the prices of the stocks, not the dividends that the underlying stocks might pay. Because the futures prices are tied directly to the index values, the futures prices do not include dividends.

To fit stock index futures, Equation 2.3 must be adjusted to include the dividends that would be received between the present and the expiration of the futures. In essence, the chance to receive dividends lowers the cost of carrying the stocks. Carrying stocks requires that a trader finance the purchase price of the stock from the present until the futures expiration. However, the trader will receive dividends from the stock, which will reduce the value of the stocks. This contrasts directly with the cost-of-carry for holding a commodity like gold. As we have seen, gold generates no cash flows, so the cost-of-carry for gold is essentially the financing cost. For stocks, the cost-of-carry is the financing cost for the stock, less the dividends received while the stock is being carried.

As an example, assume the present is time zero and a trader decides to engage in a self-financing cash-and-carry transaction. The trader decides to buy and hold one share of Widget, Inc., currently trading for $100. Therefore, the trader borrows $100 and buys the stock. We assume that the stock will pay a $2 dividend in six months, and the trader will invest the proceeds for the remaining six months at a rate of 10 percent. Table 6.5 shows the trader's cash flows. In Table 6.5, a trader borrows funds, buys and holds a stock, receives and invests a dividend, and liquidates the portfolio after one year. At the outset, the stock costs $100, but its value in a year, P_1, is unknown. From Table 6.5, the trader's cash inflow after one year is the future value

■ **Table 6.5** —————————————————————————————

CASH FLOWS FROM CARRYING STOCK

$t = 0$

Borrow $100 for 1 year at 10%.	+100
Buy 1 share of Widget, Inc.	−100

$t = 6$ months

Receive dividend of $2.	+$2
Invest $2 for 6 months at 10%.	−$2

$t = 1$ year

Collect proceeds of $2.10 from dividend investment.	+2.10
Sell Widget, Inc., for P_1.	+P_1
Repay debt.	−110.00

Total Profit: $P_1 + \$2.10 - \$110.00$

of the dividend, $2.10, plus the current value of the stock, P_1, less the repayment of the loan, $110.

From this example, we can generalize to understand the total cash inflows from a cash-and-carry strategy. First, the cash-and-carry strategy will return the future value of the stock, P_1, at the horizon of the carrying period. Second, at the end of the carrying period, the cash-and-carry strategy will return the future value of the dividends – the dividend plus interest from the time of receipt to the horizon. Against these inflows, the cash-and-carry trader must pay the financing cost for the stock purchase.

We are now in a position to determine the futures price that is consistent with the cash-and-carry strategy. From the arguments of Chapter 2, we know that Equation 2.3 holds as an equality with perfect markets and unrestricted short selling. The cash-and-carry trading opportunity requires that the futures price must be less than or equal to the cash inflows at the futures expiration. Similarly, the reverse cash-and-carry trading opportunity requires that the futures price must equal or exceed the cash inflows at the futures expiration. Therefore, the stock index futures price must equal the cost of the stocks underlying the stock index, plus the cost of carrying those stocks to expiration, $S_0(1 + C)$, minus the future value of all dividends to be received, $D_i(1 + r_i)$. The future value of dividends is measured at the time the futures contract expires. More formally:

$$F_{0,t} = S_0(1 + C) - \sum_{i=1}^{N} D_i(1 + r_i) \qquad (6.5)$$

where:

$F_{0,t}$ = stock index futures price at $t = 0$ for a futures contract that expires at time t

S_0 = the value of the stocks underlying the stock index at $t = 0$

C = the percentage cost of carrying the stocks from $t = 0$ to the expiration at time t

D_i = the ith dividend

r_i = the interest earned on carrying the Ith dividend from its time of receipt until the futures expiration at time t

FAIR VALUE FOR STOCK INDEX FUTURES

A stock index futures price has its **fair value** when the futures price fits the cost-of-carry model. In this section we consider a simplified example of determining the fair value of a stock index futures contract. We consider a futures contract on an equally weighted index, and for simplicity we assume that there are only two stocks. Table 6.6 provides the information that we will need.

Based on the data in Table 6.6, the index value is 110.56, as given by:

$$\frac{P_A + P_B}{\text{Index Divisor}} = \frac{115 + 84}{1.8} = 110.56$$

The cost of buying the stocks underlying the portfolio is simply the sum of the prices of Stocks A and B, or $199. For carrying the stocks to expiration, the interest cost will be 10 percent for 76 days or 2.11 percent. Thus, the cost of buying and carrying the stocks to expiration is $199(1.0211) = $203.20. Offsetting this cost will be the dividends

■ Table 6.6

INFORMATION FOR COMPUTING FAIR VALUE

Today's date:	July 6
Futures expiration:	September 20
Days until expiration:	76
Index:	Equally weighted index of two stocks
Index divisor:	1.80
Interest rates:	All interest rates are 10 percent
Stock A	
Today's price:	$115
Projected dividends:	$1.50 on July 23
Days dividend will be invested:	59
r_A:	.10(59/360) = .0164
Stock B	
Today's price:	$84
Projected dividends:	$1.00 on August 12
Days dividend will be invested:	39
r_B:	.10(39/360) = .0108

received and the interest earned on the dividends. For the stocks, the future value of the dividends at expiration will be:

For Stock A: $1.50(1.0164) = $1.52
For Stock B: $1.00(1.0108) = $1.01

Therefore, the entire cost of buying the stocks and carrying them to expiration is the purchase price of the stocks plus interest, less the future value of the dividends measured at expiration:

$$\$203.20 - \$1.52 - \$1.01 = \$200.67$$

In the cost-of-carry model, we know that the futures price must equal this entire cost-of-carry. However, the futures price is expressed in index units, not the dollars of the actual stock prices. To find the fair value for the futures price, this cash value of $200.67 must be converted into index units by dividing by the index divisor, 200.67/1.8 = 111.48. Thus, the fair value for the futures contract is 111.48. Because it conforms to the cost-of-carry model, this fair value for the futures price is the price that precludes arbitrage profits from both the cash-and-carry and reverse cash-and-carry strategies.

INDEX ARBITRAGE AND PROGRAM TRADING

In the preceding section we saw how to derive the fair value futures price from the cost-of-carry model. From Chapter 2 we know that deviations from the theoretical price of the cost-of-carry model give rise to arbitrage opportunities. If the futures price exceeds its fair value, traders will engage in cash-and-carry arbitrage. If the futures price falls below its fair value, traders can exploit the pricing discrepancy through a reverse cash-and-carry trading strategy. These cash-and-carry strategies in stock index futures are called **index arbitrage**. This section presents an example of index arbitrage using a simplified index with only two stocks. Because index arbitrage can require the trading of many stocks, index arbitrage is often implemented by using a computer program to automate the trading. Computer-directed index arbitrage is called **program trading**. We introduce program trading later in this section, but we reserve the fullest discussion for Chapter 7.

INDEX ARBITRAGE

Table 6.6 gave values for Stocks A and B, and we saw how to compute the fair value of a stock index futures contract based on an index composed of those two stocks. With the values in Table 6.6, the cash market index value is 110.56, and the fair value for the futures contract is 111.48, where both values are expressed in index points. If the futures price exceeds the fair value, cash-and-carry index arbitrage is possible. A futures price below its fair value creates an opportunity for reverse cash-and-carry index arbitrage.

To illustrate cash-and-carry index arbitrage, assume that the data of Table 6.6 hold, but that the futures price is 115.00. Because this price exceeds the fair value, an index arbitrageur would trade as shown in Table 6.7. At the outset on July 6, the trader borrows the money necessary to purchase the stocks in the index, buys the stocks, and sells the futures. On July 23 and August 12, the trader receives dividends from the two stocks and invests the dividends to the expiration date at 10 percent. Like all stock index futures, our simple example uses cash settlement. Therefore, at expiration on September 20, the final futures settlement price is set equal to the cash market index value. This ensures that the futures and cash prices converge and that the basis goes to zero.[3]

The profits or losses from the transactions in Table 6.7 do not depend on the prices that prevail at expiration on September 20. Instead, the profits come from a discrepancy between the futures price and its fair value. To illustrate the profits, we assume that the stock prices do not change. Therefore, the cash market index is at 110.56 at expiration. As Table 6.7 shows, these transactions give a profit of $6.32.

This will be the profit no matter what happens to stock prices between July 6 and September 20. For example, assume the prices of Stocks A and B both rose by $5, to $120 and $89, respectively. The cash market cash flows will then come from the sale of the shares, the future value of the dividends, and the debt repayment:

Sale of Stock A	+120.00
Sale of Stock B	+89.00
Future value of dividends on Stock A	+1.52
Future value of dividends on Stock B	+1.01
Debt repayment	−203.20
Futures profit/loss	−2.01

■ Table 6.7 ────────────────

CASH-AND-CARRY INDEX ARBITRAGE

Date	Cash Market	Futures Market
July 6	Borrow $199 for 76 days at 10%. Buy Stock A and Stock B for a total outlay of $199.	Sell 1 SEP index futures contract for 115.00.
July 23	Receive dividend of $1.50 from Stock A and invest for 59 days at 10%.	
August 12	Receive dividend of $1.00 from Stock B and invest for 39 days at 10%.	

For illustrative purposes, assume any values for stock prices at expiration. We assume that stock prices did not change. Therefore, the index value is still 110.56.

Date	Cash Market	Futures Market
September 20	Receive proceeds from invested dividends of $1.52 and $1.01. Sell Stock A for $115 and Stock B for $84. Total proceeds are $201.53. Repay debt of $203.20.	At expiration, the futures price is set equal to the spot index value of 110.56. This gives a profit of 4.44 index units. In dollar terms, this is 4.44 index units times the index divisor of 1.8.
	Loss: $1.67	Profit: $7.99

Total Profit: $7.99 − $1.67 = $6.32

On the futures transaction, the index value at expiration will then equal 116.11 = (120 + 89)/1.8. This gives a futures loss of 1.11 index points, or $2.01. Taking all of these cash flows together, the profit is still $6.32. The profit will be the same no matter what happens to stock prices.

If the futures price is too low relative to the fair value, arbitrageurs can engage in reverse cash-and-carry transactions. For example, assume that the futures price is 105.00, well below its fair value of 111.48. Now the arbitrageur will trade as shown in Table 6.8. Essentially, the transactions in Table 6.8 are just the opposite of those in Table 6.7. The most important difference is that the trader sells stock

■ Table 6.8

REVERSE CASH-AND-CARRY INDEX ARBITRAGE

Date	Cash Market	Futures Market
July 6	Sell Stock A and Stock B for a total of $199. Lend $199 for 76 days at 10%.	Buy 1 SEP index futures contract for 105.00.
July 23	Borrow $1.50 for 59 days at 10% and pay dividend of $1.50 on Stock A.	
August 12	Borrow $1.00 for 39 days at 10% and pay dividend of $1.00 on Stock B.	

For illustrative purposes, assume any values for stock prices at expiration. We assume that stock prices did not change. Therefore, the index value is still 110.56.

September 20	Receive proceeds from investment of $203.20. Repay $1.52 and $1.01 on money borrowed to pay dividends on Stocks A and B. Buy Stock A for $115 and Stock B for $84. Return stocks to repay short sale.	At expiration, the futures price is set equal to the spot index value of 110.56. This gives a profit of 5.56 index units. In dollar terms, this is 5.56 index units times the index divisor of 1.8.
	Profit: $1.67	Profit: $10.01

Total Profit: $1.67 + $10.01 = $11.68

short. Having sold the stock short, the trader must pay the dividends on the stocks as they come due.

The transactions give the trader a net profit of $11.68. Again, this profit does not depend upon the actual stock prices that prevail at expiration. Instead, the profit comes from the discrepancy between the actual futures price of 105.00 and the fair value of 111.48. Once the trader initiates the transactions in Table 6.8, the profit will depend only on the discrepancy between the fair value and the prevailing futures price. The profit will equal the error in the futures price times the index divisor: (111.48 − 105.00)1.8 = $11.68.[4]

Program Trading

While we have illustrated the cash-and-carry and reverse cash-and-carry transactions with a hypothetical two stock index futures contract, real stock index futures trading involves many more stocks. The MMI is smallest with 20 stocks, while the S&P 500 contains (of course) 500 stocks, the NYSE index has about 1,700 underlying stocks, and the Nikkei has 225 stocks. To exploit index arbitrage opportunities with actual stock index futures requires trading the futures and simultaneously buying or selling the entire collection of stocks that underlie the index.

If we focus on the S&P 500 futures contract, we can see that the transactions of Tables 6.7 and 6.8 call for the buying or selling of 500 stocks. The success of the arbitrage depends upon identifying the misalignment between the futures price and the fair futures price. However, at a given moment the fair futures price depends upon the current price of 500 different stocks. Identifying an index arbitrage opportunity requires the ability to instantly find pricing discrepancies between the futures price and the fair futures price reflecting 500 different stocks. In addition, exploiting the arbitrage opportunity requires trading 500 stocks at the prices that created the arbitrage opportunity. Enter the computer!

Large financial institutions can communicate orders to trade stock via their computer for very rapid execution. Faced with a cash-and-carry arbitrage opportunity, one of these large traders could execute a computer order to buy each and every stock represented in the S&P 500. Simultaneously, the institution would sell the S&P 500 futures contract. The use of computers to execute large and complicated stock market orders is called **program trading**. While computers are used for other kinds of stock market transactions, index arbitrage is the main application of program trading. Often "index arbitrage" and "program trading" are used interchangeably. Program trading has been blamed for much of the recent volatility in the stock market, including the crash of October 1987. Chapter 7 presents a real-world example of program trading and analyzes the hidden risks in this kind of index arbitrage. Chapter 7 also discusses the evidence on program trading and stock market volatility.

Predicting Dividend Payments and Investment Rates

In the example of computing fair value from Table 6.6, we assumed certainty about the amount, timing, and investment rates for the dividends on Stocks A and B. In the actual market, these quantities are highly predictable, but they are not certain. Dividend amounts and payment dates can be predicted based on the past policy of the firm. However, these quantities are far from certain until the dividend announcement date when the firm announces the amount and payment date of the dividend. In practice, there is quite a bit of variability in the payment of dividends depending on the time of year. Figure 6.2 shows a typical distribution of dividend payments through the year. Notice how dividends tend to cluster at certain days in early March, June, September, and December.

In actual practice, traders follow the dividend practices of firms to project the dividends that the stocks underlying an index will pay each day. This problem varies in difficulty from one index to the next. The MMI has only 20 very large firms with relatively stable dividend policies. By contrast, the NYSE index has about 1,700 firms. Many of these firms are small and may have irregular dividend payment patterns. Therefore, it is more difficult to predict the exact dividend

■ **Figure** 6.2

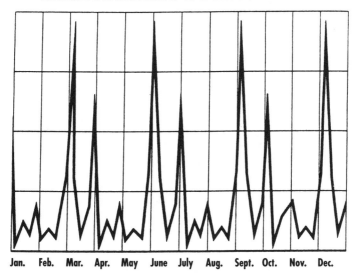

TYPICAL DISTRIBUTION OF DIVIDEND PAYMENTS

Jan. Feb. Mar. Apr. May June July Aug. Sept. Oct. Nov. Dec.

From Chicago Mercantile Exchange, "Using S&P 500 Stock Index Futures and Options," 1988. Reprinted by permission of Chicago Mercantile Exchange. © Standard & Poor's. S&P 500® is a trademark of The McGraw-Hill Companies, Inc. Reprinted by permission.

stream for the NYSE or the S&P 500 index. While the difficulties in predicting dividends may introduce some uncertainties into the cost-of-carry calculations, projections of dividends prove to be quite accurate in practice.

In our example of computing the fair value of a stock index futures contract and in our arbitrage examples, we also assumed that dividends could be invested at a known rate. In practice, it is difficult to know the exact rate that will be received on invested dividends. While knowing the exact rate to be received on invested dividends is difficult, good predictions are possible. For the most part, the futures expiration date is not very distant, so the current short-term interest rate can provide a good estimate of the investment rate for dividends.

MARKET IMPERFECTIONS AND STOCK INDEX FUTURES PRICES

In Chapter 2 we saw that four different types of market imperfections could affect the pricing of futures contracts. Those market imperfections are: direct transaction costs, unequal borrowing and lending rates, margins and restrictions on short selling, and limitations to storage. As we also saw in Chapter 2, the effect of these market imperfections is to create a band of no-arbitrage prices within which the futures price must fall. In this section we consider these imperfections briefly in the context of stock index futures.

Direct transaction costs affect stock index futures trading to a considerable extent. Relative to many goods, transaction costs for stocks are low in percentage terms. Nonetheless, stock traders face commissions, exchange fees, and a bid-asked spread. In general, these costs may be about one-half of 1 percent for stock market transactions. Even with such modest transaction costs, we cannot expect the cost-of-carry model to hold as an exact equality. Instead, these transaction costs will lead to a no-arbitrage band of permissible stock index futures prices.

Unequal borrowing and lending costs, margins, and restrictions on short selling all play a role in stock index futures pricing. In the stock market, the restrictions on short selling are quite explicit. The Federal Reserve Board will not allow a trader to use more than 50 percent of the proceeds from a short sale. The short seller's broker may restrict that usage to an even smaller percentage. As we have seen in Chapter 2, these factors all force slight discrepancies in the cost-of-carry model. The pricing relationship of Equation 6.5 holds as an approximation, not with exactitude. Thus, these market imperfections create a no-arbitrage band of permissible futures prices. However, a highly competitive trading environment and low transaction costs keep this no-arbitrage band quite tight around the perfect markets theoretical fair value of Equation 6.5.

Because the stocks of the MMI, Nikkei, S&P 500, and NYSE indexes are so widely held by financial institutions with low transaction costs, quasi-arbitrage is a dominant feature of stock index futures trading. As an example of the importance of quasi-arbitrage, consider the differential use of short sale proceeds for a retail customer and a pension fund with a large stock portfolio. Assume that the retail customer must sell a stock short through her broker. This customer will be able to use only half of the proceeds of the short sale. By contrast, we will assume that the pension fund already owns the stocks necessary to sell short for the reverse cash-and-carry transaction. In this situation, the pension fund can simulate a short sale by selling a portion of its stock portfolio. Because the pension fund is actually selling stocks, not technically selling short, it receives the full use of its proceeds. However, selling stocks from a portfolio is a perfect substitute for an actual short sale. Thus, the pension fund faces substantially lower transaction costs than the retail customer for engaging in reverse cash-and-carry arbitrage. A similar conclusion emerges from considering program trading. A small retail trader faces enormous transaction costs in attempting to engage in index arbitrage. The quasi-arbitrage opportunities enjoyed by financial institutions ensure that no individual could ever engage in index arbitrage. In Chapter 7 we review the evidence on stock index futures pricing and show that these markets approximate full carry markets. This suggests that quasi-arbitrage is a dominant feature of stock index futures pricing.

SPECULATING WITH STOCK INDEX FUTURES

Speculating with stock index futures is exciting. Futures contracts allow the speculator to make the most straightforward speculation on the direction of the market or to enter very sophisticated spread transactions to tailor the futures position to more precise opinions about the direction of stock prices. Further, the low transactions costs in the futures market make the speculation much easier to undertake than similar speculation in the stock market itself. With four different broad market indexes from two countries, the speculative opportunities are virtually endless.

One of the simplest speculative positions arises from a belief about impending market movements. If a trader anticipates a major market rally, he could simply buy a futures contract and hope for a price rise on the futures contract when the rally actually occurs. While this course of action is very simple, it does not do full justice to the complexity of the speculative opportunity. The trader might also consider which contract maturity is desirable as a trading vehicle and which of the four contracts to trade.

In major market moves, stocks of small firms tend to move more dramatically than the stocks of large well-capitalized firms. If the trader believes that a major advance is impending, then he or she has a definite reason to prefer the NYSE index to the S&P 500 index and to prefer the S&P 500 index to the MMI. Comparing the MMI and the S&P 500 index, we would expect the MMI to be more sluggish because it is more completely dominated by large firms.

With these differential responses in mind, one conservative speculation position strategy could use a spread between two indexes. If the trader anticipates a major market increase, but wishes to closely control her risk exposure, she might use a spread between the MMI and the S&P 500 indexes. Assume that she anticipates a market rise in April. Consistent with this outlook, the transactions of Table 6.9 show

■ Table 6.9

A Conservative Intercommodity Spread

Date	Futures Market
April 22	Buy 1 SEP MMI futures contract at 534.50. Sell 1 SEP S&P 500 futures contract at 333.00.
May 6	Sell 1 SEP MMI futures contract at 556.30. Buy 1 SEP S&P 500 futures contract at 342.15.

	MMI	S&P 500
Sell	556.30	333.00
Buy	534.50	342.15
Profit (points)	21.80	−9.15
× $500	$10,900.00	−$4,575.00

Total Profit: $6,325

how to initiate a spread to speculate on an anticipated market rally. The prescient speculator buys one SEP MMI futures contract at 534.50 on April 22 and sells one SEP S&P 500 futures contract at 333.00.

A few weeks later, prices have risen, with the MMI futures trading at 556.30 and the S&P 500 futures at 342.15. The wisdom in her plan is soon validated by a market rally. Not wishing to be greedy, she elects to close her position on May 6. She sells the MMI contract at 556.30 and buys the S&P 500 contract at 342.15. Her spread has worked perfectly. The MMI futures has gained 4.08 percent while the S&P 500 index contract gained only 2.75 percent. Therefore, the gain on the MMI of 21.80 index points times $500 per point is $10,900. This gain more than offsets the loss on the S&P 500 contract of $4,575, the product of 9.15 points times $500 per point. The total gain is $6,325.

Contracts farther from expiration often respond to a given market move more than the nearby contracts and the index itself. The speculator could have initiated an intracommodity spread to take advantage of this same market rally. Table 6.10 shows one possible set of transactions using the S&P contract and the same dates. The speculator believes that the more distant contracts will be more responsive to a market move than the nearby contracts. Believing that the market will rise, she buys the more distant DEC contract at 361.90 on April 22, while simultaneously selling the nearby JUN contract at 359.80.

■ **Table 6.10**

A CONSERVATIVE INTRACOMMODITY SPREAD

Date	Futures Market
April 22	Buy 1 DEC S&P 500 contract at 361.90. Sell 1 JUN S&P 500 contract at 359.80.
May 6	Sell 1 DEC S&P 500 contract at 369.75. Buy 1 JUN S&P 500 contract at 367.50.

	June	December
Sell	359.80	369.75
Buy	367.50	361.90
Profit (points)	−7.70	7.85
× $500	−$3,850.00	$3,925.00

Total Profit: $75

By May 6, the rally has occurred, so she reverses her position by buying the JUN contract at 367.50 and selling the DEC contract at 369.75. As the table shows, the JUN contract has moved 7.70 points and the more sensitive DEC contract has moved 7.85 points. The strategy has worked, in a certain sense, because the more distant contract was more sensitive. However, the difference in the price changes was not very large. In fact, the gross profit on the spread was only $75, hardly enough to cover the transaction costs.

In an important sense, both spreads were too conservative. In the example of Table 6.10, the trader correctly anticipated the market move. An outright long position in any contract would have worked well, but the conservative trader managed to protect herself completely out of the benefits that could have been obtained, given the major character of the market advance. For the speculator committed to spread trading, the stock index futures market presents a problem, because the different contracts tend to be so highly correlated.

To trade spreads in stock index futures, it is often desirable to use a ratio spread. In a **ratio spread**, the trader trades more contracts on one side of the spread than on the other. The example of Table 6.9 has a ratio of 1:1, because the trader used one MMI contract and one S&P 500 contract. A more aggressive trader might have used a higher ratio.

The Demise of Barings Bank

Theoretically, index arbitrage is risk free, and properly executed index arbitrage transactions involve very low levels of actual risk. The risk is limited because of the close relationship between a stock index futures contract and the underlying stock index itself. Thus, as we have seen, index arbitrage is a low risk strategy that seeks to capture small and temporary pricing discrepancies between stocks and stock index futures.

Nicholas Leeson, a trader for Barings Bank stationed in Singapore, was supposed to be conducting index arbitrage between Japanese stocks and futures contracts on the Japanese index. Such trading involves taking equal and offsetting positions in stocks and futures, which were traded in both Japan and Singapore. While details remain controversial, it seems apparent that Leeson did exactly the opposite in late 1994 and early 1995. Through the futures markets, Leeson made very large one-sided bets that Japanese stocks would rise. The

Kobe earthquake, however, rocked the entire Japanese economy and led to a dramatic drop in the Japanese stock market. The highly leveraged bets on a rising Japanese market turned out to be giant losers. In a short period, Leeson's trades lost about $1.5 billion. These losses completely exhausted the net worth of Barings, which declared bankruptcy and was acquired by a Dutch investment bank.

While early reports suggested that Leeson was a rogue trader who acted alone, further investigation indicates a considerable awareness of his activities on the part of senior management. Shortly after the losses became public, Leeson was arrested in Germany and held in a German jail, as Singapore pressed its extradition request. Leeson was eventually extradited to Singapore, tried, convicted, and sentenced to a six-and-one-half year jail term that he is now serving.[5]

RISK MANAGEMENT WITH STOCK INDEX FUTURES

Hedging with stock index futures applies directly to the management of stock portfolios. The usefulness of stock index futures in portfolio management stems from the fact that they directly represent the market portfolio. Before stock index futures began trading, there was no comparable way of trading an instrument that gave the price performance so directly tied to a broad market index. Further, stock index futures have great potential in portfolio management due to their very low transaction costs. In this section we consider some hedging applications of stock index futures.

A SHORT HEDGE AND HEDGE RATIO CALCULATION

As a first case, consider the manager of a well-diversified stock portfolio worth $40,000,000, and assume that the portfolio has a beta of 1.22 measured relative to the S&P 500. This implies that a movement of 1 percent in the S&P 500 index would be expected to induce a change of 1.22 percent in the value of the stock portfolio. The portfolio manager fears that a bear market is imminent and wishes to hedge his portfolio's value against that possibility. One strategy would be to liquidate the portfolio and place the proceeds in short-term debt instruments and then, after the bear market, return the funds to the stock market. Such a plan is infeasible. First, the transaction costs from such a strategy are quite high. Second, if the fund is large, liquidating the portfolio could drive down stock prices. This would prevent the portfolio manager from liquidating the portfolio at the prices currently quoted for the individual stocks.

As an obvious alternative to liquidating the portfolio, the manager could use the S&P 500 stock index futures contract. By selling futures, the manager should be able to offset the effect of the bear market on the portfolio by generating gains in the futures market. One kind of naive strategy might involve trading one dollar of the value underlying the index futures contract for each dollar of the portfolio's value. Assuming that the S&P index futures contract stands at 212.00, the advocated number of futures contracts would be given by:

$$\frac{V_P}{V_F} = \frac{\$40,000,000}{(212)(\$500)} = 377 \text{ contracts}$$

where:

V_P = value of the portfolio
V_F = value of the futures contract

One problem with this approach is that it ignores the higher volatility of the stock portfolio relative to that of the S&P 500 index. As noted previously, the beta of the stock portfolio, as measured against the index, was 1.22. Table 6.11 shows the potential results of a hedge consistent with these facts. The portfolio manager initiates the hedge on March 14, selling 377 DEC futures contracts against the $40,000,000 stock portfolio. By August 16, his fears have been realized

■ **Table 6.11** ————————————————————————

A Short Hedge	
Stock Market	**Futures Market**
March 14 — Hold $40,000,000 in a stock portfolio.	Sell 377 S&P 500 December futures contracts at 212.00.
April 16 — Stock portfolio falls by 5.40% to $37,838,160.	S&P futures contract falls by 4.43% to 202.61.
Loss: −$2,161,840	Gain: $1,770,015
Net Loss: −$391,825	

and the market has fallen. The S&P index, and the futures, have both fallen by 4.43 percent to 203. The stock portfolio, with its greater volatility, has fallen exactly 1.22 times as much, generating a loss of $2,161,840. This leaves a net loss on the hedge of $391,825. The failure to consider the differential volatility between the stock portfolio and the index futures contract leads to sub-optimal hedging results.

The manager might be able to avoid this result by weighting the hedge ratio by the beta of the stock portfolio. According to this scenario, the manager could use Equation 6.6 to find the number of contracts to trade:

$$\left(\frac{V_P}{V_F}\right)\beta_P = \text{number of contracts} \qquad (6.6)$$

where:

β_P = beta of the portfolio that is being hedged

Using this approach for our example, the manager would trade 460 contracts:

$$\left(\frac{\$40,000,000}{(\$212)(500)}\right)1.22 = 460 \text{ contracts}$$

Had the manager traded 460 contracts, the futures gain reported in Table 6.11 would have been $2,159,700 instead of $1,770,015. This higher gain would have almost exactly offset the loss on the spot position of $2,161,840. Note, however, that these excellent results depend on two crucial assumptions. First, such results could be achieved only if the movement of the stock portfolio during the hedge period exactly corresponded to the volatility implied by its beta. Second, the technique of Equation 6.6 uses the beta of the stock portfolio as measured against the S&P 500 index itself. This assumes that the futures contracts move exactly in tandem with the spot index. The assumption is clearly violated by recent market experience, because the futures contracts for all of the indexes are more volatile than the indexes themselves. This is reflected by the fact that the futures contracts generally have betas above 1.0 when they are measured relative to the stock index itself. The methodology of Equation

6.6 does not take this into account, since it implicitly assumes the index and the futures contracts to have the same price movements, which would imply equal betas. We consider more sophisticated approaches to this type of hedging problem in Chapter 7.

A Long Hedge

As with all other futures contracts, both long and short hedges are possible in stock index futures. Imagine a pension fund manager convinced that she stands at the beginning of an extended bull market. She anticipates that $6,000,000 in new funds will become available in three months for investment. Waiting three months for the funds to invest in the stock market could mean that the bull market would be missed altogether. An alternative to missing the market move would be to use the stock index futures market. The pension manager could simply buy an amount of a stock index futures contract that would be equivalent in dollar commitments to the anticipated inflow of investable funds. On May 19, with the SEP NYSE index futures contract standing at 174.40, the futures contract represents an underlying cash value of $87,200. The pension manager can secure her position in the market by buying $6,000,000 worth of futures. Since she expects the funds in three months, the SEP contract is a natural expiration to use, so she buys 69 SEP contracts, as shown in Table 6.12. By August

■ Table 6.12

A Long Hedge with Stock Index Futures

	Stock Market	Futures Market
May 19	A pension fund manager anticipates having $6,000,000 to invest in three months.	Buys 69 SEP NYSE futures at 174.40.
August 15	$6,000,000 becomes available for investment.	The market has risen and the NYSE futures stands at 178.50.
	Stock prices have risen, so the $6,000,000 will not buy the same shares that it would have on May 19.	Futures profit: $141,450

15, the market has risen, so the $6,000,000 could not buy the same shares that would have been possible on May 19. To offset this fact, the pension manager has earned a futures profit of $141,450. This gain in the futures market helps offset the new higher prices that would be incurred in the stock purchase.

CONCLUSION

In this chapter we have explored the major stock indexes on which futures contracts are traded. In addition, we have considered the structure of the futures contracts based upon them and the differences among the various futures contracts. We applied familiar cash-and-carry and reverse cash-and-carry arbitrage strategies to show that stock index futures prices should conform to the cost-of-carry model. However, we noted the cost-of-carry model must be adjusted to reflect cash dividends. In the context of the cost-of-carry model, we saw that index arbitrage and program trading are applications of cash-and-carry approaches to futures pricing.

The chapter considered some speculative trading strategies that use intracommodity and intercommodity spreads. We also considered an example of a ratio spread. In addition to speculative applications, stock index futures are useful for managing risk. We considered some examples of short and long hedges. In the short hedge example, we showed how a portfolio manager could protect against a potential bear market. With a long hedge example, we showed how a trader could capture a potential bull market by using futures as a substitute for actually buying shares.

NOTES

1. Prominent among these inactive contracts is the Value Line Contract on the Kansas City Board of Trade. Formerly, this contract was actively traded, but its construction was very complicated, being a geometric average of 1,700 stocks. Partially for this reason, its popularity faded during the late 1980s. A change in the composition of the index did little to restore its faded luster. By 1990, daily volume had fallen to a few hundred contracts and open interest in all contracts was below 2,000. Other indexes are the S&P Mid-Cap 400 and the Russell 2000.

2. In earlier times, the S&P 500 consisted of 400 industrial firms, 40 financial institutions, 40 utilities, and 20 transportation firms.

3. As we will see in Chapter 7, trading for the S&P 500 and the NYSE futures contracts ends on one day, and the final settlement price is set at the next day's opening price.

4. These calculations are sometimes off by a penny or two due to rounding.

5. In an interesting approach to the problem of Barings, one calculation insists that Barings would have made a profit of $3 billion on its position had it simply held until the end of 1995. See Numa Financial Systems, Ltd., "Barings Theoretical P/L 1995," NumaWeb home page, World Wide Web. This would have been the eventual result, although the position would also have experienced a low of −$5 billion in June 1995. For a more sober assessment, see Bank of England, "Report of the Board of Banking Supervision Inquiry into the Circumstances of the Collapse of Barings," July 18, 1995. The affair has already given rise to three books: Judith Rawnsley, *Going for Broke,* New York: HarperCollins, 1995; Nick Leeson, *Rogue Trader,* Boston: Little Brown, 1996; and Stephen Fay, *The Collapse of Barings,* New York: Richard Cohen Books, 1996.

Chapter 7

Stock Index Futures: Refinements

OVERVIEW

In Chapter 6 we saw that stock index futures prices are governed by the cost-of-carry model. Because stocks often pay dividends, we saw how to tailor the cost-of-carry model to reflect the dividends on the stocks that underlie the stock index futures. In this chapter, we explore some of the empirical evidence on the relationship between theoretical and observed market prices. As in any violation of cost-of-carry principles, arbitrage opportunities should be possible if stock index futures prices do not correspond to theoretically determined prices.

Index arbitrage is the specific name given to attempts to exploit discrepancies between theoretical and actual stock index futures prices. As we also discussed in Chapter 6, index arbitrage usually proceeds through program trading. With the advent of program trading, there has been some evidence of a link between high index price variability and the style of trading used by program traders. This chapter considers some of the evidence on volatility and explores the market concern about volatility.

Because of the perception that futures trading is responsible for stock market volatility, new concern has focused on trading practices in the futures market, leading to some changes in trading rules. This chapter also considers some of the new trading practices rules recently implemented in the S&P 500 futures pit.

Chapter 6 considered some speculative and hedging applications of stock index futures. This chapter explores some more sophisticated techniques for using stock index futures that are becoming an important tool in portfolio management. By trading stock index futures in conjunction with a stock portfolio, a portfolio manager can tailor the risk characteristics of the entire portfolio. These strategies have aspects of both speculation and hedging. Two of the most notable of these are asset allocation and portfolio insurance, which we consider in some detail.

STOCK INDEX FUTURES PRICES

In this section we consider a variety of issues related to stock index futures pricing. First, we examine the empirical evidence on stock index futures efficiency. Namely, do stock index futures prices conform to the cost-of-carry model? Evidence suggests that the market was not efficient when trading began, but that it is now efficient. Second, we consider the effect of taxes on stock index futures prices. A tax-timing option available to traders of stocks, but denied to stock index futures traders, might explain the discrepancy between theoretical and actual prices for stock index futures. Third, we consider the timing relationship between stock index futures prices and the cash market index. Does the futures price lead the cash market index, or does the cash market index lead the futures? Finally, we consider seasonal impacts on stock index futures pricing. Here "seasonal" refers not only to the time of year, but also to the time of month, time of week, and even time of day.

STOCK INDEX FUTURES EFFICIENCY

In Chapter 6, we saw that cost-of-carry principles apply directly to the pricing of stock index futures. In particular, if the spot stock index price and the futures price are misaligned, cash-and-carry or reverse cash-and-carry arbitrage opportunities will become available. We considered examples of these kinds of transactions in Chapter 6. In this section, we consider whether the stock index futures market is informationally efficient. If it is efficient, then stock index futures prices should conform to the cost-of-carry model that we developed in Chapter 6. As we will see, the general conclusion suggests that the market was inefficient in the early days of trading but that it now conforms well to the cost-of-carry model.

Exploring actual market data, David Modest and Mahadevan Sundaresan apply the carrying charges model to form permissible bounds for futures prices and try to take into account the actual transaction costs that would be incurred in trading the futures and the stocks in the indexes.[1] The bounds depend critically on the assumptions of a $25 round trip transaction cost for the futures contract and $.10 per share transaction costs for the stock itself. We must also assume that the T-bill rate is the appropriate interest rate for all calculations of carrying charges.

Modest and Sundaresan's analysis makes two additional assumptions. The first concerns the use of proceeds from short selling stocks. If a trader does not have full use of the proceeds from short sales due to margin requirements, then the interest on the proceeds that cannot be used has a marked impact on the analysis. We have already encountered this issue in our discussion of T-bill futures efficiency. Essentially, an arbitrage opportunity might require the short sale of the stock index, which means that the individual stocks comprising the index are sold short in the stock market. In this situation, the short seller may not receive full use of the proceeds from the short sale, because the broker will hold a significant fraction of those proceeds as protection against default by the short seller. Therefore, the success of any such arbitrage depends critically upon assumptions regarding the use of short sale proceeds. Modest and Sundaresan examine alternative assumptions about the use of short sale proceeds.

A second critical assumption concerns dividends. We saw in Chapter 6 that dividends are important to the pricing of stock index futures. In addition, the extreme intertemporal variation in dividends shown in Figure 6.2 means that their effect will vary dramatically from one time period to the next. For accuracy in pricing stock index futures, taking account of dividends is very important.

We begin our discussion of this issue by focusing on a paper that examined the early history of trading, ''The Relationship Between Spot and Futures Prices in Stock Index Futures Markets: Some Preliminary Evidence.'' This article by David Modest and Mahadevan Sundaresan addresses most of the issues necessary to determine the efficiency of prices in a market. For instance, we have seen that every real market has a range of permissible no-arbitrage prices. This no-arbitrage band arises because of transaction costs and restrictions on short selling. Therefore, tests of market efficiency depend critically on careful estimations of these transaction costs.

Modest and Sundaresan computed the no-arbitrage boundaries for the DEC 1982 futures contract under the assumptions outlined here and present those results in Figure 7.1. The graph tracks the futures prices from April 21 through September 15, 1982. The dotted lines on the graph show the bounds, which are adjusted for dividends and the assumption that half the proceeds from short sales are available. The solid line represents the actual futures price. Clearly, the futures price lies within the bounds except for near misses on two occasions. On the whole, these results are consistent with the rationality of futures pricing. In another part of their study, the bounds were also adjusted for dividends, but with the assumption that one has use of 100 percent of the proceeds from short sales. In this situation, arbitrage opportunities were consistently available.

In their study, Modest and Sundaresan did not attempt to include an estimate of the daily dividend payment from the S&P 500 index.

■ Figure 7.1

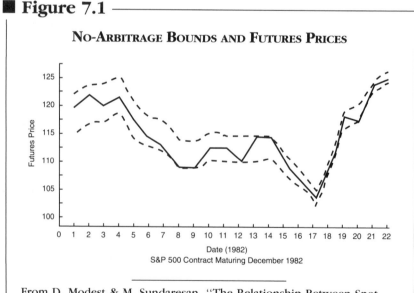

No-Arbitrage Bounds and Futures Prices

Date (1982)
S&P 500 Contract Maturing December 1982

From D. Modest & M. Sundaresan, "The Relationship Between Spot and Futures Prices in Stock Index Futures Markets: Some Preliminary Evidence," *Journal of Futures Markets*, 3:2, 1983, pp. 15–41. Copyright © 1983. Reprinted by permission of John Wiley & Sons, Inc.

Instead, they estimated the dividend rate on the index using quarterly dividend data and then interpolated that into monthly dividend data. As a result, their study does not reflect the high variability in dividends on a daily basis. The graph of Figure 7.1 applies to the DEC 1982 contract for April 21 to September 15, 1982. Over that time, dividends had very sharp quarterly peaks. Had Modest and Sundaresan been able to take these daily fluctuations into account more accurately, we would expect observed prices to lie more consistently within the no-arbitrage bounds, and their paper would be even more valuable.

Perhaps of equal importance to the exact treatment of dividends is the assumption made about the use of proceeds from short sales. In addition, we have seen that some traders face full transaction costs. By contrast, other traders face much lower transaction costs. For example, large institutions with significant portfolios can simulate short selling by selling part of their existing portfolio. In this simulated short selling, they retain full use of the proceeds. Throughout our discussion, we have referred to arbitrage activities by these low trans-action cost traders as **quasi-arbitrage**.

Modest and Sundaresan's results clearly point to quasi-arbitrage opportunities. In the early days of stock index futures trading, it appears that significant quasi-arbitrage opportunities were available. However, after the seasoning of the market, prices tended to remain within the no-arbitrage bounds. While such conclusions depend upon estimates of transaction costs, other studies substantiate the conclusion reached by Modest and Sundaresan.

Taxes and Stock Index Futures

A difference in tax treatment between futures and the stocks themselves might justify a discrepancy from the cost-of-carry model. In such a case, the market might be efficient. Comparing a long position in the stocks underlying an index and a long position in the stock index futures contract shows that there is a difference in tax treatment. The owner of a stock may have a paper gain or loss on the stock as the end of the year approaches. For example, assume that a share was purchased for $100 and that the trader pays taxes at the rate of 30 percent. If the stock sells for $90 as the end of the year approaches, the trader has the option to sell the stock for $90, realizing a $10 loss. If he or she sells the stock, taxable income will be reduced by $10. With a 30 percent tax rate, selling the stock generates a tax saving of $3. By contrast, assume that the stock price is $110 instead of $90 as the end of the year approaches. In this situation, the tax saving strategy is to wait until after the turn of the year to take the gain, thereby deferring the taxes for a full year by just waiting a few days to make the trade.

Because futures prices are marked to market at year-end for tax purposes, the futures contract possesses no tax-timing option. In the futures markets, tax rules require all paper gains or losses to be recognized as cash gains or losses each year. The tax-timing option included with the stock, but lacking with the futures contract, implies that rational pricing must reflect the value of the tax-timing option in the relationship between the cash and futures prices of the stock index.

This possibility was first noted by Bradford Cornell and Kenneth French. They showed how this tax-timing option could give extra value to the stocks relative to the futures. Cornell and French compute the value of the tax option as the difference between the observed market price and the price implied by the carrying charges model. While the tax option clearly has a value, the technique adopted by Cornell and French assumes that the stock index futures contract is priced rationally, and they compute the value of the option in accordance with that fundamental belief. For the purpose of trying to evaluate the price performance characteristics of the stock index futures contract, note that the tax-timing option would have a value, but that a trader cannot immediately assume that its value is equal to the discrepancy between the observed market price and the theoretically justified price assuming no tax-timing option. However, in an empirical study of the effect of the tax-timing option on futures prices, Cornell concludes that the tax-timing option does not appear to affect prices.[2] Cornell suggests that trading may be dominated by tax-free investors, or that other tax rules may prevent the tax-timing option from significantly affecting prices.

The Day of the Week Effect in Stock Index Futures

It has been well documented that returns on many securities vary by the day of the week. There is nothing in the financial theory to explain why returns on Thursday should be different from returns on Tuesday or Wednesday. Nonetheless, a great deal of evidence shows that returns differ depending on the day of the week. In particular, Friday returns are generally high and Monday returns (the return from Friday close to Monday close) are even negative. These return differences are substantial, and it may be possible for investors to earn a return that beats the market by timing their purchases to take advantage of these persistent differences. If so, the day of the week effect would show either that the semi-strong efficient market hypothesis (EMH) was not true or that the CAPM was not true, or both. If the CAPM is the correct pricing relationship in the market, then the EMH must be false, because it appears that prices do not adjust correctly to reflect all available information. If the EMH is true, it seems that the CAPM must be false, because there must be additional risk factors not recognized by the CAPM to explain the different returns depending on the day of the week.

The day of the week effect has also been explored in the stock index futures market. Given the strong relationship that must hold between stock index futures and the stock index itself, we would expect to find an effect in the futures market if there is one in the stock market itself. Most studies find a weekend effect – price changes from the Friday close to the Monday open are low or negative.[3]

LEADS AND LAGS IN STOCK INDEX PRICES

We have seen that arbitrage seekers force stock index cash market and futures market prices to conform to the cost-of-carry model. Thus, a movement in one price must generate a movement in the other price to keep prices in conformance with the cost-of-carry model.

At first blush, it might seem that the index should lead the futures. For example, if new information arrives in the market about a particular stock, the price of that stock will change. The index value changes to reflect the new price of the constituent stock. To keep prices in conformance with the cost-of-carry model, the index futures price must change. Under this scenario, the cash market index changes first and the futures index price changes later. Thus, the cash index leads the futures price.

However, the dominant information affecting the stock market might be more general information. If the most important information affects the general level of stock prices, rather than the price of a single firm, there may be a different transmission of stock price changes. For an example too strange to believe, assume that Iraq invades Kuwait and that this is bad news for stock prices. Traders may react to this information by trading in either the stock market or the stock index futures market. The choice of market will be affected by both the relative liquidity and the transaction costs in the two markets. If liquidity and transaction costs are most important, futures trading will be more attractive. Thus, with the invasion news, traders might first sell index futures, driving down the futures price. The cash market index must then adjust to exclude arbitrage opportunities. Under this scenario, the futures price will lead the cash market index.

These leads and lags are most likely to occur on a minute to minute basis. If the leads or lags persisted over days, for example, they could well lead to arbitrage opportunities. Whether the cash market index leads the futures, or vice versa, is essentially an empirical question. The question of leads and lags has been explored in several studies, most of which find that futures prices lead cash market prices.[4]

While stock index futures prices may lead the stock index, this differential movement does not necessarily create arbitrage opportunities. First, movements in the two prices are generally almost simultaneous. Quickly responding prices may not allow any arbitrage opportunities. Second, both prices vary constantly by small amounts as new information reaches the market. Even substantial lags would not create an arbitrage opportunity if the difference in prices is small. In other words, the futures price could always lead the cash market index. However, if the price difference is small, the difference in prices could always remain within the no-arbitrage bounds of the cost-of-carry model.

REAL WORLD PROGRAM TRADING

Chapter 6 explained the basic idea of index arbitrage through program trading. There we considered an imaginary two-stock index and showed how to engage in cash-and-carry and reverse cash-and-carry strategies to exploit mispricing of the index versus the index futures. To provide a more realistic feel for real world program trade in stock index futures, this section begins with an historical example of an actual program trade. We then consider the risks inherent in program trading that make the enterprise much more perilous than our historical example would seem to indicate. Finally, we conclude with some statistics on the extent of program trading in today's markets.

REAL WORLD PROGRAM TRADING: AN EXAMPLE

This section discusses an historical example of a cash-and-carry program trading transaction.[5] The trader buys the stocks and carries them forward while selling the futures to profit from the spot being underpriced relative to the futures. Table 7.1 shows the actual prices for the MMI stocks on February 26, 1986, when the trade began. The table also shows the MMI stock prices at the end of the trade on March 21, 1986, and the dividends that the various stocks paid between the two dates.

Faced with the prices shown for February 26, 1986, in Table 7.1, the trader bought 2,000 shares of each of 20 stocks, with a total purchase price of $2,749,000. The trader used $1,374,500 (or 50 percent) of his own funds and borrowed the same amount at 8.5

■ Table 7.1

DATA FOR INDEX ARBITRAGE

Firm	Price Feb. 26	Price Mar. 21	Dividends $/Share
American Express	64	65.625	
AT&T	22.5	22.875	
Chevron	37.875	37.375	
Coca-Cola	92	100.375	0.78
Dow Chemical	48.75	52.375	
DuPont	70.5	72.5	
Kodak	55	59.75	
Exxon	54.875	54.75	
General Electric	75.5	75.75	0.58
General Motors	78.25	83.25	
IBM	158.125	148.5	
International Paper	57	60	
Johnson & Johnson	48.375	54	
Merck	150.75	161.25	0.9
3M	97.25	104	
Mobil Oil	30.125	29.5	
Philip Morris	101.125	119.25	1.15
Procter & Gamble	67	73.5	
Sears	42.875	46.125	
U.S. Steel	22.675	22.75	
MMI Index	311.74	328.07	
MAR 86 MMI Futures	313.55	328.07	

percent. At the same time, he sold 35 MAR 1986 MMI futures at 313.55. This value implies an underlying stock value of $2,743,563 (313.55 index value × $250 multiplier × 35 contracts). (In 1986 the MMI multiplier was $250. It is now $500.) Trading this number of contracts gives the spot and futures positions very similar dollar values, which is exactly the desired relationship to profit on the relative mispricing.

RISKS IN INDEX ARBITRAGE AND PROGRAM TRADING

The index arbitrage transactions on February 26 in Table 7.2 ensure a profit, subject to a few minor risks. Because the stock index contracts are settled in cash, the spot and futures values at the close of trading for the contract must converge. For the MAR 1986 MMI, trading ended on March 21. Table 7.2 shows the transactions involved in this arbitrage. All of the values in Table 7.2 are actual market prices. Notice that the purchase of shares in Table 7.2 used 50 percent debt and 50 percent investable funds. This is necessary because of Federal Reserve Board requirements that no more than 50 percent of the purchase price of stocks can be borrowed. Table 7.2 reflects the opportunity cost of those invested funds by assuming that they could have earned the 8.5 percent interest rate that was paid to borrow money.

In computing the cash flows in Table 7.2, we consider all interest, dividends, and out-of-pocket transaction costs. The dividends totaled $3.41 from Table 7.1. With 2,000 shares of each firm, the total dividends received were $6,820. Total transaction costs were $1,100. This is about $.014 per share to buy and the same amount to sell, including the futures contracts. Notice, however, that the analysis does not reflect the daily resettlement cash flows that may have been incurred between February 26 and March 21, nor do we consider interest that might have been earned on the dividends received. In addition, the cash flow computation does not reflect the cost of searching for this opportunity.

This kind of transaction has certain elements of risk stemming from three sources. First, there is execution risk, because the trader must successfully enter and close the entire position. To establish the position, the trader must buy 2,000 shares of 20 stocks and sell 35 futures contracts. Imagine that the trader finds the opportunity and sells futures. Then the trader starts buying shares of the 20 stocks. During this time, assume that three of the stocks increase in price by $1.00

■ Table 7.2

PROGRAM TRADING TRANSACTIONS

February 26, 1986
Sell 35 MMI MAR 1986 futures at 313.55.

Use $1,374,500 of investable funds; borrow another $1,374,500 at 8.5% and use these funds to buy 2,000 shares of each of the 20 stocks comprising the MMI at a total cost of $2,749,000.

March 21, 1986
Buy 35 MMI MAR 1986 futures at 328.07.

Sell all stocks purchased on February 26, receiving $2,893,000.

Pay interest of $8,438 on borrowed $1,374,500.

Charge opportunity cost of own $1,374,500 that was invested at appropriate cost of funds of 8.5% for a total of $8,438.

Pay transaction costs: −$1,100.

Dividends received while stocks were owned: +$6,820.

Net Cash Flows:

February 26 None, because we will charge an opportunity cost for the portion of funds that were invested.

March 21		
	Futures	−$127,050
	Stocks	144,000
	Transaction Costs	−1,100
	Dividends	6,820
	Interest on Actual Loan	−8,438
	Opportunity Cost on Invested Funds	−8,438
	Arbitrage Profit	$ 5,794

each. Because the trader has sold the futures contracts, the price of that side of the position is fixed. With three stocks increasing in price by $1.00, the long position in the stocks will cost a total of $6,000 more than anticipated. If this happens, the trader pays $6,000 more than anticipated for the stocks, and the arbitrage profit turns to an arbitrage loss.

The second part of the execution risk exposure occurs on March 21 when the position must be closed. The profit or loss on the futures contract depends on the index value at the close of trading on March 21. However, the risk arbitrage strategy calls for the stocks to be sold at the end of trading on the same day. If the stocks are held until the next day, there will be considerable risk, because any kind of news could be received after the close of trading on March 21. Because of this risk, it is customary to close out such stock positions at the close of trading on the futures expiration day. To close the position, the trader enters a market on close order to sell these stocks. A **market on close order** instructs the broker to sell these shares for the market price at the close of trading. The obvious goal is to sell the shares at the settlement price of the day's trading, because that will be the share price that figures into the index, and the index value on that day determines the futures profit or loss. If the trader could be certain that the shares would be sold at the day's closing price, this element of risk would be eliminated. However, it is difficult to trade in the last 15–30 seconds to get execution at the day's final price. Therefore, there is risk involved in closing the position as well as opening the position.

In addition to execution risk, there is some risk that the dividends will not be paid as the trader anticipates. In this example, if the firms cancel their dividend payments, the trader does not receive $6,820 and the transactions will generate a loss. Such a rash of dividend cancellations is unlikely, but at least remotely possible. The final source of risk is financing risk. The trader might not be able to secure financing for the entire period at the same rate. If the stocks are financed with overnight obligations and interest rates suddenly jump, financing costs could be higher than anticipated. In summary, the index arbitrage transaction faces execution risk, dividend risk, and interest rate risk. Of these, execution risk is the most important. Nonetheless, once the transactions of February 26 are put in place, there is very little real danger of a loss.

HEDGING WITH STOCK INDEX FUTURES

In Chapter 6 we considered the basic techniques for hedging with stock index futures. We presented examples of short and long hedges and discussed a hedging strategy for hedging a portfolio with stock index futures that reflected the beta of the portfolio being hedged. The hedge position from Chapter 6 was:

$$\left(\frac{V_P}{V_F}\right)\beta_P = \text{number of contracts} \qquad (6.6)$$

where:

V_P = value of the portfolio
V_F = value of the futures contract
β_P = beta of the portfolio that is being hedged

In this section we analyze stock index futures hedging. We begin by showing that the hedge Equation 6.6 gives the futures position to establish a combined stock and futures portfolio with the lowest possible risk. We illustrate this hedging technique with actual market data. It is also possible to use futures to alter the beta of an existing portfolio. For example, if a stock portfolio has a beta of 0.8 and the desired beta is 0.9, it is possible to trade stock index futures to make the combined stock and futures portfolio behave like a stock portfolio with a beta of 0.9. Finally, we consider techniques for tailing the hedge.

THE MINIMUM RISK HEDGE RATIO

In Chapter 6 we studied the problem of combining a cash market position with futures to minimize risk. There we took the cash market position as fixed and sought to find the futures hedge ratio, HR, that would minimize risk. From Equation 3.3 we saw that the risk of a combined cash and futures position equals:

$$\sigma_P^2 = \sigma_C^2 + HR^2\sigma_F^2 - 2\,HR\rho_{CF}\sigma_C\sigma_F \qquad (3.3)$$

where:

σ_P^2 = variance of the portfolio
σ_C^2 = variance of asset C
σ_F^2 = variance of asset F
ρ_{CF} = correlation between assets C and F
σ_C = standard deviation of asset C
σ_F = standard deviation of asset F

From Equation 3.3, the risk-minimizing hedge ratio, HR, is:

$$HR = \frac{\rho_{CF}\sigma_C\sigma_F}{\sigma_F^2} = \frac{COV_{CF}}{\sigma_F^2} \qquad (3.4)$$

where:

COV_{CF} = the covariance between C and F

As a practical matter, the easiest way to find the risk-minimizing hedge ratio is to estimate the following regression:

$$C_t = \alpha + \beta_{RM}F_t + \epsilon_t \qquad (7.1)$$

where:

C_t = the returns on the cash market position in period t
F_t = the returns on the futures contract in period t[6]
α = the constant regression parameter
β_{RM} = the slope regression parameter for the risk-minimizing hedge
ϵ = an error term with zero mean and standard deviation of 1.0

The estimated beta from this regression is the risk-minimizing hedge ratio, because the estimated β_{RM} equals the sample covariance between the independent (F) and dependent C_t variables divided by the sample variance of the independent variable. The R^2 from this regression shows the percentage of risk in the cash position that is eliminated by holding the futures position.

At this point, it is important to distinguish the beta in Equation 7.1 and the beta of the portfolio in the sense of the capital asset pricing model. The CAPM beta is the beta from regressing the returns of a given asset on the returns from the "true" market portfolio. However, the returns on the true market portfolio are unobservable. Therefore, as a practical measure, proxies are used for the market portfolio and the betas of assets are estimated by regressing the returns of a particular asset on the returns from the proxy of the market portfolio. The potential confusion becomes more dangerous because the S&P 500 spot index is one of the best-known proxies for the true market portfolio.

In Equation 6.6 we computed a hedge ratio using the beta for the portfolio. This beta is the estimated CAPM beta, because it is estimated by regressing the returns from a portfolio on the proxy for the market portfolio. By contrast, the beta in Equation 7.1 is the beta for a risk-minimizing hedge ratio and is not the same as the estimated CAPM beta. The beta in Equation 7.1 is found by regressing the returns of the portfolio on the returns from the futures contract. The estimated CAPM beta is found by regressing the returns of the portfolio on the returns of the spot market index being used as a proxy for the unobservable true market portfolio. Thus, the hedging position in Equation 6.6 is not a risk-minimizing hedge. Nonetheless, such hedges can be very useful. We might think of the hedge ratio in Equation 6.6 as a rough-and-ready approximation to risk-minimizing hedging.

Having found the risk-minimizing hedge ratio, β_{RM}, we need to compute the number of contracts to trade. The solution to this problem almost exactly matches the hedging position in Equation 6.6, but we use the risk-minimizing hedge ratio, β_{RM}, instead of the CAPM beta for the portfolio, β_P. Thus, the risk-minimizing futures position is:

$$\left(\frac{V_P}{V_F}\right)\beta_{RM} = \text{number of contracts}$$

A Minimum Risk Hedging Example

In this section we consider an example of a minimum risk hedge in stock index futures using actual market data. Let us assume a trader has a portfolio worth $10 million on November 28. The portfolio is invested in the 20 stocks in the MMI. The portfolio manager will hedge this cash market portfolio using the S&P 500 JUN futures contract. We consider each step that the portfolio manager follows to compute the hedge ratio and to implement the hedge.

Organize Data and Compute Returns. The manager plans to hedge according to Equation 6.6. Therefore, she needs to find the beta for the hedge ratio. Accordingly, she collects data for her portfolio value for 101 days from July 6 through yesterday, November 27. She also finds the price of the S&P 500 JUN futures for each day. There is nothing magic about using 101 days, but these data are available and she believes that this procedure will provide a sufficient sample to estimate the hedging beta. From the 101 days of prices, she computes the daily percentage change in the value of the cash market portfolio and the futures price. This gives 100 paired observations of daily returns data.

Estimate Hedging Beta. With the data in place, the portfolio manager regresses the cash market returns on the returns from the futures contract as shown in Equation 7.1. From this regression the estimated beta is .8801, so β_{RM} = .8801. This indicates that each dollar of the cash market position should be hedged with $.8801 dollars in the futures position. The R^2 from the regression is .9263, and this high R^2 encourages the belief that the hedge is likely to perform well. Again, for emphasis, the estimated beta from regressing the portfolio's returns on the stock index futures returns is not the same as the portfolio's CAPM beta; β_P does not equal β_{RM}.

Compute Futures Position. The portfolio manager wants to hedge a $10 million cash portfolio with the S&P JUN futures contract. Having found the risk-minimizing hedge ratio, she needs to translate the hedge ratio into the correct futures position that takes account of the size of the futures contract. On November 27, the S&P futures closed at 354.75. The futures contract value is for the index times $500. Therefore, applying Equation 6.6, she computes the number of contracts as:

$$\left(\frac{V_P}{V_F}\right)\beta_{RM} = \left(\frac{\$10,000,000}{(354.75)(\$500)}\right).8801 = 49.6180$$

The estimated risk-minimizing futures position is 49.62 contracts, so the portfolio manager decides to sell 50 contracts.

Evaluate Hedging Results. Figure 7.2 shows the value of the unhedged and hedged portfolio for the next 60 days until February 22 of next year, when our trader decides to terminate the hedge. The unhedged portfolio's ending value is $9,656,090. The settlement price for the futures on February 22 is 330.60. Therefore, the futures profit is 50($500)(354.75 − 330.60) = $603,750. The futures profit results from trading 50 contracts with each index point being worth $500 and the index having fallen 24.15 points. The value of the hedged portfolio consists of the cash market portfolio plus the futures profit, so the hedged portfolio's terminal value is $10,259,840. In this example, the hedge protected the portfolio against a substantial loss.

Ex-Ante versus Ex-Post Hedge Ratios

In our risk-minimizing hedging example, we computed β_{RM} = .8801 using historical data and applied the hedge ratio to a future period.

■ Figure 7.2

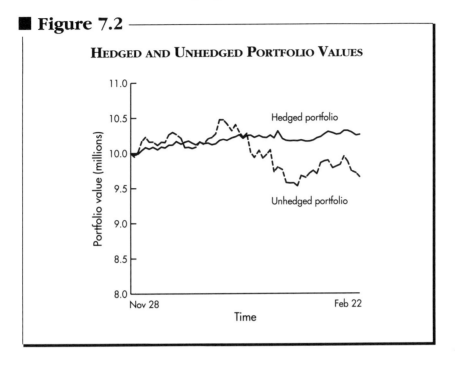

HEDGED AND UNHEDGED PORTFOLIO VALUES

It is highly unlikely that the estimated hedge ratio would equal the hedge ratio that we would have used if we had perfect foresight about the behavior of the cash market position and the futures price. This is the difference between an ex-ante and an ex-post hedge ratio. **Ex-ante**, or **before the fact**, the best hedge ratio we could find was .8801. **Ex-post**, or **after the fact**, some other hedge ratio would be likely to perform better than the ex-ante hedge ratio of .8801. In this section we consider the difference between ex-ante and ex-post hedge ratios in the context of our example.

The portfolio manager used historical returns from July 7 to November 27 to estimate the hedge ratio of .8801. She applied this hedge ratio on November 28, and maintained the hedged position until February 22 of the next year. The ex-post risk-minimizing hedge ratio was not available to her when she made her hedging decision on November 28. What would have been the ideal risk-minimizing hedge ratio, if she had complete knowledge about how prices would move from November 28 to February 22? To find this ex-post hedge ratio, we estimated Equation 7.1 using data from November to February and found an ex-post hedge ratio of .9154. This implies a futures position of 51.61 contracts. We round this to 52 contracts. Figure 7.3 shows the results from hedging with the ex-ante and ex-post hedge ratios.

In a world with perfect foresight, the ex-post hedge ratio is the risk-minimizing hedge ratio we would like to use. However, the ex-ante hedge ratio is the best estimate we can make at the time the decision must be implemented. As Figure 7.3 shows, the ex-ante hedge ratio performs quite well. The terminal value of the hedge with the ex-ante hedge ratio is $10,259,840. With the ex-post hedge ratio, the terminal value is $10,283,990. While the ex-ante hedge ratio performed well, the ex-post hedge ratio would have been even better. This is exactly the result that we would expect.

ALTERING THE BETA OF A PORTFOLIO

Portfolio managers often adjust the CAPM betas of their portfolios in anticipation of bull and bear markets. If a manager expects a bull market, she might increase the beta of the portfolio to take advantage of the expected rise in stock prices. Similarly, if a bear market seems imminent, the manager might reduce the beta of a stock portfolio as

■ **Figure 7.3**

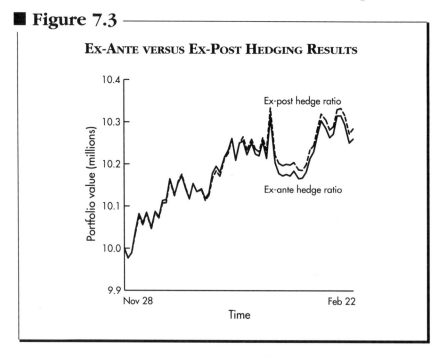

EX-ANTE VERSUS EX-POST HEDGING RESULTS

a defensive maneuver. If the manager trades only in the stock market itself, changing the beta of the portfolio involves selling some stocks and buying others. For example, to reduce the beta of the portfolio, the manager would sell high beta stocks and use the funds to buy low beta stocks. With transaction costs in the stock market being relatively high, this procedure can be expensive.

The portfolio manager has an alternative. She can use stock index futures to create a combined stock/futures portfolio with the desired response to market condition. In this section we consider techniques for changing the risk of a portfolio using stock index futures.

In the CAPM all risk is either systematic or unsystematic. **Systematic risk** is associated with general movements in the market and affects all investments. By contrast, **unsystematic risk** is particular to a certain investment or a certain range of investments. Diversification can almost completely eliminate unsystematic risk from a portfolio. The remaining systematic risk is unavoidable. Studies show that a random selection of 20 stocks will create a portfolio with very little unsystematic risk. Therefore, in this section we restrict our attention to portfolios that are well diversified and consequently have no unsystematic risk.

Starting with a stock portfolio that has systematic risk only and combining it with a risk-minimizing short position in stock index futures creates a combined stock/futures portfolio with zero systematic risk. According to the CAPM, a portfolio with zero systematic risk should earn the risk-free rate of interest. Instead of eliminating all systematic risk by hedging, it is possible to hedge only a portion of the systematic risk to reduce, but not eliminate, the systematic risk inherent in the portfolio. Similarly, a portfolio manager can use stock index futures to increase the systematic risk of a portfolio.

A risk-minimizing hedge matches a long position in stock with a short position in stock index futures in an attempt to create a portfolio whose value will not change with fluctuations in the stock market. To reduce, but not eliminate the systematic risk, a portfolio manager could sell some futures, but fewer than the risk-minimizing amount. For example, to eliminate half of the systematic risk, the portfolio manager could sell half of the number of contracts stipulated by the risk-minimizing hedge. The combined stock/futures position would then have a level of systematic risk equal to half of the stock portfolio's systematic risk.

It is also possible to trade stock index futures to increase the systematic risk of a stock portfolio. If a trader buys stock index futures, he increases his systematic risk. Therefore, if a portfolio manager holds a stock portfolio and buys stock index futures, the resulting stock/futures position has more systematic risk than the stock portfolio alone. For example, assume a portfolio manager buys, instead of sells, the risk-minimizing number of stock index futures. Instead of eliminating the systematic risk, the resulting stock/long futures position should have twice the systematic risk of the original portfolio.

We can illustrate this principle by considering the same data we used to illustrate the risk-minimizing hedge. In that example, the risk-minimizing futures position was to sell 50 contracts. Selling 50 contracts created a stock/futures position with zero systematic risk. By selling just 25 contracts, the portfolio manager could cut the systematic risk of the original portfolio in half. Similarly, by buying 50 contracts, the resulting stock/futures position would have twice the systematic risk of the original futures position.

Figure 7.4 shows the price paths of two portfolios over the 60-day hedging period from November 28 to February 22. First, the graph

■ Figure 7.4

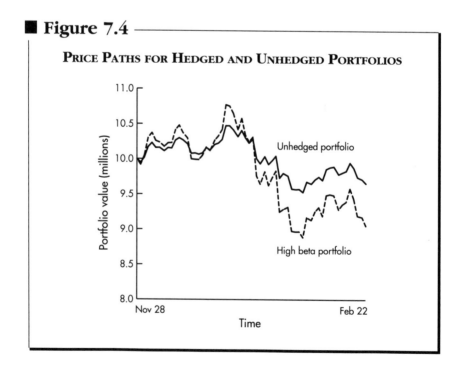

PRICE PATHS FOR HEDGED AND UNHEDGED PORTFOLIOS

shows the unhedged portfolio. Its value begins at $10 million and terminates at $9,656,090, as we have seen. Over this period, the unhedged portfolio lost about $350,000. The graph also shows the portfolio created by holding the stocks and buying 50 futures contracts. In our analysis of the risk-minimizing hedge, we found that the trader could minimize risk by selling 50 futures contracts. Buying 50 contracts doubles the systematic risk. The new portfolio of stock plus a long position of 50 contracts increases the sensitivity of the portfolio to swings in the stock market. In effect, holding the stock portfolio and buying stock index futures simulates more than 100 percent investment in the stock index. Stock prices in general fell during this 60-day period. For example, the all stock portfolio lost 3.44 percent of its value over this period.

By buying stock index futures, the portfolio manager would increase the overall sensitivity of the portfolio to changes in the stock market. Not surprisingly, then, the stock/long futures portfolio lost more than the pure stock portfolio. As Figure 7.4 shows, every move of the stock/long futures portfolio exaggerates the movement of the all stock portfolio. For the portfolio of stock plus a long position of 50 index futures, the terminal value is $9,052,340. This portfolio lost 9.48 percent of its value. However, as Figure 7.4 shows, for periods when the stock prices advanced from their initial level, the stock/long futures position rose even more. This is just what we expect, because buying futures increases the systematic risk of the existing stock portfolio.

ASSET ALLOCATION

In **asset allocation**, an investor decides how to divide funds among broad asset classes. For example, the decision to invest 60 percent in equities and 40 percent in T-bills is an asset allocation decision. The choice between investing in General Motors and Ford Motors is not an asset allocation decision. Thus, asset allocation focuses on the macro level commitment of funds to various asset classes and the shifting of funds among these major asset classes. In this section, we use the basic cost-of-carry model to show how a trader can radically adjust an initial portfolio to move from equities to T-bills or from T-bills to equities by using stock index futures. Because these portfolio maneuvers radically change the type of asset the trader holds, the maneuvers implement asset allocation decisions.

The basic cost-of-carry model we have used since Chapter 2 asserts that the futures price equals the spot price times one plus the cost-of-carry under suitable market conditions:

$$F_0 = S_0(1 + C) \qquad (2.3)$$

where:

F_0 = the futures price at $t = 0$
S_0 = the spot price at $t = 0$
C = the percentage cost of carrying the spot good from $t = 0$ to the futures expiration

The cost-of-carry includes the financing cost of purchasing the asset, plus storage, insurance, and transportation. As we have seen in Chapter 2, for financial futures the cost-of-carry essentially equals the financing cost, because storage, insurance, and transportation are negligible. Therefore, in a full carry market, a cash-and-carry strategy of selling a futures and buying and holding the spot good until the futures expires should earn the financing rate, which essentially equals the risk-free rate of interest. We can express this relationship as:

Short-Term Riskless Debt = Stock − Stock Index Futures $\qquad (7.2)$

Creating a Synthetic T-Bill

From the analysis in the preceding section, we see that the basic cash-and-carry strategy of holding the stock and selling futures gives a resulting stock/futures portfolio that mimics a T-bill. Of course, it does not create a real T-bill. Instead, the stock/futures portfolio behaves like a T-bill. We might say that the trader creates a synthetic T-bill by holding stock and selling futures.

Synthetic T-bill = Stock − Stock Index Futures

This synthetic T-bill is related to risk-minimizing hedging. In a minimum risk hedge, a trader sells futures against a stock portfolio to create a combined stock/futures portfolio that has no systematic risk. A portfolio with no systematic risk has an expected return that equals the risk-free rate. Thus, the position created by risk-minimizing hedging is essentially the creation of a synthetic T-bill.

Consider the asset allocation decision of a trader with a stock portfolio. Assume the trader believes that a bear market is imminent and that the proper asset allocation decision is to hold no equities and to invest all funds in T-bills. The trader can sell all of the equities and invest the funds in T-bills. However, selling an entire portfolio can incur substantial transaction costs. Instead, the manager can implement the asset allocation decision by selling stock index futures against the portfolio. By implementing a risk-minimizing hedge, the manager creates a synthetic T-bill.

CREATING A SYNTHETIC EQUITY POSITION

It is also possible to use stock index futures to create a synthetic stock market position. Consider now a trader who holds all assets in T-bills. We assume that this trader expects a stock market surge, and she would like to take advantage of the rising stock prices. However, she is reluctant to incur all of the transaction costs associated with buying stocks. She too can implement her asset allocation decision by using stock index futures. Rearranging Equation 7.2 shows how to create the risky stock position:

Synthetic Stock Portfolio = T-bills + Stock Index Futures

The trader can buy stock index futures and hold the futures in conjunction with T-bills to mimic a stock portfolio. Thus, she implements her asset allocation decision by trading stock index futures.

In our discussion of asset allocation, we have considered examples of using stock index futures to change from 100 percent stock investment to 100 percent T-bill investment, and vice versa. Of course, the change in the portfolio need not be so radical. When we considered hedging, we saw that a trader can implement a risk-minimizing hedge or a transaction that shapes the risk of the portfolio. For example, by trading half of the risk-minimizing futures position, a trader could cut the systematic risk of the stock position in half. Similarly, by holding stock and buying stock index futures, the trader could increase the systematic risk of the position. The same principles apply to asset allocation decisions. For the trader with an initial stock position, selling half of the risk-minimizing number of futures results in a portfolio that behaves like a portfolio that is invested half in stock and half in T-bills. Similarly, a trader with a long position in stock who buys stock index futures creates a combined stock/futures portfolio that behaves like a leveraged stock portfolio.

PORTFOLIO INSURANCE

As we have seen, traders can tailor the risk of a stock portfolio by trading stock index futures. For a given well-diversified portfolio, selling stock index futures can create a combined stock/futures portfolio with reduced risk. Holding a stock portfolio and buying stock index futures results in a portfolio with greater risk and expected return than the initial portfolio.

Portfolio insurance refers to a collection of techniques for managing the risk of an underlying portfolio. With most portfolio insurance strategies, the goal is to manage the risk of a portfolio to ensure that the value of the portfolio does not drop below a specified level, while at the same time allowing for the portfolio's value to increase. Portfolio insurance strategies are often implemented using options, but stock index futures are equally important tools for portfolio insurance. Implementing portfolio insurance strategies using futures is called **dynamic hedging**. Although the mathematics of dynamic hedging are too complex for full treatment here, we can understand the basic idea behind portfolio insurance with stock index futures.

A PORTFOLIO INSURANCE EXAMPLE

Consider a fully diversified stock portfolio worth $100 million. The value of this portfolio can range from zero to infinity. Many investors would like to put a floor beneath the value of the portfolio. For example, it would be very desirable to ensure that the portfolio's value never falls below $90 million. Portfolio insurance offers a way to control the downside risk of a portfolio. However, in a financial market there is no free lunch, so it is only possible to limit the risk of a large price fall by sacrificing some of the potential for a gain. Portfolio insurance, like life insurance, is not free, but it may be desirable for some traders.

We have seen that a risk-minimizing hedge converts a stock portfolio to a synthetic T-bill. By fully hedging our example stock portfolio, we can keep the portfolio's value above $100 million. A fully hedged portfolio will increase in value at the risk-free rate, although full hedging eliminates all of the potential gain in the portfolio beyond the risk-free rate. In dynamic hedging, however, the trader holds the stock portfolio and sells some futures contracts. The more insurance the trader wants, the more futures he or she will sell.

Let us assume that a stock index futures contract has an underlying value of $100 million and a trader sells futures contracts to cover $50 million of the value of the portfolio. Thus, in the initial position, the trader is long $100 million in stock and short $50 million in futures, so 50 percent of the portfolio is hedged. Table 7.3 shows this initial position in the time zero row. At $t = 0$, there has been no gain or loss on either the stock or futures. In the first period, we assume that the value of the stock portfolio falls by $2 million. The 50 futures contracts cover half of that loss with a gain of $1 million. Therefore, at $t = 1$, the combined stock/futures portfolio is worth $99 million. Now the manager increases the coverage in the futures market by selling five more contracts. This gives a total of 55 short positions and coverage for 56 percent (55/99) of the total portfolio. In the second period, the stock portfolio loses another $2 million, but with 55 futures contracts, the futures gain is (55/99)$2 million = $1.11 million. This gives a total portfolio value of $98.11 million.

By $t = 4$, the stock portfolio has fallen $10 million, but the futures profits have been $6.21 million. This gives a total portfolio value of $96.21 million. Also, the manager has increased the futures position in response to each drop in stock prices. At $t = 4$, the trader is short 80 contracts, hedging 83 percent of the stock market portfolio. At

■ Table 7.3

PORTFOLIO INSURANCE TRANSACTIONS AND RESULTS

	Gain/Loss $ millions		Total	Futures	Portion
Time	Stocks	Futures	Value	Position	Hedged
0	0	0	100	−50	0.5
1	−2.00	1	99	−55	0.56
2	−2.00	1.11	98.11	−60	0.61
3	−2.00	1.22	97.33	−70	0.72
4	−4.00	2.88	96.21	−80	0.83
5	−36.86	30.65	90	−90	1
6	−10.00	10	90	−90	1

$t = 5$, the stock price drops dramatically, losing \$35.86 million. The futures profit covers \$30.65 million. This leaves a total portfolio value of \$90 million. However, this is the floor amount of the portfolio, so the trader must now move to a fully hedged position. If the stock portfolio is only partially hedged, the next drop in prices can take the value of the entire portfolio below the floor amount of \$90 million. At $t = 6$, the price of the stocks drops \$10 million, but the futures position fully covers the loss. Therefore, the combined portfolio maintains its floor value of \$90 million.

Table 7.3 shows the basic strategy of portfolio insurance with dynamic hedging. Initially, the portfolio is partially hedged. If stock prices fall, the trader increases the portion of the portfolio that is insured. Had the stock portfolio risen in value, the futures position would have lost money. However, the loss on the futures position would have been less than the gain on the stocks, because the portfolio was only partially hedged. As the stock prices rose, the manager would have bought futures, thereby hedging less and less of the portfolio. Less hedging would be needed if the stock price rose, because there would be little chance of the portfolio's total value falling below \$90 million.

IMPLEMENTING PORTFOLIO INSURANCE

By design, Table 7.3 is highly simplistic. First, it does not show how the starting futures position was determined. Second, it does not show how the adjustments in the futures position were determined. Third, it considers only large changes in the value of the stock portfolio. For instance, the smallest change in the table is 2 percent of the stock portfolio's value. The exact answer to these questions is highly mathematical; however, we can explore these issues in an intuitive way.

Choosing the initial futures position depends on several factors. First, it depends on the floor that is chosen relative to the initial value of the portfolio. For example, if the lowest acceptable value of the portfolio is \$100 million, then the manager must hedge 100 percent at $t = 0$. Thus, the lower the floor relative to the portfolio value, the lower the percentage of the portfolio the manager will need to hedge. Second, the purpose of the insurance strategy is to guarantee a minimum terminal portfolio value while allowing for more favorable results. As a consequence, the futures position must take into account the volatility of the stock portfolio. The higher the estimated volatility of the stock portfolio, the greater the chance of a large drop in value that will send the total portfolio value below the floor. Therefore, the portion of the portfolio that is to be hedged depends critically on the estimated volatility of the stock portfolio. Of course, this will differ both across time and for portfolios of different risk.

Adjustments in the futures position depend upon the same kinds of considerations that determine the initial position. First, the value of the portfolio relative to the floor is critical. Second, new information about the volatility of the stock portfolio also affects the futures position. In Table 7.3, the volatility of the stock portfolio accelerates. Each percentage drop is larger than the previous. Therefore, this increasing volatility will lead to a larger short futures position than would otherwise be necessary.

In Table 7.3, the drops in the stock portfolio's values are large. In actual practice, dynamic hedging works by continually monitoring the value of the portfolio. Small changes in the portfolio can trigger small adjustments in the futures position. For many portfolios, monitoring and updating can occur many times a month. This is the reason it is called dynamic hedging – the hedge is monitored and updated continuously, often with computerized trading programs. Table 7.3 does not show that continual monitoring. Instead, we might take the different rows in the table as snapshots of the portfolio's value at different times.

Table 7.3 abstracts from some of the cash flow issues that dynamic hedging will raise. For example, it does not explicitly consider the cash flows that come from daily settlement of the futures position. There are a host of technical issues such as these that actual dynamic hedging must face.

INDEX FUTURES AND STOCK MARKET VOLATILITY

The link between stock market volatility and stock index futures trading has become important in public policy debates. Some critics of index futures have already sought limitations of index trading on the principal grounds that index trading contributes to increased stock market volatility. As we will see, the evidence supporting this proposition is far from conclusive. However, even if it were proven that stock index futures trading did increase stock market volatility, is that bad? To most economists, price volatility results from the arrival of new information in the market. Traders receive new information that causes them to reassess the true value of the good being traded. In an efficient market, the price quickly adjusts to reflect this new information. One result of this process is volatility. Thus, economists often interpret volatile prices as evidence of a properly functioning and informationally efficient market. Under this view, volatility is good, not bad. Nonetheless, if stock index futures trading contributed to volatility in a way that was not tied to information or a properly functioning market, the futures trading could be deleterious to the market.

In this section we consider the links between stock index trading and stock market volatility. Even before the Crash of October 1987, critics of index futures trading claimed that the stock index futures market was responsible for an increase in the volatility of the stock market. In essence, the argument asserts that strategies such as program trading and portfolio insurance disrupt the stock market and cause stock prices to swing wildly as they are forced into alignment with stock index futures prices. We begin by considering the evidence on stock market volatility itself. While there may be a general perception of greater stock market volatility, the evidence on this issue is mixed. Next, we consider possible links between stock market volatility and stock index futures trading, particularly index arbitrage and portfolio insurance. Finally, we analyze the Crash of 1987 and the mini-crash of October 1989 to consider the impact of stock index futures on the stock market itself.

HAS STOCK MARKET VOLATILITY INCREASED?

Here we consider whether there has been an increase in stock market volatility. While this may seem to be a fairly straightforward question, the evidence is mixed. These diverse conclusions stem in part from differences in the time periods examined. For instance, some studies compare volatility across the decades, while others focus on changes in volatility within the 1980s. Also, some studies consider volatility from month to month, others focus on day to day volatility, while still other articles examine volatility within a single day and ask whether this intraday volatility is increasing.

Stock Volatility: The Long View. Several studies have examined stock market volatility for periods of many decades, some even going into the last century. For the most part, these studies focus on monthly stock portfolio returns. The general conclusion is clear: There has been no tendency for stock market volatility to increase from decade to decade. The 1930s had the highest volatility in this century, but there is weak evidence that the 1980s was the most volatile decade since World War II. Figure 7.5 depicts this long-run pattern of volatility.

Stock Volatility in the 1980s. Even if the 1980s were not more volatile than other decades, it is still possible that volatility increased within the decade. With the 1980s, we consider conclusions using daily data and intraday data. Within the 1980s, October-December 1987 show high volatility. (The Crash occurred on October 19, 1987.) However, there appears to be no general tendency for volatility to have increased over the 1980s.

Becketti and Sellon suggest that we distinguish normal volatility and jump volatility. The ordinary variability of stock returns, perhaps

■ Figure 7.5

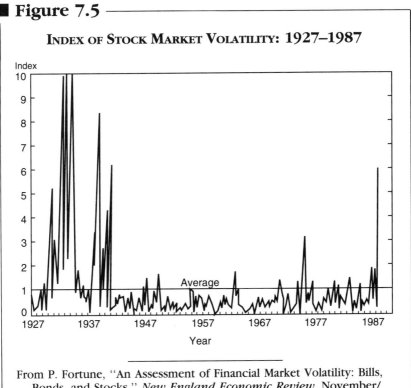

INDEX OF STOCK MARKET VOLATILITY: 1927–1987

From P. Fortune, "An Assessment of Financial Market Volatility: Bills, Bonds, and Stocks," *New England Economic Review,* November/ December 1989, p. 16. Reprinted by permission of Federal Reserve Bank of Boston.

measured best by the standard deviation, is **normal volatility**. By contrast, **jump volatility** is the occasional extreme jump in prices. Figure 7.6 shows the frequency of large jumps in stock returns from 1962–1988.[7] Sellon and Becketti conclude that 1986–1988 exhibit high jump volatility, but they are quick to point out that this evidence does not suggest a permanent shift to a market with higher jump volatility. More data are needed to answer that question. Further, even in terms of jump volatility, the 1980s were not high compared to other decades before the 1960s. For example, only four of the 34 largest daily drops in 105 years occurred in the 1980s.[8] This is approximately the number of observations one would expect to find by chance.

Schwert also considered intraday data in his analysis of stock market volatility. He examined returns over 15-minute intervals for February

■ Figure 7.6 ───────────────

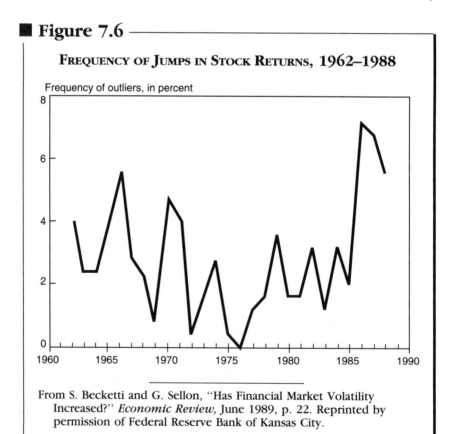

FREQUENCY OF JUMPS IN STOCK RETURNS, 1962–1988

From S. Becketti and G. Sellon, "Has Financial Market Volatility Increased?" *Economic Review*, June 1989, p. 22. Reprinted by permission of Federal Reserve Bank of Kansas City.

1, 1983 through October 19, 1989. He found that October 19–31, 1987, and October 13, 1989, stood out. (Friday, October 13, 1989, was the date of the "mini-crash.") However, volatility quickly returned to normal levels after these episodes of high volatility. From this review of a century of stock prices, we can conclude that there has been no increase in long-term volatility. Jump volatility seems to have been high in 1986–1988 compared to the 1960–1988 period. However, jump volatility for the 1980s appears to be about normal compared to the rest of the century.

DO STOCK INDEX FUTURES CAUSE MARKET VOLATILITY?

There are two main practices in stock index futures trading that are alleged to cause stock market volatility. These are index arbitrage (particularly program trading) and portfolio insurance. Both practices contribute to volatility, critics say, because they quickly dump large orders on the market at critical times. These large orders can reinforce existing trends in prices, thereby contributing to stock market volatility. We consider each in turn.

Index Arbitrage and Stock Market Volatility. In index arbitrage, traders search for discrepancies between stock prices and futures prices. When the two prices differ from the cost-of-carry model enough to cover transaction costs, index arbitrageurs sell the overpriced side of the pair and buy the underpriced. Typically, the arbitrageur holds the combined stock/futures position until expiration. At expiration, the cash settlement procedures for index futures guarantee that the stock and futures prices will converge. This convergence is guaranteed to hold at the open of trading on the expiration day, because the last futures settlement price is set equal to the opening cash market index value on that day. Some stock index futures also use the closing price as the final settlement price. In that case, to take advantage of convergence, index arbitrageurs often unwind their positions by entering market-on-close orders for the last trading day of the futures. A market-on-close order sells or buys a stock at the market price prevailing at the close of trading.

Consider now an index arbitrageur who is long stock and short futures. We assume that the futures settles based on the closing price and that the trader enters a market-on-close order to sell the stocks. Assume also that other arbitrageurs are also long stock and short futures and seek to unwind their positions in a similar manner. All of these stocks will come to market at the same time, so there could be an extremely large number of stocks to be sold all at once at the close of trading. Critics fear that this practice can lead to dramatic volatility in the market in a way that disrupts trading. Particularly, they fear that such high jump volatility might scare away some investors.

Notice that this effect occurs only if there is a substantial order imbalance among index arbitrageurs. There may be a very high level of index arbitrage with no serious order imbalance. Assume for a moment that, over the life of the futures, the stock and futures prices vary in being high or low relative to the cost-of-carry model. Some traders will initiate their index arbitrage transactions by buying stocks, while others will arbitrage by selling stocks. At the expiration of the futures, the unwinding could result in roughly equal numbers of buy and sell orders for stocks. In such a situation, we would not expect index arbitrage to have any effect on prices, and it could not contribute to volatility.

Portfolio Insurance and Stock Market Volatility. Portfolio insurance can also contribute to potential order imbalances that might affect stock prices. From our example of a portfolio insurance trade in Table 7.3, we see that a drop in stock prices requires the portfolio insurer to sell additional stock index futures. Similarly, when prices rise, the insurer buys stock index futures. A potential problem for market volatility arises because portfolio insurance generates trading in the same direction that the market happens to be moving. Thus, portfolio insurance can contribute to the existing momentum of the market.

To see the potential effects of portfolio insurance in exacerbating an existing trend, assume that the stock and futures prices are tightly linked by the cost-of-carry model. Due to this linkage, a drop in stock prices will quickly stimulate a drop in futures. The same transmission will occur from a drop in futures to a drop in stock prices. Now assume that there is a large drop in stock prices.

In response to the drop in stock prices, the futures price will have to fall. The cost-of-carry model requires this adjustment. However, the drop in stock prices also stimulates a large number of orders from portfolio insurers to sell index futures. This is clear from our example in Table 7.3. Critics fear that the sell orders from portfolio insurers might temporarily depress the futures price below the price justified by the cost-of-carry model. Assuming this happens, stock prices must again fall to match the depressed futures price. Now, with this next drop in stock prices, the portfolio insurers must again sell futures. Critics of portfolio insurance fear that this selling – price fall – selling scenario could create a spiral of falling prices and more sell orders, putting the entire market into a tailspin that could be disastrous.

Summary. According to critics, unrestricted stock index futures trading can contribute to stock market volatility, or even panics, by creating order imbalances that force stock prices below the prices justified by economic fundamentals. For index arbitrage, the feared order imbalance is most likely to occur at the expiration of the futures. Critics fear that portfolio insurers will respond to a sudden drop in stock prices by dumping sell orders onto the stock index futures market, thereby depressing prices. These depressed prices will feed into the stock market causing another drop in prices. The portfolio insurer will again sell stock index futures, and perhaps help create a downward price spiral. (On the other hand, if prices fall too much, the stocks will be cheap, and value-oriented investors will be attracted to buy. This buying would help restore prices to their rational levels.)

VOLATILITY AND STOCK INDEX FUTURES BEFORE THE CRASH

Long before the Crash of October 1987 and the mini-crash of October 1989, critics charged that stock index futures increased volatility. Here we consider the empirical evidence on this issue that is not related to the Crash or mini-crash. The Crash and crashlet we discuss later. We begin by considering the pre- and post-futures trading periods in general. Later, we consider the expiration days for the futures.

Volatility and the Introduction of Stock Index Futures. To determine whether stock index futures increase stock market volatility, some studies have compared the volatility of the stock market before and after the introduction of stock index futures in 1982. Santoni computed the means and standard deviations of percentage changes in the S&P 500 index before and after the introduction of S&P 500 futures in April 1982. Table 7.4 presents his key results. Focusing on the standard deviations, we see that weekly and daily standard deviations changed little. The weekly standard deviations rose slightly, while the daily standard deviations fell just a little. Neither difference is statistically significant. Santoni also considered intraday variability and concluded that it fell slightly, but statistically significantly, after the introduction of the S&P 500 futures. Other studies have examined the issue using a similar approach. Most of these

■ **Table 7.4**

S&P 500 Index Statistics: Before and After Futures Trading

	Before April 1982		After April 1982	
	Mean	**Std. Dev.**	**Mean**	**Std. Dev.**
Weekly	0.13	1.68	0.306	1.74
Daily	0.004	0.95	0.069	0.88

From G. Santoni, "Has Programmed Trading Made Stock Prices More Volatile?" *Review*, May 1987, pp. 18-29. Reprinted by permission of Federal Reserve Bank of St. Louis.

studies find no increase in overall volatility after the introduction of futures trading. However, some do find increases in volatility for intraday data.

While comparing pre- and post-index futures trading may shed some light on the volatility effect of futures trading, the technique has some dangers. For example, if volatility increases, might there be some other factor that explains the increase, such as inflation or deficits? Also, even if volatility does not change, it is still possible that stock index futures stimulated volatility and some other factors offset the increase in volatility caused by futures.

Stock Volatility on Expiration Days. Even if index futures trading cannot be charged with a general increase in stock market volatility, it might still be associated with episodic increases in volatility – the jump volatility that Santoni considered. In particular, the unwinding of index arbitrage programs at the futures expiration might cause an order imbalance that could increase volatility. Accordingly, this section focuses on stock index futures and expiration day volatility.

In 1985-86, stock index futures, options on the stock index, and options on the stock index futures had common expiration dates four times per year and generally settled based on closing prices. (Now some instruments settle based on opening prices.) The convergence of these three expirations gave them the name of the **triple witching hour** – witching because of the fear of high volatility. For these expiration days, most studies find higher volatility than on other days. For the most part, the higher volatility is concentrated in the last hour of trading. (Recall that this study covered a period when the final settlement price was determined at the close of trading. Now there is a trend for the opening price to be used as the final settlement price for the futures.)

Table 7.5 summarizes some key results from the Stoll and Whaley (1986) study of expiration day volatility. The table shows the mean and standard deviation of returns computed from minute by minute price data. As the table shows, the standard deviation was higher when the futures expired than when nothing expired. However, when the Chicago Board Options Exchange (CBOE) S&P 100 option expired, but the futures did not, the volatility was not significantly higher than on days when nothing expired. Also, stock prices tend to fall on expiration days. If we compare the behavior of the S&P 500 index on expiration days with its behavior on nonexpiration days, the price effect and the volatility effect are both statistically significant.

Figure 7.7, also drawn from the Stoll and Whaley study, illustrates the dramatic price movements that can occur as the futures expires. Figure 7.7 traces the minute by minute level of the S&P 500 index for the last 30 minutes of trading on December 20, 1985, and for the first 30 minutes on the next trading day. This figure gives a visual impression of the kinds of swings the index can take in a very short period of trading time. Stoll and Whaley found also that stock prices tend to rise in the first 30 minutes of trading on the first trading day after expiration. In summary, higher volatility does appear to be associated with futures expirations, particularly in the final hour of trading when many index arbitrage positions are being closed.

■ **Table 7.5**

EXPIRATION DAY STOCK PRICE VOLATILITY
(FINAL HOUR OF TRADING)

S&P 500	Expiring Instrument		
	Futures	CBOE S&P Options	Nothing
Mean	−0.352	0.026	0.061
Std. Dev.	0.641	0.261	0.211
Observ.	10	16	97

From H. Stoll and R. Whaley, "Expiration Day Effects of Index Options and Futures," New York University: Monograph Series in Finance and Economics, 1986. Reprinted by permission of New York University.

■ **Figure 7.7**

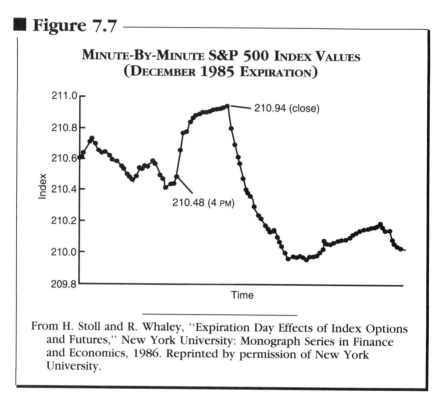

MINUTE-BY-MINUTE S&P 500 INDEX VALUES
(DECEMBER 1985 EXPIRATION)

From H. Stoll and R. Whaley, "Expiration Day Effects of Index Options and Futures," New York University: Monograph Series in Finance and Economics, 1986. Reprinted by permission of New York University.

INDEX FUTURES AND STOCK MARKET CRASHES

Even if futures expirations cause higher volatility for an hour once per quarter, the effect cannot be very serious. However, if futures are somehow responsible for market crashes, the matter has a completely different and more ominous character. In October 1987, the Crash led some to believe that the entire financial system was threatened. The events of October 19, 1987, touched off a series of debates and policy discussions that still continues. This section analyzes the relationship between stock index futures and stock prices during October 1987. Later we consider the mini-crash of October 13, 1989.

The Crash of October 19, 1987, is as controversial as it is dramatic. The Dow Jones Industrial Average lost 22.61 percent of its value that day. Trading volume was so heavy that it brought the trade processing divisions of brokerage houses to a virtual halt. During the day, it was often impossible to trade or even obtain accurate price quotations. In many respects, there was no stock market on that Black Monday. No sooner did trading cease than finger pointing started. Some fingers pointed at the trade deficit, while others pointed at the budget deficit. Still others pointed to the futures market as the cause of the crash. Here are a few choice quotations. Anis C. Wallace: "Investors knew that stocks were overpriced by any traditional valuation measure such as price/earnings ratios and price to book value. They also knew that the combination of program trading and portfolio insurance could send prices plummeting." David E. Sanger: "On Monday, October 19, Wall Street's legendary herd instinct, now embedded in digital code and amplified by hundreds of computers, helped turn a sell-off into a panic." Donald Regan: "In my mind, we should start by banning index option arbitrage and then proceed with other reforms which will restore public confidence in the financial markets." Marshall Front: "Futures and options are like barnacles on a ship. They take their life from the pricing of stocks and bonds. When the barnacles start steering the ship, you get into trouble, as we saw last week."[9]

In the aftermath of the crash, the government formed a presidential task force under Nicholas Brady, who later became Secretary of the Treasury, to study the crash and its causes. The report of the task force is widely known as the Brady Report. While most observers agree that the inability of cash markets to handle the incredible order flow contributed to the market turmoil, the Brady Report attributed the fall in prices to index arbitrage and portfolio insurance. This view of the Crash has become known as the **cascade theory**. According to the Brady Report, portfolio insurers sought to liquidate their equity exposure by selling stock index futures. This selling action drove futures prices below their equilibrium price. In terms of the cost-of-carry model, the selling by portfolio insurers created a reverse cash-and-carry arbitrage. Seeing a profit opportunity, index arbitrageurs implemented reverse cash-and-carry strategies by buying futures and selling stocks. This action depressed prices further, and with new lower equity prices, portfolio insurers dumped more stock index futures, depressing prices still further. The vicious cycle was started. The repeated action of index arbitrageurs and portfolio insurers caused a downward "cascade" in prices. Thus, the Brady Report maintained that "mechanical, price-insensitive selling" by institutions was a key cause of the crash.[10]

THE STOCK/FUTURES BASIS ON OCTOBER 19

The cascade theory, and thus the conclusions of the Brady Report, rest on the view that the stock/futures basis on October 19 was disrupted by the actions of "mechanical, price-insensitive" trading systems. Specifically, the Brady Report alleges that futures prices that day were too low relative to stock values. Therefore, the stock/futures basis became a critical empirical issue. The price relationships between stocks and stock index futures have been studied on a minute-to-minute basis for both the S&P 500 and the MMI.[11] Both markets reveal a similar story. At first glance, the usually tight relationship of the cost-of-carry model apparently failed completely. However, in large part, this appearance was due to the inability to trade or even to know the current value of individual shares. For instance, even though the market opened at 9:30 New York time, some stocks did not trade for more than an hour. Among the MMI stocks, Exxon was the last one to start trading at 11:23 A.M. With stocks failing to trade in New York, traders were forced to use Friday prices as guides to Monday values. Such an estimate was, to say the least, imprecise.

Figure 7.8 shows the spread between the cash and futures using Chicago time. The extremely large difference at the open was due largely to the late opening of the individual stocks in New York. Until the stocks began to trade, there was no cash market for the traders in Chicago to use as a guide to proper values for the futures. However, it appears that the futures and stock did track each other with some accuracy during the middle of the day when prices were somewhat more available. The situation in the S&P 500 was similar. Lawrence Harris summarizes: "Nonsynchronous trading explains part of the large absolute futures-cash basis observed during the crash. The remainder may be due to disintegration of the two markets."[12] Thus, even in the madness, the cost-of-carry model was functioning with the available information. There was simply very little information flow. However, the stock/futures basis did seem to respond to the information that was available.

ORDER IMBALANCE, INDEX ARBITRAGE, AND PORTFOLIO INSURANCE ON OCTOBER 19

Even if the basis held to the cost-of-carry model as well as one could expect given the dramatic events on October 19, there is still a residual concern about the role of index arbitrage and portfolio insurance. That day, 16 firms accounted for almost all stock index arbitrage and portfolio insurance trading. Twelve firms concentrated on index arbitrage, while four focused on portfolio insurance. About 9 percent

■ Figure 7.8

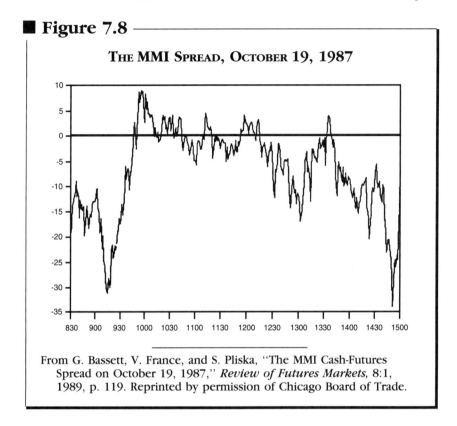

THE MMI SPREAD, OCTOBER 19, 1987

From G. Bassett, V. France, and S. Pliska, "The MMI Cash-Futures Spread on October 19, 1987," *Review of Futures Markets,* 8:1, 1989, p. 119. Reprinted by permission of Chicago Board of Trade.

of NYSE volume was generated by index arbitrage trading. For stock index futures, 12 to 24 percent of selling originated through portfolio insurance activity.[13] As a percentage of activity, these numbers suggest the possibility that futures related activity was large enough to significantly affect the day's trading.

One interesting piece of evidence comes from comparing S&P 500 stocks with non-S&P 500 stocks. Blume, MacKinlay, and Terker found that S&P stocks fell about seven percentage points farther than non-S&P 500 stocks on October 19. By mid-morning during the recovery on October 20, the difference had been almost eliminated. In other words, stocks in the S&P 500 fell more during the crash, but bounced back to parity with other stocks very quickly.[14] Also, Blume, MacKinlay, and Terker found that the fall in S&P 500 stock prices was positively correlated with order imbalances on October 19. With heavy sell orders awaiting execution, stock prices fell more than at other times.

If this order imbalance was related to futures trading, then the futures market could share some responsibility for the drop in the market.

Some evidence appears to show that futures trading is not necessary to start a panic in a given market, but this theory does not really absolve futures of all responsibility. The Crash was a worldwide phenomenon, as Richard Roll points out.[15] Of 23 markets worldwide, 19 fell by more than 20 percent. Further, the Crash seems to have begun in non-Japanese Asian markets, spread to European markets, then North American, then Japanese. This progression took place around the clock as trading developed on October 19 and 20. Comparing market performance and the presence of computer-directed trading in isolation, Roll found that, if computer trading had any impact at all, it actually helped reduce the market decline.

The fact that the Crash started in markets with limited futures trading does appear to show that other factors were at work besides futures trading. This opens the possibility of a **contagion theory** of the Crash. A crash develops in one country's market for some unknown reason. News arrives in other markets carrying the disease of the crash, which helps a crash develop in the second market. This kind of contagion theory was developed by King and Wadhwani.[16]

Assume that the U.S. market is infected and a crash starts to develop. The U.S. crash is then intensified by order imbalance resulting from futures trading. Now other countries could catch the crash disease from the U.S. in its more heightened and virulent form. Yet this does not seem to fit the facts for October 1987. First, the U.S. lost less than most other markets, both those that had crashed before and those that crashed later. Based on the version of the contagion theory just explained, we would expect the U.S. Crash to be deeper than that of countries that crashed earlier.

Summarizing the portion of evidence related to futures, the Crash did not start in the U.S., so the futures markets could not have been the original source of the problem. The Crash in the U.S. was not relatively more severe, even though futures markets are more developed in the U.S. than elsewhere. There was no tendency for the crashes in markets trading after the U.S. Crash to be more severe than crashes in markets trading before the U.S. Nonetheless, if futures contributed to the U.S. Crash and if the contagion theory has merit, then the U.S. Crash could have contributed to crashes that occurred later.

Thus, residual suspicion about the role of futures remains, even though there is no compelling evidence to show that futures trading, whether index arbitrage or portfolio insurance, caused the Crash.[17] Study continues and the issue remains controversial. However, there does seem to be fairly widespread rejection of the Brady Report's main conclusion that the Crash was caused by index arbitrage and portfolio insurance leading to a cascade in stock prices.[18]

POLICY RECOMMENDATIONS AND CHANGING TRADING RULES

In proposals for reform, the Brady Report recommended that the regulatory system be modified to have a single agency, that there be a unified clearing system for all financial markets, that margins be consistent between cash and futures markets, and that information systems across markets be improved. The Report also recommended that exchanges implement **circuit breakers** - systems of planned trading halts - in times of volatility. There is continuing action on all of these fronts and much has already been implemented.

Since the Crash, circuit breakers have been put in place and refinements to the system continue. In essence, a circuit breaker is a planned decoupling of the stock index futures market and the stock market through price limits and trading halts. The system also permits delaying program trades. The idea is to halt trading when prices fall below their fundamental values. During the pause in trading, the effect of mob psychology will dissipate, and when trading resumes, prices will return to rational levels. These circuit breakers are controversial and their value is unknown.

However, even if trading is halted, prices can continue to fall and traders will be stuck with additional losses. According to market lore, the worst fear of many traders is to be stuck in a position. Some scholars believe that trading halts may create more panic than calm and consequently assert that trading halts are unwise. Nonetheless, futures markets already embody something like circuit breakers in the form of daily price limits. Also, defenders of circuit breakers believed they performed well in the mini-crash of October 13, 1989.

Probably the most controversial recommendation of the Brady Report is that there be "consistent margins" between stock and futures markets. This has been interpreted as calling for a large increase in futures margins. Such a policy would destroy the futures market as it now exists. According to defenders of futures, this policy recommendation shows a complete lack of understanding of futures margins.[19] Futures margins are not a partial payment for a good as they are in the stock market. Instead, futures margins serve as a security bond for the changes in the futures price that day. The bond is payable daily and renewable daily. In the ensuing debate, margin levels have become a political football in the struggle between the CFTC and the SEC. Also, stock index margins have been raised by the futures exchanges in an apparent effort to deter any move for even higher margins. In defense of the futures margining system, it is important to realize that no customer funds were lost due to failure to meet margin calls and no clearinghouse failed because of the Crash.

THE MINI-CRASH OF OCTOBER 13, 1989

Almost exactly two years after the Crash, it seemed that history would repeat itself. On October 13, 1989, a Friday the thirteenth, stock prices began a sickening slide. That day, the Dow dropped 190 points, with a 135 point drop in the final hour of trading. This mini-crash provided an opportunity to test some of the procedures instituted after the Crash.

Falling prices triggered a circuit breaker at 2:15 P.M. for the MMI futures and at 3:07 P.M. for the S&P 500 futures. For both contracts, trading could resume only at prices above the price that triggered the circuit breaker. Trading resumed and the circuit breaker was hit again for the S&P 500. In assessing the performance of the circuit breakers, both the CFTC and the exchanges seem to feel that they performed well.[20] Further efforts to refine the system continue and the market awaits further, perhaps more severe, tests of the system.

CONCLUSION

This chapter reviewed a wide range of issues related to stock index futures. We began by examining stock index futures pricing. We considered the efficiency of the stock index futures markets, the effect of taxes on stock index futures prices, the influence of seasonal factors on prices, and leads and lags between the futures market and the stock market. Next, we considered a real-world example of program trading, focusing on an index arbitrage example. This example showed the hidden risks in the apparently riskless strategy of index arbitrage. We also reviewed the level of program trading in recent years.

To extend the introduction to hedging in Chapter 6, we worked through an example of minimum risk hedging in detail, and we considered the difference between ex-ante and ex-post hedge ratios. We also saw how to use a hedging approach to adjust the beta of a portfolio. Adjusting the beta by a small amount may be a hedging activity, but we also explored asset allocation using stock index futures. Using stock index futures, traders holding riskless bonds can simulate full investment in equities. Similarly, a trader fully invested in equities can use stock index futures to make the combined stock/futures portfolio behave like a riskless bond.

This chapter also focused on the connection between stock index futures and stock market volatility. As we saw, the main arguments for a connection rely on order imbalances that might be caused by index arbitrage or portfolio insurance. We saw some evidence of these order imbalances and increased volatilities on expiration days. Finally, we considered the Crash of 1987 and the mini-crash of 1989. Although futures do not appear to be responsible for the price changes observed on these days, the events have been important in changing the institutional arrangements in the futures market.

NOTES

1. D. Modest and M. Sundaresan, "The Relationship Between Spot and Futures Prices in Stock Index Futures Markets: Some Preliminary Evidence," *Journal of Futures Markets*, 3:1, Spring 1983, pp. 15–41.

2. B. Cornell and K. French, "Taxes and the Pricing of Stock Index Futures," *Journal of Finance*, 38:3, June 1983, pp. 675–94; and B. Cornell, "Taxes and the Pricing of Stock Index Futures: Empirical Results," *Journal of Futures Markets*, 5:1, 1985, pp. 89–101.

3. See, for example, E. Dyl and E. Maberly, "The Weekly Pattern in Stock Index Futures: A Further Note," *Journal of Finance*, 41:5, December 1986, pp. 1149–52.

4. For a more extended survey of these studies, see R. Kolb, *Understanding Futures Markets*, 5e, Cambridge, MA: Blackwell Publishers, 1997.

5. This example was the focus of a *Business Week* article, "A Real Life Strategy for Making 14% Risk-Free," April 7, 1986.

6. Strictly speaking, there is no return on a futures contract because a position in a futures contract requires no investment. By the futures return we mean the percentage change in the futures price.

7. The definition used for large jumps is somewhat complex, but essentially a large jump is a daily return that is substantially larger than the typical change in prices.

8. C. Jones and J. Wilson, "Is Stock Price Volatility Increasing?" *Financial Analysts Journal*, 45:6, November-December 1989, pp. 20–26.

9. All quoted in G. Santoni, "The October Crash: Some Evidence on the Cascade Theory," *Review*, Federal Reserve Bank of St. Louis, May/June 1988, pp. 18–33.

10. *Report of the Presidential Task Force on Market Mechanisms*, 1988, p. v. See also G. Santoni, "The October Crash: Some Evidence on the Cascade Theory," *Review*, Federal Reserve Bank of St. Louis, May/June 1988, pp. 18–33 for a thoughtful critique of the Brady Report. P. Tosini, "Stock Index Futures and Stock Market Activity in October 1987," *Financial Analysts Journal*, 44:1, January/February 1988, pp. 28–37 also discusses the cascade theory.

11. See L. Harris, "The October 1987 S&P 500 Stock-Futures Basis," *Journal of Finance*, 44:1, March 1989, pp. 77–99; G. Bassett, V. France, and S. Pliska, "The MMI Cash-Futures Spread on October 19, 1987," *Review of Futures Markets*, 8:1, 1989, pp. 118–38; G. Wang, E. Moriarty, R. Michalski, and J. Jordan, "Empirical Analysis of the Liquidity of the S&P 500 Index Futures Market During the October 1987 Market Break," Commodity Futures Trading Commission Staff Working Paper #88-6, February 1989; G. Santoni, "The October Crash: Some Evidence on the Cascade Theory," *Review*, Federal Reserve Bank of St. Louis, May/June 1988, pp. 18–33.

12. L. Harris, "The October 1987 S&P 500 Stock-Futures Basis," *Journal of Finance*, 44:1, March 1989, p. 77. This view is supported by A. Kleidon and R. Whaley, "One Market? Stocks, Futures, and Options During October 1987," *Journal of Finance*, 47:3, July 1992, pp. 851–77. Kleidon and Whaley find that the market conformed well to cost-of-carry relationships in early October, but very poorly during the crash.

13. These values are drawn from P. Tosini, "Stock Index Futures and Stock Market Activity in October 1987," *Financial Analysts Journal,* 44:1, January-February 1988, pp. 28-37.

14. M. Blume, A. MacKinlay, and B. Terker, "Order Imbalances and Stock Price Movements on October 19 and 20, 1987," *Journal of Finance,* 44:4, September 1989, pp. 827-48.

15. R. Roll, "The International Crash of October 1987," *Financial Analysts Journal,* 44:5, September-October 1988, pp. 19-35.

16. M. King and S. Wadhwani, "Transmission of Volatility Between Stock Markets," *Review of Financial Studies,* 3:1, 1990, pp. 5-33.

17. The Office of Technology Assessment, U.S. Congress, studied the Crash and reported on it in its study, "Electron Bulls & Bears: U.S. Securities Markets & Information Technology," September 1990. The study concluded that the responsibility of futures for the Crash could not be resolved by statistical analysis.

18. Among those who reject the Brady Report conclusions of a futures-induced cascade are: G. Santoni, "The October Crash: Some Evidence on the Cascade Theory," *Review,* Federal Reserve Bank of St. Louis, May/June 1988, pp. 18-33; J. Hill, "Program Trading, Portfolio Insurance, and the Stock Market Crash: Concepts, Applications and an Assessment," Kidder Peabody, January 1988; R. Roll, "The International Crash of October 1987," *Financial Analysts Journal,* 44:5, September-October 1988, pp. 19-35; D. Harrington, F. Fabozzi, and H. Fogler, *The New Stock Market,* Chicago: Probus Publishing Co., 1990; M. Miller, B. Malkiel, M. Scholes, and J. Hawke, "Stock Index Futures and the Crash of '87," *Journal of Applied Corporate Finance,* 1:4, Winter 1989, pp. 6-17.

19. See, for example, M. Miller, B. Malkiel, M. Scholes, and J. Hawke, "Stock Index Futures and the Crash of '87," *Journal of Applied Corporate Finance,* 1:4, Winter 1989, pp. 6-17.

20. See "CFTC Reviews Friday the 13th," *Futures Industry Association Review,* November/December 1989, pp. 10-11.

■ Chapter 8

Foreign Exchange ■
Futures

OVERVIEW

Foreign currencies are traded in both a highly active forward market and a futures market. The foreign exchange market is the only one in which a successful futures market has grown up in the face of a robust forward market. The forward market for foreign exchange has existed for a long time, but the foreign exchange futures market developed only in the early 1970s, with trading beginning on May 16, 1972, on the International Monetary Market (IMM) of the Chicago Mercantile Exchange (CME). Without doubt, the presence of such a strong and successful forward market retarded the development of a futures market for foreign exchange. This dual market system means that the futures market cannot be understood in isolation from the forward market. The conceptual bond arises both from the similarity of the two markets and from the fact that the forward market continues to be much larger than the futures market. Because many traders are active in both markets, familiar cash-and-carry and reverse cash-and-carry strategies ensure that the proper price relationships between the two markets are maintained.

As discussed in Chapter 2, forward and futures markets for a given commodity are similar in many respects. Because of this similarity, specific price relationships must hold between the two markets to

319

prevent arbitrage opportunities. While any observer might be more impressed by the similarities in the two markets, the forward and futures markets differ in several key respects. Particularly important are the differences in the cash flow patterns (due to daily resettlement in the futures market) and the different structures of the contracts with respect to their maturities.

To understand foreign exchange futures trading, this chapter begins with a brief discussion of the markets for foreign exchange: the spot, forward, and futures markets. Against this institutional background, we analyze no-arbitrage pricing relationships, such as the Interest Rate Parity Theorem (IRP) and the Purchasing Power Parity Theorem (PPP). These theorems essentially express the pricing relationship of the cost-of-carry model. We also examine the accuracy of foreign exchange forecasting. As always in the futures market, the twin issues of specula-tion and hedging play an important role, and we consider them in detail.

PRICE QUOTATIONS

In the foreign exchange market, every price, or exchange rate, is a relative price. To say that one dollar is worth 2.5 Deutsche marks (DM 2.5) also implies that DM 2.5 will buy $1.00, or that DM 1 is worth $.40. All foreign exchange rates are related to each other as reciprocals, a relationship that is quite apparent in Figure 8.1, which shows the foreign exchange quotations as they appear daily in *The Wall Street Journal*. The quotations consist of two double columns of rates, one for the U.S. Dollar Equivalent of the foreign currency and one set of two columns for the amount of foreign currency per U.S. dollar. Each set of quotations shows the rates for the current and the preceding business day. We focus only on the two columns of current quotations. The rate in one column has its reciprocal in the other column. (Sometimes these are not exact due to transaction costs.) The value of $/DM($ per DM) is just the reciprocal of the value of DM/$(DM per $). For some countries, such as Australia, the quotations show only the spot rate, the rate at which Australian and U.S. dollars may be exchanged at the moment.

For many major currencies, such as those of Germany, England, Japan, and Canada, the quotations show forward rates for periods of 30, 90, and 180 days into the future. The 30-day forward rate, for example, indicates the rate at which a trader can contract today for

■ Figure 8.1

FOREIGN EXCHANGE QUOTATIONS

CURRENCY TRADING

EXCHANGE RATES

Tuesday, April 23, 1996

The New York foreign exchange selling rates below apply to trading among banks in amounts of $1 million and more, as quoted at 3 p.m. Eastern time by Dow Jones Telerate Inc. and other sources. Retail transactions provide fewer units of foreign currency per dollar.

Country	U.S. $ equiv. Tue	U.S. $ equiv. Mon	Currency per U.S. $ Tue	Currency per U.S. $ Mon
Argentina (Peso)	1.0012	1.0012	.9988	.9988
Australia (Dollar)	.7900	.7868	1.2658	1.2710
Austria (Schilling)	.09371	.09374	10.671	10.668
Bahrain (Dinar)	2.6525	2.6525	.3770	.3770
Belgium (Franc)	.03204	.03210	31.210	31.150
Brazil (Real)	1.0152	1.0152	.9850	.9850
Britain (Pound)	1.5170	1.5123	.6592	.6612
30-Day Forward	1.5162	1.5116	.6595	.6616
90-Day Forward	1.5150	1.5103	.6601	.6621
180-Day Forward	1.5131	1.5085	.6609	.6629
Canada (Dollar)	.7339	.7338	1.3625	1.3628
30-Day Forward	.7343	.7342	1.3618	1.3621
90-Day Forward	.7350	.7349	1.3606	1.3608
180-Day Forward	.7524	.7528	1.3290	1.3283
Chile (Peso)	.002455	.002453	407.25	407.65
China (Renminbi)	.1198	.1198	8.3502	8.3500
Colombia (Peso)	.0009671	.0009671	1034.00	1034.00
Czech. Rep. (Koruna)	...	...	...	...
Commercial rate	.03610	.03610	27.697	27.702
Denmark (Krone)	.1708	.1710	5.8536	5.8469
Ecuador (Sucre)	...	...	...	...
Floating rate	.0003277	.0003282	3052.00	3047.00
Finland (Markka)	.2081	.2095	4.8059	4.7740
France (Franc)	.1946	.1948	5.1380	5.1335
30-Day Forward	.1949	.1950	5.1306	5.1269
90-Day Forward	.1954	.1956	5.1168	5.1127
180-Day Forward	.1962	.1964	5.0961	5.0923
Germany (Mark)	.6572	.6592	1.5215	1.5170
30-Day Forward	.6585	.6604	1.5187	1.5143
90-Day Forward	.6608	.6627	1.5134	1.5089
180-Day Forward	.6648	.6666	1.5043	1.5001
Greece (Drachma)	.004134	.004134	241.91	241.91
Hong Kong (Dollar)	.1293	.1293	7.7362	7.7356
Hungary (Forint)	.006685	.006686	149.59	149.57
India (Rupee)	.02923	.02921	34.215	34.230
Indonesia (Rupiah)	.0004298	.0004297	2326.50	2327.00
Ireland (Punt)	1.5657	1.5613	.6387	.6405
Israel (Shekel)	.3153	.3147	3.1720	3.1775
Italy (Lira)	.0006436	.0006436	1553.75	1553.70
Japan (Yen)	.009375	.009378	106.67	106.63
30-Day Forward	.009415	.009420	106.21	106.16
90-Day Forward	.009489	.009493	105.38	105.34
180-Day Forward	.009604	.009605	104.13	104.12
Jordan (Dinar)	1.4124	1.4124	.7080	.7080
Kuwait (Dinar)	3.3333	3.3322	.3000	.3001
Lebanon (Pound)	.0006327	.0006327	1580.50	1580.50
Malaysia (Ringgit)	.4003	.4014	2.4980	2.4915
Malta (Lira)	2.7435	2.7435	.3645	.3645
Mexico (Peso)	...	...	...	...
Floating rate	.1350	.1353	7.4100	7.3900
Netherlands (Guilder)	.5874	.5894	1.7023	1.6967
New Zealand (Dollar)	.6838	.6870	1.4624	1.4556
Norway (Krone)	.1532	.1534	6.5257	6.5210
Pakistan (Rupee)	.02915	.02915	34.310	34.310
Peru (new Sol)	.4241	.4241	2.3582	2.3582
Philippines (Peso)	.03820	.03818	26.180	26.190
Poland (Zloty)	.3790	.3793	2.6388	2.6365
Portugal (Escudo)	.006429	.006431	155.54	155.50
Russia (Ruble) (a)	.0002023	.0002032	4942.00	4922.00
Saudi Arabia (Riyal)	.2667	.2667	3.7501	3.7498
Singapore (Dollar)	.7097	.7098	1.4090	1.4088
Slovak Rep. (Koruna)	.03285	.03285	30.446	30.446
South Africa (Rand)	.2361	.2352	4.2350	4.2525
South Korea (Won)	.001284	.001284	779.05	778.75
Spain (Peseta)	.007919	.007938	126.28	125.98
Sweden (Krona)	.1489	.1491	6.7174	6.7078
Switzerland (Franc)	.8107	.8137	1.2335	1.2290
30-Day Forward	.8133	.8161	1.2296	1.2254
90-Day Forward	.8179	.8210	1.2226	1.2181
180-Day Forward	.8252	.8285	1.2118	1.2070
Taiwan (Dollar)	.03681	.03683	27.170	27.155
Thailand (Baht)	.03956	.03964	25.280	25.228
Turkey (Lira)	.00001351	.00001351	74001.50	74001.50
United Arab (Dirham)	.2757	.2723	3.6270	3.6725
Uruguay (New Peso)	...	...	...	...
Financial	.1314	.1314	7.6100	7.6100
Venezuela (Bolivar)b	.002058	.002024	486.00	494.00
Brady Rate	.002062	.002020	485.00	495.00
SDR	1.4468	1.4484	.6912	.6904
ECU	1.2381	1.2375	...	...

Special Drawing Rights (SDR) are based on exchange rates for the U.S., German, British, French and Japanese currencies. Source: International Monetary Fund.

European Currency Unit (ECU) is based on a basket of community currencies.

a-fixing, Moscow Interbank Currency Exchange. b-Changed to market rate effective Apr. 22.

the delivery of some foreign currency 30 days hence. If the trader buys the foreign currency, then he or she agrees to pay the 30-day forward rate in 30 days for the currency in question, with the actual transaction taking place in 30 days. This kind of transaction exactly fits the description of forward markets in Chapter 1.

The quotations shown in Figure 8.1 are provided by Bankers' Trust Company, a major participant in the foreign exchange market. The market from which these quotations are drawn is made up of large banks in the U.S. and abroad. This market is known as the **interbank market**. As Figure 8.1 notes, the quotations pertain to transactions in amounts of $1 million or more. As is typical of forward markets, there is no physical location where trading takes place. Instead, banks around the world are linked electronically with each other. The large banks in the market have trading rooms elaborately equipped with electronic communications devices. A trader in such a room may have access to 60 telephone lines and five or more video quotation screens.[1] The market has no regular trading hours and is open somewhere in the world 24 hours per day. In addition to banks, some large corporations have access to the market through their own trading rooms.

Regional banks are unlikely to have their own trading rooms. Instead, they clear their foreign exchange transactions through correspondent banks with whom they have the appropriate arrangements. Corporations that are too small to have their own trading room, as well as individuals, make foreign exchange transactions through their own banks. As Figure 8.1 notes, the rates quoted are not available to small retail traders. Instead, retail transactions will be subject to a larger bid-asked spread that allows the bank providing the foreign exchange service to make a profit.

Geographical and Cross-Rate Arbitrage

A number of pricing relationships exist in the foreign exchange market, the violation of which would imply the existence of arbitrage opportunities. The first two to be considered involve **geographical arbitrage** and **cross-rate arbitrage**. One of the best ways to learn about the relationships that must exist among currency prices is to explore the potential arbitrage opportunities that arise if the pricing relationships were violated.

Geographical arbitrage occurs when one currency sells for two prices in two different markets. Such pricing would be a simple violation of the law of one price. As an example, consider the following exchange rates between German marks and U.S. dollars as quoted in New York and Frankfurt. These are 90-day forward rates.

New York	$/DM	.42
Frankfurt	DM/$	2.35

The New York price, quoted as $ per DM, implies a DM/$ price equal to the inverse of the $/DM price:

$$\frac{1}{.42} = DM/\$ = 2.381$$

In New York, the DM/$ rate is 2.381, but in Frankfurt, it is 2.35. Since these are not equal, an arbitrage opportunity exists. To test for a geographical arbitrage opportunity, simply take the inverse of the price prevailing in one market and compare it with the price quoted in another market.

To conduct the arbitrage, the trader purchases the currency where it is cheap and sells it where it is expensive. In New York, a trader receives 2.381 DM per dollar, but only 2.35 DM per dollar in Frankfurt. Therefore, the DM is cheaper in New York. To exploit this pricing discrepancy, the trader transacts as shown in Table 8.1. These transactions represent the exploitation of an arbitrage opportunity since they ensure a profit with no investment. At the outset, there is no cash flow. The only cash flow involved in the transactions occurs simultaneously when the commitments initiated at $t = 0$ are com-

■ Table 8.1

GEOGRAPHICAL ARBITRAGE

This is an arbitrage transaction since it has a certain profit with no investment. Notice that the arbitrage is not complete until the transactions at $t = 90$ are completed.

$t = 0$ (the present)
  Buy DM 1 in New York 90 days forward for $.42
  Sell DM 1 in Frankfurt 90 days forward for $.4255.

$t = 90$
  Deliver DM 1 in Frankfurt; collect $.4255.
  Pay $.42; collect DM 1.

$$
\begin{array}{ll}
\text{Profit:} & \$.4255 \\
& -\ .4200 \\
\hline
& \$.0055
\end{array}
$$

pleted at $t = 90$. The profit, however, was certain from the time of the initial transactions.

Arbitrage is also possible to exploit misalignments in cross rates. To understand a cross rate, consider the following example. In New York, an exchange rate is quoted for the dollar versus the German mark. There is also a rate quoted for the dollar versus the British pound. Together, these two rates imply an equilibrium exchange rate between the German mark and the British pound. This implied exchange rate is a **cross rate**. Therefore, the exchange rates in New York involving the dollar imply an exchange rate between the mark and pound that do not involve the dollar. Figure 8.2 shows quotations for cross rates from *The Wall Street Journal.*

If the direct rate quoted elsewhere for the mark versus the pound does not match the cross rate in New York, an arbitrage opportunity exists. As an example, assume that the following rates are observed, where SF indicates the Swiss franc, and all of the rates are 90-day forward rates:

New York	$/DM	.42
	$/SF	.49
Frankfurt	DM/SF	1.2

■ Figure 8.2

CROSS RATES

Key Currency Cross Rates
Late New York Trading Apr 23, 1996

	Dollar	Pound	SFranc	Guilder	Peso	Yen	Lira	D-Mark	FFranc	CdnDlr
Canada	1.3625	2.0669	1.1046	.80039	.18387	.01277	.00088	.89550	.26518	....
France	5.1380	7.7943	4.1654	3.0183	.69339	.04817	.00331	3.3769	....	3.1110
Germany	1.5215	2.3081	1.2335	.89379	.20533	.01426	.00098	....	.29613	1.1167
Italy	1553.8	2357.0	1259.6	912.74	209.68	14.566	....	1021.2	302.4	1140.4
Japan	106.67	161.82	86.478	62.662	14.395	....	.06865	70.108	20.761	78.29
Mexico	7.4100	11.241	6.0073	4.3529	....	.06947	.00477	4.8702	1.4422	5.4385
Netherlands..	1.7023	2.5824	1.3801	....	.22973	.01596	.00110	1.1188	.33132	1.2494
Switzerland..	1.2335	1.8712	....	.72461	.16646	.01156	.00079	.81071	.24007	.90532
U.K.	.65920	....	.53441	.38724	.08896	.00618	.00042	.43325	.12830	.48381
U.S.	....	1.5170	.81070	.58744	.13495	.00937	.00064	.65725	.19463	.73394

Source: Dow Jones Telerate Inc.

From *The Wall Street Journal,* April 24, 1996, pp. C22, C16. © 1996 Dow Jones & Company, Inc. Reprinted by permission of The Wall Street Journal. All Rights Reserved Worldwide.

The exchange rates quoted in New York imply the following cross rate in New York for the DM/SF:

$$DM/SF = \left(\frac{1}{\$/DM}\right) \$/SF = \left(\frac{1}{.42}\right) .49 = 1.167$$

Because the rate for the directly quoted DM/SF in Frankfurt differs from the cross rate quoted in New York, an arbitrage opportunity exists. To exploit the arbitrage opportunity, one can trade only the exchange rates actually shown. For example, in New York there may not be a market for DM in terms of the Swiss franc.[2] To exchange DM for SF in the New York market involves two transactions. First, a trader sells DM for $ and then buys SF with $.

To know how to trade, one must know which currency is relatively cheaper in a given market. In New York one receives DM 1.167 per SF, but in Frankfurt SF 1 is worth DM 1.2. The DM, therefore, is cheaper in Frankfurt than in New York. Table 8.2 shows the transactions required to conduct the arbitrage.

FORWARD AND FUTURES MARKET CHARACTERISTICS

The institutional structure of the foreign exchange futures market resembles that of the forward market, with a number of notable exceptions. While the forward market is a worldwide market with

■ **Table 8.2**

CROSS RATE ARBITRAGE TRANSACTIONS

$t = 0$ (the present)
Sell SF 1 90 days forward in Frankfurt for DM 1.2.
Sell DM 1.2 90 days forward in New York for $.504.
Sell $.504 90 days forward in New York for SF 1.0286.

$t = 90$ (delivery)
Deliver SF 1 in Frankfurt; collect DM 1.2.
Deliver DM 1.2 in New York; collect $.504.
Deliver $.504 in New York; collect SF 1.0286.

Profit: SF 1.0286
−1.0000
SF   .0286

no particular geographical location, the principal futures market is the International Monetary Market (IMM) of the Chicago Mercantile Exchange (CME). In the futures market, contracts trade on the most important currencies, such as the German mark, the British pound, the Canadian dollar, the Swiss franc, and the Japanese yen. All of the contracts trade on the MAR, JUN, SEP, DEC cycle with expiration on the third Wednesday of the expiration month. By contrast, forward market quotations are stated for a given number of days into the future.[3] In the futures market, the exchange determines the maturity date of each contract. With each passing day, the futures expiration comes one day closer. In the forward market, contracts for expiration 30, 90, and 180 days into the future are available each trading day. In the futures market, contracts mature on only four days of the year; in the forward market, contracts mature every day. In the forward market, contract size is negotiated. In the futures market, the rules of the exchange determine the contract size. Table 8.3 summarizes the differences between forward and futures markets for foreign exchange. The most important differences are the standardized contract, the standardized delivery dates, the differences in daily cash flows, and the differences in the ways contracts are closed. It is particularly interesting to note that less than 1 percent of all foreign exchange futures are completed by delivery, but delivery occurs on more than 90 percent of all forward contracts.

The forward market for foreign exchange dates back to beyond the reaches of history, while the futures market began only in the 1970s. The major center for the forward market continues to be London, but New York has been gaining in importance as the market for foreign exchange in the U.S. has grown rapidly. While foreign currency futures trading has grown dramatically, the forward market still dwarfs the futures market by a factor of about 20 to one, as measured by the U.S. dollar volume of trading. Since banks are the major participants in the forward market, it is not too surprising that their level of activity in the futures market is rather limited.

Figure 8.3 shows foreign exchange futures price quotations. The columns of quotations follow the pattern set for other types of contracts, showing the open, high, low, and settlement prices, and the change in the settlement price since the preceding day. The next two columns present the high and low lifetime prices for each contract, while the final column shows the open interest in each contract. The final line of data for each contract shows the estimated volume of

■ Table 8.3

FUTURES VS. FORWARD MARKETS

	Forward	Futures
Size of Contract	Tailored to individual needs.	Standardized.
Delivery Date	Tailored to individual needs.	Standardized.
Method of Transaction	Established by the bank or broker via telephone contract with limited number of buyers and sellers.	Determined by open auction among many buyers and sellers on the exchange floor.
Participants	Banks, brokers, and multinational companies. Public speculation not encouraged.	Banks, brokers, and multinational companies. Qualified public speculation encouraged.
Commissions	Set by "spread" between bank's buy and sell price. Not easily determined by customer.	Published small brokerage fee and negotiated rates on block trades.
Security Deposit	None as such, but compensating bank balances required.	Published small security deposit required.
Clearing Operation (Financial Integrity)	Varies across individual banks and brokers. No separate clearinghouse function.	Handled by exchange clearinghouse. Daily settlements to the market.
Marketplace	Over the telephone worldwide.	Central exchange floor with worldwide communications.
Economic Justification	Facilitate world trade by providing hedge mechanism.	Same as forward market. In addition, it provides a broader market and an alternative hedging mechanism via public participation.
Accessibility	Limited to very large customers who deal in foreign trade.	Open to anyone who needs hedge facilities, or has risk capital with which to speculate.
Regulation	Self-regulating.	April 1975 – Regulated under the Commodity Futures Trading Commission.
Frequency of Delivery	More than 90% settled by actual delivery.	Less than 1% settled by actual delivery.
Price Fluctuations	No daily limit.	No daily limit.
Market Liquidity	Offsetting with other banks.	Public offset. Arbitrage offset.

From International Monetary Market, "Understanding Futures in Foreign Exchange Futures," pp. 6-7. Reprinted by permission of Chicago Mercantile Exchange.

■ Figure 8.3

FOREIGN EXCHANGE FUTURES QUOTATIONS

CURRENCY

	Open	High	Low	Settle	Change	Lifetime High	Low	Open Interest
JAPAN YEN (CME)-12.5 million yen; $ per yen (.00)								
June	.9450	.9479	.9422	.9446	– .0002	1.3130	.9259	68,687
Sept	.9564	.9588	.9555	.9558	– .0002	1.2085	.9390	2,034
Dec	.9695	.9700	.9680	.9669	– .0002	1.0500	.9520	1,180
Est vol 16,261; vol Mn 14,971; open int 71,998, –3.								
DEUTSCHEMARK (CME)-125,000 marks; $ per mark								
June	.6613	.6620	.6592	.6596	– .0017	.7315	.6592	81,550
Sept	.6652	.6655	.6633	.6635	– .0017	.7312	.6633	3,285
Dec	....	....	....	.6676	– .0017	.7070	.6698	388
Est vol 20,262; vol Mn 21,455; open int 85,244, +1,777.								
CANADIAN DOLLAR (CME)-100,000 dlrs.; $ per Can $								
June	.7341	.7353	.7341	.7346	+ .0001	.7500	.6930	34,723
Sept	.7360	.7361	.7355	.7353	+ .0001	.7490	.7170	1,834
Dec	.7367	.7367	.7362	.7359	+ .0001	.7460	.7130	1,676
Mr97	....	....	....	.7364	+ .0001	.7395	.7117	439
June	....	....	....	.7365	+ .0001	.7395	.7185	197
Est vol 2,765; vol Mn 2,857; open int 38,871, –173.								
BRITISH POUND (CME)-62,500 pds.; $ per pound								
June	1.5100	1.5170	1.5090	1.5164	+ .0054	1.5870	1.4910	59,363
Sept	1.5080	1.5160	1.5080	1.5148	+ .0054	1.5840	1.4910	146
Est vol 10,234; vol Mn 5,200; open int 59,547, –1,748.								
SWISS FRANC (CME)-125,000 francs; $ per franc								
June	.8180	.8208	.8156	.8157	– .0025	.9120	.8140	40,170
Sept	.8262	.8270	.8229	.8231	– .0025	.9188	.8212	1,521
Dec	....	....	....	.8306	– .0025	.8999	.8290	670
Est vol 13,480; vol Mn 12,233; open int 42,364, –853.								
AUSTRALIAN DOLLAR (CME)-100,000 dlrs.; $ per A.$								
June	.7845	.7890	.7845	.7870	+ .0025	.7904	.7260	11,697
Est vol 840; vol Mn 1,398; open int 11,725, –85.								
MEXICAN PESO (CME)-500,000 new Mex. peso, $ per MP								
June	.12950	.12960	.12880	.12930	– .0005	.13400	.09020	10,522
Sept	.12135	.12160	.12050	.12100	– .0025	.12700	.08600	3,994
Dec	.11310	.11410	.11310	.11370	– .0035	.11500	.09900	1,322
Mr97	.10650	.10750	.10600	.10700	– .0045	.10800	.10070	408
Est vol 2,863; vol Mn 3,276; open int 16,246, –152.								

From *The Wall Street Journal,* April 24, 1996, pp. C22, C16. © 1996 Dow Jones & Company, Inc. Reprinted by permission of The Wall Street Journal. All Rights Reserved Worldwide.

the current day, the actual volume of the preceding day, the current open interest across all contract maturities for each contract, and the change in the open interest since the preceding day.

While the price quotations for each currency are similar, there are some differences. First, different contracts trade a different number of units of the foreign currency. For instance, one contract is for 12.5 million yen but only 125,000 marks. The difference in quantity reflects the vast difference in the value between a single mark and a single yen. In 1996, one U.S. dollar was worth slightly more than 100 yen but less than two marks. Notice also that the quotations for the yen have two zeroes suppressed.

The foreign exchange futures market grew rapidly until 1992, with total volume falling from that high, as depicted by Figure 8.4. From

■ **Figure 8.4**

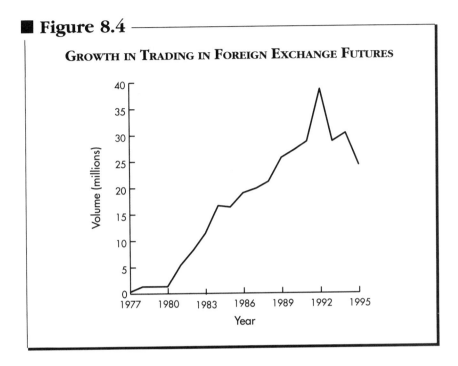

GROWTH IN TRADING IN FOREIGN EXCHANGE FUTURES

a level of only 199,920 contracts in 1975, the total trading volume on foreign exchange futures climbed to just over 38 million by 1992. By 1995, volume was down to 24.3 million. Figure 8.5 shows the share of volume for key currencies in 1995.

In 1993, the CME introduced a new foreign exchange concept called the "rolling spot." As we have seen, the forward market in foreign exchange dominates the futures market, yet futures markets have some advantages over the forward market in terms of default risk control and financial integrity. In essence, a rolling spot contract trades like a regular cash market transaction with a five-day horizon, but any fluctuations in the foreign exchange rate must be realized in cash through the customary futures market resettlement and margining process. In essence, the rolling spot contract performs like a typical spot agreement in the foreign exchange market with the financial backing of the CME clearinghouse. Further, the contracts have a standard size and expiration date, like a futures, and all transactions are publicly reported like any futures. British pound rolling spot contracts began trading on June 15, 1993, with contracts scheduled to follow in the Canadian dollar, the German mark, the Japanese yen, and the Swiss franc. These have not been as successful as the CME had hoped.

■ Figure 8.5

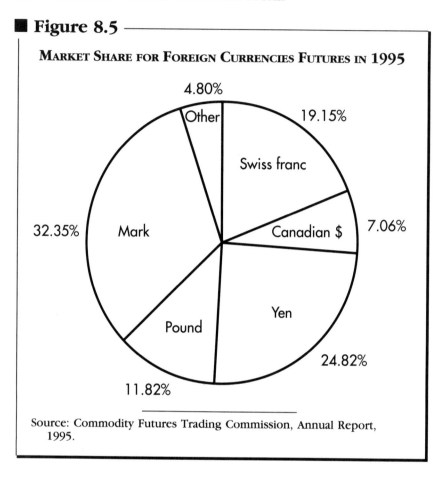

MARKET SHARE FOR FOREIGN CURRENCIES FUTURES IN 1995

Source: Commodity Futures Trading Commission, Annual Report, 1995.

MORE FUTURES PRICE PARITY RELATIONSHIPS

Earlier in this chapter, we noted the geographical or cross-rate arbitrage opportunities that occur when foreign exchange rates are improperly aligned among single contracts. The arbitrage examples of Tables 8.1 and 8.2 arose from a pricing discrepancy in the foreign exchange rates for a single maturity of 90 days forward. Other price relationships are equally important and determine the permissible price differences that may exist between foreign exchange rates for delivery at different times. These relationships are expressed as the **interest rate parity theorem** (IRP) and the **purchasing power parity theorem** (PPP). As we will see, the IRP is simply the cost-of-carry model in a very thin disguise.

INTEREST RATE PARITY THEOREM

The interest rate parity theorem asserts that interest rates and exchange rates form one system. According to IRP, foreign exchange rates will adjust to ensure that a trader earns the same return by investing in risk-free instruments of any currency, assuming that the proceeds from investment are repatriated into the home currency by a forward contract initiated at the outset of the holding period. We can use the rates of Table 8.4 to illustrate interest rate parity. Faced with the rates in Table 8.4 and assuming interest rate parity holds, a trader must earn the same return by following either of two strategies:

Strategy 1: Invest in the U.S. for 180 days.
Strategy 2: (a) Sell $ for DM at the spot rate.
(b) Invest DM proceeds for 180 days in Germany.
(c) Sell the proceeds of the German investment for dollars through a forward contract initiated at the outset of the investment horizon.

With our sample data, the following equation expresses the same equivalence:

$$\$1(1.20)^5 = [(\$1/.42)(1.323)^5](.40)$$

In the equation, Strategy 1 is on the left-hand side. There one dollar is invested at the 20 percent U.S. rate for one-half year. For Strategy 2 on the right-hand side, the dollar is first converted into marks at the spot rate of $.42 per DM. The trader invests these proceeds at the German mark rate for one-half year. This 180-day rate is 32.3

■ Table 8.4

INTEREST RATES AND EXCHANGE RATES TO ILLUSTRATE INTEREST RATE PARITY

Exchange Rates	$/DM	Interest Rates U.S.	Germany
Spot	0.42	–	–
30-day	0.41	0.18	0.576
90-day	0.405	0.19	0.33
180-day	0.4	0.2	0.323

percent. Investment of the German funds will pay DM 2.7386 in 180 days. The investment proceeds are sold for dollars using the 180-day forward rate of .40. For this 180-day horizon, the equivalence between the two strategies holds, so no arbitrage opportunity is available. In this example, the interest rate parity theorem holds.

INTEREST RATE PARITY AND THE COST-OF-CARRY MODEL

In essence, the interest rate parity theorem is simply the exchange rate equivalent of the cost-of-carry model. To see this equivalence, consider the cash-and-carry strategy for the interest rate market. In a cash-and-carry transaction a trader follows these steps: Borrow funds and buy a bond, carry the bond to the futures/forward expiration, and sell the good through a futures/forward contract arranged at the initial date. The cost-of-carry is the difference between the rate paid on the borrowed funds and the rate earned by holding the bond. Our familiar cash-and-carry strategy is known as **covered interest arbitrage** in the foreign exchange market. In covered interest arbitrage, a trader borrows domestic funds and buys foreign funds at the spot rate. The trader then invests these funds at the foreign interest rate until expiration of the forward/futures contract. The trader also initiates a futures/forward contract to convert the proceeds from the foreign investment back into the domestic currency. The cost-of-carry is the difference between the interest rate paid to borrow funds and the interest earned on the investment in foreign funds.

Thus, a trader borrows the domestic currency, DC, at the domestic rate of interest, r_{DC}, and exchanges these funds for foreign currency, FC, at the spot exchange rate. The trader receives DC/FC units of the foreign currency and invests at the foreign interest rate, r_{FC}. This rate, r_{FC}, is the interest rate applicable to the time from the present to the expiration of the forward or futures. At the outset of these transactions, $t = 0$, the trader also sells the forward or futures contract at price $F_{0,t}$ for the amount of funds $(DC/FC)(1 + r_{FC})$. With these transactions, the trader has no net cash flow at $t = 0$. At expiration the trader receives $(DC/FC)(1 + r_{FC})$ units of the foreign currency from the investment of foreign funds. The trader delivers this foreign currency against the forward or futures contract and receives $F_{0,t}$ in the domestic currency. The trader then must pay the debt on the original borrowing, which is DC$(1 + r_{DC})$. If IRP, or equivalently, the cost-of-carry model, holds, the trader must be left with zero funds. Otherwise an arbitrage opportunity exists.

Applying this notation to our previous example of the cost-of-carry transactions for the 180-day horizon, we can generalize this example to write an equation for IRP or the cost-of-carry model as it applies to foreign exchange. For convenience, we begin with $1 as the amount of the domestic currency, DC. Before, for our example, we wrote:

$$\$1(1.20)^{.5} = [(\$1/.42)(1.323)^{.5}](.40)$$

In the new notation this translates as:

$$DC(1 + r_{DC}) = (DC/FC)(1 + r_{FC})F_{0,t}$$

Remember that r_{DC} and r_{FC} are the interest rates for the specific period between the present, $t = 0$, and the expiration of the futures at time t.

Isolating the futures price on the left-hand side gives:

$$F_{0,t} = \frac{DC(1 + r_{DC})}{\left(\dfrac{DC}{FC}\right)(1 + r_{FC})} = FC\left(\frac{1 + r_{DC}}{1 + r_{FC}}\right) \quad (8.1)$$

Equation 8.1 says that, for a unit of foreign currency, the futures price equals the spot price of the foreign currency times the quantity:

$$\left(\frac{1 + r_{DC}}{1 + r_{FC}}\right) \quad (8.2)$$

This quantity is the ratio of the interest factor for the domestic currency to the interest factor for the foreign currency. We can compare this to our familiar Equation 2.3 for the cost-of-carry model in perfect markets with unrestricted short selling:

$$F_{0,t} = S_0(1 + C) \quad (2.3)$$

where:

$F_{0,t}$ = the futures or forward price at $t = 0$ for a foreign exchange contract to expire at time t

S_0 = the spot price of the good at $t = 0$

C = the percentage cost of carrying the good from $t = 0$ to time t

Equations 2.3 and 8.1 have the same form. Therefore, the quantity in Expression 8.2 equals one plus the cost of carry, $(1 + C)$. The cash-and-carry strategy requires borrowing at the domestic rate, r_{DC}, so this is an element of the carrying cost. However, the borrowed domestic funds are converted to foreign currency and earn at the foreign interest rate r_{FC}. Therefore, the foreign earnings offset the cost being incurred through the domestic interest rate. The net result is that the quantity of Expression 8.2 gives the value for one plus the carrying cost. As a simpler approximation, we note that:

$$1 + \text{Cost-of-Carry} = \left(\frac{1 + r_{DC}}{1 + r_{FC}}\right) \approx 1 + (r_{DC} - r_{FC}) \qquad (8.3)$$

Therefore, the cost-of-carry approximately equals the difference between the domestic and foreign interest rates for the period from $t = 0$ to the futures expiration. To complete this discussion, let us apply this equation for the 180-day horizon using the rates in Table 8.4. We have already seen that there is no arbitrage possible for this horizon. For this example data we have:

$F_{0,t}$ = .40
S_0 = .42
r_{DC} = .095445 for the half-year
r_{FC} = .150217 for the half-year

Applying Equation 8.1 to this data, we have:

$$.40 = .42\left(\frac{1.095445}{1.150217}\right)$$

This equation holds exactly. The cost-of-carry is −0.047619. For this example, the approximate cost-of-carry for the half-year is:

$$r_{DC} - r_{FC} = .095445 - .150217 = -0.054772$$

Thus, the cost-of-carry for the half-year is approximately −.05. The cost-of-carry is negative because the cash-and-carry trader pays at the domestic rate but earns interest at the higher foreign rate. For the same reason, the futures price of the foreign currency must exceed the spot price. If the foreign rate of interest had been lower, the futures price of the foreign currency would have to be lower than the spot price to avoid arbitrage.

EXPLOITING DEVIATIONS FROM INTEREST RATE PARITY

The analysis of the values in Table 8.4 shows that there is not an arbitrage opportunity in the 180-day contract. If the interest rate parity theorem is to hold in general, there cannot be an arbitrage opportunity for any investment horizon. In Table 8.4, the rates allow an arbitrage opportunity in the 90-day contract. This is apparent when one realizes that the strategy of holding the U.S. dollar and DM investment does not yield the same 90-day terminal wealth in U.S. dollars when the marks are converted into dollars by issuing a forward contract. The following computation illustrates the different terminal dollar values earned by the two strategies:

Strategy 1: (hold in U.S.)
$$\$1(1.19)^{.25} = \$1.0444$$

Strategy 2: (convert to DM, invest, and use forward contract)
$$(\$1/.42)(1.33)^{.25}(.405) = \$1.0355$$

Strategy 1, investing in the U.S., gives a higher payoff than converting dollars to marks and investing in Germany. This difference implies that an arbitrage opportunity exists.

This is also evident by applying the cost-of-carry model for foreign exchange to the 90-day values in Table 8.4. For this horizon, the values in Table 8.4 imply:

$$F_{0,t} = .405$$
$$S_0 = .42$$
$$r_{DC} = .044448 \text{ for the quarter-year}$$
$$r_{FC} = .073898 \text{ for the quarter-year}$$

With these values, the futures price should be 0.408482:

$$\text{FC}\left(\frac{1 + r_{\text{DC}}}{1 + r_{\text{FC}}}\right) = .42\left(\frac{1.044448}{1.073898}\right) = .408482$$

Because the futures price is less than this amount, an arbitrage opportunity exists. With our example data, it is clearly better to invest funds in the U.S. rather than Germany. Table 8.5 shows the transactions that will exploit this discrepancy, assuming that the transactions begin with $1.00.

This kind of arbitrage in foreign exchange is covered interest arbitrage. With these transactions, the trader uses a forward contract to cover the proceeds from the DM investment. The proceeds are covered, because the trader arranges through the forward contract to convert the DM proceeds into dollars as soon as the proceeds are received. The IRP theorem asserts that such opportunities should not exist. The section on market efficiency explores whether the IRP theorem actually holds.

PURCHASING POWER PARITY THEOREM

The purchasing power parity theorem (PPP) asserts that the exchange rates between two currencies must be proportional to the price level

■ **Table 8.5**

COVERED INTEREST ARBITRAGE

$t = 0$ (present)
 Borrow DM 2.3810 in Germany for 90 days at 30%.
 Sell DM 2.3810 spot for $1.00.
 Invest $1.00 in the U.S. for 90 days at 18%.
 Sell $1.0355 90 days forward for DM 2.5571.

$t = 90$ (delivery)
 Collect $1.0444 on investment in United States.
 Deliver $1.0355 on forward contract; collect DM 2.5571.
 Pay DM 2.5571 on DM 2.3810 that was borrowed.

$$\begin{array}{rl} \text{Profit:} & \$1.0444 \\ & -\ \underline{1.0355} \\ & .0089 \end{array}$$

of traded goods in the two currencies. Purchasing power parity is intimately tied to interest rate parity, as we discuss later. Violations of PPP can lead to arbitrage opportunities, such as the following example of "Croissant Arbitrage."

For croissant arbitrage we assume that transportation and transaction costs are zero and that there are no trade barriers, such as quotas or tariffs. These assumptions are essentially equivalent to our usual assumptions of perfect markets. The spot value of the French franc is $.10 and the cost of a croissant in Paris is FF 1, as Table 8.6 shows. In New York a croissant sells for $.15, so this price creates an arbitrage opportunity. A trader can exploit this opportunity by transacting as shown in the bottom portion of Table 8.6. Given the other values, the price of a croissant in New York must be $.10 to exclude arbitrage.

Over time, exchange rates must also conform to PPP. The left column of Table 8.7 presents prices and exchange rates consistent with PPP at $t = 0$. The right column shows values one year later at $t = 1$, after a year of inflation in France and the United States. During this year, French inflation was 20 percent, so a croissant now sells for FF 1.2. In the U.S. inflation was 10 percent, so a croissant is now $.11. To be consistent with PPP, the exchange rates must also have adjusted to keep the relative value of the franc and the dollar consistent with the relative purchasing power of the two currencies. As a consequence, the dollar must now be worth FF 10.91. Any other exchange

■ Table 8.6

CROISSANT ARBITRAGE

	FF/$	Cost of One Croissant
Paris	10	FF 1
New York	10	$.15

Arbitrage Transactions:
Sell $1 for FF 10 in the spot market.
Buy 10 croissants in Paris.
Ship the croissants to New York.
Sell 10 croissants in New York at .15 for $1.50.

Profit:	$1.50
	− 1.00
	.50

■ Table 8.7

PURCHASING POWER PARITY OVER TIME		
Expected Inflation Rates from $t = 0$ to $t = 1$: $ .10		
FF .20		
	$t = 0$	$t = 1$
Exchange Rates FF/$	10	10.91
Croissant Prices		
Paris	FF 1.00	FF 1.20
New York	$ .10	$ .11

rate would create an arbitrage opportunity. The requirement that PPP holds at all times means that the exchange rate must change proportionately to the relative price levels in the two currencies.

PURCHASING POWER AND INTEREST RATE PARITY

The intimate relationship that exists between the purchasing power parity theorem and the interest rate parity theorem originates from the link between interest rates and inflation rates. According to the analysis of Irving Fisher, the nominal, or market, rate of interest consists of two elements, the **real** rate of interest and the **expected** inflation rate. This relationship can be expressed mathematically as follows:

$$(1 + r_n) = (1 + r^*)[1 + E(I)] \qquad (8.4)$$

where, r_n is the nominal interest rate, r^* is the real rate of interest, and $E(I)$ is the expected inflation rate over the period in question. Since the expected inflation is the expected change in purchasing power, the purchasing power parity theorem expresses the linkage between exchange rates and relative inflation rates. A difference in nominal interest rates between two countries is most likely due to differences in expected inflation. This means that interest rates, exchange rates, price levels, and foreign exchange rates form an integrated system.

FOREIGN EXCHANGE FUTURES PRICES AND EXPECTED FUTURE EXCHANGE RATES

Throughout this book, and particularly in Chapter 2, we have stressed the relationship between futures prices and expected future spot prices. If risk-neutral speculators are available in sufficient quantity, their profit seeking activity will drive the futures price toward equality with the expected future spot price. The same process occurs in the foreign exchange market. The linkages among interest rates, price levels, expected inflation, and exchange rates merely emphasize the fundamental relationship that exists between forward and futures foreign exchange prices, on the one hand, and the expected future value of the currencies, on the other.

To investigate these relationships, consider the exchange rates and price levels of Table 8.8. In the left panel, a set of consistent exchange rates, interest rates, expected inflation rates, and croissant prices are presented for March 20, 1998. The right panel presents the expected spot exchange rate for March 20, 1999, along with expected croissant prices, consistent with the expected levels of inflation in France and the United States.

■ Table 8.8

PRICE LEVELS, INTEREST RATES, EXPECTED INFLATION, AND EXCHANGE RATES

March 20, 1998		March 20, 1999	
Exchange Rates FF/$		Expected Spot Exchange Rate	
Spot	10.00	10.45	
MAR 1999 Futures	10.45		
Interest Rates (1-year maturities)			
United States	.12		
France	.17		
Expected Inflation Rates (for the next year)			
United States	.10		
France	.15		
Croissant Prices		Expected Croissant Prices	
United States	$ .10	United States	$ .11
France	FF 1.0	France	FF 1.15

Assume that all of these values hold and that the expected spot exchange rate in one year is FF 11 per dollar. With the MAR 1999 futures price of 10.45 FF/$, a speculative opportunity exists as follows. A speculator might buy a futures contract for the delivery of dollars in one year for FF 10.45 per dollar. If the expectation that the dollar will be worth FF 11 in one year is correct, the speculator will earn a profit that results from acquiring a dollar via the futures market for FF 10.45 and selling it for the price of FF 11. If we assume that avaricious risk-neutral speculators are present in the foreign exchange market, the discrepancy between the futures price of 10.45 FF/$ and an expected spot exchange rate of 11 FF/$ (at the time the futures contract matures) cannot exist. In fact, given a profusion of risk-neutral speculators, the only expected spot exchange rate to prevail on March 20, 1999, which would eliminate the incentive to speculate, would be 10.45 FF/$. Of course, different market participants have different expectations regarding inflation rates and expected future spot exchange rates, and this difference in expectations is the necessary requirement for speculation.

FOREIGN EXCHANGE FORECASTING ACCURACY

In this section we examine the evidence on the accuracy of foreign exchange futures and forward prices as forecasts of future spot exchange rates. As we have just argued, the presence of risk-neutral speculators should drive the futures and forward prices into equality with the expected future spot rate of exchange. If today's expectation of future exchange rates is unbiased, and if the forward and futures prices equal that expectation, we would find that today's forward or futures exchange rate should, on average and in the long run, equal the subsequently observed spot exchange rate. Thus, there are two parts to this equivalence. First, does the forward or futures price equal the market's expectation of the future spot exchange rate? Second, is today's expectation of the future spot exchange rate unbiased? That is, does today's expectation of the future spot exchange rate, on average and in the long run, equal the actual subsequently observed spot rate?

METHODOLOGY FOR TESTS OF FORECASTING ACCURACY

Unfortunately, there is no truly accurate way to observe today's market expectation of future exchange rates. Therefore, most tests assume that the market expectation is an unbiased estimate of the future spot exchange rate. Under this assumption, scholars test the relationship between the forward and futures price today and the subsequently observed spot rate. In our notation, they test the following equivalence:

$$F_{0,t} = S_t \qquad (8.5)$$

where:

$F_{0,t}$ = the forward or futures price at $t = 0$ for a contract expiring at time t

S_t = the spot exchange rate observed at time t

Testing the equivalence in Equation 8.5 determines whether the forward or futures price is a good estimate of the future spot rate of exchange. Even if there are large deviations between the two prices in Equation 8.5, it is still possible that the forward or futures price could provide an unbiased prediction of the future spot rate. An **unbiased predictor** is a predictor whose expected value equals the variable being predicted. In other words, if the quantity $F_{0,t} - S_t$ equals zero, on average, the forward or futures price would provide an unbiased estimate of the future spot rate of exchange.

No predictor is perfect. Therefore, it is possible that the forward or futures price may seem to be error ridden. However, the most relevant test of any predictor comes from testing the accuracy of the predictor against alternative predictors. As we will see, forward and futures prices do not provide very good predictions of future spot rates – unless we compare them to alternative forecasting schemes.

Earlier in this chapter, we reviewed the evidence on the relationship between futures and forward prices of foreign exchange. There we saw that the evidence strongly suggests that the two are equal. We rely on that equivalence in this section. In the discussion that follows, we speak of futures and forward prices in general, without distinguishing the two.

TESTS OF MARKET-BASED FORECASTS

A **market-based forecast** is a forecast of a future economic value derived from an examination of current market prices. In the context of foreign exchange, we ask whether the current futures price provides a good market-based forecast of the future foreign exchange rate. As we have seen, this essentially amounts to testing the equivalence of futures prices and subsequently observed spot exchange rates.

While earlier studies generally found that futures prices were unbiased predictors of future spot rates, later studies clearly find bias and large errors in the futures forecasts of subsequent spot prices. However, most studies do not find biases that are sufficiently large or consistent to allow profitable trading strategies. In summary, the errors in forecasts of future exchange rates appear to be large, and biases do seem to exist in these forecasts, although the biases appear to be too small to allow profitable exploitation.[4]

COMPETITORS OF MARKET-BASED FORECASTS

If we consider the futures price as a forecast of the future spot rate of exchange, we must conclude that the forecast is likely to have large errors, and we must acknowledge that the forecast may be biased. These two features do not appear to recommend market-based forecasts of future spot exchange rates. Perhaps some other type of forecast is better. The usefulness of market-based forecasts of future exchange rates depends, however, on a whole range of factors, including availability, cost, extent of bias, size of the forecast error, and performance of the forecast relative to other methods. In this section, we compare market-based forecasts with the performance of commercial forecasting firms. As will become apparent, in spite of their limitations, the futures forecasts have important advantages.

Clearly, the futures forecast has an advantage in availability and cost. Both are readily available every day for the price of *The Wall Street Journal.* If forward and futures prices provide the best forecast of the future spot rate that is available, the biases in the forecasts are probably not too serious. Even if the biases are substantial, the futures forecast may still be the best forecast available. Perhaps the most severe challenge to the market-based forecasts comes from the forecasting services that prepare and disseminate forecasts of exchange rates. However, market-based forecasts appear to have smaller errors than forecasts from commercial firms.[5]

THE EFFICIENCY OF FOREIGN EXCHANGE FUTURES MARKETS

The efficiency of the foreign exchange market has been explored by numerous researchers over an extended time. In spite of this attention, the efficiency of the market remains an open question. This situation is not unusual when a complex empirical issue in finance is at stake. If arbitrage opportunities such as geographical, cross-rate, or covered interest arbitrage exist, then the foreign exchange market is inefficient. Reflection on the structure of the market helps support the case for efficiency. With a worldwide network of active traders, all linked by sophisticated information systems and all aware of the profits implied by arbitrage opportunities, we might expect any incipient arbitrage opportunities to be detected very early. As quasi-arbitrage opportunities appear, we would expect traders to adjust their trading patterns to exploit even the slightest opportunity. This activity, we expect, should eliminate any observable arbitrage opportunities.

On the other hand, the foreign exchange market is unique in attracting central bank intervention from a variety of countries. If central banks cannot leave their hands off the market and insist on managing floating rates, the character of the market could be affected. If the market is subject to the actions of well-capitalized governmental agencies with agendas that are not profit-determined, then we might expect profit opportunities to arise from betting against central banks. In this section, we explore the evidence on market efficiency, beginning with an example of interest rate parity.

We have seen that deviations from interest rate parity create opportunities for cash-and-carry and reverse cash-and-carry trading strategies. With transaction costs, slight deviations from interest rate parity are possible, because transaction costs make it unprofitable for traders to exploit minor discrepancies. The arbitrage opportunity depends upon finding deviations from interest rate parity large enough to cover all transaction costs and still leave a profit. As a result, one way of searching for the existence of violations of the interest rate parity theorem is to look for the occurrence of large deviations from interest rate parity. Table 8.9 shows deviations from interest rate parity for some major currencies on which futures contracts trade. Richard M. Levich selected .25 percent as a permissible deviation from interest rate parity, which would still be consistent with the absence of arbitrage opportunities. He believed that this fourth of one percent would be a reasonable bound for transaction costs to form a no-arbitrage band around the price exactly consistent with IRP. As Table 8.9 shows, a high percentage of Levich's observations fall within that band. From this, Levich concludes, "Therefore, the Eurocurrency market is efficient in that there are few unexploited opportunities for risk-free profit through covered interest arbitrage."[6]

■ Table 8.9

PERCENTAGE OF DEVIATIONS FROM INTEREST PARITY WITHIN
+/− .25%
(ALL ASSETS ARE FOR 3-MONTH MATURITIES)

Country	Percentage within Bounds
Canada	93.43
United Kingdom	96.68
Germany	98.82
Switzerland	78.59

Source: Richard M. Levich, "The Efficiency of Markets for Foreign
Exchange: A Review and Extension." Reprinted in Kolb and Gay,
International Finance: Concepts and Issues, Richmond, VA: Robert
F. Dame, 1982.

To what extent do deviations outside the band of .25 percent represent arbitrage opportunities? If we find only few opportunities, it may still be worthwhile to look for them. Based on Table 8.9, it seems potentially worthwhile to follow the Swiss franc, since over 20 percent of the observations appear to lie outside the stated boundaries. The critical question here is the selection of the no-arbitrage boundaries. If transactions costs exceed .25 percent, then the bounds are too narrow. By the same token, perhaps transaction costs are really less than .25 percent, and the no-arbitrage boundaries are too lax. These questions are not easy to answer, since it is virtually impossible to know what measure of transaction costs to use. The most striking feature of Table 8.9, however, appears to be the prevalent tendency for so many opportunities to fall within .25 percent of exact interest rate parity. While it may not be possible to say that no arbitrage opportunities are to be found in the foreign exchange market, it is much more impressive to note how closely the observations tended to correspond to interest rate parity.[7]

Levich's study characterizes the earlier evidence on the efficiency of foreign exchange markets. Nonetheless, more recent evidence on forward and futures markets for foreign exchange suggests that the markets are not efficient. Most studies of foreign exchange market efficiency find significant departures from theoretical pricing relationships. Further, some studies find that speculative strategies can earn significant profits. Part of the findings seem to be due to intervention in the foreign exchange markets by central banks. As a tentative explanation, it seems possible that central banks intervene to stabilize currencies. In the process, they provide profits to savvy speculators. However, most of these opportunities appear to be quite small.[8]

SPECULATION IN FOREIGN EXCHANGE FUTURES

We have seen that the market for foreign exchange has some significant inefficiencies. This inefficiency appears to open the door to speculative strategies. Nonetheless, we should not expect gross inefficiencies in the market. For example, it still appears that market-based forecasts outperform professional forecasts. This suggests that attempts to "beat the market" may still be hazardous. In this section, we illustrate strategies to speculate with foreign exchange. These strategies presume that the trader has well-developed expectations about the value of foreign exchange rates.

SPECULATING WITH AN OUTRIGHT POSITION

In speculation, the most important single point to remember is that the trader opposes his or her wisdom to the opinion of the entire market, since prices available in the market reflect the consensus opinion of all participating parties. The dependence of speculative profits on superior estimation of future exchange rates is demonstrated in Tables 8.10 and 8.11. Imagine a speculator who confronts the exchange rates of Table 8.10 between the U.S. dollar and the German mark on April 7. As an expression of the market's beliefs, these exchange rates imply that the mark will rise relative to the dollar. The speculator, however, strongly disagrees. She believes that the price of the mark, in terms of dollars, will actually fall over the rest

■ Table 8.10

FOREIGN EXCHANGE PRICES – SPOT AND FUTURES, APRIL 7

	$/DM
Spot	0.414
JUN Futures	0.4183
SEP Futures	0.4211
DEC Futures	0.4286

■ Table 8.11

	SPECULATION IN FOREIGN EXCHANGE	
	Cash Market	**Futures Market**
April 7	Anticipates a fall in the value of the DM over the next 8 months.	Sell 1 DEC DM futures contract at .4286.
December 10	Spot Price $/DM = .4211	Buy 1 DEC DM futures contract at .4218.
	Profit:	$ .4286 − .4218
	Profit per DM	$ .0068
	Times DM per contract	× 125,000
	Total Profit	$ 850

of the year. Table 8.11 shows the speculative transactions she enters to take advantage of her belief.

Since the speculator expects the mark to fall, she sells the DEC futures contract for .4286. If the subsequent spot price is less, she makes a profit. The speculator does not actually need to be correct in the stated belief that the spot exchange value of the mark will fall over the next eight months. A profit is assured if the mark is worth less than the DEC futures price. On December 10, as Table 8.11 shows, the DEC futures is .4218 and the spot exchange rate is 0.4211. Notice that the belief that the mark would fall in value was incorrect. The December 10 spot price still exceeds the original spot price, as does the price of the DEC futures contract. Nonetheless, the drop in the futures price from .4286 to .4218 generates a profit of $.0068 per mark. Since the DM contract calls for delivery of 125,000 marks, the total profit is $850.

SPECULATING WITH SPREADS

In addition to outright positions, such as the position in the previous example, various spread strategies are also possible. These include intracommodity and intercommodity spreads. Some intercommodity spreads are important, because they allow positions that might not be easily attainable in other markets. The only U.S. futures market for individual foreign exchange contracts is the IMM. In the IMM all prices are stated in terms of dollars. A speculator might believe that the Swiss franc will gain in value relative to the German mark but might also be uncertain about the future value of the dollar relative to either of these currencies. It is possible to speculate on the SF/DM exchange rate by trading on the IMM futures market.

Table 8.12 presents market prices on the IMM for June 24 for the $/DM and $/SF spot and future exchange rates. The futures prices imply cross rates between the mark and franc as well, as shown in the right column. The rate structure is peculiar, with the DM/SF rate dipping first and then rising. In particular, a speculator finds the implied cross rate for December to be too low. The speculator believes that the Swiss franc will tend to appreciate against the mark over the coming year. Even though it is impossible to trade the mark against the Swiss franc directly on the IMM, given the available rate quotations, the speculator can use a spread to achieve the desired speculative position.

Since the speculator believes that the value of the mark will fall relative to the Swiss franc, he must also believe that the value of the mark relative to the dollar will perform worse than the value of the Swiss franc relative to the dollar. In other words, even if the mark appreciates against the dollar, his belief about the relative value of the Swiss franc implies that the Swiss franc would appreciate even more against the dollar. Likewise, if the mark falls against the dollar, the speculator would believe that the Swiss franc would either gain or not fall as much as the mark. It is important to realize that the speculator need not have any belief regarding the performance of the dollar relative to either of the European currencies. He is merely

■ Table 8.12

SPOT AND FUTURES EXCHANGE RATES, JUNE 24

	$/DM	$/SF	Implied DM/SF Cross Rate
Spot	0.3853	0.458	1.1887
SEP	0.3915	0.4616	1.1791
DEC	0.4115	0.4635	1.1264
MAR	0.4163	0.4815	1.1566
JUN	0.418	0.51	1.2201

going to trade through the dollar to establish a position in the DM/
SF exchange rate.

Table 8.13 shows the transactions necessary to exploit the belief
that the December cross rate is too low. If the speculator is correct,
the mark will fall relative to the Swiss franc. Therefore, he sells 1
DEC mark contract at .4115 and buys 1 DEC Swiss franc contract at
.4635. This spread is equivalent to speculating that the implied cross
rate of 1.1264 is too low, or that it will require more than 1.1264 DM
to buy 1 SF by December. By December 11, the two contracts are
approaching expiration, and the speculator offsets both contracts. He
buys the DEC DM contract at .3907 and sells the SF contract at .4475.
This generates a profit of $.0208 per DM and a loss of $.0160 per SF.
Both contracts are written for 125,000 units of the foreign currency,
so the net profit on the spread transaction is $600.

As a final example of currency speculation, consider the spot and
futures prices for the British pound in Table 8.14. A speculator
observes these relatively constant prices, but believes that the British
economy is even worse than generally appreciated. Specifically, she
anticipates that the British inflation rate will exceed the U.S. rate.
Therefore, the trader expects the pound to fall relative to the dollar.
One easy way to act on this belief is to sell a distant futures contract,
but this position trader is very risk averse, and she decides to trade

■ Table 8.13

A Speculative Cross-Rate Futures Spread

Date	Futures Market
June 24	Sell 1 DEC DM futures contract at .4115. Buy 1 DEC SF futures contract at .4635.
December 11	Buy 1 DEC DM futures contract at .3907. Sell 1 DEC SF futures contract at .4475.

Futures Trading Results:

	DM	SF
Sold	.4115	.4475
Bought	− .3907	− .4635
	$.0208	−$.0160
× 125,000	= $2,600	−$2,000

Total Profit: $600

■ **Table 8.14** ————————————————————

	SPOT AND FUTURES PRICES, AUGUST 12
	$/British Pound
Spot	1.4485
SEP	1.448
DEC	1.446
MAR	1.446
JUN	1.447

a spread instead of an outright position. She believes that the equal prices for the DEC and MAR contracts will not be sustained, so she trades as shown in Table 8.15, selling what she believes to be the relatively overpriced MAR contract and buying the relatively underpriced DEC contract. By December, the speculator's expectations have been realized and the pound has fallen relative to the dollar, with the more distant futures contract falling even more. The speculator then closes her position on December 5 and realizes a total profit of $150, as Table 8.15 shows. As a result of her conservatism, the profit is only $150. Had the trader taken an outright position by selling the MAR contract, the profit would have been $517.50. In these examples of successful speculations it must be recognized that the

■ **Table 8.15** ————————————————————

TIME SPREAD SPECULATION IN THE BRITISH POUND

Date	Futures Market
August 12	Buy 1 DEC BP futures contract at 1.4460. Sell 1 MAR BP futures contract at 1.4460.
December 5	Sell 1 DEC BP futures contract at 1.4313. Buy 1 MAR BP futures contract at 1.4253.

	December	March
Sold	1.4313	1.4460
Bought	−1.4460	−1.4253
	−$.0147	$ .0207
× 25,000	= −$367.50	+ $517.50

Total Profit: $150

speculator pits his or her knowledge against the collective opinion of the entire market, as that opinion is expressed in market prices.

Hedging with Foreign Exchange Futures

Many firms, and some individuals, find themselves exposed to foreign exchange risk. Importers and exporters, for example, often need to make commitments to buy or sell goods for delivery at some future time, with the payment to be made in a foreign currency. Likewise, multinational firms operating foreign subsidiaries receive payments from their subsidiaries that may be denominated in a foreign currency. A wealthy individual may plan an extended trip abroad and may be concerned about the chance that the price of a particular foreign currency might rise unexpectedly. All of these different parties are potential candidates for hedging unwanted currency risk by using the foreign exchange futures market.

If a trader faces the actual exchange of one currency for another, the risk is called **transaction exposure**, because the trader will transact in the market to exchange one currency for another. Firms often face **translation exposure**, the need to restate one currency in terms of another currency. For example, a firm may have a foreign subsidiary that earns profits in a foreign currency. However, the parent company prepares its accounting statements in the domestic currency. For accounting purposes, the firm must translate the foreign earnings into the domestic currency. While this procedure does not involve an actual transaction in the foreign exchange market, the reported earnings of the firm expressed in the domestic currency can be volatile due to the uncertain exchange rate at which the subsidiary's foreign earnings will be translated into the domestic currency. In the examples that follow, we consider hedges of both transaction and translation exposure.

Hedging Transaction Exposure

The simplest kind of example arises in the case of a vacationer planning a six-month trip to Switzerland. Our vacationer plans to spend a considerable sum during this trip, enough to make it worthwhile to attend to exchange rates, as shown in Table 8.16. With the more distant rates lying above nearby rates, the vacationer fears that spot rates may rise even higher, so he decides to lock in the existing

■ **Table 8.16**

SWISS EXCHANGE RATES, JANUARY 12	
Spot	0.4935
MAR	0.5034
JUN	0.5134
SEP	0.5237
DEC	0.5342

rates by buying Swiss franc futures. Because he plans to depart for Switzerland in June, he buys 2 JUN SF futures contracts at the current price of .5134. He anticipates that SF 250,000 will be enough to cover his six-month stay, as Table 8.17 shows. By June 6, our recreationist's fears have been realized, and the spot rate for the SF is .5211. Therefore the vacationer delivers $128,350 and collects SF 250,000. Had he waited and transacted in the spot market on June 6, the SF 250,000 would have cost $130,275. Hedging his foreign exchange risk has saved $1,925, which is enough to finance a few extra days in Switzerland.

In this example, the vacationer had a preexisting risk in the foreign exchange market, since it was already determined that he would acquire the Swiss francs. By trading futures, he guaranteed a price of $.5134 per franc. Of course, the futures market can be used for

■ **Table 8.17**

THE VACATIONER'S SWISS FRANC HEDGE		
	Cash Market	**Futures Market**
January 12	Vacationer plans to take a six-month trip to Switzerland, to begin in June; the trip will cost about SF 250,000.	Vacationer buys 2 JUN SF futures contracts at .5134 for a total cost of $128,350.
June 16	The $/SF spot rate is now .5211, giving a dollar cost of $130,275 for SF 250,000.	Vacationer delivers $128,350 and collects SF 250,000.
Savings on the Hedge = $130,275 − 128,350 = $1,925		

purposes even more serious than reducing the risk surrounding a Swiss vacation.

HEDGING IMPORT/EXPORT TRANSACTIONS

Consider a small import/export firm that is negotiating a large purchase of Japanese watches from a firm in Japan. The Japanese firm, being a very tough negotiator, has demanded that payment be made in yen upon delivery of the watches. (If the contract had called for payment in dollars, rather than yen, the Japanese firm would bear the exchange risk.) Delivery will take place in seven months, but the price of the watches is agreed today to be Yen 2850 per watch for 15,000 watches. This means that the purchaser will have to pay Yen 42,750,000 in about seven months. Table 8.18 shows the current exchange rates on April 11. With the current spot rate of .004173 dollars per yen, the purchase price for the 15,000 watches would be $178,396. If the futures prices on April 11 are treated as a forecast of future exchange rates, it seems that the dollar is expected to lose ground against the yen. With the DEC futures trading at .004265, the actual dollar cost might be closer to $182,329. If delivery and payment are to occur in December, the importer might reasonably estimate the actual dollar outlay to be about $182,000 instead of $178,000.

To avoid any worsening of his exchange position, the importer decides to hedge the transaction by trading foreign exchange futures. Delivery is expected in November, so the importer decides to trade the DEC futures. By selecting this expiration, the hedger avoids having to roll over a nearby contract, thereby reducing transaction costs. Also, the DEC contract has the advantage of being the first contract to mature after the hedge horizon, so the DEC futures exchange rate should be close to the spot exchange rate prevailing in November when the yen are needed.

■ Table 8.18

$/YEN FOREIGN EXCHANGE RATES, APRIL 11	
Spot	0.004173
JUN Futures	0.0042
SEP Futures	0.004237
DEC Futures	0.004265

The importer's next difficulty stems from the fact that the futures contract is written for Yen 12.5 million. If he trades three contracts, his transaction will be for 37.5 million. If he trades four contracts, however, he would be trading 50 million, when he really only needs coverage for 42.75 million. No matter which way he trades, the importer will be left with some unhedged exchange risk. Finally, he decides to trade three contracts. Table 8.19 shows his transactions. On April 11 he anticipates that he will need Yen 42.75 million, with a current dollar value of $178,396 and an expected future value of $182,329, where the expected future worth of the yen is measured by the DEC futures price. This expected future price is the most relevant price for measuring the success of the hedge. In the futures market, the importer buys three DEC yen contracts at .004265 dollars per yen.

On November 18, the watches arrive, and the importer purchases the yen on the spot market at .004273. Relative to his anticipated cost of yen, he pays $342 more than expected. Having acquired the

■ Table 8.19

THE IMPORTER'S HEDGE

	Cash Market	Futures Market
April 11	The importer anticipates a need for ¥42,750,000 in November, the current value of which is $178,396, and which have an expected value in November of $182,329.	The importer buys ¥3 DEC futures contracts at .004265 for a total commitment of $159,938.
November 1	Receives watches; buys ¥42,750,000 at the spot market rate of .004273 for a total of $182,671.	Sells ¥3 DEC futures contracts at .004270 for a total value of $160,125.
	Spot Market Results: Anticipated Cost $182,329 − Actual Cost − 182,671 −$342	Futures Market Results: Profit = $187
	Net Loss: −$155	

yen, the importer offsets his futures position. Since the futures has moved only .000005, the futures profit is only $187. This gives a total loss on the entire transaction of $155. Had there been no hedge, the loss would have been the full change of the price in the cash market, or $342. This hedge was only partially effective for two reasons. First, the futures price did not move as much as the cash price. The cash price changed by .000008 dollars per yen, but the futures price changed by only .000005 dollars per yen. Second, the importer was not able to fully hedge his position, due to the fact that his needs fell between two contract amounts. Since he needed Yen 42.75 million and only traded futures for Yen 37.5 million, he was left with an unhedged exposure of Yen 5.25 million.

HEDGING TRANSLATION EXPOSURE

Many corporations in international business have subsidiaries that earn revenue in foreign currencies and remit their profits to a U.S. parent company. The U.S. parent reports its income in dollars, so the parent's reported earnings fluctuate with the exchange rate between the dollar and the currency of the foreign country in which the subsidiary operates. This necessity to restate foreign currency earnings in the domestic currency is **translation exposure**. For many firms, fluctuating earnings are an anathema. To avoid variability in earnings stemming from exchange rate fluctuations, firms can hedge with foreign exchange futures.

Table 8.20 shows DM exchange rates for January 2 and December 15. Faced with these exchange rates is the Schropp Trading Company of Neckarsulm, a subsidiary of an American firm. Schropp Trading expects to earn DM 4.3 million this year and plans to remit those funds to its American parent. With the DEC futures trading at .4211 dollars per DM on January 2, the expected dollar value of those

■ Table 8.20

EXCHANGE RATES FOR THE GERMAN MARK

	January 2	December 15
Spot	0.4233	0.4017
DEC Futures	0.4211	0.4017

earnings is $1,810,730. If the mark falls, however, the actual dollar contribution to the earnings of the parent will be lower.

The firm can either hedge or leave unhedged the value of the earnings in marks, as Table 8.21 shows. With the rates in Table 8.20, the 4.3 million marks will be worth only $1,727,310 on December 15. This shortfall could have been avoided by selling the expected earnings in marks in the futures market in January at the DEC futures price of .4211. Table 8.21 shows this possibility. With a contract size of DM 125,000, the firm could have sold 35 contracts at the January 2 price. This strategy would have generated a futures profit of $84,875 (35 contracts × 125,000 marks × $.0194 profit per mark). This futures profit would have almost exactly offset the loss in the value of the mark, and Schropp Trading could successfully make its needed contribution to the American parent by remitting $1,812,185.

CONCLUSION

This chapter began by exploring the foreign exchange spot and forward markets. Of all goods with futures markets, the foreign exchange market is unique in the strength of the forward market. In fact, the forward market is much larger than the futures market. Nonetheless,

■ Table 8.21

SCHROPP TRADING COMPANY OF NECKARSULM

January 2

Expected earnings in Germany for the year		DM 4.3 million
Anticipated value in U.S. dollars (computed @ .4211 $/DM)		$1,810,730

Schropp Trading Company's Contribution to Its Parent's Income

	Unhedged	Hedged
Contribution to parent's income in U.S. dollars from DM 4.3 million earnings (assumes spot rate of .4017)	$1,727,310	$1,727,310
Futures profit or loss (closed at the spot rate of .4017)	0	$84,875
Total	$1,727,310	$1,812,185

as we discussed, forward prices and futures prices for foreign exchange are virtually identical.

Because foreign exchange rates represent the price of one unit of money in terms of another unit of money, every foreign exchange rate is clearly a relative price. Because of this unique character of foreign exchange markets, we considered the determinants of foreign exchange rates, such as the balance of payments. With modern money being a creation of governments, government intervention in the foreign exchange market is more dominant than in most other markets. Governments attempt to establish exchange rate systems that either fix the value of a currency in terms of another currency, or allow the value of currencies to float. Even when the value of a currency is allowed to float, governments often intervene to manage the value of their currency.

As we have seen for all markets, no-arbitrage conditions constrain foreign exchange rates. One of the most famous of these relationships is the interest rate parity theorem. As we discussed in detail, the IRP theorem is just the cost-of-carry model for foreign exchange. Thus, foreign exchange pricing principles match the concepts we have developed for other markets.

Compared to many other markets, there have been a number of studies of the forecasting accuracy of futures and forward exchange rates. These studies ask whether the futures price is a good forecast of the spot price that will prevail at the futures expiration. In general, most of these studies find significant errors or biases in the futures-based forecast. However, compared with most professional forecasting services, the futures price still provides a superior forecast of future spot prices.

The evidence on the efficiency of the foreign exchange market is probably more negative than the evidence for any of the other markets we have considered. Most studies seem to agree in finding significant departures from efficiency. These range from violations of parity conditions to finding successful speculative strategies. The reason for this apparent inefficiency is unclear, but several studies point to central bank intervention as a possible explanation: Central banks enter the market to pursue policy objectives, thereby providing speculators with profit opportunities. Whether this tentative explanation can be sustained is not totally clear.

As with all futures markets, the foreign currency futures market has numerous hedging applications. We showed how to use foreign currency futures to hedge risk for importers and exporters. Also, we considered the problems of transaction and translation exposure. In transaction exposure, a trader actually faces the exchange of one currency for another and wishes to hedge the future commitment of funds. In translation exposure, funds received in one currency will be restated for accounting purposes in another currency. Because it concerns only accounting, translation exposure need not require the actual exchange of one currency for another. Nonetheless, firms can hedge translation exposure to avoid the volatility of reported earnings in the home currency.

NOTES

1. One such trading room was featured in the film, *Rollover,* starring Kris Kristofferson and Jane Fonda. In this story of international financial intrigue and panic, Kristofferson played the brilliant hard-nosed manager of the trading room, who saves the world from financial collapse.

2. Actually, in major foreign exchange centers such as New York, some traders will make markets in the major cross rates. For many currencies in many markets, however, a separate quotation for cross rates is not available.

3. Although maturities of 30, 90, and 180 days are normally listed, forward market transactions may be arranged with different maturities to suit the needs of the customer.

4. For representative studies in this area, see the following articles: L. Hansen and R. Hodrick, "Forward Exchange Rates as Optimal Predictors of Future Spot Rates: An Econometric Analysis," *Journal of Political Economy,* 88:5, 1980, pp. 829-53; R. Hodrick and S. Srivastava, "Foreign Currency Futures," *Journal of International Economics,* 22:1/2, 1987, pp. 1-24; L. Kodres, "Tests of Unbiasedness in Foreign Exchange Futures Markets: The Effects of Price Limits," *Review of Futures Markets,* 7:1, 1988, pp. 139-66; S. Kohlhagen, "The Forward Rate as an Unbiased Predictor of the Future Spot Rate," *Columbia Journal of World Business,* 14:4, Winter 1979, pp. 77-85.

5. See, for example, R. Levich, "Evaluating the Performance of the Forecasters," in R. Ensor (ed.), *The Management of Foreign Exchange Risk,* 2e, Euromoney Publications, 1982, pp. 121-34.

6. See R. Levich, "The Efficiency of Markets for Foreign Exchange: A Review and Extension," in G. Gay and R. Kolb, *International Finance: Concepts and Issues*, Richmond, VA: Robert F. Dame, 1982, p. 406.

7. Many other empirical tests tend to confirm the conclusion of efficiency reached by Levich, and a number of these are included in the bibliography to his article.

8. For studies of foreign exchange market efficiency, see K. Cavanaugh, "Price Dynamics in Foreign Currency Futures Markets," *Journal of International Money and Finance*, 6:3, 1987, pp. 295–314, and D. Glassman, "The Efficiency of Foreign Exchange Futures Markets in Turbulent and Non-Turbulent Periods," *Journal of Futures Markets*, 7:3, 1987, pp. 245–67.

INDEX